Vidaluz Meneses

Flame in the Air:
Bilingual Poetry Edition

Translated & Edited by María Roof

Second Edition

First Edition, 2013 ©
Second Edition, 2015 ©
Vidaluz Meneses *Flame in the Air*
Copyrights® to the poems is held by Vidaluz Meneses
Translation Copyright © 2015 by María Roof
All Right Reserved
Cover photo and Design by: Mario Ramos/Casasola Editores
Interior design by: Oscar Estrada/Casasola Editores
Printed in the U.S.

Meneses, Vidaluz.
    Flame in the Air: Bilingual Poetry Edition, Translated and Edited by Maria Roof — 2st ed.
    English and Spanish text on facing pages.
    ISBN-10: 1942369093
    ISBN-13: 978-1-942369-09-7
    1. Meneses, Vidaluz — Translation into English. I. Roof, María. II Title.

Casasola LLC
1619 1st Street NW Apt. C Washington DC 20001
Apartado 2171, Tegucigalpa, Honduras

❧

casasolaeditores.com
info@casasolaeditores.com

Vidaluz Meneses

Flame in the Air:

Bilingual Poetry Edition

CONTENTS

Dedication / 17
Preface / 19
On the Translation / 21
Acknowledgements / 23
Nicaragua: Brief Contemporary Chronology / 27
I. Vidaluz Meneses on her Life / 33
II. Vidaluz Meneses on her Works / 145
III. Poems in Spanish and English / 181
Llama guardada (1975) / 182
Guarded Flame (1975) / 183
I. Del acontecer cotidiano: Del acontecer cotidiano / 184
I. On Everyday Events: On Everyday Events / 185
Llama guardada / 186
Guarded Flame / 187
Solitario transeúnte de la noche/ 186
Solitary Passerby in the Night / 187
Paradoja / 188
Paradox / 189
Inventario de un hombre moderno / 188
Inventory of A Modern Man / 189
La trampa / 190
The Trap / 191
"Quien tenga oídos" / 190
"He Who Has Ears to Hear" / 191
Ahora deambulamos solos / 192
Now We Wander Alone / 193
Alfonso / 192
Alfonso / 193
Tú dijiste / 194
You Said / 195
Intuyo / 194
I Intuit / 195
Escarnio / 196
Contempt / 197
Ellos reirán de vuestra hambre / 196
They Will Laugh at Your Hunger / 197
A Pavel / 198
To Pavel / 199

He visto / 200
I Have Seen / 201
Poema para sobrevivir / 202
Poem for Survival / 203
Bonanza / 204
Bonanza / 205
Abuela / 206
Grandmother / 207
Hoy / 206
Today / 207
Rama / 208
Rama / 209
Llueve / 208
It Rains / 209
Hoy no soy más / 210
Today I Am Nothing More / 211
Encontrar los amigos / 210
Meeting with Friends / 211
II. Instantáneas: High life en tres movimientos / 212
II. Snapshots: High Life in Three Movements / 213
Advertencias / 214
Warnings / 215
Instantánea conyugal / 216
Snapshot of a Marriage / 217
III. Páginas de una nueva desposada: Cuando yo me casé / 218
III. Pages of a New Bride: When I Married / 219
En el llano / 220
On the Plain / 221
Pequeño canto de la buenaesperanza / 220
Short Song of Good Hope / 221
Apuntes para una primeriza / 222
Notes for Her, A First-timer / 223
Pájaro en tres cantos / 222
Bird in Three Songs / 223
Ninguna campesina madre crea / 224
Let No *Campesina* Mother Believe / 225
Pequeña muerte / 226
Small Death / 227
Yo amanezco persiguiendo un canto / 228
I Awake Chasing A Song / 229

Sol en la playa / 230
Sun on the Sand / 231
Mujer estéril / 230
Barren Woman / 231
Ahora poseo el tiempo / 232
Now I Have Time / 233
Acto de fe / 232
Act of Faith / 233
Alguna noche insomne / 234
On A Sleepless Night / 235
IV. Oficina: Oficina / 236
IV. The Office: The Office / 237
Fugaces, intermitentes / 238
Fleeting, Intermittent / 239
Siento el suave rumor / 240
I Sense the Soft Murmur / 241
Es la vida / 242
That's Life / 243
Abandono, adrede y concientemente / 244
I Abandon, Purposely and Consciously / 245
Todos los días / 244
Every Day / 245
V. Tríptico de la muerte / 246
V. Triptych on Death / 247

El aire que me llama (1982) / 250
Air that Calls Me (1982) / 251
I. De ineludible memoria y otros poemas: Apunte/ 252
I. Of Unavoidable Memory and Other Poems: Sketch / 253
Las niñas Valle / 254
The Valle Girls / 255
Verano / 256
Summer / 257
Invierno / 258
Winter / 259
Pax / 258
Pax / 259
Bajamar / 260
Ebb Tide / 261
Mayo Nicaragua / 262
May in Nicaragua / 263

Madre / 264
Mother / 265
Epitafio / 264
Epitaph / 265
II. Hijos-juegos: Karla Dolores / 266
II. Children-Games: Karla Dolores / 267
Hijos / 268
Children / 269
Canto para un invierno que no comienza / 270
Song for a Winter that Does Not Begin / 271
Fauna nica / 272
Nican Fauna / 273
Hubo una vez / 274
Once There Was / 275
III. Notas de viaje: Notas de viaje / 276
III. Travel Notes: Travel Notes / 277
Mujer cachikel / 278
Cakchiquel Woman / 279
Antigua / 280
Antigua / 281
IV. Sobrevida: Golpeas impotente la puerta de la Nochebuena /282
IV. Survival: Helpless, You Knock on Christmas Eve's Door/ 283
Abril casero / 284
Familiar April / 285
La falda nueva / 286
The New Skirt / 287
Los que no han muerto / 286
Those Who Have Not Died / 287
Comerciales / 288
Commercials / 289
Mínimo homenaje / 290
Small Homage / 291
En el nuevo país / 290
In the New Country / 291
El vuelo / 292
Flight / 293
Epístola / 292
Epistle / 293
A los técnicos / 294
To the Technical Experts / 295

La tierra recobrada / 294
Land Recovered / 295
La Primera Dama / 296
First Lady / 297
Diciembre 7 / 298
December 7th / 299
Advertencia / 300
Notice / 301
Compañera / 300
Compañera / 301
Nota para Ángela / 302
Note for Angela / 303
Pedro: Ahora he estado recordando... / 304
Pedro: Just Now, I Have Been Remembering / 305
Hija / 304
Daughter / 305
Última postal a mi padre, General Meneses / 306
Last Message to My Father, General Meneses / 307
V. Porque amor no es aureola: La propia insurrección / 308
V. Because Love is Not a Halo: Private Insurrection / 309
Inmersa en las multitudes / 310
Immersed in the Multitudes / 311
A fin de cuentas / 312
All in All / 313
Encontrarte en el momento adecuado / 314
Finding You at the Right Time / 315
He ido creciendo / 316
I Have Been Growing / 317
Canción de amor para vos / 318
Love Song for You / 319
Las palabras nos precedieron / 318
Words Preceded Us / 319
Llama en el aire (1990) / 320
  I. Selección de poesías de *Llama guardada*
  II. Selección de poesías de *El aire que me llama*
  III. En el costado más frágil
Flame in the Wind (1990) / 321
  I. Selected Poems from *Guarded Flame*
  II. Selected Poems from *Air that Calls Me*
  III. On the Side Most Fragile

Eva de siempre / 322
Forever Eve / 323
Mi tía Adelina / 324
My Aunt Adelina / 325
Salomón / 326
Salomon / 327
Poeta o ángel terrible / 328
Poet, or Terrible Angel / 329
Si no es por un polvazal de los Barrios Orientales / 330
If Not for A Dust Whirl in the Eastern Neighborhoods / 331
Niño de siempre / 332
Always a Child / 333
Mujer, años 50 / 334
Woman, 1950s / 335
Mayaya la June Beer / 336
Mayaya June Beer / 337
Evocaciones de Mayo ya/86 / 338
Evocations of May Day/86 / 339
Mirando su fotografía / 340
Looking at Her Photograph / 341
Evasión / 342
Evasion / 343
Evocación de Ernesto / 344
Evocation of Ernesto / 345
Esa mujer / 346
That Woman / 347
Monet en el almanaque / 348
Monet on the Calendar / 349
En el costado más frágil / 350
On the Side Most Fragile / 351
IV. Con las mismas manos: Vigilia / 352
IV. With the Same Hands: Night Duty / 353
Te escribo ahora / 354
I Write to You Now / 355
Recuento / 356
Reckoning / 357
Sorprendido, feliz / 358
Surprised, Happy / 359
Nuestro amigo Semionov / 358
Our Friend Semionov / 359

Ciclo fatal / 360
Fatal Cycle / 361
Sueño submarino / 362
Underwater Dream / 363
Nombres / 364
Names / 365
Baraja / 366
Tarot / 367
Vista Casablanca con ojos nuevos / 368
Casablanca Viewed with New Eyes / 369
Paseo en otoño / 370
Autumn Stroll / 371
V. A los hombres futuros:
Del revolucionario y algunas de sus debilidades/ 372
V. To Future Men and Women:
About the Revolutionary and
Some of His Weaknesses / 373
Postal para Alba Azucena / 374
Message for Alba Azucena / 375
Estampas de Jalapa (La Limonera) / 376
Scenes from Jalapa (La Limonera Military Unit) / 377
Trabajo voluntario / 378
Voluntary Labor / 379
A mis hijos, Carlos y Karla, en su autoexilio / 380
To My Children, Carlos and Karla, in their Self-exile / 381
Reportaje de una brigada de cortadores de café
(Cosecha de 1984-1985) / 384
Report of a Coffee Brigade (1984-1985 Harvest) / 385
El sexto signo / 388
The Sixth Seal / 389
Tríptico para recordar / 390
Triptych to Remember / 391
Muro de lamentaciones / 392
Wailing Wall / 393
Todo es igual y distinto (Poemas 1992-2001) (2002)
All is the Same and Different (Poems 1992-2001) (2002)
Neoliberalismo / 396
Neoliberalism / 397
¿Dónde estás? / 396
Where Are You? / 397

Oficinistas / 398
Office Girls / 399
Síntesis del encuentro / 398
Synthesis of the Encounter / 399
Evocación Jurásica / 400
Jurassic Evocation / 401
Amor en cualquier tiempo, I / 402
Love at Any Time, I / 403
Amor en cualquier tiempo, II / 404
Love at Any Time, II / 405
Confidencia / 406
Confiding A Secret / 407
Dueña del canto / 410
Mistress of Her Song / 411
Canción de cuna de mayo / 412
May Lullaby / 413
Canción interior / 414
Internal Song / 415
Evocación / 416
Evocation / 417
Paco / 418
Paco / 419
Vida con vida / 422
Life with Life / 423
Esquelas mortuorias que corona la fama / 424
Death Notices Crowned by Fame / 425
Homenaje / 426
Homage / 427
Aquí estarías / 428
Here You Would Be / 429
Indagaciones / 430
Inquiries / 431
Itinerario/97 / 438
Itinerary/97 / 439
Hoja de diario / 442
Diary Page / 443
Interrogantes / 444
Questions / 445
Vivas estamos / 446

Alive Are We / 447
Convocatoria a la belleza / 450
Beauty Contest / 451
Poema del desamor / 450
Poem on Disaffection / 451
Esa mujer está loca / 452
That Woman Is Crazy / 453
Virgo / 454
Virgo / 455
La María Shangai / 456
María Shanghai / 457
Cuando sólo un árbol te sostiene / 458
When Only a Tree Sustains You / 459
Viaje hacia el interior / 460
Journey toward the Interior / 461
In extremis / 462
In extremis / 463
Poems and Poetic Publications Not in Collections / 465
Invocación en días calurosos / 466
Invocation on Hot Days / 467
Analiza tu vida / 466
Analyze Your Life / 467
A Guillermo, Guardafronteras y hermanos / 468
To Borderguard Guillermo and His Brothers and Sisters / 469
Guardafrontera / 468
Borderguard / 469
Maestro, tu voz / 470
Master, Your Voice / 471
Corazón en pampa / 472
Heart in the Open / 473
Reflexión en blue sobre New Orleáns / 478
Reflection in Blue on New Orleans / 479
Palabras para el último encuentro / 484
Words for the Last Encounter / 485
References in the Poems / 490
Annotated Bibliography / 496
Index / 517

DEDICATION

We dedicate this book to the women who will find their voices and bring about the globalization of justice.

PREFACE

This volume introduces to English readers the life and work of Vidaluz Meneses (b. 1944), one of the most acclaimed poets writing in Central America and a public figure of distinction during the Sandinista regime in Nicaragua (1979-1990), when she held leadership positions in the new Ministry of Culture. Although poems from her first books appear in anthologies published around the world —Great Britain, Switzerland, Denmark, Germany, Italy, Mexico, Cuba, Dominican Republic, and the United States— no selection in English has included more than a five-poem sampling of her work, and the total number available in English from all published sources is under twenty.

Hispanophone literary critics know and savor her work, yet only a few critical treatments (university theses) have appeared in the United States. Familiarity with her poetry and life story will trigger revision of the accepted interpretations of Nicaraguan history and letters. This volume presents her poetic works and their translation on facing pages, in addition to my substantial interviews with Meneses conducted between 2005 and 2013, which affirm the centrality of her life experiences in her works and highlight the choices confronting her and her peers.

Vidaluz Meneses enjoyed a rather carefree and comfortable life as the eldest of six children in the family of a National Guard officer whose early assignments took them to the small cities and towns of rural Nicaragua. When they later settled in the capital, Managua, Meneses was sent to a Catholic "school for rich girls," where acts of charity were part of the curriculum, but many students developed a profound commitment to the poor that questioned the political and social order. As was the custom, Meneses married and began a family, but, against custom, she joined a new wave of women who sought a university education.

Her increasing conviction during the 1960s and 70s of the need for radical change and overthrow of the military dictatorship ruling her country since 1933 led to a valiant struggle to transform herself from a traditional woman into an active participant in the dangerous process of revolution. Her story exemplifies the series of passionate life choices made by others of her generation who, like Father Ernesto Cardenal, defined themselves as faith-based revolutionaries, defied their own families, and challenged the values of their class.

When the Sandinistas lost the 1990 national elections to an alliance of conservative factions, the decade of revolutionary changes came to an abrupt halt. Out of work, divorced, economically destabilized, and fearful of possible retaliations against Sandinista officials, Meneses was disillusioned and shaken by the failure of the potentially transformational revolutionary project. Her perceptions mirrored those of novelist and Sandinista Vice-President Sergio Ramírez: "I always thought the revolution would be a transcendental story in human development, but it wasn't, was it?" (qtd. in Garvin). After 1990, Meneses embarked on a difficult, and continuing, search to reconcile historical sacrifices with contemporary reality, to recast her social role as person, woman, poet, and to find ways to build a new society outside the paradigm of revolution.

Vidaluz Meneses provides powerful insight into the poetic process as she identifies particular episodes from which specific poems emerged and explains how she reworked those experiences and turned them into poetry. She presents her perspective as a daughter, wife, and mother whose marriage and family were split apart by political events. She provides her unique access to the "inside story" as a founding official of the Ministry of Culture (1979-1988), and then as university department chair and dean (1991-1996), ecumenical center executive director (1997-2002), and national codirector of a coalition of over 600 independent NGOs (2002-2005).

In the 2006 and 2010 elections, she was on the unsuccessful Sandinista Renovation Movement Party´s slate as representative to the Central American Parliament. She was a founding member and first executive director of Anide, the Nicaraguan Association of Women Writers, and is president of the Nicaraguan Writers Center (CNE).

Meneses's life and work form a continuum, her intellectual and personal engagement in issues continuously overlapping. In these interviews, she talks about: the female body as a mystery to girls; feminism and its impact among her peers; generational differences between her mother, herself, her daughters; Afro-Caribbean culture; disruptions of traditional family relations before, during, and after the revolutionary period of the 1970s and 1980s; and her deeply-felt connection between religious beliefs, social commitment, poetry, and personal coherence.

Meneses reviewed and approved the edited Spanish transcription of the interviews, which were translated by the editor as the first two chapters here, "Vidaluz Meneses on Her Life" and "Vidaluz Meneses on Her Works." Especially in the first chapter, many of the questions were eliminated for easier reading. Very little reordering of the material was done, and the presentation is roughly chronological, although memories triggered by associations are generally left in the order presented. The oral nature of the interviews has been preserved.

Flame in the Air includes the information necessary for historical, literary, and geographical references in the poems, in the form of brief notes appended to the translations. Each translation, then, is a self-contained text, with notes as a first step for deriving an accurate framework for the poem's messages and meanings. A final reference section elaborates on main historical and literary topics and figures that might be unknown to English readers. An annotated bibliography summarizes interviews and scholarly articles.

On the Translations

The translation of poetry presents unique challenges, especially from a rhythmic, Latin-based language like Spanish to a direct, monosyllabic-tending, Germanic and Anglo-Saxon language like English. Our guiding principle has been to maintain fidelity to the original and respect the poet's choice of words from among other options available to her. The translations are accurate, then, but are not the only possible "correct" versions of the poems.

Certain nuances particular to Nicaraguan Spanish have been reflected as much as possible in English. Some aspects of this form of Spanish cannot be conveyed in English, such as the "you" singular pronoun, "vos." Howard University linguist Alberto Rey has done extensive research on the use of "vos" throughout Central America and establishes the contexts in which it signals more or less intimacy than "tú," and, certainly, less distance than the formal "usted." In practice, however, Meneses's poetic contexts tend to suggest the level of intimacy that is absent in the English "you," and the poet is consistent with her culture in using the formal "usted" only three times (in "Tarot," "I Sense the Soft Murmur," and "Pedro: Just Now, I Have Been Remembering"), as would be appropriate in the business contexts there. The familiar "tú" pronoun is used only three times, all in poems written between 1965 and 1973 (in one about her daughter, "Karla Dolores," and when addressing Austrian poet Rainer Marie Rilke in "You Said," and a Russian literary character in "To Pavel"), but verb forms corresponding to "tú" appear in several poems written between 1968 and 1974. Elsewhere, "vos" prevails in all contexts in poetry dated after 1978. As witnessed in Meneses's texts, the use of "vos" corresponds to evolving cultural changes reflected in language: prior to the Revolutionary period "vos" was considered inappropriate and improper in poetry, whereas it later became an indicator of social egalitarianism, and "tú" is now considered an affectation (Rodríguez Rosales).

Like many Nicaraguans, Meneses uses the phrase "in the years of the Revolution" to include the period of revolutionary struggle in the 1960s and, especially, the 1970s, led by the Sandinista National Liberation Front, as well as the period of the majority-Sandinista governing junta (1979-1984) and the elected Sandinista government (1984-1990).

The translations are mine unless otherwise indicated.

María Roof

ACKNOWLEDGEMENTS

The greatest support for this project was offered by the poet herself, who generously set aside time for our discussions at literary conferences, during trips for other purposes, and even at a son's wedding reception. During one marathon week, Vidaluz Meneses granted over thirty hours of interviews, which became the largest part of the sections on her life and works in this edition, and recited poems for taping and website use. She reviewed the edited interview transcriptions and provided additional information where she thought her statements should be enhanced. On a trip to the U.S., she toted a heavy bag of family photograph albums and spent days identifying people, events, and contexts for those pictures, some of which appear here, as well as clarifying some of the more hermetic passages in her poetry. My respect and admiration for Vidaluz Meneses, as a person and a poet, converted this endeavor from a literary project into a passionate labor of commitment, so that readers of English might grasp what it means in Central America and elsewhere when a poet not only has no "room of her own," but also, no "poetic space of her own," yet she creates poetry, even as she leads campaigns for social and political reforms.

Sonia Celerín proved a highly efficient transcriber of the taped interviews. Her attuned Panamanian ear readily perceived linguistic nuances that might confound less knowledgeable listeners, such as the difference between "No está aquí"—She's not here— and "No, está aquí"—No, she's here. Sonia describes the transcription process as an incredibly enriching experience. Her years of working on cultural issues in Panama and elsewhere provided her with the necessary background in Central American history, politics, geography, literature, culture, and folklore, as well as Spanish oral and written syntax, to comprehend readily the dialogues. When speaking, people often use a shorthand way of making references, and Sonia turned those allusions into comprehensible statements.

I applaud the editors of early bilingual anthologies and anthologies in translation that sparked interest in Nicaraguan poetry at crucial historical moments: Zoë Anglesey, Amanda Hopkinson, Dinah Livingstone, Alejandro Murguía and Barbara Paschke, Nora Jacquez Wieser, and Marc Zimmerman. I am especially indebted to Nora Jacquez Wieser, whose *Open to the Sun* gave me my first glimpse of what I now consider a miniboom of women poets in Nicaragua. Margaret Randall's interviews with Nicaraguans during the 1980s were crucial for bringing their life stories to a U.S. public at a time when official policy demonized them.

Jorge Román Lagunas has been pivotal in the development of this project. He founded the Central American Literature Congress (CILCA) in 1992 and has maintained its annual sponsorship by the University of Purdue-Calumet—no small task in these budget-slashing times. CILCA became instrumental in stimulating new scholarship on the region, and its meeting is now the major forum where writers, critics, students, and the general public convene for mutually enlightening discussions. At the 8th CILCA meeting in Antigua, Guatemala, Vidaluz Meneses and I first discussed publishing a translation of her works. The organizers of the 9th CILCA in Belize invited us to do a bilingual reading and share her works with the English-speaking public there. In the context of the 12th CILCA in Liverpool, England, Astvaldur Astvaldsson and the Windows Project gave us the opportunity to participate in a dialogic bilingual reading and writing workshop, along with Manlio Argueta of El Salvador. The Windows writers' fervent reaction to the translations encouraged us in our work and helped us keep non-U.S. English readers in mind.

Jo Anne Engelkirk has been an inspiration to me as a translator, because of her consistent art and skill in turning Central American poetry into resonant English. The breadth and quality of her work sets the standard for translators of poetry.

For background material on Nicaraguan authors, I found the website maintained by Yolanda Blanco very helpful (www.dariana.com), as was Sergio Ramírez's online essay on Nicaraguan literature, and Julio Valle-Castillo's new monumental anthology with critical assessments on poetry from 1880 to 1980. Daisy Zamora's encyclopedic anthology of women poets in Nicaragua provided insightful details on the explosion of women poets onto the literary scene in the 1960s. Essays by Nicasio Urbina, Jorge Eduardo Arellano, and José María Mantero were rich sources of information and interpretations. In English, Steven F. White has made significant contributions with his important studies and translations of Nicaraguan poetry. John Beverley and Marc Zimmerman began a debate on poetry and politics in Central American revolutions that continues to resonate and established a critical dialogue that Greg Dawes has continued with respect to Nicaragua. David E. Whisnant brings attention to literature and popular culture in his fascinating broad study of the politics of culture in Nicaragua.

For assistance in language use, from Spanish meaning to English phraseology, I thank: María Pilar Polo Iglesias, Mercedes Vidal Tibbits, Piedad Frías Nogales, Nicasio Urbina, Amelia Mondragón, Graciela Maglia Vercesi, James Roof, Philip Roof, Marthe Diogo, Margaret Bonds, Kimberly Kerr, Guadalupe Gámez de Rodríguez, and Cheryl Ann Spray Grospitz. Bible references were researched by Gwendolyn Jones and Bertha Roof. Carol Hall, Josephine Woll, and Vidaluz Meneses provided material for the notes. Cynthia Burton's commitment to this project and use of her expert bibliographical talents were appreciated, as was concrete technical support provided by: Mike Jensen, Juan Egea Montes, Rita Manning, Claire Mallicotte, Debbie Grauel, Wendy Nutwell, and Linda Poe. I appreciate the generosity of Cristina Guzzo, Alba Fabiola Aragón, Frances Jaeger, and Rick Mc Callister in sending me their literary criticism. I thank Alba Fabiola Aragón and Andrés G. Tucker for permission to use their translations. Karleesha Wright and Michelle Neely stepped in at a critical juncture to provide valuable assistance in word processing.

For providing nurturing spaces in which to work, I thank James and Bertha Roof, Roberta Huch Alberts and D.J. Alberts, Jessica White and Mariano Icaza. I am especially grateful to Françoise and Marie-Hélène Pfaff, in whose comfortable Washington, DC, living room we taped the greater part of the interviews.

I appreciate the enthusiasm of James J. Davis, Chair of the Department of World Languages and Cultures, Howard University, who sponsored a bilingual poetry recital in which Vidaluz Meneses and I first explored the effectiveness of some of the translations. I value that university's further support for my research through its Fund for Academic Excellence Travel Grants for my participation in CILCA conferences and the granting of a sabbatical leave so that I could complete this book.

NICARAGUA: BRIEF CONTEMPORARY CHRONOLOGY

[Bold type: See further information in References]

1833-1910	Repeated U.S. military interventions.
1912-1925	Occupation by U.S. Marines to protect U.S. interests.
1926-1933	Return by U.S. Marines to attempt to quell rebellion by **Augusto César Sandino** and almost continual occupation
1933	**Anastasio "Tacho" Somoza García** named head of newly-created National Guard by President Juan Bautista Sacasa.
1934	Assassination of Sandino and his men, under a safe-conduct agreement during peace talks, on orders of Anastasio Somoza García.
1936-1956	Power seized by "Tacho" Somoza García; elected and reelected president, occasionally alternating with civilian surrogates; assassinated.
1956-1963	"Tacho" Somoza's presidential term completed by his son, Luis Somoza Debayle, later elected.
1961	**FSLN (Sandinista National Liberation Front)** founded by **Carlos Fonseca,** Tomás Borge, and Silvio Mayorga.
1963-1967	Somoza associate René Schick Gutiérrez president.
1967-1979	**General Anastasio "Tachito" Somoza Debayle**, the other son of "Tacho" and head of National Guard, elected and reelected president, alternating in presidency with civilians; severe repression of opposition.
1972 Dec.	Earthquake in Managua: 10,000 dead, 20,000 injured, 300,000 homeless; international relief aid pocketed by Somoza; city not rebuilt.

1978 Jan.	Pedro Joaquín Chamorro, owner and editor of anti-Somoza *La Prensa* newspaper and leader of conservative opposition party, assassinated.
1979 July	Somoza into exile.
1979-1990	Sandinistas in power.
1979-1984	Five-person governing Junta of National Reconstruction, with Sandinistas Daniel Ortega (coordinator) and Moisés Hassan, novelist Sergio Ramírez, *La Prensa* publisher Violeta Barrios de Chamorro (widow of Pedro Joaquín Chamorro), and businessman Alfonso Robelo.
1979	Founding of the Ministry of Culture under **Ernesto Cardenal.**
1980	Literacy campaigns: illiteracy reduced from 52% to 13%.
1980	Barrios de Chamorro and Robelo reject Sandinista political program and leave ruling junta; replaced by conservative lawyer Arturo Cruz and banker Rafael Córdova Rivas.
1980-1990	U.S. funds counterrevolutionary war led by the "Contras," operating from bases in Costa Rica and Honduras; Nicaragua's ports mined and total trade embargo imposed by U.S.
1985-1990	FSLN President Daniel Ortega, Vice-President Sergio Ramírez (Nov. 1984 elections).
1988	Ministry of Culture compacted into Ministry of Education.
1990-1997	President Violeta Barrios de Chamorro, of U.S.-backed coalition UNO (National Opposition Union); defeat of FSLN candidate Daniel Ortega (Feb. 1990 elections).
1997-2002	President Arnoldo Alemán, of Liberal Alliance (AL), later Liberal Constitutionalist Party (PLC); defeat of FSLN candidate Daniel Ortega (Nov. 1996 elections).

1998 Oct.	Hurricane Mitch: record amounts of rainfall dumped on Honduras and Nicaragua; massive flooding and mudslides; second deadliest Atlantic hurricane in history; in Nicaragua, at least 3,800 dead and 500,000-800,000 left homeless.
2002-2007	President Enrique Bolaños, of the Liberal Constitutionalist Party (PLN); defeat of FSLN candidate Daniel Ortega (Nov. 2001 elections).
2007-	President Daniel Ortega (FSLN) elected and reelected (Nov. 2006, Nov. 2011 elections).

I. VIDALUZ MENESES ON HER LIFE

I. Vidaluz Meneses on Her Life

Interviews with Vidaluz Meneses invariably cover her political commitment to the Sandinista Revolution. Before addressing that, could you tell us something about the child who would become one of the best known poets in Nicaragua?

Multicultural, nomadic childhood

My first memories from childhood are of Matagalpa and the home of my great-aunts, "The Three Valle Girls," who appear in several of my poems, and of my mother, a very beautiful young woman. She worked as a copyist at the courthouse and was known for the uniquely personal style of her lovely handwritten script. I remember when my Great-Aunt Virginia came for a visit. She was married to a mining engineer from the United States, Leslie N. Hoey, and they also became figures in my poetry. Aunt Virginia invited me to stay with her for a while in Bonanza, a town in the northern part of the country known as Nicaragua's Atlantic or Caribbean region. The night before the trip—I don't know why I remember certain phrases, especially this phrase which is not easy for a child—she asked me during dinner:

"You're coming with me tomorrow, right, honey?"
"Yes...," I answered and smiled, but I felt worried because I was going to have to leave my mother. My aunt said,
"She's answering me 'between the tooth and the lip.'"

It surprises me because I remember that strange phrase, "between the tooth and the lip," and it's true, I wasn't very eager to go with her. I was about three or four at the time.

A poet's early sensitivity to language?

Perhaps so. In the morning, when I saw the truck ready to take us to the plane for my first flight, from Matagalpa to Bonanza, I did what I had planned the night before: I held tight onto my mother's skirt and screamed, "Noooo!" I think that's a universal scene in children's lives! But I quickly realized it was futile, and no matter how much I might yell and cling to my mother, I had to go, because that was the will of the adults. My mother cried a little and told me I was going to have a good time with my great-aunt and my godmother, who was waiting for me in Bonanza.

They loaded me into the truck, and we went in a Lanica Company plane with two engines that spit fire behind the propellers as they started. I threw up the whole way! I think it was because I was so nervous, and air pockets violently tossed the plane up and down. There were some paper bags in the seat backs, and I used them all up, mine and all my neighbors'.

When we landed at the Bonanza airstrip, which was quite rustic and still is—I was there recently, and it hasn't changed much—waiting for us was my Great-Uncle Leslie, always a very warm figure in my memories. He greeted us cheerfully, we piled into his Willys jeep and headed for town. We stopped at the public school where one of the teachers was his oldest daughter, Anna Bessie Hoey, my mother's first cousin and my godmother. She came running out and was very pretty and tall, with blue eyes and black hair. She hugged and kissed me, and they left me right there at the school. They sent me to school with her every day, even though I was too young, just to give me something to do. I wasn't enrolled, because that wasn't the custom. My grandchildren have gone to school since they were very little. Preschools are everywhere now, but back then, you started kindergarten at age five and the next year, first grade.

When I returned to Matagalpa, happy to be back with my mother, she introduced me to a warm, slender man with a thin nose and honey-colored eyes, saying, "This is your father." She explained that I hadn't seen him before because he was a cadet at the Military Academy, named Edmundo Meneses Cantarero. I lived at home with them and returned to Bonanza for vacations, back and forth. My first sister, Ulda, was born when I was five years old, and they would sit me down on a rocking chair and give her to me to hold. But one day she died of gastroenteritis. At the time, I didn't have a clear sense of death. I only remember that she looked like a doll placed on the altar with a veil like mosquito netting covering her. The next morning, I don't know in what words, someone explained it to me, my mother, or someone else. I cried for that strange event, a little sister of mine had suddenly died, and we buried her and didn't see her again. She must have been about six months old. In those times there weren't a lot of vaccines in Nicaragua, and a high percentage of babies and children died.

I had a mild form of polio

Something happened to me when I was about two or three, though I don't really remember it, but I allude to it in the autobiographical poem "Confiding A Secret." My mother tells me that I had very high fevers, and after I recovered, she noticed I was limping. Mother asked what had happened, and I said I had fallen in a ditch. I don't know if I really had fallen, but she says that's what I answered. Time passed, and I always walked with a slight limp. When I was about 15, we were marching in a school parade, and I began to feel sharp pains in my lower back, in the kidney area. I'd had a serious kidney infection and was hospitalized in Bonanza when I was seven, but I got over it and never had another problem. With the back pain, they thought I was having kidney problems again and did X-rays. When doctors examined my bones, they discovered that I'd had a mild form of polio, apparently more or less back when I had the fevers. In later years, I have met people my age who were seriously affected by polio and need crutches to get around, and others who had a mild case, like me. That's why I have one leg slightly shorter than the other.

Although it affected my pelvis, I birthed my children with no problem. They had normal deliveries, except my second child, Carlos Rodolfo, who was born bottom first, but I didn't have any complications. Of course, for dancing…! In "Confiding A Secret," I admit that I can't do all the steps. When I walk, the tendons in my right foot don't stretch enough to step normally, so I have a distinct way of walking.

Those are my early memories, and I remember first grade in Matagalpa, at the Ramona Rizo School. When my father finished his courses, he was transferred from Matagalpa to Boaco, a town in north central Nicaragua, Chontales Department. We made the move in trucks, with all the household goods piled up, beds, folding chairs. I was six or seven, and they put me in a small school for little girls. I was always either in school or on vacation between Bonanza, Matagalpa, and Boaco. My brother Jairo was born in Matagalpa and Edmundo in Boaco. After that, we went to another town, Camoapa, where I went to the San Francisco Institute.

Nicaragua is an agricultural country, and most of it is quite rural. I was born in Matagalpa in the north and lived in all those pretty rural towns. The north is different from Managua, Granada, and León, which are more urban. And the Caribbean Coast is completely different. Nicaragua has distinct cultures, markedly different, and perhaps that influenced me. I am a Gemini, therefore versatile, and our lifestyle offered a multicultural formation that, in my opinion, gives me a certain advantage in the contemporary world.

"Distracted" from early on

As a child, I had the reputation of being distracted. The joke in my family is that I was mentally "elsewhere" some of the time. In fact, when I was a teenager, my father and mother were sitting on a hammock, resting, and father told me to go get something from their room. He and mother smiled like accomplices when he said it, and I went off thinking they were laughing because they thought I was going to forget what I had been sent for. Sure enough, I was so concerned with what they were smiling about, I forgot what my father had said! When I got to their room, I didn't know if I was supposed to fetch the slippers, a shirt, or what. It turned out they were right! [Laughter]

I remember another episode, when we lived in Camoapa, and they gave me money to pay the monthly tuition at the Institute, and I put it on the car seat and forgot it there. But luckily, the teacher or someone else found it and returned it to my mother, who said, "You see! You forgot the money I gave you to pay for your school!" And I felt bad.

Do you remember what you were thinking about when you walked around in your own world?

No, but I remember I used to be quiet for long periods of time. I was a little nostalgic too, when I was in Bonanza. I imagine it was part of the poetry that was gestating, and the rain and mist in the moutains made me cry. Also, when I would leave Matagalpa, I cried for my mother, and when I came back from Bonanza, I missed my family there.

That's an experience that people in exile describe too, a sense of uprootedness and the resulting nostalgia. You were being shifted around.

Well, now that you mention that, I remember the theory of post-traumatic stress syndrome in Nicaragua that Martha Cabrera and her team of psychologists explained to us. They spoke of an international stress scale in psychology where you rate what affects you emotionally, even something like moving to a new house. I think that human beings usually create a certain habitat, a routine. In Managua, imagine the consequences of the 1972 earthquake: from one day to the next, even in just a few hours, people lost their homes, their families, all the reference points in the city, because the center city was gone, the street you usually walked down, where you used to see your neighbors. It was totally disorienting. I imagine those are the sorts of things that affect you and maybe you are not prepared for them. Some people have more fragile psychologies, others, stronger ones, I believe. Now, those good-byes are funny to me because there I was, screaming when I had to leave my mother, and then, coming back from Bonanza, crying because I was leaving my great-aunt and uncle and my godmother!

Living the "American Way of Life"

In Bonanza, I lived in the staff area, the family residential section for U.S. employees of the Neptune Gold Mine Company, which operated a mine up in the hills. The town where the mestizos, Miskito and Sumo Indians, also called Mayagnas, and Chinese workers lived was lower down. In contrast to the Pacific Coast in the 1940s, where Catholics prevailed, on the Atlantic side there were two churches, Catholic and Moravian.

U.S. workers had brought their whole "American Way of Life" with them. The houses were large and comfortable, made of wood and built on pylons, with shiny, polished floors, carpets in the living and bedrooms, linoleum in the kitchen and bathrooms, bathtubs with hot water, inside toilets, electric ranges, and washing machines. The commissary was stocked with gringo products—Gold Medal flour, Fleishman's yeast, Del Monte fruit cocktail and vegetables, Campbell's soups, Corn Flakes.

Bread was baked every three days at home. There was a cook, but my aunt and godmother often did the baking themselves. I especially remember the delicious apple pie we used to eat, and I mention it in the poem "On the Side Most Fragile" dedicated to my Uncle Leslie, which I wrote when I learned he was on his deathbed in the U.S. Also in that poem, I talk about the movies we went to see at the local theater, mostly cowboy films with Roy Rogers as the hero. A few days ago, I was touring Frederick, Maryland, with my son Mariano, and I was moved seeing restaurants named for this actor. Movies and newspapers came by plane every three days. Sometimes during our winter rainy season, flights would be suspended for several days, and then we had no newspapers and no films. In Matagalpa with my great-aunts, the Valle Girls, I assimilated Catholic Christmas traditions, such as the *posadas* celebration with prayers and processions, and the arrival of Baby Jesus. In Bonanza, I experienced the Anglo-Saxon traditions of Santa Claus, Easter eggs, and Halloween celebrations.

We invented our own games

From Camoapa my father was transferred to Ocotal, capital of the department of New Segovia, the area where General Sandino waged war against the U.S. Marines. Before we moved, we went with my pregnant mother to Matagalpa, where Meriulda was born. Annabella was born in Ocotal, and her birth was a local event. She weighed 14 pounds at birth, and the clothes my mother had taken for a three-month old didn't fit her, and she sent for clothes for a six-month old. In small towns, family life is public knowledge, and everyone talked about the size of the baby born in their hospital.

We lived in Ocotal twice. The second time, my brothers and sisters were older, and I had to take care of them, but I invented ways to play with them that were fun for me too. Dolls were never of much interest to me, actually, they bored me. When I had one, I would rock her to sleep very quickly and then put her straight to bed. But I loved playing with cups and saucers. I would sit all my brothers and sisters down at a little table and cook beans and ripe bananas fried in butter and eat them with hard cheese or curds and cream.

I used to organize events and circus parties, and we would charge our family admission. We would perform the acts we saw at the circus. My cousin, César Suazo, who was the son of another National Guard general, was the king of the circus, and I was the queen. A boy taken in by my aunt and uncle, a black child from Pearl Lagoon in the South Atlantic area, was the trapeze artist "Black Eagle." His real name was José Bailón Dixon, and he was an adolescent, older than me, and merrily went along with us. He would don a black cape and swing on the trapeze.

From Ocotal we went for a year to El Jícaro, a town more to the north. I went to the public school there, which I mention in the prose piece "Sketch" published in *Air that Calls Me*. The teacher was Juliet, a stout woman with light-colored eyes, and one day she disappeared. People said that she had taken off with the driver of the local bus, the only bus that connected the municipality to Ocotal and the rest of the towns in the area. In "Sketch" I talk about a cart pulled by oxen that passed every morning in front of our house that was next to the military headquarters. I would wait for it and run after it to lift my brothers and sisters on and then jump on myself. We would ride across town on the cart, and at the edge of town, hop off. One morning, I was taking a bath when the cart passed, and I don't know how my little brothers and sisters got on, but they did. They kept riding and never got off. When we started looking for them at home and couldn't find them, everyone was alarmed and sent guards off looking for the commandant's children. They found them all sweaty at a neighboring farm, quietly watching sugarcane juice run from the sugar press.

After the last stay in Ocotal, we kids went with mother to León, where her sister Lila was married to the military commandant of that city, and mother gave birth to her last child, Dalila. Father went ahead to Managua, his next duty post, to find a house for us. In León I had a very brief relationship with a boyfriend, an adolescent boy. With him and a group of boys and girls we would play the game of "Sweethearts," a sort of flirting game to see who liked whom. A girl would say, "Oh, oh, oh, I'm going to leave in a little while," and the group would say, "Who are you going with?" She would answer, "With my beloved," and they'd ask, "Who's your beloved?" You would say the name of the boy that you liked, and if he was asked and liked you, he would say your name. I was enrolled at the Asunción School, where upper class Nicaraguan girls were educated, and this facilitated my admission into a branch of the school when we moved to Managua, because nuns of the same order ran both schools. This school was decisive in deepening my Christian identity and establishing the bases for my later social commitment.

Living in those small towns was very joyful, we would go play at the river and ride horses. My cousin César and I used to play all the time with little medicine bottles that we would dress up. I would make the clothes, and we put them on the bottles, and it wasn't because we didn't have plastic soldiers or other toys. César was an only child, and my uncle had money, so there was always a certain high standard of living in their household. Although he had soldiers, we preferred to play with the medicine bottles.

Your creativity was sparked, in a sense, right?

I imagine so. My memories of childhood are happy, because all those worlds brought me joy. With my great-aunts in Matagalpa, I liked living their life, going to church, the *posadas* tradition, Baby Jesus, and in Bonanza, Santa Claus, and the other traditions. We were a happy family, my parents and little brothers and sisters, you know? I think childhoods were fun in those small towns, because there was no television, and we had to use our imagination to amuse ourselves.

That was a discovery I made later, as an adult, suddenly worried about what my grandchildren could see on television, although my daughters try to keep them involved in sports and other activities. Once, I tried to remember what I watched as a child, and I realized that I never watched television! I wondered why we had no television at home. Didn't my parents have enough money to buy a TV set? Why not? I asked other people of my generation, and sure enough, television didn't come to Nicaragua until I was in Managua, already an adolescent.

The female body, a mystery

I was not very clear about some things, like menstruation. I remember when I was about 11 years old, I went to spend a vacation in Somoto, a town near Ocotal in Madriz Department, where my cousin César lived. Later, I went to stay at his house in León, but I am talking about earlier, when we were younger. I went for vacation to Somoto, that's where the Mejía Godoys are from, the famous Nicaraguan musicians and singers. We were all little then, and that's where we played with the medicine bottles. When my mother was dropping me off, my Aunt Lila spoke to her, and I heard her say, "Tell her"— for my mother to talk with me. So mother sits me down and tells me that at a certain age women start to bleed. She didn't say where from, but she lowered her eyes to my belly. That this happens every month, it's called menstruation, and that I should get ready for it and not be afraid.

So, I had a vague idea of what was going to happen, but it didn't during that vacation, only later, when I was living in Ocotal and organizing circus shows. My cousin César was there on vacation, and we would play in the mango tree in the patio. He would climb up on a branch, and I would pull it up and down; then I would climb up, and he would pull on it. One of those times, the branch snapped from the weight, and I fell to the ground but wasn't injured. That night, when I took off my underwear, I could see a dark shadow in my panty, and I thought it must be dirt or mud and didn't want to turn on the light to check it out. I dropped it into the dirty clothes basket and went to bed. The next morning, I looked, and, oh! I see blood as dark as coffee! Oh, no! I go to my mother to ask if that's what it is, and she says yes and gets me some sanitary napkins. I put one on, and that whole day I stayed sitting in a chair and moved only as much as necessary, because I felt like I had a mattress between my legs and couldn't budge! [Laughter] It was terrible! But I didn't start then. It came just that once, went away for a year, then came back for real.

I realize that even with the preparation I had, things were not very clear, and it was all mysterious, like you are never really ready for that. Also, with the nuns and the atmosphere in which you were raised, everything about your body was a mystery, and you had to be careful. Virginity was a huge issue, right? Of course, in my childhood, with my cousins in Bonanza, we would check each other out, with all the sensations and curiosity there is at that age, look and see what we had, but it was something that had to be hidden.

When I was 14, and we were living in León, my father brought me a really pretty blouse from a military school in Venezuela. I remember this because it is related to the fact that I was starting to develop breasts and was quite a shy girl. The blouse was made of T-shirt material with a logo, to advertise the school where the military went for training, but it was for a girl, very pretty. One day I put it on and went out like I did every day to play baseball in the street with the other kids, all of us teenagers. When I picked up the bat and raised my arms, the shirt stuck to my chest, and you could see my breasts, even though I was skinny and my breasts were tiny, just beginning to develop, and this friend of mine who was very sharp said, "Hey, you pig! You don't use a bra?" [Laughter.] I threw the bat down and ran home dying of embarrassment and went to tell my mother to buy me a brassiere. My mother, of course, had several smaller children, and I imagine she was taking care of the little ones, so she gave me some money and told me to go buy it myself. I was so embarrassed, but I set out to buy my first bra. I went to the corner where the mother of a friend of mine had a little *pulpería* store where they sold all sorts of cheap products and basic necessities for everyday use. I said to my friend, "I need to buy a bra and am embarrassed. Do you have any?" Yes, they did, but homemade from plain cloth for the local women, pink bras with a piece of netting and a snap, no elastic, and she put one on me. I couldn't breathe! The first bras I bought were like that, and I couldn't breathe, they asphyxiated me!

There was always something mysterious about women's bodies, and that is why I find so interesting what Gioconda Belli did and what her critics are doing now, analyzing how she demythologizes the body and confers value upon it. I enjoy all that, and I think it is quite healthy. I really like Gioconda's attitude in her literature, and I appreciate the honesty she shows with sexual topics. We were educated at the same school, Gioconda was at Asunción, as was Michèle Najlis, both poets with whom I identify closely. Gioconda is four years younger than me, and I like her approach. I think she is establishing an important vindication.

The worst part of my life; I started to write more: Adolescence, the 1960s

I think my childhood was happy, but I didn't like my adolescence at all. Probably it was the worst period in my life, although I went to lots of parties and enjoyed them, but actually I used them as a means of escape, first, I think, because mine was a melancholic adolescence. Maybe a lot of things came together at once for me—a sense of searching, worry, concern about social issues…, and living in a country with a dictator, where my father was a National Guard officer and, therefore, supported the dictatorship. Secondly, perhaps because of the awareness the school nuns instilled in us. Hormonal changes too, I imagine, menstruation and all that, affect your character. That's when I started to write more. I also fell in love, and then the repression set in—you can't calmly experience your sexuality because you have to be careful. The double standard—girls had to stay virgins until marriage, and the boys, the more girls they had, the higher esteem they earned as macho men. An absurd double standard! There were so many things I didn't like.

Talking gifts to the poor

I transferred to the Asunción School in Managua, and it influenced me, the charitable mission outings, for example. The school was quite elegant, next to the lake, and we would go to a poor neighborhood on the other side of the lake. There was a school for rich girls and a school for poor girls called "The Asunción Annex," where the daughters of domestic workers went, girls with few resources, and the school was maintained with contributions from our school. At a ceremony once a year we would walk over and meet the line of poor children, and in front of the Mother Superior, we would give the poor girls a gift. We also went to a neighborhood on the other side of the school named "La Tejera." One of the first poems I wrote, titled like the first line, "To Be in the Nothingness of a Neighborhood," was sent to the magazine *Presencia* published by a group of poets in the city of Diriamba who invited me to contribute. The poem relates what I knew about the poor neighborhood, where there were dead animals, trash, and entrails, and people picked through them to find something to eat.

We would go there once a week to distribute meat with a French nun, Mother Mireille, an excellent person who died just a few years ago at a very old age. I loved her a lot and admired her saintliness. There was also a Mother Celia who they said was crazy; she painted and always stayed on the top floor of the school. But I have very nice memories of her, despite her reputation for having a bad temper, because with me, she was always very sweet. Once, I was supposed to be in a celebration dressed as one of the Three Kings, and my parents didn't have money to buy me an elegant costume like the other girls had. I imagine there wasn't a lot of money at home, and none for an expensive outfit, you know? Mother Celia told me to bring in a bedspread, and I brought a real pretty one that she turned into a cape worthy of a king. She helped me make a crown out of gold cardboard, and I looked great. I thought it was very sweet of her, because my classmates all had elegant costumes specially made for them out of silk, but mine looked just as good. I also remember Mother Julia from El Salvador, wise in her advice, and Mother Sonia, younger and more dynamic. In general, I have good memories of the nuns, but I had classmates who spoke ill of them, generally girls who had been at the school since they were little, and some of them were very rebellious and couldn't stand the nuns.

"Raise your hand if you've ever kissed your boyfriend"

Of course, the discipline was strict. The sexuality part was a disaster! On the one hand, the nuns, and on the other, the type of parents some of the girls had. My parents were never too ridiculous about the sexual part, but there were certain rules that absolutely could not be violated, for example, adolescent girls had to be protected. Between 1959 and 1962 all of us were turning 15, so there were lots of "sweet fifteen" parties, and the custom was for you to be given a diamond ring and a party at your home or a club, with 15 boys dressed in suits, and 15 girls in pink dresses. I went to lots of those parties, and usually, your mother or your aunt or grandmother, someone like that, would chaperone you. In my case, my mother was always taking care of a bunch of younger kids, but she would entrust me to certain mothers. So-and-so was going with her mother, and I could go with them. They would come by and pick me up, and I would go to the party, but my father would come get me at a set time. That's how I went to the parties of my best friends, Ángela Saballos, for example, who is a journalist now; her "sweet fifteen" party was wonderful, but at eleven p.m., my father came to pick me up. She lived on the outskirts of Managua, and it was a far out, so I started saying my good-byes and thanked the mother who had accompanied me. She said, "What a distrustful man!" because father didn't want to let me stay later. But I was a submissive girl, not rebellious, and I didn't insist, so there was nothing more to say, and I left with him at the time I had to leave.

One of the anecdotes from that time was once when the nuns told us, "Raise your hands if you have ever kissed your boyfriend." You can imagine that no one reacted, but then, one of my classmates, Auxiliadora Román, a very sweet girl, raised her hand. The nuns grabbed her, took her to a room to lecture her, and made her give confession to a priest. It was such a huge thing, almost like an exorcism! Some girls thought they could get pregnant from a kiss. A thousand ridiculous things like that we had in our adolescence.

I could not be indifferent to the world

Did you have a sense then of the changes that were coming?

The changes were already on our doorsteps. We lived our social reality, and besides, I had poet friends who came to see me. Julio Cabrales and Beltrán Morales were the first poet friends I had during my teen years, and they would visit me at my house in the military neighborhood. And it's curious, both of them suffered insanity; one died, Beltrán in 1986, and the other is still alive, but he walks around the streets completely crazy. It's so terribly sad.

Did other girls at the school become socially aware, as you did?

A good number of my classmates from Asunción School worked for the Revolution, Angelita Saballos and Michèle Najlis, among others. Michèle was in the vanguard; she walked out of the school for rich girls. After her "sweet fifteen" party, she took to the streets and joined the people's struggle, slept in the street with them. It was a drastic step, and the nuns had us pray for her because she was going to turn communist! [Laughter]

The nuns were creating revolutionaries without knowing it!

Yes, without knowing it. Some of the other girls, no; they got married, left the country, so not everyone. But a certain number from my generation, a few of us, embraced the Revolution, and younger girls too, many of the younger girls… Gioconda Belli, Gloria Carrión, Telma Argüello, Lourdes Mayorga, María José Alvarez, Rossana Lacayo, Margarita Montealegre, the Vijil Teyssere sisters….

As time went on, the nuns were more open to change. Liberation Theology arrived, and there was more of a stimulus, and the younger girls became more clearly committed. The upper class in Nicaragua was committed too, and many of the revolutionary commanders came from the upper class, people who left their homes and went to live in poor neighborhoods like El Riguero, where Father Uriel Molina was the priest at the Santa María de los Ángeles Church. Like them, several of the young girls from Asunción.

I could not be indifferent to the world. Later, I wrote an essay about a painter, Leonel Vanegas, an academic paper that I turned into a homage to him, and in it, I wanted to describe the context for his work. I did a review of what I mentally wanted to explain to myself: What happened during my years as an adolescent? What made me opt for radical changes in Nicaragua? Because it wasn't just Nicaragua that needed and wanted change; it wasn't just almost 50 years of dictatorship by the same family, repression by one sector of the population. Obviously one sector was well off, but at the expense of the other. It wasn't just that, because there were winds of change in the world, and not only in Latin America, where military dictatorships were the rule.

Winds of change: The 1960s

You can imagine, then, the enormous impact that the triumph of the Cuban Revolution in 1959 had on our continent.

You were almost 15 at the time, right?

Yes. Afterwards, in 1968, you have the student rebellion in Paris and at the Tlatelolco Plaza in Mexico City—we didn't know much about it at the time, but it had a huge impact inside Mexico, where it was covered up. Then, Allende in Chile in the 1970s, but all that was grounded in the 1960s, and changes were taking place in other areas too: a new pedagogy appears, a whole new philosophy with the Beatniks, existentialism, Simone de Beauvoir, Sartre, the hippies....

But to return for a moment to my adolescence, the developed countries were not happy. I think that the young people in the developed countries wanted a more natural world, because the hippies represented that—they didn't cut their hair, walked around with no shoes on, didn't want to drink Coca-Cola... They wanted to recover an ideal society, a paradise, not live in an industrialized society. In the United States, you have Elvis Presley, and, from what I've been told, rock and roll and Elvis Presley were promoted as the white figure of a black success story. The blacks are the ones who created rock and roll, that music of forceful protest, but Elvis is promoted and becomes one of the popular singers in my adolescence. Then come the Beatles with their beautiful sounds and revolutionize music. Also, drugs begin to appear in the 1970s. In the '60s, when you and I are 15, 16 years old, there was not a lot of drug use yet, at least not in Nicaragua. That comes at the end of the '60s and beginning of the '70s, with marihuana, LSD, and other stronger drugs.

But in my youth there were winds of change, and many new theories came to the university in the 1970s, like Marcuse and his new theory of communication. In Latin America, winds of political and economic change prevail, and intellectuals there also produce theories of change: prestigious economists come out with their dependency theory; sociologists of the stature of Edelberto Torres Rivas with a reinterpretation of Central American development; his Guatemalan compatriot Severo Martínez Peláez with his broad study, *The Homeland of the Creole*. Much new thought appears. Marxism as a philosophical tendency is assimilated. In pedagogy, Paulo Freire, a Christian, revolutionizes education with his *Pedagogy of the Oppressed* and *Education, the Practice of Freedom*, and his international counterpart, philosopher Erich Fromm, publishes *The Art of Loving*.

This epoch of ours is really incredible, with very important changes taking place from the 1960s to now. There is the whole sexual revolution. The modern form of feminism started in Europe in the 1950s and comes to us later, as a lot of feminist tendencies begin to arrive. I think that taking into account this context, we can explain why we no longer belong to the previous world and adopt a new way of thinking and being. All this, I believe, I lived and experienced during my adolescence, if not in a totally conscious way, at least, unconsciously.

I fell head over heels in love

"Sweet fifteen" parties were the norm back then, but I didn't have one because we had just moved to Managua, and I didn't have a lot of friends. I was just starting at the school and hadn't gotten into all the social activities. So, they made me a new rainbow-colored dress, one of those puffy styles that were popular at the time, my parents took me out to dinner, and afterwards, we walked around, getting to know Managua. Later, I started to go to parties for my classmates and friends. I went to the one for María Antonieta Gutiérrez and noticed a very handsome boy who was a poet, and I knew he was going out with Indiana Valle—that "sharp" friend of mine from León who had said, "What? You don't wear a bra?" I met him at the party, and he asked me to dance. We danced to a bolero called "Memories of Ipacaraí".... I have never forgotten the details of that moment! He suddenly asked me, "Do you want to be my girlfriend?" You were not supposed to say "yes" immediately, because you'd look easy; you had to say you would think about it, and that's what I answered. But before that, I asked, "And Indiana?" "We're through," he said.

So I felt free, because in my time, at least for some of us girls, we were superstrict, and you were never supposed to steal a boyfriend from another girl, never ever! But if he was free, then you could go out with him. Later on, he visited me at home, and a week later, I said "yes" and became his girlfriend. I don't remember how I told my mother that I had a boyfriend who wanted to come visit me, but she told my father. It was incredible, because I was already 16, and the boy was 17, one year older than me, and my father said it was okay, that he could visit me three times a week between seven and nine p.m.! [Laughter]

One of my father's weaknesses was "skirts." He was not a drinker; he was loving with all of us; he was financially responsible, and with my mother was always the great romantic. She was in love with him all his life and forgave his adventures to such an extent that she says if my father were still alive, she would marry him all over again; he was the only man for her. But he was unfaithful, and since military officers have certain duties, he would pull duty or be elsewhere and often was not at home at seven in the evening. My boyfriend started to come every day, and my mother didn't say anything, but at nine, the windows would begin to rattle so he'd leave. And, María, I have to tell you, I fell deeply in love. That was my first love. I kissed him too, but with permission. There was a priest at school, Father Álvaro Oyanguren, with a new mentality, very open, very broad, a Jesuit, and the chaplain told us it was not a sin to kiss.

He authorized it?

Yes. My father once had a talk with me about this. It was really humorous because he wanted to give me advice and fulfill his role as a father and said I had to be careful, that trust should be limited. He, in the most delicate way, tried to advise me on things by putting limits on me, and I answered him in reverse. I said, "But, father, love is like a tree, you have to water it so that it grows...," so on and so forth, reversing everything he told me. It was a really funny conversation, because he did what he could as a parent, and I did what I could as a daughter to be right, and that's as far as the conversation went!

This boy and I kissed and embraced, and, wow! I was transported to another world! Head over heels in love! He was handsome; he was intelligent; he had won a prize for oratory; he was a good poet and a good story writer and won a poetry prize with the literary magazine *Ventana* and, for short story, the Mariano Fiallos Gil Prize, the most important prize for my generation offered by the UNAN University. He was just about to graduate from high school. For several months, we were sweethearts and would see each other every day, go to parties, always with a chaperone, of course, but I was deeply in love with him. He was very good with me too, but I heard constant rumors that he went to León to see Indiana or another girl and that he wasn't totally faithful. He graduated and left to study in Mexico. We said good-bye. Several other boys we knew finished school at the same time and went abroad to study.

Angelita Saballos, who was my close friend, and I later talked and compared our experiences. She had such a strong love for her first boyfriend that she can't ever forget it either. Angelita is the same age as me, and she remembers Marvin like it was the first day. He also left to study. Carlos, my boyfriend, studied law, and Marvin, medicine. Marvin would write three letters a day! Angelita had a ton of letters like no one had ever seen before! [Laughter]

Carlos wrote to me, I answered. I got a letter only about every 10 days, but those letters were important to me. I would put the last letter under my pillow and leave it there until the next one came and read it over and over again. He sent some beautiful poems. One day I had the flu, and my father was going to give me a shot and told me to boil the hypodermic needles in the kitchen. I go to boil the needles, and my father moves my pillow, calculating that he is going to give me the shot with his right hand in my left hip. He moves the pillow to get the bed ready and discovers the letter underneath.... My mother comes into the kitchen and says to me, "Are you crazy or what? Your father is in there reading your letter!" "Oh, no! I'm so embarrassed!" I said. Of course, they were beautiful letters, but I was worried that my father was reading one. I waited until he finished reading, stuck it in the envelope, and put it back, then I came in. He said not one word, nor did I, didn't even open my mouth, and he gave me the shot.

Several months later I heard that Carlos had a girlfriend in Mexico. People started telling me things that completely undermined my confidence in him. Besides, I thought some of his letters sounded strange. I wrote to him and said, "Look, honestly, if you don't want to continue, let's end it now." I remember that I wrote the card to him with deep pain but great pride. And I added, "It's too bad you have such little confidence in yourself," or something like that, because he had been saying he was unsure about his future, this, that, and the other. What I concluded was that he was trying to tell me, in an indirect way, that we should end our relationship, so I ended it right then and there. Afterwards, he came home for vacation, and I was dying to see him, but I acted like it didn't matter. I never, ever forgot him. He married a Mexican woman, and I dreamed about him for years!

I married forever (1966): Happy marriage, children, activism

Afterwards, the man whom I eventually married, Carlos Rodolfo Icaza, courted me, and I fell in love with him. But at first, I was still in love with the other Carlos, and I told him, "Look, the truth is that I can't forget my other love, and why should I lie to you? You seem like a nice person, and I like you, but I'm not sure." I told him I was going to Bonanza on vacation, and he visited me there. That really impressed me—the difference between the one I adored, but who was distancing himself from me, and this one who came to see me in Bonanza, which was a long and expensive plane trip. Besides, he was a great singer with an excellent voice and sang romantic songs to me. He was intelligent too, studying law, and was very polite and sensitive with me. He had a jeep and would pick me up from work at the office and take me to the university. He dedicated himself to me, called me every day, and that's how he won my heart. I appreciated him and fell in love. The other one fascinated me; it was something that came spontaneously into my life, a first love, but it went just so far, because that man was not faithful or anything like it. But this other man loved me, pursued me, and finally convinced me. I was really in love with him and got married at age 22.

In the chapel and with the Monsignor officiating?

Yes, precisely. You are referring to the poem "When I Married," and you can see there that I have an intuition about what was going to happen…

In what sense?

Because the whole tone of the poem is between real and ironic.

When I married
the chapel was tiny
Monsignor recited the traditional psalms:

> *"May you be diligent like Martha,*
> *prudent like Rachel,*
> *of long and prolific life, like Sarah."*

In that poem, I think I leave a testimony about my period. I mean, those are the commandments I received, and I submitted to them conscientiously, because that is how I had been brought up, and those were the values. Being diligent in my home was being responsible…, although it's not exactly true that I was very diligent at home because I had a housekeeper, and my mother-in-law lived with us and helped me while I worked in an office. Being prudent was not hard for me because I was calm by nature. I was never impulsive or ill-mannered, and I imagine that helped my husband feel comfortable with me, because it was not easy to enter into conflict with me. I was much calmer and more mature and didn't get into conflicts despite his character, which over time, grew intolerable. I had the children I was supposed to have, though later on, we controlled the fertility somewhat. In that first period, then, I married seriously and sincerely forever.

And were you happy?

For 10 years I managed to be happy. There were problems, but they were all surmountable until a later point, when it was awful.

I always wanted to work outside the home: Women enter the university

What you have said about working surprises me, because the image in the media of Nicaragua during that period was that there was not a strong middle class. But you are talking about yourself and other women from the middle and upper middle class who worked outside the home. You worked after you were married and had children. Was this due to economic conditions?

In the 1960s and 1970s, above all in the '70s, under Somoza, even when there was a 52% illiteracy rate in Nicaragua, a good number of us entered the university, and there were many bookstores. Of course, only the privileged class could read, but there was a certain boom. I once consulted with a Nicaraguan economist and sociologist Óscar-René Vargas, and said, "You know, I am writing about that period of the 1970s, and I remember some very positive things about the economy then. As director of the Central American University [UCA] Bookstore, I earned 2,500 *córdobas* [$360], which was not a bad salary—the exchange rate was seven *córdobas* to one U.S. dollar—and things were cheaper. Buying power was high; I could hire a housekeeper, and there was money left over for many other things." He told me I was right, because there was an economic resurgence based on a boom in cotton. International cotton and coffee prices rose and brought a marked economic improvement in Nicaragua. The contradiction, I say, is that authoritarian governments, dictatorships, have the advantage of imposing order, but you have to weigh the price of that order. There was a flourishing economy, then, that increased and fortified the middle class.

Besides, the Revolution itself was not made by workers and farmers but by university students. The Ortega brothers are middle class, not proletarians. Their father was an exporter, as Humberto Ortega mentions in his book, an export firm representative. There was a strong middle class, although right now, a huge problem in practically all of Latin America is this neoliberal economic system that is accused of impoverishing the entire middle class.

I saw that in Chile in 1999, the result of the mislabeled "Chilean Miracle."

The same happened in Nicaragua, but in the 1970s, there was a flourishing middle class.

Did middle class women work because they needed the household income? As you say in the poem "When I Married," women of a certain class were married in the chapel and took certain traditional vows related to homemaking. But did they then work outside the home? And you worked with a husband and children. Was it for financial reasons, or because it strengthened you personally?

In my case, it was my choice. I always wanted to work. My income was not a significant factor in the lifestyle we led, because I was just a secretary, but at least I earned enough for my personal needs and could pay a housekeeper to do the domestic work that I didn't want to do. The amount of money was not significant, but work gave me interesting contacts at the university, and besides, I studied and worked there. My husband had graduated from law school and was a good lawyer; he had many clients and managed to earn money even in the midst of tragedies. After the 1972 earthquake that devastated Managua, many supermarkets were looted, and he was their lawyer. He filed and processed all the insurance claims and lawsuits and had a significant income at that time. Of course, much of that money went to pay for my father-in-law's operation in Miami; it took an enormous amount of money to try to save him. But my husband really began to earn a good income; we took out a loan for 350,000 *córdobas* [$50,000] to build a house, the large house we were living in at the triumph of the Revolution, and we were able to cover the loan payments and all the household costs with his income.

Did your husband ever object to your working? He didn't prefer for you to stay at home?

Those were issues we had discussed explicitly, and there was no problem. On my own, after I graduated as a librarian, I decided that I would work part-time in the library at the Jesuit Centroamérica School, where my sons were studying. That allowed me to be at their school for a year, but then the war came. That was my last job before the Revolution, because my husband had a better income, his work was more stable, and I wanted to spend more time with my children. There was always time to write, since I had housekeepers.

"You know, Vidaluz is collaborating with the communists": Public visibility

There was a colonel with a terrible reputation, Colonel Orlando Villalta, Somoza's pilot and the father-in-law of one of my sisters who was very young when she married his son. I didn't like the father or the son and have a very bad opinion of them both. When the father was older, he had a bad opinion of me too. I wrote under my married name in the newspapers and had a certain amount of autonomy. In the 1970s, Pablo Antonio Cuadra gave space in *La Prensa* for a column he baptized "Voice of the Nicaraguan Woman," that I wrote with Ligia Guillén and her sister, Adriana Guillén, who used the pen name of "Carla Rodríguez." Our purpose was to raise consciousness about the need for change in Nicaragua among middle and upper class women. I think each of us wrote two columns and didn't continue, probably because of the onrush of events. I remember that in one of my columns, I used irrefutable data from the first sociological research study carried out here by Reynaldo Antonio Téfel and his team that was published in a book titled *Poor People's Hell*. For me, this type of research, as well as theological and humanistic studies, strengthened me and deepened my commitment. I was not a member of a political party, I didn't engage in anti-Somoza polemics or utilize strictly political language. But I was convinced that the rampant corruption had to be stopped and Somoza had to be removed, as the only way to transform our reality.

That column, "Voice of the Nicaraguan Woman," was it based on Christian principles?

No, Adriana and Ligia were not so Christian, in fact, I think Adriana was more of a Marxist, I believe, or she had a humanist or rationalist background. The point of view of the column came from a little feminism and a little humanism. I would sign "Vidaluz de Icaza," which was a version of my married name, in order to put some distance between it and my father's surname and not cause problems for him. But this man, Villalta, was shrewd; he noticed what I was doing and kept track of it. I was also on the editorial board of a journal published by the Jesuits, a journal of acute political analysis. And I got involved in a few other things, for example, the crisis when they fired poet

Luis Rocha from the Central American University, because the rector, Father León Pallais, was pro-Somoza. The director of the Department of Culture was poet Pablo Antonio Cuadra, the secretary was Luis Rocha. Luis and Ernesto "Tito" Castillo, a law professor, published a Christian oppositional newspaper, *Testimony*, and I helped by typing it. A huge crisis ensued when the Jesuits fired Luis Rocha, they kicked him out, and Pablo Antonio Cuadra resigned because they had disrespected him; they didn't consult him, as Rocha's immediate supervisor, and after Pablo resigned, so did I and left the university because I agreed with all their work promoting change. The resignations were published in the daily *La Prensa* newspaper, which Pablo Antonio codirected with Dr. Pedro Joaquín Chamorro, Somoza's eternal opponent. Certain things, then, made me slightly more visible, despite, as I mentioned, my signing the columns with my married name.

This colonel said to my father, "You know, Vidaluz is collaborating with the communists." And my father said to me, "Look here, my dear, uh… who are you working with?.... Look, you need to be a little careful." My father was timid that way; he never said things to me very directly. He just expressed his concern that the communists not use me. He was worried about that.

His was a healthy and loving concern in a sense, right?

Absolutely. I have always recognized his concern for me personally. He said, "Be careful so the communists can't use you." That's why in the poem "Last Message to My Father, General Meneses," I say, "because history did not allow you to / glimpse this moment, / much less understand it."

And did you ever feel that you had been used?

No. I always had a reason and explanation for my actions, and it was like when I was with my first boyfriend, and my father told me to be careful about being too trustful and so forth, and I gave the example of the tree and said just the opposite, that I was for the liberation of love. On this occasion, I talked to him about Liberation Theology and said, "No, it's about a Christian commitment, father; I work with priests, with religious people, and really with the gospel that speaks of equality…," and I went on and on about Liberation Theology. He just kept quiet.

Unarmed women at mass tear-gassed

The Chamorro family has survived terrible tragedies. I admired Dr. Pedro Joaquín Chamorro, and my mother says that my father thought well of him, because when they sent father to the Dominican Republic with OAS troops, Pedro Joaquín went along as a journalist, and they shared a tent at the camp and had a chance to talk. When Pedro Joaquín was killed in 1978, it affected my father. Stories and speculations abounded that it had been the Sandinista Front, but it was ultimately attributed to Somoza—someone sent by Somoza had killed him.

Your father wouldn't have a way of finding out, since he was a general?

I suppose so, but I don't know; we never talked about it.

An incident of support among women from different social classes occurred just after the assassination. Many men from the countryside had been disappeared, and rural women occupied the United Nations headquarters in Managua. We were called to take turns accompanying them—they were inside the building, and we were outside praying. We would take them urgently needed items and be present as an act of solidarity. One day we learned a mass was going to be celebrated outside the U.N. building for Pedro Joaquín Chamorro and for the disappeared. Since my father was in Guatemala as ambassador, I felt freer—he was not in the country, he was a diplomat and no longer a military officer, and I knew I would not come face-to-face with him if there were problems. For more support, I invited my mother-in-law who was from an anti-Somoza family, an almost-70-year-old lady who was very fond of me, and we went together.

When we arrived, lots of people were already there, including a large number of upper class women, and when the priest was halfway through the mass, National Guard patrols began arriving in their Becats, a type of jeep named for the infamous Special Battalion against Terrorist Acts. They drove up and down in front of the crowd, armed with tear bombs, coming and going, surrounding us and trying to intimidate us. We began to shout, "Who killed Pedro Joaquín? Ask El Chigüín!" "El Chigüín," "The Kid," was the nickname for Somoza's son who was head of the army's Special Forces at the time. Somoza named his son to that position, even though he was not in line for it. "El Chigüín" is a slightly pejorative Nahuatl term used informally for young children. "Who killed Pedro Joaquín? Ask El Chigüín! Where are our rural cousins? Ask the assassins!" That's what we shouted.

Were the shouts intentional provocation?

It was more of a denunciation, because it was true that people out in the country disappeared as soon as they were captured by the National Guard. When mass was almost over, we were singing, and men started arriving to pick up their wives, sisters, relatives, but some of us remained. My husband did not show up, nor did other family members, to try to persuade us to leave or take us away.

Suddenly, they started throwing tear-gas bombs at us. I was sitting on the grass with my mother-in-law and a friend from my prayer group, María Elena Fletes de Chamorro, wife of Rafael Chamorro, later president of the Central American Supreme Court of Justice. Standing behind us was the widow of Iván Mojica, the son of the military attaché who was at the embassy in Guatemala with my father. Behind us on a wall was the Nicaraguan flag, and the tear bombs were the size of a water glass, made of tin, covered with red cloth like felt, and one that they threw at us stuck to the flag. A friend of mine, Tere Cardenal de Delgadillo—Ernesto Cardenal's cousin and mother of César Delgadillo, who had been the assistant supreme Army Chief but later left the Armed Forces, a large woman who was wearing pants that day, she turns around, grabs the bomb off the flag, walks up to the front, stretches one leg up like a baseball pitcher, and, *chac!*, tosses the bomb back at the Guard! [Laughter] They responded by firing more and more bombs! I put my arms over my head, because I thought a tear-gas canister could split our heads open. A wave of smoke came over us, and I got really angry at the point, because we were a bunch of unarmed women at a mass, and what was the justification for such an unnecessary show of force? "Let's sing," I shouted. And we all did, my mother-in-law calmly singing, my friend too.

But tear gas tends to rise, and the friend behind us, Ruth, was suffocating: "Vidaluz, I can't take any more!" she said gasping, tears running down her face, and she was choking, because they were throwing bomb after bomb at us, and smoke was everywhere. I grabbed my mother-in-law by the arm, and we took off running. My friend María Elena hurt her leg, we weren't sure how, maybe on the spiny leaves of a plant. We turned a corner and ran toward some houses, because people in the neighborhood had opened their doors to offer refuge if the Guard arrived and started arresting people, and they had tubs full of water ready inside so people could wash their faces. We were the last to arrive, and I was worried about my mother-in-law who had high blood pressure and heart problems, and I felt responsible for her. I see that all the tubs are empty, and there is no water anywhere; we go to the bathroom, no water at the sink, no water at the shower, because the Guard had cut off the water. Oh, no! Then someone gives me a piece of ice, thank goodness! I wash my mother-in-law's nose and face and my own.

We waited there inside, and they took care of my friend's leg wound. "When can we leave?" people were asking. I said, "Not now, because if we walk out now, the Guard will be waiting and will arrest us. Let's wait a while." I didn't want to be arrested because they would tell my father that his daughter had been involved, and I didn't want him to get mixed up in it. That was my biggest worry, not about getting arrested, but that it was going to complicate his life. "No, let's wait."

When we were informed that the Guard was gone and we could leave, my mother-in-law and I got in the car, drove another woman home, and finally got to my mother-in-law's house. My children ran out to greet us and had sneezing fits, because our clothes were full of tear gas. My husband came from his office just up the street, we gave him a quick summary, and he shook his head, worried and resigned. I said good-bye and headed home with the children. Guess what! My father was in the neighborhood! I didn't know he was in Nicaragua! My sister was married to the son of some neighbors who lived on the corner, and my father was at her in-laws' house when the rest of the family came home from the mass. Everyone in my neighborhood was involved. The women went in, clothes full of gas, eyes red, and said:

"Greetings, General. What they did to us is an outrage! Would you believe we were at mass, and the guards threw tear bombs at us!" My father was very embarrassed.

"And Vidaluz? Was Vidaluz there too?"

"Yes."

The rest of the day I waited for my father to come over, but he didn't.

They called me, it was a Saturday…: Ambassador father assassinated in Guatemala, 1978

When your father was shot in Guatemala and you went there, did you find yourself surrounded by National Guard troops?

Yes, they called me, it was a Saturday, almost noon. My uncle, Octavio Gutiérrez, a colonel in the Navy—husband of my mother's sister Pastora, the same family that later took care of my son Carlos when he went to New Orleans, was on vacation in Guatemala with my aunt. They were going to go out with my parents, and my father went to get a shave at a barbershop a few blocks away. Then they heard the shots. My mother said she was almost ready when she heard the gunfire and some movement and noise in the street, and shortly thereafter, they told her my father had been shot a few blocks from home and an ambulance had been called. My uncle phoned me:

"Vidaluz, your father has been shot."

"Where?," I asked.

"At the street corner," he said.

"No, I mean, where on his body was he shot? In the head, in the back?" I don't remember what he answered, but it was something like:

"Call the president's office." So I hung up and called and said:

"I want to inform you that the Nicaraguan ambassador to Guatemala, General Edmundo Meneses Cantarero, has just been shot."

"Understood. Where? Give me all the details." I told them what I knew and added:

"Please, do something quickly so he can get help and be brought back as soon as possible." Then I called my husband, and I imagine he contacted other officials right away, because when I got a call back, it was from the minister of Health, my husband's cousin, Edmundo Bernheim Espinosa, and he said:

"Vidaluz, what happened?"

"My father has been wounded, they say. He's not dead, but they shot him, and I don't know much more," I said. "Someone has to call Somoza, tell him to send help…, or whatever should be done." He said to me:

"We're going to make arrangements for you to go."

"Good," I said.

He got us a small plane, and I went with my son Carlos and my youngest sister, Dalila. When I got there, I went directly to the private clinic where they took him run by a German doctor. The atmosphere was extremely tense. There were men patrolling the clinic grounds, and when I went to where my father was, I noticed glass windows all around, and he was sitting up and alert. I greeted him and gave him a kiss, and said:

"Father, how do you feel?"

"I'm okay," he said.

"I'm glad."

I stayed with him for a while, but I was worried about the windows, because I know that Guatemala is extremely violent. It has always been a violent place, and I had heard it wouldn't be the first time killers would go into a hospital to "finish off" someone they wanted dead, and I was frightened by the windows all around the area. I think we talked about this among the family members, that security was moving all around. By the next day, they had moved him to the end of a corridor, to a room where I thought he was better protected. When you looked out the window, there were security patrols in the garden and everywhere. It was all very tense.

The family took turns each day staying with him. Father Amando López, who was in my Christian study group in Nicaragua, recommended a Jesuit priest in Guatemala to me, Father Amán, and I spoke with him. He said he would be glad to sit with me for a while, and he took confession from my father and gave him communion. After he left, my mother or someone said to me:

"Listen, it seems that the guards don't want you to bring those priests around here for security reasons," because they thought they were communists. I asked him not to come again and explained:

"Father, I thank you very much, but you should not come back because this comment was made to me, and I don't want to cause more problems, or create more tension, or complicate things for you, and I don't want my family to feel uncomfortable."

"Don't worry," the father said very humbly. Then a nun started coming and gave my father communion.

There was a colonel working at the embassy, and I would talk with him, Otto Mojica, the father of a poet younger than I who died very early in an accident, Iván Mojica. The first week my father got better, his condition improved. But I thought it wasn't a good idea for them to turn on the television; security people would come from the embassy and talk with him and give him information, and they would turn on the TV where you could see the cities being bombed by Somoza's troops. I don't know if it was because my father ordered them to keep him informed, or if they thought it was a good idea, or if military officers just act like that, but I always thought it wasn't appropriate for a person in such a delicate state to get terribly stressful news and, in addition, for him to see those awful scenes of the bombing of cities and the civilian population.

One night they called us urgently because my father's condition had worsened, and he was doing poorly. First, skin ulcers had appeared, as a reaction to the operation, and then he suffered a hemorrhage, and at the same time his chest became congested. I remembered that my father-in-law had died of a cerebral tumor; they operated on his brain in Miami, and as a postoperative reaction, he suffered a massive, uncontrollable hemorrhage, as if there were nervous shock to the system. My father's condition worsened, and they did a tracheotomy on him, but he died. I saw how he died little by little on that machine where you see clearly how the heartbeats finally turn into a flat line. I saw death there, and it was a very moving and extraordinary experience. He died very peacefully, and I will always remember his serene face.

My uncles, his brothers, had their doubts and wondered whether he had received good medical care, whether the doctor had been threatened and failed to treat him aggressively enough and just let him die, because during the first week he began to recover, but during the second his condition deteriorated. I must admit that these doubts weighed on me too, wondering if something like that was a factor, but we will never know. This type of political attack is surrounded by so many possibilities that you can never be sure about anything. What I felt was that two things could have affected him: one, that they kept him informed on the terrible progress of the war; and two, the possibility that he might become an invalid. One of the times that a priest friend of his from Jinotega visited, a priest or a doctor, or two people visited him, I really don't remember, but I was there. His friend took a pencil and touched his leg and foot, and there was no feeling, so it's possible that he realized that he was going to lose the use of both legs. My father was a very handsome man and very masculine, and maybe it was too hard for him to accept becoming an invalid.

Well, such scenes happened, and Rosa María Britton, the Panamanian author, said, "Write a novel with all that!" I told her for me, that moment was too distressing, too intense, too terrible. They take my father down to the morgue because the body has to be prepared. The rest of the family is leaving, and I don't have the strength to move, so I tell them, "I'm going to stay here, you can pick me up later." I go down to the morgue and am there with my father where they are going to prepare him. Some men with a camera come in…, in a short poem I talk about this…, and they lift the sheet and clack, clack, clack, photos for the file, you know, practical things.

And "Case Closed," as the poem "Triptych to Remember" says?

Yes, photos for the record and all that, and I am sitting there. My mother went to the beauty parlor, because you have to follow class protocol, right? The wake for the ambassador was going to take place, so she went to get her hair done. The whole family went to get ready, the wake was in a funeral home, and the next day a special plane came, and we took him back to Managua. The funeral procession went through streets that were in the middle of a war. We went to the Military Academy, and he was given full military honors for those who die on duty; the bugle played as he was buried, they gave the widow the folded flag…, very impressive rituals…, and we lived through all of that.

Back at the hospital when he could still talk, my mother had asked him, as if it were the most natural question, "Where do you want to be buried?" He answered, "In the crypt for officers." My elderly grandparents were at the funeral, and my grandmother wanted him buried in Jinotega, but my father had said in the officers' crypt, a section in the general cemetery where military officers were usually buried, with the statue of a soldier on top, and that's where we buried him, with a plaque underneath. I didn't want him put there, because I thought it was better for him to go back to Jinotega, back to where his parents were, detached from all this, from the National Guard, from Somoza. But we respected his wishes.

When the Revolution triumphed, some people went into that crypt and destroyed the top part; they didn't touch the coffins, but they demolished the statue of the soldier. That had a horrible impact on me, and I dreamed people went there and dragged his coffin out. I had nightmares, and six months later my uncles in Jinotega asked me, "Vidaluz, could you help us get Edmundo moved?" "Oh, yes," I immediately replied.

I very happily asked for permission from the Ministry of Health and quickly got it. I removed him, and we went to bury him in Jinotega. I thought it was a good thing because we left him in a safe place, in a grave that was cared for, which was like putting him in a clean, orderly room, immersed in a good environment, and he was with his grandparents and his ancestors who loved him.

A group did assume responsibility for your father's assassination, right?

Yes, after my father died, about 15 days or a month later a newspaper published a communiqué from the Guerrilla Army of the Poor (EGP) saying that they assumed responsibility for the attack, carried out as a gesture of solidarity with the struggle of the Sandinista Front in Nicaragua, a gesture of support from revolutionaries in Guatemala to those in Nicaragua.

But there were a lot of rumors in my family that the assassins were not from the EGP. At first, the family was suspicious, and I posed some direct questions to find out. When the Revolution triumphed, people were saying it had been Doris Tijerino. "I don't think so," I said, but I mentioned it to poet Erick Blandón, Erick talked with Doris, and she absolutely denied it. I believe she told the truth. Later, they linked it to Commander Henry Ruíz, but it turned out he wasn't involved either. The infamous Colonel Villalta, apparently my endless pursuer, had the nerve to insinuate to my mother that I had something to do with the attack, based on what could be read into the poem that I dedicated to my father, "Last Message." I told my mother that only a twisted mind like Villalta's could make that sort of interpretation. The poem was published during the Revolution in the daily paper *Barricada* and in the Casa de las Américas journal, one of the Latin American left's most prestigious publications. It was a homage to my father to whom I felt special sense of gratitude.

For me, it was clearly logical that it had been a cell of the Guerrilla Army of the Poor. Guatemala is still an extremely violent country. My mother was told that members of the commando group that carried out the assault were hunted down and killed by Guatemalan security forces.

Because it had been a terrorist act?

For me, it was cold-blooded murder, because they attacked an unarmed person from behind while he was walking into a barbershop. My mother's chauffeur, Pedro, drove him and was waiting in the car. My father got out, and as he went up the steps, they drove by and machine-gunned him in the back. I said it was not an act that rose to the level of the revolutionary struggle of the Nicaraguan people, because the Sandinista Front had never committed that type of attack, just the opposite, many young people fell in lopsided confrontations.

In my family we have another horrible case of war violence, against the father-in-law of my brother Jairo, who married Eunice Pérez, daughter of General Reynaldo Pérez Vega. It was a terrible episode. In 1978, Nora Astorga, later the revolutionary government's ambassador to the United Nations, participated in what was supposed to be the kidnapping of the general, the chief of security. From what I learned later, the intention was to kidnap him and demand freedom for Sandinista prisoners. Besides Nora, who played the role of seductress in the context of the military man's known pursuit of women, there was a guerrilla commander, Walter Ferreti, who used the name of "Chombo" and had joined the guerrillas after living and working in a restaurant in California for several years; and Hilario Sánchez, a famous commander from Monimbó, Masaya, a young man of indigenous origins. I knew Nora from when she was quite young and came to study law at the UCA college where I was a secretary. She always impressed me as a refined, sweet person. I was surprised when the news item appeared in the paper, first the terrible news of the execution of my brother's father-in-law, and then the photo of Nora dressed in camouflage in the middle of the jungle, making her role public.

It is curious that before the revolutionary government lost the election in 1990, all three of the people in this episode lost their lives. Nora died of cancer very young, her oldest daughter died soon afterwards, and her other children were raised most unselfishly by her sister Lidia, the first woman airline pilot in Nicaragua. Walter Ferreti died in a terrible automobile accident. Hilario Sánchez, a bold and brave commander, drowned during a rescue mission on Lake Nicaragua.

For my sister-in-law, Eunice, the experience was very difficult. In my brother's house in New Orleans hang the portraits of my father and of her father, both generals and both assassinated. An enormous, terrible weight hangs over our family. Eunice and Jairo have two sons, but between the birth of those two, she lost a child and suffered deeply. They kept the baby's ashes, and once when I went to the United States, they gave them to me so that I could put them in my father's tomb in Jinotega, and I did.

In 2002, all my brothers and sisters went to Managua for the first time in a long while, and all six of us children got together with my mother and wanted to bring my father back to Managua, because my grandmother had died, and my grandfather was close to death, and put him in the family crypt that has 12 places for the six children plus whoever else wants or needs to be buried there. My great-aunt and uncle are there. We transferred my father's remains again, and the ashes of my brother's child, from Jinotega to a final resting place, the family crypt in Managua, where my mother hopes to be buried next to my father. My father has been a traveler after death and has had no rest! But now I think he's where he should be and where my mother, the woman who loved him always, is going to keep him company.

I considered my father a victim

I considered my father a victim. I said so once in an interview, and perhaps it was misunderstood. I saw him as a victim of the system, since he and many military men went into the Guard like your young men in the U.S. join the Army.

Was it a way for him to generate opportunities? One of the few options for a young man at the time?

His family had 10 children, and they tell me he left home at a young age and headed for the Caribbean Coast. He left when he was a teenager in high school and wanted to be a doctor. From the coast he went to Managua with no support.

He left home for the Caribbean Coast to do what?

To work at whatever he could find. I don't remember how he survived, how he said he lived during that time, but I imagine he did any job he could find to eat and live. When he was still young, he went to Managua and joined the Guard. Really, a young man who leaves his family home has no financial support. In any case, I imagine that his father tried to force him to return home, and he saw the Guard as the only way he could keep his freedom. As a National Guard officer, it's probably similar to what you have in the States, on a different scale, of course—there are lots of possibilities, and the privileges of military officers are always a factor. He got an education, finished high school, and graduated as a military officer, in the Mullins Class, which was the fourth class graduated from the academy, named for a U.S. officer. Once he graduated, he came out with a rank, an assignment, and a salary. He graduated and married my mother, and when I met him, he was Lieutenant Meneses, I don't remember if it was Second or First Lieutenant. He had various assignments and did specialized training courses. He never went to the States, but he was in Panama at the School of the Americas and later went to Venezuela to a school called White Rabbit.

When they transferred him to El Jícaro and I stayed in school in Matagalpa, there was an border conflict with Honduras that Sandinista General Humberto Ortega talks about in his book, *The Epic of the Insurrection*. On May 1st, 1957, the same day he assumed office as president, after elections boycotted by the Conservative Party because it considered them fraudulent, that night, Luis Somoza Debayle went to the National Stadium to organize the first battalion armed with Sherman tanks. An Infantry company of 74 soldiers went with each tank, for a total of 400 men under the command of National Guard Major Carlos Reyes, supported by Captain Napoleón Ubilla Baca, who later rebelled against Somoza, and Lieutenants Guillermo Conrado and Edmundo Meneses Cantarero, my father. This episode was known as the Mokorón War, named for the disputed geographical area in the north of our national territory. The conflict was eventually resolved, but my father was in the border war zone and prepared for combat. As a strategy he ordered some sticks tied together and dressed in olive drab uniforms to look like soldiers in a truck, so the enemy would think there were more soldiers than there actually were. General Ortega mentions a curious fact, that "university students Carlos Fonseca and Silvio Mayorga, members of the Nicaraguan Democratic Youth, proposed to the president of the Republic that he mobilize the Nicaraguan young people to defend the Nation." That is, a sort of patriotic military service proposed by future leaders of the anti-Somoza opposition and founders of the FSLN, the Sandinista National Liberation Front. But, in the end, war did not break out.

It must have been hard on the family.

My mother was rather calm, or maybe unaware, perhaps she was a little nervous about it, but she trusted my father, who was very responsible and left the household well-prepared. Bailón, the teenaged boy from the coast who was living with us, was in charge of going to headquarters to get provisions for the family, making sure nothing was lacking, that there were candles and everything, in case of war. Yes, there was a little bit of tension.

Another international episode was with the OAS in the Dominican Republic in 1965, when a group of young officers tried to restore the constitutional government of Juan Bosch, elected after the assassination of Rafael Leónidas Trujillo. Bosch had been ousted by a faction of the Army. The OAS went to mediate, and several countries with military governments sent troops. My father was in charge of the Nicaraguan contingent. That's where he talked with journalist Dr. Pedro Joaquín Chamorro, housed in the military tent, and was impressed by him. A photo was published in *Novedades* when the troops returned and paraded on the plaza in front of the Cathedral. We went to welcome him home and are pictured there with him, in his combat fatigues.

Another incident occurred in 1967, when he was sent to Pancasán in the Matagalpa hills, where the guerrilla forces were operating, a conflict that the Sandinista Front considers a military loss but political and moral victory. My father was there for a while. I later learned that a Coronel [Óscar] Morales had been sent as my father's superior officer—"Moralitos," notoriously remembered for the assassination of David Tejada. I know that whoever was captured was to be sent to jails in Managua, and my father was supposed to do this. I never heard of him torturing anyone in the mountains. At the time, I was recently married, living separately, and trying to maintain some distance from these events, because it was too painful to think that my father was on one side, and on the other were young men whom I might have met at the university and who were disappearing from the classrooms to join the clandestine struggle.

You told me once that being a National Guard member was insecure. In what sense?

My mother told me, "Remember that the Guard is insecure." I don't know if it was because my father could be killed or he could leave the Guard, with no job security if he did.

Might it have been like in the U.S., where you have to win promotion within a certain time frame or be forced out?

Well, there were two types of military men at the time—the older group was the Guard that Somoza formed under U.S. military guidance, which they called "Constabulary," made up of people who became military men in the process. But my father was in the fourth graduating class from the academy, so he was part of an echelon through which you advanced, unless you got a dishonorable discharge for some reason, but generally, my father was highly disciplined in his work.

I don't know in what sense my mother felt insecure, because the probabilities were that father would be promoted, since he was an academy graduate. When we left León for Managua, he was a captain, and later he kept getting promoted. Economically, I believe, she may have thought it was a little insecure because within the Guard, there were positions that paid more or less, depending on the jobs you were assigned. There were some famous appointments, chief of police, for example. That was part of the criticism made of Somoza's army and a topic I discussed with my father. The actual salaries of Guard members were low, but they gave them extra pay for many things on top of the fines they collected, the taxes, money from brothels.... I asked him, "Why don't they put some order in the Guard and pay a decent salary; for example, a commandant in a town has a position equivalent to that of a company manager and is supposed to maintain good relations with the community, send his children to certain schools, etc., so why not pay him a manager's salary?" He responded that there was a military officer doing just such an economic study to reorganize the Guard.

Safe house for guerrillas, then, for National Guard officers, 1979

The jubilation on the main square on July 20th, the day after the Sandinista triumph, I saw on television. I took seriously Commander Tomás Borge's guiding maxim, "Implacable in combat, generous in victory." My home had been a transit point for popular combatants who needed temporary refuge or were waiting for exile through the Mexican or Colombian Embassies. The Colombian Embassy, located in Chema Castillo's house, held a number of Sandinistas, several of them wounded, and could not suddenly receive National Guard members who sought asylum at the moment of defeat. The embassy affixed its national shield on my house and asked us to open it to the new asylum seekers. My reflection was that few persons would be able to find the emotional equanimity in those moments to put the commander's maxim into practice. And in my father's memory, I thought, I am going to receive these National Guard people into my home.

And you did that conscious of the implications?

Absolutely, totally. The father of my children agreed, and our shocked housekeepers, Teresa Pérez and Leopoldina Hernández, collaborated. We were suddenly invaded by 80 people—military men, their wives and children. That was our situation when Dr. Alejandro Lara Manning, director of the Military Hospital, showed up, bag in hand, in a Red Cross vehicle, and asked to stay. I explained that it was materially impossible to house him, and I was sure he would be able to get help, considering his rank, and besides, he was being supported by the Red Cross. He turned pale and left with the people who had brought him. Dr. Lara was the father of my childhood friends in Somoto, the twins, María Auxiliadora and María Elena, and I had met him there, but he didn't appear to remember me. I should have taken him in, but I realize that I never thought he was in danger, in fact, he was being protected by the Red Cross, and I was fully convinced that a humanistic regime was going to take over, grounded in social justice. The higher echelons were always more likely to have their lives respected, while the lower-ranking military were going to need protection during the first days, because of the thousands of deaths during the war between brothers and sisters that was drawing to a dramatic close. There was so much pain and hatred.

We really did not have the physical capacity to house so many people, and we spoke with our neighbor, one of Carlos's cousins, Marina Icaza, who was married to a Britisher named Colin Brown. They had the consulate in their home, only that country could not offer asylum, but it could take in refugees, which was the status of the wives and children. We took immediate action. By six in the afternoon, the Colombian Embassy had rented the neighboring house and came to collect the majority of my guests. I was left with some 10 military men of all ranks, from the cook at the Military Casino to a Coronel Soto, who had a law degree. I had studied at the UCA and worked as a secretary at the Law School for three years [1968-1971]. Several Guard officers enrolled in classes, and I had met this Colonel Soto. I said to him:

"Look, you studied law. I can understand that my father, who did not have an alternative profession, never left the Guard, but you were a lawyer. Didn't you realize what was happening? Didn't you understand Somoza's circumstances?" He answered:

"Of course. I specialized in political warfare, and I did an analysis of the correlation of combatant forces that showed the FSLN was about to win and sent it to Somoza."

"And what did he say?"

"He said, 'Stop talking shit and get back to work.'" That's how he answered him, with vulgarity.

"You should have left then," I said, but he didn't answer. He stayed there and was granted asylum.

So, it was with this "contingent" that we watched the televised scenes of the 19th of July that actually took place on the 20th, but it doesn't end there. The jails freed all the Sandinista prisoners, and the combatants from Masaya whom I had housed clandestinely began to show up—Carlos Alberto Gutiérrez, alias "You," from San Juan de Oriente, who had survived a bullet to the head, and from Catarina, the Carballo brothers and Carlos Nicaragua. Of that group, we had been able to keep out of jail only "Pablo," Raúl Vásquez, who posed as our gardener. Boris Vega Sánchez, may he rest in peace, and Juanita Bermúdez had brought them to us because they were wounded and needed to be treated by a doctor in Managua, or because they had been identified and could be arrested. They came rushing in with their red and black scarves, and we hugged very joyfully. Only later did I realize the terror that invaded our transitory guests when they saw them burst in wearing the adversary's symbol, red and black scarves around their necks!

I also had the minister of Public Health in my house, and that comes out in a poem. The Somoza government's last minister of Health was Edmundo Bernheim Espinosa, also my husband's cousin. He was a great internist and excellent private doctor. He was not a politician and had no reason to be a minister, but he accepted the appointment from Somoza during his last period. Toward the end, we were engaged in an endeavor to debilitate Somoza's government by convincing his officials to resign. We would call Edmundo and say:

"Mundo, leave. Why are you a minister? You were never a politician, you were a successful doctor, and you are sharing responsibility for a corrupt government with a terrible reputation." But he didn't leave, and when the government fell, he went straight home. Somoza notified all the government officials of an airplane waiting to take them out of the country, but Edmundo didn't feel responsible or guilty and thought, "Well, I did my job, and now I am going home." My husband called him and said:

"Look, Mundo, don't you want to come over to our house? We have a shield from the Colombian Embassy. I think you should come, because you were minister of Health, and people are not going to ask if you were honest or not, a good or bad minister, just whether you were in favor of Somoza."

He convinced him, and Edmundo came and stayed for a week. Another friend of ours from the Christian group came over, Dr. Juan Ignacio Gutiérrez Sacasa, who became the first vice-minister of Health for the Revolution when Dr. César Amador Kühl was minister of Health. Juan Ignacio came over, and Edmundo gave him the key to the Ministry of Public Health right there in my house.

Edmundo Bernheim had been a personal friend of Doña Hope, Somoza's wife. Doña Hope was a Nicaraguan brought up outside the country and given the name of "Hope" in English instead of "Esperanza." They were good friends, and the rumor was that they were lovers. He says it was not true, and I think maybe it wasn't. Somoza always had a very famous mistress who was featured in magazines in Nicaragua—Dinorah Sampson, a beautiful Nicaraguan woman. But Doña Hope was a classical woman in her dress and demeanor, and I imagine her model was Jackie Kennedy. She wore very sober, impeccable suits and was a very tall, elegant woman. Somoza's mistress was quite attractive, short, exuberant, pretty, and younger, but Doña Hope was an elegant and refined woman. However, her mentality was foreign. To her credit, she built the Rubén Darío National Theater in Nicaragua, a significant contribution, although at the time it was rejected as elitist, because the social problems of the country's poor people were being ignored. While I was at the university, I attended a street performance of a dramatic piece by Roberto Sánchez, another student, writer, and journalist, that was performed in protest at a nearby square on the same day as the inauguration of the National

Theater. It was ironically titled "What an Honorable Family."

Doña Hope was a good friend of Edmundo, and after he had taken refuge in my house, I asked him:

"Edmundo, is it true that you were Doña Hope's lover?"

"No."

"Then why did you agree to be minister of Health? Why did you join that government and at that stage? You didn't need the money. You were a successful doctor and had a good practice. You have never been a politician, so why?"

"Look, what happened was that when Somoza had his last heart attack, Hope called and asked me, please, as a favor, to go with him, so I traveled with him on the plane to Miami for treatment. I stayed during his convalescence, and we would talk. I said to him, 'You have a bunch of thieves in your government, that's why people are attacking you.' He said to me, 'Why don't you help me? Go take charge of the Ministry of Health.' And I accepted."

"Too bad," I said, "what a mistake!"

In my book *Air that Calls Me* there is a poem titled "First Lady." In that poem, I am speaking to him, although I start out talking about the first lady when I say, "She knew not how to tempt the faun." The faun is Somoza, who always had mistresses.

She knew not how to tempt the faun.
Foreign to her own people,
with the criteria of an investor in "gross countries"
and socially motivated like a philanthropic tourist.

There is another part of the poem that says something that was real, because at the triumph of the Revolution, we went looking for a place to install the Ministry of Culture, which did not exist before. We went to Somoza's home and decided to stay there. We went inside and walked through, curiously examining things. On a shelf in one of the rooms, there was a little book titled in English *My Favorite Birthdays*, as I say in my poem. Edmundo Bernheim was a medical doctor, but in my imagination, for the poem I make him a psychiatrist to Doña Hope, because really a good friend is sometimes the best therapist, and one of the sections of the poem says:

She enjoyed those tactical ways of yours
of serving whiskey on the rocks and
your Freudian analysis of her moments of domestic malaise.
She sent you timely bottles of "cologne for men"

I am imagining that part, because of her personal friendship with him:

*and carefully noted your daughters' birthdays
in her neat book of My Favorite Birthdays.*

*I ask myself, does she still wonder about your fate
from her comfortable exile?*

The poem was inspired by the dialogue I had with Somoza's last minister of Health, at the end of the Somoza regime. I think they were probably not lovers, but close friends. I wrote the poem based on that and the album we found, where I saw written the names of Edmundo's daughters, who were my children's cousins, that's why I knew their names and that of their mother, Kate Parker.

Working for the poor: Christian commitment to the Revolution

Getting back to values and options, when the Revolution triumphs, there is a pluralistic governing junta that I see as natural and appropriate, because I am not an ideologue. In the new Ministry of Culture was Claudia Chamorro, Pedro Joaquín Chamorro's daughter, the first director of the Department of Plastic Arts, and we talked and shared some things at the time. I thought it was normal and positive that Doña Violeta, Pedro Joaquín Chamorro's widow, was a member of the junta, and that Alfonso Robelo was there also representing business interests, that it was pluralistic, because the Revolution was successful, as Humberto Ortega's book says now, because of the alliance of all the people who opposed Somoza.

Obviously, however, the vanguard was in the hands of the armed military front, the Sandinista Front, and the Front people were Marxist-Leninist, at least founders like Tomás Borge. Distinct Front tendencies were involved, but I didn't give them a lot of importance at the time. There were: Jaime Wheelock's proletarian Marxist tendency, in which Christians were not especially welcome at first, although later many joined it; and the GPP, the Prolonged Popular War tendency that had more to do with war strategies and tactics and was the group of Tomás Borge, Bayardo Arce and Lenin Cerna. Humberto Ortega and company's so-called "third" tendency opened the possibility of participation by many progressive and Christian men and women. The person who spoke most explicitly about the potential for Christians was Ricardo Morales Avilés, a major leader and former National University Psychology professor and the husband of Doris Tijerino, one of the Revolution's legendary women commanders. That gave us an opening and allowed me to find a place too. If that possibility had not been opened, I imagine I would have stayed timidly on the margins. But since a more open attitude was expressed, and the politics of alliances was clearly defined, I began to lend support, first through prayer groups, then in first aid brigades to care for those wounded in the fighting, and later using my home as a safe house.

At the hour of the triumph, I see that the plural government junta is appropriate, but it quickly became clear that the Front's most radical tendency, the Marxist one, intended to prevail. The deepest sense of the envisioned changes involved social justice, and that provided common ground for practice by both Marxists and Christians, because if we follow the gospels, the message of Jesus Christ is radical.

I thought, if Robelo, who is a businessman, does not want to radicalize the Revolution because it affects his interests, then he does not have a place, because really what we are going to do is vindicate the poor. I decide that I'm going to work for the poor, and that fits with my way of thinking. I understand the radicalization and what came as a counterrevolutionary war, which further polarized the situation. I incorporate the radicalization, and I understand it more as a struggle between interests—the rich are not going to allow their wealth to be distributed to the poor—and I stay with the Revolution, but not out of hatred for the counterrevolutionaries.

Never a party member, though it was a privilege to be invited: Political commitment vs. family obligations

I never became a party member, though I was invited twice. Just after the triumph of the Revolution they called me and asked me to go to meetings. I went to the first couple of what was called Sandinista Base Committees. I was not very aware of what was going on, and suddenly I found myself involved in the meetings of a party cell. But what was with me? When I explain this, I say that when the Revolution triumphs, I am 35 years old, I am an adult, I have four children, and I come from two rich and deep experiences and options in my life. First, as a young person, I went to the Asunción School, where, as I told you, for me, the pious readings every morning, when they brought us together and gave us profound talks about spirituality and commitment, were a rich experience that formed and marked me.

Then, after I was married, for about seven years we had a prayer group of Christian couples that would meet weekly. There were six to eight couples at any one time, including my neighbors, Pepe Barreto and María del Socorro Gutiérrez, sister of Juan Ignacio Gutiérrez, who became the first vice-minster of Health after the triumph; he and his wife, Irene; Jaime Chamorro, later director of *La Prensa* and his wife, Hilda Argeñal; Morris and Jeannette Sallick;

Jeannette's sister, Ileana Ramírez, and her husband Ernesto Robelo. Ileana died at age 43 of a cerebral aneurysm in the first years after the triumph of the Revolution, and she was considered a saint, people even say she performed miracles. She was a charming woman who played the guitar and sang and seemed to have the gift of healing, as witnessed by some of the poor people who were her neighbors in Esquipulas, on the road to Masaya. My younger son is divorced from a niece of hers; we never imagined we were going to be family! I pray to her for my grandchildren, Arián and Maité. Also in the group was a gynecologist, Álvaro Avilés, and his wife, Graciela, from Peru. Their oldest son Álvaro died doing Patriotic Military Service, and one of the short poems that make up "Triptych to Remember" is about him. His death was so painful, a boy we had watched grow up with our children. Also, Rafael Chamorro, later president of the Central American Court of Justice, and María Elena Fletes; my husband Carlos Rodolfo and I.

The group changed later on, because after the Revolution, some left the country, others withdrew their support for the Revolution, some of us divorced. Other couples joined those of us who remained: Edgar Parrales, a former priest and member of the political group "The Twelve," and his wife, Carmen Dolores Córdova; former priest Ricardo Chavarría and his wife, Milagros Lanzas; Lorenzo Cardenal and Nadina Sevilla. Several extraordinary priests guided and accompanied us, including Father Amando López, one of the Jesuits killed in El Salvador on November 16, 1989. Father Fernando Cardenal would join us for long periods. We met for years, and you can imagine the quality of our reflections on the gospels, on our commitment, and on coherence in our lives. Our decisions were very important and deeply based. We shared our joys and sorrows.

That was the sort of meeting I was used to. So when I started to go to political meetings, I went because I was invited, and when I got there to see what it was all about, I found that they commented on the commanders' speeches, about this and that, and the analyses were not very consistent. The political secretary was a young man, a very young man, and I remember he wore a comb stuck in his Afro haircut; I don't know if he worked for a circus or one of the popular houses of culture. More than commentaries, what came out of the meetings was orientation for political work. They talked about the particular stage of the Revolution that was coming, the orientations that were appropriate, that is, the orders sent down by the leadership and the content of the commanders' speeches.

At some point, they decide to hold these meetings at six o'clock in the morning. I was already feeling some tensions at home—four children, my husband, who was starting to disagree with the Revolution and, on top of that, trying to make my children think that the Revolution was more important to me than they were, when what I wanted was for my children and all of us to live the Revolution. Considering this, I say to myself, "No, I am not going to go to any more meetings. It causes tensions at home when I go. And besides, I spend all day at the Ministry of Culture, can't come home for lunch, don't get back until late in the evening, and, now, they want me to leave home earlier in the morning? No." Daisy Zamora, vice-minister of Culture, was at the next meeting, also some other leaders, and I said, "I want to thank you for inviting me to these meetings, but I have to tell you that I am not coming back. I will do the work that I have to do, and you can count on me. But for these meetings, I think you need to have a certain level of commitment, and not everyone is ready for that." Total silence..., because it was a privilege to be invited to join the party, and here I am, saying I'm not ready! I imagine they thought I was crazy. But Daisy, who is very understanding and is a friend who knows me perfectly well, said, "That's okay, Vidaluz. No problem." "Thank you," I said. That was that, and I stopped going.

About a year later, the political secretary was from a different level. Martha Sandoval was much better prepared, daughter of a famous professor, Julio César Sandoval, who led classes on the TV and radio, an important intellectual, and her mother was a distinguished radio actor. Martha was different, then, and said to me, "Listen, Vidaluz...," and I remembered exactly when the nuns thought that I could become a nun and were after me to join a convent. They invited me into an organization that was like one step prior to becoming a nun, but I realized that I had been in love and did not want to become a nun. I thought, if they send me on missions, surely I am going to fall in love with the mission doctor.... "No, no," I said, "I don't have the calling to be a nun." It was the same with Martha, who said to me, "Listen, Vida, I'm inviting you, come to the Base Committee meeting" on a certain day. She was given the task of pursuing me. That's how they were in the party. So I say to her, "OK, I'll try it." I thought I would give it another try. I am divorced, I don't have a husband causing me any more tension, I can organize things to take the least time away from my children, so I will try it again. What do I want from the meeting? For them to teach me Marxism, since I had not studied Marxism, give me an ideological base, then. What are the Revolution's ethical principles? Explore the values and theory of the Revolution.

What I found was more of the same, read the commanders' speeches, when I could just as well read them at home. The meetings were never up to my expectations, and I left again. I also realized that the leaders were militants, and that bothered me a bit. I think I have a certain sense of personal freedom that I have protected. I don't know if I haven't been somewhat anarchic. I think maturity has helped me. Maybe if I had been younger, they could have gotten me into militancy. I left and decided to volunteer for all the activities I could handle, but I didn't want anyone telling me what I had to do. Perhaps that is why I took on so many commitments: I went to pick coffee and cotton, went with a cultural brigade to the war zones and volunteered for lots of tasks to support the Revolution.

I suffered physical and emotional abuse: Families split apart by the Revolution

Before I married, I had been told about Carlos's difficult character, which became much worse toward the end, with the Revolution. He became unbearable to the point that he attacked me physically, and I also suffered psychological abuse. I was able to avoid the trap for so many women who cannot get free because the cycle of violence is complex and dangerous. Well, all this I had to experience too, as a writer and as a woman. There was a struggle between values also in my own development as a woman.

My father was dead at the time. He really could have been a source of support for me, because under patriarchy, after all, the male figure is respected. My mother now asks why I didn't tell them when the trouble began, but I felt that when I had problems, they were my responsibility, and I had no reason to get them involved. Besides, Carlos attacked me physically after my father had died and my mother and brothers were in exile.

I managed to get free of that, and the context of the Revolution helped me. It's not simply by chance that many women got a divorce after the triumph of the Revolution; it was a factor, because there was an atmosphere of moving outside, of liberation, of making decisions. I felt calm when I separated from my husband, because living with a violent man worried me and made me fearful for my children and for myself. Besides, I felt freer to do whatever I wanted. I was 35 when the Revolution triumphed. I was separated at 36 and legally divorced a year later, in 1981. When I review my life, I think that after age 37, after I had made the definitive separation from my husband, that's when I lived my life most fully. Why? It was not just because of the divorce, but because I have become my own person. I feel that at this stage, there is a synthesis of life, a certain accumulated maturity. I am responsible for myself, my criteria, I make my own decisions, I am sure, pretty sure, about everything I am doing. And as a woman, I feel happy to live my life. Afterwards, I went out with friends, began to act like a single woman, and live my life with total freedom and coherence.

Were your children with you at that time?

Well, certain things started to happen. During the first months, my four children were with me. I had financial difficulties because I stayed in the large house that we were paying off, and the monthly mortgage was half my salary at the ministry, and after that, I had to pay for food, schools, clothes, etc. I couldn't keep up with the level to which the children were accustomed, and their father was totally irresponsible. The first month, he gave me 1,000 *córdobas* [$140], then nothing.

Was your mother-in-law still with you?

No, no one. My mother, my mother-in-law, my aunts, everyone had gone into exile. The month before the Revolution, all my immediate family left. Within a year after the triumph, my whole, entire family had left. No one remained in the country, except my Great-Aunt Adelina and two great-uncles in Matagalpa. After I was divorced and single, I learned that one of the uncles had died, his son notified me, and my Aunt Adelina was left all alone, so I went and got her, and she came to live with me.

My husband, as a lawyer, had drawn up the first contract for a mixed enterprise between the government and private entrepreneurs of La Colonia Supermarkets, a well-known company in Nicaragua owned by the Mántica family. His legal fees were more than a million *córdobas* [$143,000], an enormous amount of money. But they couldn't pay him, they said, because Somoza had sacked the treasury, there was no money, and everything was in upheaval at that moment. He was angry, and besides, he was beginning to dislike a lot of things about the Revolution, and didn't insist. He came from an anti-Somoza family and had supported the struggle, but afterwards, he did not like many of the things that were happening. The takeovers of land and such things shocked him, and besides, his clients were rich people. He couldn't handle a lot of things because he lacked ideological consistency and coherence, in my opinion.

I said to him, "Carlos, don't bother trying to collect your legal fees, because the country has no money," which was true, "but why don't you talk with Nicho Marenco?" Nicho was a friend of ours, minister of the Interior and poet Daisy Zamora's husband. "Talk to Nicho and tell him instead of paying you those fees, cancel the house mortgage in exchange and give us a clear and free title. That way we won't have that house expense. I can't pay it with my salary, and you don't have the money either." But he wouldn't listen to me, he was so enraged, he didn't want to do anything, and he didn't. I now realize that I had still not achieved my self-affirmation at that point. The house was in my name, and if Carlos didn't want to talk to Nicho, I should have explained the situation, I now think, and they probably would have accepted my proposal. But I didn't, I was too respectful of my husband and, in the end, he had earned the legal fees, but I should have considered my children's stability.

What I did was talk with junta member Sergio Ramírez, who was a friend, his wife too, and they knew our family, and we lived across the street, because Sergio was assigned a house in my neighborhood. And I said, "If I give the government this house, can you give me enough to buy a small one?" They gave me the money, I turned over the large house and went to a place half its size. That meant having a decent place to live. I bought a house in the same neighborhood but much smaller. I had to reduce all the costs I could, instead of two housekeepers, one, and I moved in with my four children and my great-aunt.

Not just a few people from the middle class lowered our life style, and in tandem, many proletarians moved into residential neighborhoods. But I thought this was natural, the Revolution was carried out for the poor, and if this should have been implemented through orderly government programs, the immediate reaction of those sectors was in line with that logic.

"It is good that the house of Somoza become the House of Culture"—Cardenal

What happened next? I organized my life and began to feel I was in control of my world. I had my house, my children, my job, everything, and I was going to work for the Revolution. I loved libraries, which were my field, so I was in charge of the library program, and we started training people, opening libraries all around the country to support the literacy campaign. The work was exciting for me, and it was amazing how much had to be done. But then my two older children went to live with their father and the two younger ones stayed with me.

When you worked for the Ministry of Culture, what positions and responsibilities did you have there? You told me that you worked as acting vice-minister but without an official appointment, yet you traveled as an official representative of the ministry.

When the Revolution triumphed, there was no Ministry of Culture. In Nicaragua, as in many countries, and I think it was the same throughout Central America, what you had was a Department of Cultural Extension, part of the Ministry of Education, a very small entity. The great dream was to create a Ministry of Culture after the Revolution, and of course, since it didn't exist, there was no building for it. Even the House of Government, where would it be established? Just after the triumph of the Revolution, the directorate of the new government moved into the Inter-Continental Hotel. Later they settled in what had been a Central Bank building that the 1972 earthquake had lowered by several floors, and only four were left. The different leaders set up their offices there, and Ernesto Cardenal had an office, but just one room with a carpet on which we would sit to plan the creation of the ministry.

One day in early July, Daisy Zamora called me. She had just returned from Costa Rica, like several others. Ernesto, Daisy, and others had gone to Costa Rica to fight on the southern front, and they returned with the new revolutionary junta. Daisy called me because people were talking to Ernesto Cardenal about creating the Ministry of Culture. Since it was about culture, I in turn called several other people: Antonina Vivas, a guitarist and singer, to consider the music aspect; Adilia Moncada, who had studied history at the university—friends of mine, because we had studied together. I called Adriana Guillén, with whom I had written the newspaper column "Voice of the Nicaraguan Woman" in the 1970s; she was married to a pediatrician and enjoyed a certain economic level and supported musician Carlos Mejía Godoy; and a group of doctors, the "Harmonic Scalpels," who played instruments and sang and had carried out an important recovery of popular Nicaraguan music through an organization called Popular Sound Workshops.

I called them because they were writers or people involved in the arts or culture, so that we could talk about how we were going to create the ministry with Ernesto. Other writers were there, also filmmaker Carlos Alemán Ocampo and painter Ramiro Lacayo, both in military uniforms, and two foreign "internationalists" who had joined to fight during the Revolution or had simply joined us. There was a Mexican dancer, Rodolfo Reyes, and a Colombian we knew only by his pseudonym—lots of people used pseudonyms then—"Katari," his *nom de guerre*. We never knew his real name.

All of us sat there on the carpet in the office, because there were no chairs or tables, to talk with Ernesto and see how we were going to create a Ministry of Culture. Rodolfo had a good sense of organization, I imagine from his experiences in Mexico, and used a board to draft the organizational charts we made for areas the ministry would be responsible for. Suddenly, someone came up from the basement, where there was a printing press, with a sheet of paper that said "Ministry of Culture of Nicaragua." What efficiency! But I remember noticing a detail—the sheet had the national seal of Nicaragua and "Ministry of Culture," and below that, a black line and a red line. I mentally questioned it, because those were the colors of the Sandinista Front, and it was logical, in a way, because the Revolution had triumphed and the vanguard had been the Front, but this letterhead was for national use. That was just a slight intuition I had—that something had to be resolved, or the difference defined between what was the party's business and the State's. But I must say, it was just an intuition that sensed a political issue, not something that my mind was explicitly telling me.

Right then, Ernesto Cardenal asked, "Who printed this?" It was as if Lope de Vega's town of Fuenteovejuna had answered, "Fuenteovejuna, sir! All for one!" People just did things, no one was giving orders, everyone took the initiative. Someone just printed it and brought it up. "No," Ernesto said, "it has to have blue and white, the colors of the national flag." Of course, I thought, because it is the State that represents the nation. Well, these were just subtleties. Afterwards we said, "We have to set up somewhere. Where is it going to be? Let's go try to find a place." Several houses belonging to Somoza and his allies had been confiscated, we looked at them for the ministry, and Ernesto said when we entered Somoza's private residence, "It is good that the house of Somoza become the House of Culture," that is, that the house of the tyrant, his private home, become the people's House of Culture. So we settled in there.

When you went into Somoza's family home, there were still personal items there, such as the My Favorite Birthdays *album mentioned in your "First Lady" poem.*

Yes, lots of personal items. We looked around, and there were so many bathrooms. "Oh, oh," we said, "lots of rooms for washing.... Must be the guilt!" In one of the bathrooms we came across an object shaped like a half moon, and you could pull it out from the wall. "What's this? Could it be for putting someone's neck in here? It must have been used for torture!" That's what we were thinking. But no, it was a device explained by Gladys Ramírez de Espinosa, Ernesto's friend and my children's aunt, an upper class cultural activist who was later head of the Culture Institute for Doña Violeta in the 1990s. It was a sort of coiled spring that ended in a half moon where there was supposed to be a mirror, so that you could see yourself up close if you were in the bathroom shaving or putting on make-up. The mirror had fallen out, and what was left was that half moon made of metal that we didn't recognize. Our imaginations ran wild in the home of the deposed dictator! [Laughter]

The house was very sober, with simple architecture. Ernesto talks about the house in his memoirs. It had two floors, and upstairs was a small area for two offices. At first, Ernesto moved in there as minister of Culture, but later, I imagine the steps must have given him problems, because he moved downstairs, and finally, I assumed the functions of vice-minister and moved to the second floor. But when we first went to the house, there was a Colombian whose pseudonym was "Juan Meza," and that boy was a little crazy, because when we arrived, we didn't have the house keys, and he shot the door open! That meant it was destroyed, but we were able to enter. He went out into the streets, confiscated cars, and brought vehicles to the ministry; he assumed that as his task.

Everything happened at a dizzying pace, every day was very intense, and we worked like ants. We moved in and started to create certain areas. Ernesto was the founding minister of Culture and his vice-minister was Carlos Fernando Chamorro. Carlos Fernando stayed only about two months as vice-minister before he moved to a different area, I think it was to the party's Department of Education and Political Promotion. He was a young journalist and later founded *Barricada*, the official newspaper of the Revolution. Daisy Zamora succeeded him as vice-minister. More as librarian than as a writer, I took charge of the main office for an area that I thought was important, libraries. Poets came, painters appeared, and we made a survey of the existing installations. In Dambach Colony north of Managua, we established the School of Plastic Arts close to the lake. Several architects joined us too, including Amelia Barahona, a very skilled young professional, a specialist in the restoration of monuments. It was surprising to me that we actually had people like that in the country. She came with several other architects—Nelson Brown, Jaime Vásquez, Rita de Franco.

We joined together naturally, and that first year, created a section that was the Office, or Direction, of Historical Heritage, which included historical sites, museums..., well, not really museums, because there was only one national museum, in Managua, and it was in very precarious condition, and a few other very modest municipal museums created on the initiative of provincial intellectuals, like the Gregorio Aguilar Barea Museum in Juigalpa. Chontales, and one in Nindirí. The National Library, the National Archive, all that came under the Office of Historical Heritage, and I took charge of it and called on my fellow librarians. Before the Revolution, some 35 librarians, men and women, more women than men, had graduated from our one university course of study in library sciences. Several had left the country, and I think there were some 12 of us left.

We went to assess the situation at various institutions. The National Library was established in 1882, and our great poet Rubén Darío worked there. I found that at the National Library, the personnel was untrained, and the collection was very poor. Conditions at the National Library were shameful, and at the National Archive, even worse, because the most valuable documentation was totally disorganized and neglected. For the directorship of the National Library I invited Francisco Valle, a magnificent poet and the only senior librarian who had attained his degree in library sciences outside the country. Francisco is a very good writer, but he suffers from a tormented personal life, a complex internal world, and is depressive. He's a person who seldom leaves his house, even now you hardly see him, but he is always writing. Truly, because of his academic training and his integrity, because he was a good person, naming him was correct, but he really did not have the energy to head the library and organize all there was to do.

Conditions at the National Library were terrible. Everything had to be done to update and modernize the infrastructure, train personnel, organize collections, procure financing, everything. It was a huge project to undertake. Jorge Eduardo Arellano, a great bibliographer, also a writer, poet, and essayist—he's a very prolific man—was there and full of energy. We must recognize that a publication brought out by the National Library while Francisco Valle was director owed much to Jorge Eduardo, who was very supportive, and together they produced the library's first publications and organized the files. But Jorge Eduardo's vocation is more as a researcher than a director; the director had to be a self-starter, a person determined and willing to invest a lot of energy and time in the position. We moved both of them and promoted Jorge Eduardo to advisor to the Office of Libraries and Archives, because that program was in transition. It was a dynamic institution that we created empirically, as we went along, but afterwards, we put some order into it and strengthened it as an institution. We received a lot of outside advice offered in solidarity. In my area, we got very valuable advice from Virginia Betancourt, daughter of Venezuelan statesman Rómulo Betancourt. She was an authority in Caracas and had done a wonderful job with the Autonomous Institute of the National Library of Caracas, and she urged us to prepare a Nicaraguan bibliography as soon as possible.

We wanted to accomplish everything in a single day! I considered most urgent the need to train personnel in basic concepts of library management. We met in the office that was assigned to me, three rooms and a little reception area. We all met there—the architects, the librarians, the archivists. Of course, later, the person in charge of the archive went over to the National Archive, the building next to the library, but the rest of us stayed in the main office.

"They don't need salaries, they're all volunteers!"—Cardenal

Things just appeared at the ministry. I think Juan Meza, the young man who rounded up vehicles, brought a truck that had been confiscated, and if there was fuel, we filled it up and went out to collect books and archaeological objects. At the time, we had no salaries. Once, there was a meeting of all the government ministers... it's an anecdote that flew around the entire country: at the cabinet meeting, the ministers are asked how much each of them needs for his ministry. When Ernesto Cardenal speaks, he says, "Nothing," he doesn't need anything because we all came to work voluntarily. Everyone laughed, and they gave him something like 50,000 *córdobas*, which was around $7,000 in those days. He took the money and kept it in the hotel room where he stayed.

The Pancasán musical group was four young men and a young woman who sang, and several of them were married with children. At the ministry, there was a dining room where we all ate lunch for free, because provisions came from somewhere and were prepared; we received fuel and food, but no salary. After a while, some people needed more, because they had small children. The Pancasán members came to me and said:

"Sorry, but we need some money."

"You're right," I replied and said to Ernesto:

"Let's give money to the Pancasáns, Poet. We should give them something."

"For what?"

"Well, because they have families. They have children, and we have to give them some money."

"All right. How much?"

"2,500 pesos for now to split between them, 500 pesos [$70] for each."

And we gave them the money. Later on, of course, the ministry got organized—accounting, an administrative department, the different sections, the annual budget, but this is the way it was during the first days. After a few days, another friend of mine who is a business manager came, María Elsa Vogl, and she says to me:

"They sent me to be the business manager at the Ministry of Culture. Please ask the poet to give me the money so I can deposit it in the bank and start organizing the administration." I tell him:

"Poet, María Elsa Vogl has come to take charge of the administration, so please give her the money to open a bank account and organize the administrative section."

"No," he says, "I can't do that because we need it for a lot of things right now."

"Of course," I say, "You will tell her what you need," because we had just moved into the first house, and there were repairs needed, like the door that the crazy Colombian had destroyed, and many other things.

Well, he was not very convinced, but he gave her the money to deposit. He was coming from Solentiname, from managing an economy based on the sale of paintings by country people and members of his community of the poor. He was very practical and methodical; he taught the farmers in Solentiname to paint, then he took the paintings to New York, sold them at a good price, and brought the money back to the farmers, who began to earn much more for their paintings than they could from harvesting a field of corn. Also, Ernesto took the paintings and was backed in Managua by the supermarket chain owned by the Mántica family, which strongly supported culture, and by Jaime Morales Carazo, later vice-president under Daniel Ortega, who was in charge of INDESA, a company that supported artists and artisans. Ernesto had bought and sold things, so he was not "up in the air" about financial matters, but had experience only on a practical, small scale level. He was not familiar with the bureaucracy of a ministry. The next Saturday, he says:

"And the truck?" asking about the truck he used that had a problem and was at a garage. "Isn't the truck ready?"

"Yes," says his assistant, Luz Marina Acosta, "but we have to pay the repair bill."

"Well, pay it right away and tell them to bring it over because we need it now."

"Yes, we're getting the check ready."

"You see?" he says, frustrated, "That's what I was saying; everything moves slowly now because we have to write a check." From that point on, he was divorced from the inevitable State bureaucracy.

I used to meet with librarians around a large table in one corner of the patio under a big *guanacaste* tree, and we got a lot of good advice and support from Fidel Coloma, a Chilean specialist on Darío, who had been teaching in Nicaragua for 30 years and had educated many Nicaraguans. He made valuable contributions and later was director of the National Library. He was a university professor and husband of writer-professor Margarita López Miranda. Coloma, with his vast academic background, very generously met with us, and we began to talk about creating a national system of documentation. We would organize public libraries throughout the country, and for me, in addition to supporting the literacy campaign in order to stimulate scholastic and academic preparation, this was a way to democratize information.

The experience communicated to us by Venezuela was very helpful for this endeavor. In poor areas, like up in the mountains, there was a type of public library service designed so that people could go there to read and also to get practical information—how to pay taxes, pay water, electricity, telephone bills. I thought that was very useful, especially if the Revolution was about people participating in what we thought would necessarily be a democratic system. So we went about establishing the bases and forming networks of school libraries and public, specialized, and university libraries. With those networks, we developed a proposal to create a national system of documentation connected to the president's office, specifically to an information systems department within that office. A very skilled man worked there, Paul Oquist, from the U.S., married to a Nicaraguan, who later worked in Africa and Asia for the U.N. and is now an advisor to the Ortega-Murillo administration. Sociologist-writer Manuel Ortega Hegg was also in that office.

We discussed all these plans with them, and it seemed there was an infinite amount of work that needed to be done. I was there for about three years

[1979-1981], the first in the Office of Historical Heritage, and I enjoyed working with the architects. I learned that their profession is integral, because they know now to make plans and develop a budget, they know about art, many of them are artists themselves, and some, like Amelia, were specialists in the restoration of monuments, which was very important to us.

The Revolution in general was run by young people, and because of their age, they lacked much professional preparation, and also, people coming from the general populace had had little access to formal education, so education and training were fundamental. A lot was invested in that process, and I attached great importance to people's training. Cuba was of invaluable help, a truly fraternal country. Perhaps the one-sided political reading was that the Cubans were going to spread communism among us, but that was overly simplistic, the easiest thing to say. We should not underestimate Cuba's contribution, for example, its very generous support in health. The island has sent many medical doctors, even under governments hostile to its system, like those after the revolutionary period. Reality forces us to accept this support humbly, because Cuban men and women doctors are still arriving and go to remote places where Nicaraguans often will not.

In health, in culture, in education, the Cubans contributed a great deal, and culture was especially important for me, because that is the field in which I worked. Many people benefited from scholarships and the extraordinary art, dance, and music professors coming from Cuba. Three people from my area went to study museum sciences in Cuba: Luis Morales, who is a great painter now and co-director of the Nicaraguan Institute of Culture and owner of his own plastic arts gallery; Armando Mejía Godoy, winner of the national prize in plastic arts; his wife, Claudia Díaz, a young woman who was a primitivist painter and died of cancer in the 1990s. We also sent a young man from the country, a high school graduate in Darío City, who oversaw Rubén Darío's boyhood home; he also went to Cuba and learned how to restore documents.

As I said, we looked for other ministerial offices after the first year and moved to a place that the Mánticas, the supermarket owners, had donated, a very beautiful building that is now the Julio Cortázar Museum. It houses a very valuable art collection donated to the Revolution by the best Latin American painters at the urging of Ernesto Cardenal, with administrative support from Chilean Carmen Waugh, later director of the Salvador Allende Museum of Solidarity in Santiago, Chile, who died recently, and Virginia Espinosa Ramírez, art critic and diplomat. We moved in with all our books, well, the books that had been confiscated. When houses were confiscated, we would go collect the books in the private collections and found precious archaeological works, including very important books by Hildeberto María, a Christian brother. He was a Spaniard named Joaquín Matillo Vila, a teacher at the La Salle Pedagogical Institute, one of the schools for people of means, where the Somozas had studied, as had many others previously in power. Three private schools, La Salle, Central American, and Calasanz, were where the upper class in the country studied. Hildeberto María's passion was archaeology. He had already written several books, such as *Acahualinca*, and other important archaeological studies that were done practically in an *ad hoc* manner, because they were not funded endeavors, or foreigners came to do studies, and the Banco de América cultural office supported the works and published them.

In 1981, we separated the Office of Cultural Heritage, which included archaeology, museums, and historical sites, from the General Direction of Libraries and Archives. I stayed in libraries and archives, which was my area of specialization and a big enough universe for me, and architect Amelia Barahona took over Museums and Historical Sites. I stayed there for three years [1981-1983] and saw the need to strengthen the Rubén Darío National Library and was appointed director [1984]. A colleague of mine, Mayra Miranda, took over as director of Libraries and Archives. I stayed at the National Library for some nine months. During that time, we organized the symposium "Darío-Martí—New Latin American Literature and the Caribbean," which brought together recognized literary theorists from all over the continent.

Democratize the arts or not: Murillo vs. Cardenal

Internally during this time, Minister of Culture Ernesto Cardenal was confronting the type of strife common in all government agencies—internal personnel problems, coordinating task forces. Political life was very intense, and there was always a contradiction between the Sandinista party and the State, a subtle but obvious difference. I am speaking more about the work world, the internal aspect, and that world was not at all calm. It was always stirred up by internal political problems within the Revolution and relations between people.

I was a relatively older person in comparison to many others, but I had some administrative ability and experience as director of the UCA Bookstore [1972-1976] and tried to go to various offices to help consolidate the ministry. When the director of Art Promotion, Antonina Vivas, left to work for the United Nations, I replaced her, since it was an area of the arts [1984-1985]. Art Promotion had four departments that supported four schools—theater, dance, music and plastic arts—and a department of literature headed by Julio Valle-Castillo. We also had poetry workshops, which Ernesto Cardenal ran himself, because that was his passion, and he introduced a program that became very controversial and was the subject of much discussion, internal arguments, criticisms, and fear that his experiment would have us reproduce Socialist Realism. The debates were fiery, and I will offer my personal view of the issues.

I thought, there are many people who play musical instruments or sing well by ear; others have natural grace for dancing; the average Nicaraguan is talented in theater performance. Parallel to the Ministry of Culture, the ASTC had been created, the Sandinista Association of Cultural Workers, an umbrella group made up of the various unions of artists, with Rosario Murillo as secretary general. It included the unions of artists from several disciplines—Writers, Plastic Artists, Dancers, Musicians, even Circus Workers. It was our form of trade union life. Like many others, I belonged to the Writers' Union and, at the same time, was a government official in the Ministry of Culture and on the Editorial Board of the *Barricada* cultural supplement *Ventana*, which Rosario also directed. Writer Guillermo Rothschuh Tablada was the delegate from the Ministry of Education and I, from the Ministry of Culture.

Tensions existed around different concepts of culture. Ernesto had a concept that he wanted to promote with his team, and Rosario Murillo held a different concept. Both should have been supported. I thought it was useful to have a professional union, and, given the limited resources, for Rosario, with her concept of modern plastic arts, to pay more attention to professional artists. I thought it was appropriate for her to give priority to professional plastic artists and for Ernesto to work more in the area of primitive painting, because he prioritized the less-favored social sectors and thought culture should be democratized for their benefit.

Ernesto promoted both primitivist painting and the poetry workshops. I ask, why did that have to be criticized and undermined? He should have been allowed to develop those useful fields; besides, he is an outstanding artist, a writer of international acclaim, and a visionary, and those were his ways of democratizing plastic arts and literature. That was not the only approach, we all agree. It was fine that Rosario Murillo, with her power as the wife of Daniel Ortega, the head of government—power itself—also gave support to professional artists. The problem was that she competed and tried to sabotage another revolutionary institution by attacking Ernesto and destroying the work of the ministry.

What sort of confrontations took place?

At first, there were just criticisms, especially criticism of the poetry workshops. I myself and several other writers were somewhat concerned that one way of writing poetry might be taught as the only way to create poetry. During the discussions, I went to observe a workshop to comprehend objectively, despite all my respect and fondness for Ernesto. Julio Cortázar and Claribel Alegría got involved in the criticism when Rosario, Francisco de Asís Fernández and others argued that Ernesto was promoting Socialist Realism and was going to box people into a dogmatic process, which is horrible for art.

Actually, this turned out to be a phantom concern based on prejudices, and very quickly these renowned writers corrected their stances, and those of us who were close to it came to understand Ernesto's theory. In my opinion, there was no reason for concern, and I began to see positive aspects. For example, Fidel Coloma, professor to generations, with his vast experience as an educator, said, "I find intriguing what Ernesto achieves with those workshops, because recently literate people are able to write and synthesize, and it is not easy to make a synthesis of thoughts. I have students in their final year of university studies who write pages and pages, and you never can figure out what they're trying to say. They write and write but cannot synthesize a thought. That's what is remarkable to me, that recently literate people are capable of synthesizing their ideas and feelings."

Actually, I had a similar experience myself. Ernesto drafted a sort of literary precept, some rules for writing poetry, the type of exteriorist poetry that he promoted in the workshops. A while ago, my grandson Alejandro had an assignment for school, and my daughter Karla phoned me and said:

"Can you help me? Alejandro has to write a poem. Do you think you could give him a little bit of guidance?" I was very busy at work that day and said:

"Let's see, what I am going to do is send him right now, by e-mail, some rules that Ernesto Cardenal wrote. Tell him to read them, and I will call in a few minutes so we can talk about them." I called later and asked:

"Alejandro, did you read the rules?"

"Yes."

"Okay, then, keep those explanations in mind because they are very clear." Ernesto had written them so that everyone could understand them. "Let's have you write about what you like. What do you like?"

"Soccer."

"Well, you could write about soccer. What other things do you like?"

"The sea."

"Now the sea is an interesting topic. Many writers in the world have written about the sea, and it's a good topic for you. Calmly write things you like about the sea and try to express them following the poet's recommendations, and then we will go over it together."

He wrote his poem about the sea, guided by his grandmother over the Internet using Ernesto's rules. That's how I had the experience myself in my family, in addition to the results I saw from the workshops—a truly original first poem written by my grandson.

There were unnecessary internal arguments, discussions, accusations that Ernesto was being dogmatic, wanting to box people in, that he was vain, that he wanted to turn them all into "little Cardenals." The comments were rude and offensive, but the truth lies in a very well-crafted magazine of poetry published on newspaper stock donated by a wealthy woman from Caracas, an outstanding supporter in solidarity with the Revolution, Graciela Gil Yépez, who died a few years ago. That magazine published what the people in the workshops had written; half the magazine was national production, and the other half had other poems, even epigrams by the Ancient Roman poet Catullus. People in the workshops, then, could read universal poetry of the highest quality and also see their own works published. It was a useful endeavor, but the tensions were terrible. I went to meetings of the *Barricada* Editorial Board and tried to maintain a balance between Rosario Murillo's efforts and Ernesto Cardenal's.

You asked me about the types of confrontations, and I can give you one small example. The prime minister of a socialist country donated a circus tent that was going to be very useful at the time, since we were in a war economy, and there were very few resources. It was sent to Ernesto with a message saying that the prime minister, with great fondness and respect for Ernesto's prestigious work, greeted him cordially and was sending him a circus tent as a gift. Ernesto didn't know about it ahead of time, and when the message came, he said, "This is wonderful!" and had his staff inquire whether it had arrived at customs. He found out that Rosario Murillo had claimed it, because there was an order from her that it be delivered to her office.

We should be clear that Rosario was in charge of the Association of Circus Professionals, but she could have called Ernesto and said, "Poet, look, please remember that the Circus Association is over here…," or asked him, "I hear a tent has arrived for you. Do you want to donate it?" Do it in a decent manner. But no, she just claimed it. Finally, they called from the ministry to Daniel Ortega's office and said, "The poet received this donation, but they say Rosario is going to take it." In the end, Ernesto had to send Daniel Ortega a copy of the message that said it was being given to him. Finally, Daniel, embarrassed, had to tell them to deliver the tent to Ernesto. That type of problem.

Those are details that can create resentments.

Right. When Daisy Zamora was at the ministry, Rosario attacked her constantly. Carlos Fernando Chamorro left after some two months, and Daisy Zamora replaced him as vice-minister of Culture. Rosario never accepted Daisy's appointment to that position and attacked her again and again until she was removed. Daisy got sick from the constant harassment and was treated in Cuba. When she returned, she faced another difficult situation. They put her in the Sandinista Front Party secretariat, and there again, she had to put up with very ugly treatment by the party. Francisco Lacayo Parajón, who had been vice-minister for Adult Education, was named to replace Daisy at the ministry, and he came with the best intentions of harmonizing relations between Rosario Murillo and Ernesto Cardenal, but within a short time, he also crashed into Rosario's attitude.

Did she wield her own power, derived from her work in society and politics or her reputation as a poet, or only what she derived from the position of her husband, Daniel Ortega, president of the Republic?

Poet Erick Blandón, who later also cut ties with Rosario, attempted to improve relations with her and invented some mini-meetings for which he invited us to his house—Rosario and some four writers at a time. My turn came with Lizandro Chávez, Alejandro Bravo, and another writer, and we went to talk with her. Lizandro is very direct, and he said some things to her. Then I said, "Look, Rosario, when we talk about Somozaism, it's more about an attitude that should be eradicated from the country, and it won't be eradicated overnight. Still operating here is the culture of the 'man in charge,' and the question of power is very delicate. Commander Daniel Ortega is the president of the Republic, he is the man in charge, and you are the wife of the man in charge. In the Ministry of Culture, I can tell you that everyone is quite competent, and most area directors are women with great initiative. But it is not the same if woman director X from the Ministry of Culture makes a request to the mayor's office: 'Can you give us a truck to transport a cultural brigade or a musical group?,' that sort of request, and if you call, because you are the wife of the man in charge. As soon as you call, there is a tremendous boost in terms of power. They answer you immediately, and you get the truck. Your request is expedited and handled quickly."

When we all finished speaking, Rosario said she was concerned by what Lizandro and I had said to her. She was a little bothered, but in any event, it was just one more conversation. That sort of dialogue was attempted with her, but the situation grew more and more tense, and I think she really wanted to be Nicaragua's minister of Culture, but for Daniel Ortega it would have been scandalous and uncomfortable to remove Ernesto Cardenal and name his wife. I understood, then, Rosario's ambition for power, even to cogovern with her husband.

Cardenal anointed me acting vice-minister of Culture

Francisco Lacayo came on board to replace Daisy as vice-minister of Culture, and he brought new energy and a positive attitude and wanted to resolve the difficulties, but he realized it was impossible. He was finally sent off as an ambassador to get rid of him. Nevertheless, the way to debilitate Ernesto's institution was already charted, because no vice-minister was named to replace Francisco. Ernesto requested that a replacement be appointed, because as minister of Culture, he traveled a lot, and the ministry was already enormous. It had grown quite a bit, since throughout the country there were houses of culture, public libraries, the National Archive, the Library, all the areas of plastic arts, schools, workshops, the publishing branch, the Film Institute.... It was a huge ministry, gigantic, and Ernesto brought money to it. When he traveled, people would stuff checks and money into his pocket; he would come back and turn that money over to the State to maintain the ministry and for other necessities.

There was no justification, then, for saying that the Ministry of Culture should be closed due to the war economy when the order came, the so-called "compaction"—they say an engineer gave it that name—to compact and reduce the ministries, and the war economy was set. But at the Ministry of Culture, we said, "Ernesto brings in a lot of money to finance this ministry! What the government gives us is not a significant amount," because our salaries were modest, and we were highly disciplined. No salary was above 10,000 *córdobas* [$1,400] a month, and that was Ernesto's. I was earning 7,000 [$1,000] a month as the director of a ministry department. When we traveled, we never had more than $100 per diem allowance, because the poet said that we'd be invited, and it was true; when we'd go to a seminar or workshop, we were given food and lodging, but you always wanted to have something in your pocket, and at times, we suffered hardships with so little money. But we were really a very honest ministry, and Ernesto set the example with his lifestyle as a priest. All of us were very careful with money. There was no justification, then, for closing the ministry for economic reasons. Ernesto traveled a lot, and besides, he couldn't take care of everything himself; the team at the head of the ministry helped him, and he began to delegate responsibilities to me and give me the duties of vice-minister of Culture [Nov. 1986].

At one point, a high level delegation came from Sweden, and when you have high level visitors, you cannot have them hosted by a lower-ranking official, because it is a great lack of courtesy, a grave error in international protocol. Ernesto needed to have a corresponding vice-minister and put his hand on my shoulder and told the Swedish delegation, "She is not the vice-minister, but it's as if she were." I say that he anointed me vice-minister of Culture!

[Laughter.] Daniel Ortega never appointed me. There is a letter from Ernesto to René Núñez, minister secretary to the presidency, where he requests that I be given the official appointment and authorized the salary of a vice-minister, because I had been carrying out the duties without the appointment or the salary. It was never done.

A high-ranking woman official arrived from an African country where there is a strict hierarchy. She came as a prime minister with an impressive revolutionary record and was accompanied by other women officials who served her, in accordance with her country's customs. A celebration in homage to her was planned. At a meeting with Rosario Murillo that Lea Guido told me about, she was the minister of Health at that time, Lea said:

"Let's organize a meeting of the women officials in the revolutionary government to honor her." They made a list of the women who had appointments: Mónica Baltodano, secretary to the presidency, Lea at Health, and all the other women who were ministers or vice-ministers, and Lea put me on the list as vice-minister of Culture. Rosario said,

"She is not the vice-minister of Culture." Lea responded:

"But everyone considers her the vice-minister of Culture."

"Yes, but she does not have the appointment and never will."

"Well," said Lea, "that may be, but right now, she is the one with the duties of vice-minister of Culture, and we are going to put her on the list." And they invited me to participate in the celebration.

When I heard about Rosario's statement, I realized there was a political will to not name me, and Daniel Ortega was yielding to it. That gave me a sense of Rosario Murillo's influence over Daniel Ortega, and I understood that those two had begun to wield the power in the Revolution. I thought, if they are going to judge me from the party's point of view, they're right, because I am not a member. I left the base committees twice. I have given my honest work to the Revolution and offered all the positive contributions that I can and to the full extent of my abilities. If they don't value that, if what is most important for them is the question of the party, fine, that's OK with me. But I knew that was not really the problem; the problem was there was no longer any willingness to support Ernesto.

During all that time [Nov. 1986-Apr. 1988], I made decisions, signed proposals, agreements; thousands of things were accomplished. I think Ernesto's leadership was very beneficial, because in León and Granada important projects were begun to restore the town center, churches, for example, the beautiful church in Subtiava, the Convent of San Francisco in Granada, undertaken with Swedish cooperation. Many very important projects were completed.

Like living in another dimension of reality: In the war zones

I have a war diary from 1983, called a "Campaign Notebook," that I published in 2006 as *Struggle is the Highest of Songs* [*La lucha es el más alto de los cantos*], a verse by Fernando Gordillo. Cultural brigades went to the war zones as a commitment to maintaining high morale among the combatants. We'd already had some disagreements with Rosario Murillo, but she persuaded ex-guerrilla commander Hugo Torres to speak to artists and writers in the ASTC about joining brigades and going to the war fronts, "in solidarity with our brothers and sisters."

I went with the Leonel Rugama Cultural Brigade. Each cultural brigade was named for a revolutionary hero or martyr. Leonel Rugama was a poet who died fighting alone against the National Guard. I organized everything at school for my children. The older two had already left: Karla, the oldest, was in the United States, and Carlos Rodolfo lived in Managua with his father. I left my two younger children at home with the trusted housekeeper who had worked many years for me, her son, and my great-aunt.

I was in the war zone from May 20 to June 6. The brigade included: three painters, Leonel Vanegas, Arnoldo Guillén, who is an excellent portrait painter, both of them talented painters, and Francisco Rueda, younger than the others; the Justo Rufino Garay Theater Group; the Ruth Palacios Folkloric Dance Group, composed mainly of adolescents; the Pancasán group of musicians and composer-singers, famous for their revolutionary songs; and yours truly. The writer in each brigade had the responsibility of keeping the brigade journal. We went to Las Segovias and to Jalapa, where I wrote several poems at the La Limonera military unit included in *Flame in the Wind*.

The theater group had an original drama called "The Sweating Virgin," which they wrote to expose an invention by the Catholic right wing to attack the Revolution, a statue of the Virgin that appeared to sweat, but it was discovered to be a trick. It was a humorous piece, an open-ended play, as literary theory would say, right? The theater people had a lot of imagination, and they would add things, funny, sharp, clever additions, depending on the group of combatants where they were performing. We often went to five different sites, five different war fronts, and I saw 43 performances of the play, but I laughed every time because they invented new things. One day the Revolution was paying homage to a hero, I think that day it was Germán Pomares, and the group was given a manifesto that had to be read, and they had the intelligence and creativity to insert it and read it as if it were part of the play.

It was such an intense experience, and as I review the brigade diary now, I think the experience of the Revolution was awe-inspiring for many people at the time and for several years afterwards, like living in another dimension of reality. The cultural brigades actually went into areas of real danger. Once, we were supposedly headed for Jalapa, on the border with Honduras, but first we stopped to sleep in Ocotal, then proceeded to Condega and to Somoto, but no one said why we didn't get to Jalapa that day. Later, we learned that conditions were not secure enough for us there. A truck finally took us, and when we arrived, we learned there had been fierce confrontations.

We set up in the town's main square and could hear bombs going off at the front while we were getting ready. Around one p.m. we were told to go to the movie theater because the governing junta was about to arrive by helicopter to make a presentation. At that time, the junta was composed of Daniel Ortega, Sergio Ramírez, and a conservative leader, Rafael Córdova Rivas. Daniel Ortega gave a speech and saluted the brigade that was accompanying the combatants, and after the event ended, they left by helicopter. A group that had arrived by land for the event, which included reporters from the *Washington Post*, several international and national newspapers, and others, returned by land. We were told to use the theater for our performance and went out to invite people so that we could begin at four p.m. We went walking around talking with people and announcing our formal event, and you could see sandbags at the street corners and other security measures in the town to fend off a possible attack.

We went back to the theater and at four p.m. were about to begin the program, when the group traveling overland came back, and at the theater entrance, I saw Roberto Sánchez, a writer and captain in the Army then, now also a historian, with his arm bandaged. He told us that on the way to Managua, they had been attacked at a hacienda called La Mía. Several people were wounded, including Roberto. But he was very calm, and we learned later that it was his birthday, so we went to a place to have a beer to celebrate, and he spoke with us very calmly. He said the important thing at that time was to control fear in order to control the situation. We stayed with him for a while and then left for the military unit.

In Jalapa, we were at the La Limonera camp, and there were large installations, huge sheds for drying tobacco being used as dormitories for the combatants, and we were going to sleep there. You had to carry your own hammock, and I had a big one a friend had loaned me, but I had only one hook and was missing the one for the other end. It was my mistake, and I should have gotten another one in Managua, because at the camp, I couldn't ask a combatant to loan me a hook, when they were fighting a war and were terribly fatigued. One of them heard me saying I was missing a hook, and he said to me in popular argot:

"You're going on the sweater,"—a sweater is to keep warm, we use the English word in Spanish, and I said:

"Oh, you know, I didn't bring a sweater, but I do have a blanket." He laughed. He was saying to me "suelo," ground, in a slang called "escaliche"—"you're going on the 'suelo,'" not on the sweater, and we got a kick out of his joke.

We had a political guide, a combatant who went from Condega with us to Jalapa; we called him "The Politician," and he didn't have a hammock either. Another woman in the brigade sang with the Pancasán musical group, Auxiliadora Espinosa, and in other places we had put the hammock on the ground and slept on it, so I proposed we do the same in Jalapa, and we did. Before we went to bed, they called us to formation. Our instructions were that at all times, we had to adopt military discipline for security reasons. If they called formation, you had to go to formation. You had to obey orders, and they teach you some military terms like "circular defense." When they called formation, I lined up but noticed that some people from the brigade did not. Since we were supposed to follow orders, I went to bring the group over and found them staring at the back of a truck that had two bodies in it, bodies of counterrevolutionaries with their legs sticking out. We eventually lined up, although we were deeply affected, and the politician spoke to us. He gave us instructions, but I noticed that at his feet was a bag covered with blood and a cap next to it. Those were signs of the war close by.

I thought to myself, I have to stay calm, although you could hear "BOOM," "BOOM," the artillery, the bombs, what you hear in a war. They ordered us to go to bed, and I got down on the hammock with Auxiliadora and the politician, and above me was the hammock of one of the dancers from the folkloric group. During the night, I was dreaming about the legs of the counterrevolutionaries hanging out of the truck, when the dancer turned in his hammock and one of his legs came over the side and hit me in the stomach! I jumped up terrified and covered my mouth so I wouldn't scream! I was wide awake and could hear all the bombing and shots being fired and a lot of movement of people in the unit, in and out. I couldn't fall back asleep and decided to take half a Diazepam. I didn't want to use sleeping pills, but I thought, I'm getting too nervous and tense, so I'll take a half, and I did. I realized that I didn't think much about my family, my children, how they were, because it was the only way to stay calm and not be overly anxious about what could happen to me and them.

In the poem "Scenes from Jalapa (La Limonera Military Unit)" I include part of a conversation I had with a young man who was the medic in charge of the unit's health center. I went with Auxiliadora, who wasn't feeling well, and talked with him about dealing with fear:

> When I asked you
> what to do
> with fear felt
> in the midst of combat, you answered:
> "You can't remember
> the happy times,
> all that can't mean a damn!"

He added that he thought if people like Carlos Fonseca, Germán Pomares, had given their life, who was he not to give his? I turned that conversation into part of the poem.

Children cruelly manipulated to terrorize me

As our mission was coming to an end, we were in a very hot place, Somotillo, and I was worried about the relationship between my former husband and his new wife, the U.S. Embassy, and people against the Revolution. After we divorced, my ex-husband began to go out with Mercedes Stadthagen, a friend of mine who was divorced from a rich businessman with the Dreyfus Company, a famous commercial house in Nicaragua. All those families were against Somoza. Mercedes was also Gioconda Belli's very good friend, and under Somoza, they were investigated. When Gioconda went into exile, Mercedes was taken to a military tribunal for questioning, but she was helped by her class and her relations and was not arrested. She supported the Revolution and was named international relations officer at the Ministry of Culture. On the first trip I took to Cuba with Ernesto Cardenal, she went along with several others, including Adriana Guillén. Later, Adriana left the Revolutionary and joined the counterrevolution, as did her sister Ligia Guillén, both friends of mine, especially Ligia. We have reestablished contact now, and I hope to see her soon. In the counterrevolution they worked at a radio station in Miami supporting the Miskitos.

Getting back to Mercedes Stadthagen, she was a friend, but given her economic and class interests, she became disaffected with the Revolution. She left the Culture Ministry and began a relationship with Carlos, my ex. I had no problem with that, because she didn't interfere in my marriage, and we continued to be friends. They later married and joined a circle that included the manager of Coca-Cola and Conservative Party member, Adolfo Calero Portocarrero, who later led the counterrevolution, and they also had contacts with the U.S. Embassy. Rumor had it that they were connected to those circles, whereas I was more and more committed and involved in the Revolution, which was becoming more radicalized.

The day in Somotillo, toward the end of the cultural brigade's mission, the television news said that my former husband and his wife were among the conspirators who planned to assassinate the chancellor of the Republic, Father Miguel d'Escoto. I never learned the truth, but a story came out about a bottle of Benedictine wine they were going to use and U.S. Embassy involvement. An arrest order had been issued for both of them. I was worried, nervous, when I was informed that I was being recalled to Managua. I thought, something has happened, and it's better for me to be there to protect my children, because their father could be mixed up in who knows what. They took me in a military truck, and I arrived early in the morning, bought the newspaper at the corner, went to my house, and asked my housekeeper, Teresa, a really good person who had been with us for years:

"Teresa, what about Carlos Rodolfo?"—that's my son.

"He's been arrested," she says. I think she must mean my ex-husband, and I say:

"No, I mean Carlos, my son."

"Yes, your son," she says. "Doña Juanita Bermúdez," Sergio Ramírez's assistant, "said for you to call as soon as you came back." I called immediately.

"Vidaluz," she says, "Sergio said to tell you to come in right away."

They came to pick me up, and I went to the president's office. Sergio explained to me:

"It seems that Carlos and Mercedes, your ex-husband and his wife, got involved in this matter and are at the American Embassy," or they had left a car at the embassy. "And your son, Carlos Rodolfo, was detained for interrogation because he was with his father." My son was 14. "But considering that he is a minor, and there is a conflict…, you are a militant in the Revolution, and they are going to turn your son over to you."

"Thank you, Sergio," I say, "but I want you to talk with him now when you set him free."

I asked him that because Carlos was at the age of adolescent rebellion, and I was aggrieved by what had happened but grateful they were giving me my son. I think the weight of responsibility was on his father, but I also needed to teach him a lesson so he would not play around in serious matters. He was a teenager, he had no defined ideology, he was caught in a struggle between what his father and his mother were saying, and he had to take the situation seriously. Sergio knew him from when he was a kid and a friend of his own children, and in a paternal voice he very gently said:

"Carlos, you got involved in this problem, but out of respect for your mother, who is a militant in the Revolution, we are going to let you go home with her."

"Do you see what happened to you?" I said to him, instead of embracing him which he must have expected. My son Carlos still resents what I said to him on that occasion. It's true that I hugged him later, but right then I said:

"It's important to me that you realize that you got wrapped up in issues between adults that are very serious, and you have to be very careful. Thank God, they are doing me this favor, and I appreciate it. But if you get involved like this again, you will have to face the consequences. You are a minor, but you must think about what you are getting involved in."

What had your son done, exactly?

It seems he put up some flyers, some counterrevolutionary flyers or something like that. I suppose he wanted to earn points with his father. Security detained and interrogated him. They did not torture him, but just being captured was traumatic for him. I think he has felt resentment against me for years because I didn't just embrace him like a loving mother. Perhaps I should have done only that, I don't know, I'm still not sure, but I remember that I acted as I did because he was a rather rebellious child, and at that moment, he had to realize what he had been involved in.

So that he would learn, to turn the experience into a lesson for him?

Precisely. They gave me my son, and his father and Mercedes sought asylum at the Venezuelan Embassy. He was there for 11 months, but Mercedes had collaborated with Gioconda Belli in support of the Revolution, and Tomás Borge was a witness to that. Tomás lent a hand, and she got a safe conduct pass and left first for Venezuela, then for the United States. From there, she began to work on getting her husband out, but they would not give him a safe conduct pass.

I talked with State security, because I wanted my children to be able to visit their father at the embassy, but I wanted to make sure my children and I would be safe. I was willing to allow that because it was the lesson I had learned in my own family. I thought, since my father, who was a military officer, respected my option, and my mother did too, I will respect my children's choices, because one thing is personal sentiments and another, my ideological option. Besides, my son Carlos doesn't like the Revolution, and I have no reason to force him, on top of that, to feel bad about his father and not be able to see him. Fortunately, they were able to go visit him.

At some point, the father got sick, or at least that was a factor, and after 11 months the Revolution authorized his departure from the country, and he left. Shortly thereafter, my son Carlos decided he no longer wanted to live in Nicaragua and wanted to leave. Karla had already gone to Miami, and both of them went to live with their father, but just for a short time, because his relationship with his wife was terrible, and my poor children had a really difficult time. Karla then went by herself to an uncle's home in Miami, and Carlos went to New Orleans with my mother, aunts and uncles, and they helped him. Carlos married at a very young age, 17. Karla stayed in the United States and worked until she came back at 21, about a year before the end of the Revolution. Those were very tense years, when everything was exceedingly difficult.

There was another episode in 1987 when Carlos, my former husband, went over to the counterrevolution. He was an advisor to the Human Rights Commission, and I understand he had a lot of contacts in the United States, with the CIA, I imagine, but he was in Honduras, and I was acting vice-minister of Culture. Every year I would give the two children who were with me, Vidaluz and Mariano, permission to go visit their father, and they would come back. Vidaluz was a revolutionary young woman, a militant in the Sandinista Youth, committed, living the Revolution, and sharing a lot of things with me. My son was not so sure; he went to pick coffee, but he didn't like the experience and was not committed. In 1987 the war was more intense, and security was tighter. I saw there was a risk in the visit, because Vidaluz had already been identified as a young revolutionary in the Sandinista Youth, and I told them, "You are not going to Honduras this year. If your father wants to see you, he can send you tickets to go to Panama and see you at your grandmother's house," because his mother and sister, the children's grandmother and aunt, lived there. They went to Panama for their month of vacation and their father went, everything was okay. When it was time to come back, Vidaluz came, but not Mariano.

"Where's Mariano?"

"He wanted to stay. His aunt and uncle told me to tell you to leave him with them for a while because he's taking classes that will help him improve at school." Well, all right, I thought at first. But a friend of mine said:

"Don't let him stay. It's risky, and they might try to take him from you." I called them.

"Why didn't Mariano come back?" I asked my ex-sister-in-law.

"He was taking some classes, Vidaluz. Look, we wanted to tell you that the boy wants to stay here...," and then she began to talk in a way that I thought was dangerous, as if they wanted to take him from me.

"No," I said. "Please, send him to me on Wednesday. He has to come."

"But, Vidaluz, the boy doesn't want to go back."

"He is a minor child. I am his mother. He is to come back on Wednesday."

Wednesday came and went, and no Mariano. My friend said:

"You'd better go get him yourself." I requested permission and asked for help. I spoke with poet Ernesto, my boss, and said:

"I need to go to Panama because my ex-husband is a counterrevolutionary, and it seems that they want to take my child away, and I need to go get him." Ernesto immediately authorized the trip.

I went to Panama and stayed at our embassy there. The embassy car was put at my disposal, and I went to my ex-in-laws' house. My former mother-in-law was someone who loved me a lot, but she had just had an operation and was still hospitalized. My former sister-in-law had just given birth to a little girl and was at home when I arrived. I said:

"Hello. How are you? I am here for Mariano."

"He's not here. We don't know anything."

"But where is he?" I ask. "How can you not know anything when he lived here in this house with you?"

"No, his father came, and I don't know where he took him." Then an old housekeeper came into the room, a person my children love a lot and call Granny, and I asked her:

"Granny, where is Mariano?"

"We don't know. Carlos Rodolfo came, Vidaluz, and I don't know, we don't know where he took him." I'm supposed to believe that! I said:

"This is impossible! He's a minor child! How can you just let him leave like that?"

I went out into the street, but that friend of mine in Nicaragua had told me, "Look, the one thing these people fear is a public scandal, so don't let yourself be silenced." Once I got outside, I yelled back at them, "I am going to accuse you of being conspirators in this kidnapping!" I went back to the embassy weeping and sobbing and reported, "They have kidnapped Mariano."

They called in the army, the police, the government, my rank as vice-minister helped. I called Chuchú Martínez, a figure from the time of Torrijos, his advisor, whom I had met in Managua, and he was a very entertaining and cultured man, who spoke several languages. When Torrijos assumed the presidency, he wanted to be his bodyguard. I called him and said:

"Chuchú, this is Vidaluz Meneses from Nicaragua. I want to request a special favor from you."

"Of course, *compañera*!" I explained what had happened and said:

"I think my son has been kidnapped."

"Don't worry!" I give him the address of the house where he had been staying, the names, and the details. An order was sent to all the border crossings and exit points that the child was not to leave.

"And Chuchú," I said, "if you could do me the favor, they told me he was not there, but maybe if you dropped by the house in your uniform to see...."

I also talked with Esther María Osses, a very important Panamanian writer who died recently; she was head of the Casa Azul Foundation, and companion to Carlos Wong, another Panamanian intellectual in solidarity with the Sandinista Revolution. Many leftist writers there were very supportive—Rogelio Sinán, Moravia Ochoa and others—all very generous, very much in solidarity. I told them what had happened to me, and Esther María said, "No! Impossible! Of course we're going to help you!" She asked a member of the taxi drivers' union, a big, strong man, to take me to different places to look for my son. I remembered all the addresses of people in Panama who had been friends of the family. My husband's father had been a doctor in Chitré, Panama, and they knew a lot of families in Panama who even sent their children to live at my in-laws' house in Managua. I tried to remember all the names and addresses. We searched high and low for two days, and I would get back to the embassy late at night and totally disconsolate. Finally, my older daughter Karla called from the States and said:

"Look, mother, my father says for you to stop causing a scandal. Mariano wanted to go with him. He did not kidnap him. Mariano doesn't want to stay in the Revolution and said he wants to live with his father." Oh, well, then, if Mariano really didn't want to be in the Revolution, there was nothing I could do. Karla says to me:

"Mother, why don't you come too?"

"What? Why would I go to the United States?"

"Well, if you don't like the States because of the war, imperialism, and all that, then leave for a neutral country! Can't you see that three of your four children have left? And you, why do you have to be there?"

"Because this is my country, and this is my history," I told her. "You are the ones who left...." But I didn't keep arguing with her. I just cried for a while.

It pained me deeply because it was really another failure—three children who didn't embrace the Revolution. I surrendered, because I knew Mariano had not been very happy. I stayed in Panama the rest of the day, and the next day, said good-bye, and returned to Nicaragua. I had only Vidaluz left with me.

Their father did another terrible thing to me. After several months, Mariano stopped calling and writing me, and I was informed one day:

"One of Vidaluz's friends is on the line." Vidaluz is a very brave person, a girl who has always been courageous. It surprised me that instead of her calling, it was one of her best friends, and she says:

"Doña Vida, Don Carlos called from Honduras, and it seems that a bomb exploded at their house."

"What happened?"

"I don't know; we need to find out."

"And Vidaluz?"

"She's here."

Oh, no, I thought, something must have happened to Mariano, something happened if Vidaluz, who is a brave person, couldn't call me, what happened? I phoned the Nicaraguan Embassy in Honduras with fear in my heart and said to the ambassador:

"*Compañero*, this is Vidaluz Meneses, and I need to know what happened, at the home of my ex-husband, Carlos Icaza, who is with the counterrevolution…," and I told him what I knew.

"Yes, there was a bomb," he said, "but we have no news of any deaths or injuries. It seems only the house was damaged."

Then I called a number that Vidaluz gave me and got a young woman on the line, apparently at an office where my former husband worked, and I said:

"Please, miss, I want you to understand me and answer me as a woman, because maybe you are a mother or you have a mother. I am the mother of Dr. Carlos Icaza's son, and they told me a bomb went off at their house. I just want to know about my son, nothing more, and I would be truly grateful if you would tell me what happened."

"That's what they told you?" she says.

"And that my son had been injured."

"No, a bomb exploded but what got broken was just a window," she said.

I noticed her tone of voice was sort of mocking or unappreciative of my ex-husband, and that's not impossible, because he is a difficult person who fights with the people he works with. But I didn't care, I just wanted the correct information. I calmed down knowing that no one had been injured. I finally got the home phone number and talked with my son:

"Mariano, how are you?"

"Okay…"

"What's wrong? Did something happen? Was there a problem?"

"Yes."

"Did you get hurt?"

"Yes."

"Where?"

"On my foot."

"How do you feel?"

"Okay, I'm okay."

But it was a lie; he was never injured, and nothing was wrong with him. The father and his wife made him tell me he was hurt just to bother me, can you imagine? But, in the end, nothing had happened to him.

Who placed the bomb?

I never knew. Vidaluz said his wife called later, the wife he had at that time, his third wife, a very beautiful woman, Adela Kalthoff, from Chinandega, who had been at the Asunción School in León, where I studied, but was younger. Adela called Vidaluz and said that they held me responsible for the bomb, because it had been placed by a commando named for the Honduran intellectual Froylán Turcios. Tell me if I would blow up a house and hurt my own child! Destroy the house where my own child is living! Not even crazy! That was the end of it. My son had not been injured. I don't know who placed the bomb, and the episode ended there, but it was used to try to terrorize me. Those were very trying incidents.

Orphaned by my children

Years later, I went to New Orleans to meet with my four children after all these episodes, after the war had calmed down, and the peace accords process had begun. I got together with Karla, Carlos, Vidaluz, and Mariano, and the five of us had a chance to talk. Vidaluz said to Mariano, "You should never have done that to my mother. Never, ever." And I think he was embarrassed about it.

They had taken advantage of a child's innocence, right? He was a pawn in a cruel game.

Yes, exactly. Something strange used to happen when I'd dream about my children: I dreamed of being worried about the boys, not the girls, although Karla had left on her own. Even as a child Karla was very mature, very serious, and I was always confident that she would be successful in life. I wasn't so sure about Carlos, because he was a restless child, highly intelligent but very impulsive, and I was horrified at the possibility of drug use because of his instability and lack of support in the United States. My salary was paid in *córdobas*, and I couldn't send him money. His father Carlos cut him adrift. My family was very good to him. The home that Carlos found in the States was with a military uncle, a naval officer, Octavio Gutiérrez, husband of my Aunt Pastorcita, my mother's younger sister, and they were more than real parents to him. They had left for exile with their children and gave Carlos a home for over three years, from the time he was 14 until he turned 17 and married at that young age.

Do you have a good relationship with them now?

Yes, excellent. What I regret, María, is that my children left home too soon, I mean, the Revolution forced.... In my poem, "That Woman," there is an intertextuality with Rosario Castellanos, because I loved a line of hers that fit my sentiments to a T. I wrote, "The mother orphaned of offspring," because really, they were the ones who left me, I never left them. I wanted them to live the Revolution, to experience the construction of a new society. I firmly believed in the possibility of a new form of society, and I hoped that with their Christian values, they would appreciate that and make a commitment just as I had done, but they didn't.

Do you think it was because they were too young?

Too young, and I lost the battle. It is curious in human beings, I don't know how certain sentiments are forged..., they weren't ideologies, but values and affections, and that was what prevailed. I was the crazy one, or my process was too deep and personal and was valid only for myself and for one of my children, Vidaluz; it was difficult to extend it to the rest of my children because of their other close relationships.

"Why, if grandpa was good, did he work for Somoza, who was bad?": Children's and grandchildren's questions

When my father was killed in Guatemala in 1978, they shot him the back, and he lived for 13 days, from September 16th to the 29th. I flew in a private plane with my son Carlos and my sister Dalila. When we got there, my son said he wanted to stay with me, but for him, it must have been terrible that his grandfather had been shot. His grandpa was an affectionate person with them—the figure of the grandfather in a family is generally that of affection, right? But "Somoza is bad, and grandpa works for him...." There were too many problems for children's minds.

At one point, I had to talk with my brother Edmundo's children in Spain. My sister-in-law Elisa is a superintelligent and sensitive woman, whom I am encouraging to become a writer and pen a biography of her mother; she's already written a nice biographical essay on me. She was listening when I spoke with her children and said, "Edmundo has never talked with them about this at all." That is why I had to answer the large questions that almost all our children and grandchildren had:

"Why, if grandpa was good, did he work for Somoza, who was bad? Why did you support the Revolution, and why was my grandpa killed?" You have to try to explain everything, tell them:

"Well, Nicaraguan Sandinistas did not kill your grandfather. It was a commando of Guatemalan revolutionaries, and they didn't kill your grandpa the person, but the representative of Somoza's government, which for them was bad."

But it's complicated! My children's love for their grandfather was natural. They used to spend vacations with him. When my parents lived in Managua, we would go to their country home that had a swimming pool where my children learned to swim. We went to Guatemala when my father was ambassador there. My mother-in-law, the kids, their father, and I all drove over to spend two weeks with them. We went boating, visited little towns in Guatemala, and had a wonderful time with them.

All my children's relatives had left. The cousins who were my sons' and daughters' contemporaries were the children of my Aunt Pastorcita, who is seven years younger than my mother and married at 30. Her kids and mine were the same age, and they were very fond of one another, and those children had to go into exile too. My children lost all the people they were close to. It was hard for them, I know, and everything was conflictive, and I imagine a factor that influenced them too, it's logical, was that their father was saying this and that and didn't like many things about the Revolution, and they felt confused.

Was it a sort of brain-washing?

I think so. I was interviewed once on TV and talked about the family contradictions. I said two of my children were in the United States, one was in Honduras; also, the loss of class privileges changed things, that the Revolution was being made for the poorest among us, but that affective relationships still count. One New Year's, for example, when Carlos and Mariano were still with me, their father was a lawyer earning a good income and had just married Mercedes Stadthagen, a rich woman, and they were going to the coast for the holiday with wonderful food, coolers full of hams, sandwiches, Coca-Colas.... And I said to the kids, "Let's go pick coffee with the country folk and eat beans and tortillas." My older son went with his father! I thought, if adults yield to temptations, it's harder to counteract in a child, because values are abstract. Solidarity is beautiful, but it is not easy to counterbalance the other. When my children went on vacations with their father, he'd buy them bicycles, they'd eat chocolate....

I remember the year when I was acting vice-minister, with the responsibilities but not the salary. Nonetheless, Ernesto Cardenal requested the Christmas bonus for me that vice-ministers received, and it was $125. I went to a store for diplomats where you could buy in dollars, thinking that I was going to buy something really special for each one of my children, and when I got there, just a blue jean skirt for my daughter and another something for Mariano, and all the money would be gone! And I still had to buy for my great-aunt, the housekeeper, and her son. I didn't have enough. So I thought, let's all have a grand meal, then, because a skirt is a trifle, anyhow, and I can buy it some other time.

I filled the supermarket basket for a Christmas dinner as if everything were normal, because lots of things had become scarce, and I thought I had bought very special things. I realized that I had bought butter, which we hadn't been able to buy for a while, and I filled the cart with a canned ham that I loved—memories of Bonanza! Virginia ham! I bought those things and took them home to have a great Christmas dinner together.

Dismantling the Revolution: End of the Ministry of Culture

While Ernesto was on a trip to Japan, the compaction of the ministries continued, and we got a notice. Fortunately, since it would be a little less difficult, the minister of Education at the time was Fernando Cardenal, a Jesuit priest and Ernesto's brother, and they call me and tell me from the office of the president of the Republic that we have 48 hours to turn the Ministry of Culture over to the Ministry of Education, to "compact" it with Education. I go to a meeting with Fernando Cardenal, and I say:

"Father, the Ministry of Culture is enormous; if your ministry is going to be responsible for it, can it become a vice-ministry of the Education Ministry? Transform the Ministry of Culture into a vice-ministry?"

"No," he says, "they don't want to do that; it has to be an office, a direction in the Ministry of Education." That means reduced.

"Oh, but this thing is enormous, Father, even if we call it a direction. I would like to propose that you invite the directors of your main areas, and I will bring all the Ministry of Culture directors, and we will explain what we are turning over to them."

"Okay, that's fine." And I asked him,

"Does Ernesto know about this? Does the poet know?"

"I don't know."

"Well, then, I am going to call him. Why don't you call him?"

"No. Daniel knows the number."

I saw that Fernando was uncomfortable. He felt bad, but, of course, Daniel Ortega was the one who should call his minister and say, "Look, you are no longer going to have a Ministry of Culture, because it is going to become a direction." So, I called Ernesto in Japan and told him:

"Poet, look, they called me from the president's office informing me that they are compacting the Ministry of Culture; it will become a direction within the Ministry of Education. I am here with your brother, Fernando."

"Can't it be a vice-ministry?"

"No, I proposed that. I was just explaining to the Father here that the ministry is enormous, and it is quite illogical to reduce it into a direction, but they say that's what they want done. And we have 48 hours to turn it over, so I would appreciate your giving me some instructions about which areas you want to keep."

"No, no, no, no, no," he said, "turn it all over."

"You don't want anything special?" I thought he would keep his office, primitivist painting, and the area of publications.

"No, no. Just leave me my secretary," who was Lesbia Rodríguez.

"All right."

Were you surprised by his reaction?

No, it's what I expected from him. I know him, and I'm glad he was like that, very drastic, and he was right. I felt that it was a very offensive, really, a huge lack of respect. I left and held a meeting of the ministry's Directors Council and told everyone, "I wish to inform all of you that so and so has happened. I talked with Ernesto, who had not been informed." Their reaction: "Incredible! Who could believe it?" some of them said.

About two months before, strong rumors were circulating, we recognized that there was no political will to preserve the Ministry of Culture, but we made a last ditch attempt. I went outside Managua with 80 people from the institution—the main directors from Managua and directors of all the libraries and cultural centers in the country—for a workshop retreat to reflect on the future of the ministry. I had discovered Néstor García Canclini, an Argentine theorist living in Mexico, whose work I appreciated. I read his book, *Cultural Politics in Latin America*, which has a very interesting graph of different systems of government and ideologies charted with the cultural policies characteristic of each system. I photocopied it and distributed it to the directors. I also invited two specialists who are excellent theorists, very cultured people, Ileana Rodríguez and Julio Valle-Castillo, and said to them, "You are going to be 'terrorists' because I need a shock. Please come and give a presentation on culture and the current context as a preamble before we start the workshop."

Ileana said something that shocked party members, "We are witnessing the dismantling of the Revolution." She is superbly deep and analytical. It was tough to hear but true, and Sandinista Front Party members were deeply offended by those terrible words. Then Julio Valle said, "What cultural project do you want us to talk about, since this government's leadership does not believe in culture? There is no cultural project here!" That was the tone of both presentations, and it disturbed everyone. I had told Ileana and Julio, "Come make the presentations, and if you would like to stay with us, please do; if not, you can leave." They gave their presentations and took off, so I was left facing everyone alone! I said, "You can agree or disagree with these presentations, but the point is that the Ministry of Culture can no longer continue the way it has up to now; there is a war economy situation and a threat that the Ministry of Culture will be compacted with the Ministry of Education or disappear altogether. Let's develop proposals about what we can do on our own initiative to reduce our costs to a minimum and still carry out our duties." We ended up with a very good set of proposals, some 15 or 20 measures that could be taken, and we needed government authorization for only three of them.

With those results, I drafted a letter to Daniel Ortega, with a copy to Vice-President Sergio Ramírez and all other pertinent government officials, and signed it along with all the ministry directors. We said we were aware of the situation and had made this type of effort, these were the results, and, as they could see, of the proposals, most were within our power to implement, and we needed support for only three. We sent the proposals and got no answer. Two months later, what I told you happened, they closed the Ministry of Culture, "compacted" it.

This hurt me because I could see what was happening all around—the sense that the Revolution was dissolving, you could feel it. What was going to happen? And the real factor, permanent warfare? Then I saw it: what triumphed here was the power of Rosario Murillo. Ernesto is a renowned figure, he will transcend all these things that are happening, but I no longer have any interest in working for this revolutionary government. Then I went to talk with Father Uriel Molina at the Friar Antonio de Valdivieso Ecumenical Center, to see if he wanted me to work for the center. I thought to myself, I want to go back to a Christian place that lives up to its commitment to the people and see if there is a place for me there. Uriel took me in.

Everything was in order when we turned over the Ministry of Culture. I wrote my letter of resignation to Fernando Cardenal and thanked him for the confidence and opportunity they had given me to make a contribution through the revolutionary government. He said:

"Vidaluz, we were thinking of offering you the directorship of the National Library." I responded:

"Father, I appreciate it a lot, and I could work perfectly well with you, because I like you and respect you, but I no longer want to work in the cultural area because Rosario Murillo has her plans. I am not exactly clear about what she wants to do, but I do not want to work for her and Daniel Ortega, and they're the ones in charge. I'll have to see what I'll do, because I need to earn a living for my family, and I believe I can go work in another sector."

Back to a Christian environment: Valdivieso Ecumenical Center

The minister of Education respected my decision. I forwarded my formal letter of resignation and went to talk with Father Uriel, who was wonderful to me, welcomed me with open arms, and told me to take charge of the center's international relations. The center was founded by him and a group of protestant ministers and Catholic lay people—I was a member of the founding assembly—as a place for Christians within the context of the Revolution, to offer a space for reflection. A great Italian theologian came to the center every year up until a few years ago, Giulio Girardi. Giulio wrote an important book that no one in Nicaragua paid much attention to, *Sandinism, Marxism and Christianity: The Confluence*, which sought to derive a theorization of the experiment of the Sandinista Revolution that mixed Marxists and Christians. In Nicaragua, however, activism prevailed over theory, and people worked with very little theory. Afterwards, the book was slightly more appreciated, and in the future, it will be considered important, but at the time, no one paid the proper attention to the deep and exhaustive study done by Giulio. The Valdivieso Center channeled aid for social projects that were a strong support for the Revolution.

Were the aid funds from external sources?

From outside the country. The center was founded in 1980, just one year after the triumph of the Revolution, and the mission, established in its founding document, was to provide a space for theological reflection for Christians who were immersed in a Revolution headed by Marxists, yet continued to retain their Christian faith. Each year it held theological weeks that were quite stimulating, and the best Latin American liberation theologians came: Pedro Casaldáliga, Leonardo Boff, Gustavo Gutiérrez, Jon Sobrino, for example, the top scholars in Liberation Theology. In Nicaragua Father Uriel Molina, a Catholic priest, is really the pioneer of ecumenism, which was popularized by Pope John Paul II, and then Ratzinger wanted to follow that tradition, despite his conservatism on other social issues. The current Pope Francis I has given positive signs that the Catholic Church will advance in this area.

But ecumenism in our countries of Latin America has had little resonance, because the Catholic Church has been sectarian. It was imposed as the only one, and that continues, to a great extent, with the rejection of the contributions by evangelical churches, and now protestant sects have proliferated everywhere. Why? Because they are more democratic than the Catholic Church. They educate a lot of people and go into areas to work with the poor, and besides, they do not deal exclusively with spiritual life, but also pay attention to people's material problems. Ecumenism is a worthy approach, and I spent a year at the Valdivieso Center [1989] observing the swift progress of the peace accord discussions to answer the questions: Where is the Revolution headed? What will happen now with the Revolution? I didn't know.

Maybe we can preserve some aspect of the Revolution: Solentiname

I saw many signs that, as Ileana Rodríguez had said, we were witnessing the dismantling of the Revolution. And I thought, how is it possible to lose this? I wanted to go work in the first community founded by Ernesto Cardenal, the Christian community in Solentiname. I knew I would like to work with culture, always, but on a smaller scale, because we had to start over again. Ernesto had formed the Association for the Development of Solentiname, a non-governmental organization (NGO). There was an office in Managua headed by Alejandro Guevara, from one of the Solentiname families in which everyone was a writer or painter. Alejandro was a guerrilla commander and resident delegate in that region. I told him, "Alejandro, I'd like to work to support Solentiname, and I believe that with the experience I have, maybe I could work as a cultural advisor to the Río San Juan Department, to see if we can preserve some aspect of the Revolution. That was the first territory to be freed from illiteracy, that is the place where Ernesto began his labor, and you are commander of the region. We should try to preserve that focus and continue work there." He liked the idea, so I resigned from the Valdivieso Center and explained to Father Uriel, "I want to work there, Father, because I believe it is a corner where we can preserve something that started with the Revolution."

I moved to Alejandro's office in 1990. They paid me $300 from a project, but in order to pay me, since it was an NGO, one of my duties was to serve as reference person for a book on Río San Juan for which I gathered material. It was a book that Ernesto compiled on all the texts that had been written about Río San Juan, from the first Spanish conquistador, Alonso Calero, to Julio Cortázar and other contemporary authors who visited Solentiname before and after the triumph of the Revolution.

Since I had worked as a librarian, it was easy to find the texts, and that's how I justified my salary, but there were tons of other duties. When you work in a support office for a place like Río San Juan or the Caribbean Coast of Nicaragua, which is far away, the infrastructure is deficient. There is a road and air service, boats on the lake, but service is slow, intermittent, and costly, and many things are needed. From the office I would buy what was needed in Río San Juan and San Carlos, like tractor and boat parts, turbos, all kinds of pieces of equipment that were sent to San Carlos, and from there, to Solentiname. The job involved administrative support and the gathering of documents and bibliography for Ernesto's project, which became the anthology *Río San Juan: Doubtful Strait in the Center of America* [*El Río San Juan: estrecho dudoso en el centro de América*]. Our friend Janet Gold appreciated the information I gave her about the existence of the book, because it was an important reference item for her valuable work on Río San Juan presented at one of the International Congresses on Central American Literature (CILCA).

We didn't know if we'd be thrown in jail: 1990 elections, loss and changes

After the loss of the 1990 elections, Cuban poet Roberto Fernández Retamar extended me an act of kindness: he called and told me, in solidarity, that I could count on him. I see it as a highly generous gesture, though I have not had to ask for his support, but I appreciated the message, because it is true that in the history of our countries, it has not been easy to surrender power peacefully. Revenge-taking could follow, and we didn't know what was coming, whether those of us who worked for the Revolution would be thrown in jail. So many things could happen to us, and no one knew. I think it was excellent, then, that Retamar offered his help.

After the 1990 elections I went to Cuba and talked with Retamar on two occasions. In February Doña Violeta won the elections, and in March, during Holy Week, I went to Cuba for the last time, to the home of Ileana Rodríguez, who had married a Cuban. We had dinner, and I noticed Retamar was extremely nervous and tense. We said good-bye at the airport, and I knew that was the last time we would see each other. Although the relationship we had during the Revolution was very beautiful, I came back feeling like a weight had been lifted from my shoulders, because I had not gone there to live, although I had invented in my mind that I could get an appointment, perhaps with my embassy in Cuba, and would have a salary to maintain my house in Nicaragua, where my great-aunt was still living with me, and pay for the housekeeper. Vidaluz possibly would go with me to study at the university in Cuba, those were my plans. But, now, with no Revolution or anything, I knew it was unlikely I would be given a job there, and also, the deepest and most radical separation would be from my children in the United States, and I wouldn't be able to tolerate that.

I returned to Nicaragua and fell into a depression. It was logical to be depressed, although I didn't want to be. I wanted to feel full of energy, because I needed to work, move forward, see what was going to happen next. But the loss of the Revolution, the loss of that beautiful affective relationship, and the return to the same situation in the country, despite all the sacrifices, despite all the loss of life, that was really dreadful. In the 1990s Doña Violeta's government began to establish the bases for democracy, first, because pacification was necessary, and then, to organize the postwar economy. And I had no job.

We lost the 1990 elections…, the Sandinista Front lost…, which ended the revolutionary project and also my contract with Alejandro at the Association for the Development of Solentiname. He was very kind, very decent, and told me…, of course he was giving me information for militant party people like him, and I had no reason to be aware of it…, that there was a political willingness to provide us with some stability, and he asked whether I owned the home I was living in, because if not, you could get a title for it and stay there. "Yes," I said, "I turned my original house over to the State, and they gave me enough to buy a smaller house; I have paid taxes on it, and everything is in order."

Of course, when my daughter Karla, who had not been in the Revolution, returned to Nicaragua, she asked, "Mother, why aren't they going to give you back your house? Lots of people who never paid anything are getting their houses…." I had paid part of what was owed on the house I turned over to the Revolution, and the land was mine. I had paid $140,000 on the $350,000 loan. I wrote to Sergio Ramírez and said that Alejandro told me there was a political willingness to provide stability for those of us who had worked in the Revolution, and I was not going to ask for anything special, but I proposed that they return the house I had turned over to the government, and I would return the house I bought with the money they gave me. The taxes had been paid, improvements made, and all. No, wait, I didn't write that to him yet, that was my intention, but I tell him that if they give me a house that is equivalent to the one I turned over, I'll give them back the one I was living in. I didn't want to ask for my original house back, because a Sandinista woman was living there.

Then, my daughter said, "Why are they going to give you a confiscated house? Afterwards, they'll say you are a thief!"—she had the mentality of the people returning from the outside. "Tell them to give your original house back to you." I tried and told Tulita, Sergio Ramírez's wife, what Karla thought, and she said:

"She's right." It was fair for me to recover my original house that was larger, when a lot of people are getting houses and didn't pay anything. I'll return the house I have, and they can use it to help other people.

"Go talk with the person who's living there now," Tulita advised. And when I did, the lady said:

"Where am I supposed to go?"

"No, since there is this willingness…. Sergio gave his OK, that they could give me an equivalent house, but the only one I want is this one, my original house, and I'll return the one I have now." But she didn't want to go live in my house, which was half the size of the other one. There are people with different mentalities.

"Well," she says, "all right, but I don't want a house out on the highways," and she mentioned the residential neighborhoods she preferred. I said:

"All right, then, I will go see which houses are available and let you know, because you're not going to want to move to a house that I pick out." I went to a lawyer who told me:

"Go right to the registrar and get the certification." Imagine, my original house was still in my name, because there had been a government error, and the title had not been transferred. So I could easily turn over my house legally to the State and get back the original one with everything in proper order.

Well, that was very favorable to me, and I was going the next day to get the certification, because it was going to be easier with that in hand. But I was unable to go to the registrar because I was called from Granada, a large, beautiful city, and told that some people wanted to take a boat from Solentiname, the rural community, a boat named "Peace Boat" that had been donated during the Revolution. I went to Granada to try to keep them from taking the boat away from the Solentiname residents. When I did go to the registrar the very next day, I saw that the woman living in my house had raced there and put it in her name. It would no longer be so easy for them to return the house to me, and I understood her intention to not vacate the house.

That was a terrible disappointment for me. I was really upset about it, and my daughters accused the woman in the street of being a thief. She was offended, and her husband showed up one day to complain about what he considered an insult to his wife by my daughters.

"No," I said, "you have no right to come here and say anything to me." He insists:

"Well, maybe your daughters are not well informed."

"Of course they are!" I said. "My daughters are perfectly well informed, although I accept that my daughters should not call your wife a thief or insult her, because that is not our way, and I didn't bring them up that way, but they are truly indignant and were swept up in the injustice and said what they did. But it's not that they have no information; they are perfectly well informed, and you will leave my house immediately." And I threw him out.

This disillusioned me a lot, because it was a symbol for me of the people in every revolution who go in it with different mentalities. Afterwards, they both took gravely ill, got divorced, and were not well. I felt sorry for them later, especially for her. He got very rich.

Unemployed and depressed... What to do?

In the 1990s, I sat in my little house unemployed and very worried. That's when I ran into Sergio Morazán again. We had seen each other at different moments over the years but didn't keep in touch. I went out one day with Angelita Saballos to a really nice club where the father of her children was co-owner. They were good friends of Sergio, and we met there by chance. He asked me to dance, and, you know what? I liked it when I danced with him, first of all, because he's an excellent dancer, and second, because his embrace was very pleasing. [Laughter.] I think it's very important to feel "chemistry," as they say. It was not exactly sexual attraction, but I liked his personality, his openness and directness. I was attracted by his frankness.

Men have won me over on two occasions by being direct. I wouldn't say that my former husband was that way exactly, but going from my first boyfriend, whom I deeply loved but did not completely trust, to a man who dedicated himself to me, that had won my heart. Morazán, with his clear, frank attitude, told me everything; he likes to talk and says everything, keeps nothing to himself. I trusted him explicitly, like I had trusted my husband too, I trusted my husband totally, and when he was with his fourth wife, a wonderful person whom my daughters liked a lot—and I was sincerely glad that he had a good home, because, after all, that was my children's other home—his wife grew jealous and insecure. I sent her a message, "Tell Adilia not to be jealous, because this man has a bad temper, but if he treats her right, she should not be jealous, because he is faithful as a husband, and I always trusted him." Would you believe that about a year later a boy showed up, a son born from an affair he had between the births of my daughter Vidaluz and my son Mariano! What a shock! And me, putting my hand in the fire for him!

You didn't suspect a thing?

Never in my life! It never crossed my mind! Supposedly, it was a surprise for him too, because he says he never knew he'd had that son. The girl was a secretary where he used to do business as a lawyer; he had that affair, she got pregnant, and he says she never told him, and I heard the same. She was married to someone for many years, and the boy didn't appear here until he was grown. He was born between my third and fourth children, a clear and absolute infidelity! No, I say, I'll never put my hand in the fire for anyone ever again! What an idiot! [Laughter] I trust Morazán now, but I'm not going to put my hand in the fire, although his direct way of approaching things gives me a lot of confidence in him.

Did you have any relationship with that young man, your children's half-brother?

None so far, nor do I think it necessary. I've only seen him from a distance. Besides, he's not responsible for anything, nor is his mother. It's the father who had the commitment to me.

How does Nicaraguan society deal with the children of affairs like that one? Do the children have the right to make any demands of the father?

Of course, they have inheritance rights now. Advances have been made, and the term "natural children" is not longer used for children born outside of marriage. Materially, fathers are obligated by law to provide for them, but in Nicaragua it is not very strict. Irresponsible paternity abounds.

And it was not within your understanding of marital obligations to be unfaithful to your husband?

Fidelity and loyalty are two of my unalterable principles.
Anyhow, there I was in my house, unemployed, and, just imagine, I was in a deep depression. Then an uncle showed up, one of my father's brothers, who told me he was back in the country importing supplies for supermarkets. I told him I needed a job, and he said, "My wife is coming, and I'm going to ask her to hire you." She gave me a job selling advertising space in an international phone directory. I have never been a good salesperson. I sold a tiny little ad to a shipping firm and earned almost nothing. My uncle later asked me to sell fax paper. Morazán is very sharp at selling and had ample experience selling agricultural products before the Revolution. I said, "Help me sell." Well, that was hilarious, and we managed to sell all the fax paper to a university.

Two things were returned to me after 1990, and one was my parents' house outside Managua, the only house my parents had owned. I told my daughters what I had in mind, "Let's go out to the house and accept its return officially, with the keys and everything." But I receive it in very dramatic conditions. The day I go out there, a man's body is lying less than half a kilometer away. I report it to the police, and they come. It was someone who had been murdered and dumped at the side of the road. That made me afraid of living in the area. When we went inside, the house was totally destroyed! It would have required a huge investment to make it livable. I managed to get Herty Lewites to look at it for me. He was the former Sandinista mayor of Managua and later ran against Daniel Ortega and died during the campaign. He was a very accomplished man who had been minister of Tourism in the revolutionary government. I said to him:

"Herty, the government returned this property to me because it belonged to my parents. What should I do? Please help me because I am out of a job and don't know what I can do here." He says:

"Just invest $60,000, and everything will be fine."

Where was I going to get that kind of money? I could take out a mortgage from the bank, because it was some 19 acres of land, enough as a guarantee, but how was I going to repay it, without a dime to my name? My whole family was all on salaries, no one had extra money, no one wanted to invest. Everyone was happy that I got the family property back, but no one had the means to make an investment. I thought, well, I'll go live there with my daughters. I can rent out my house in Managua, and with that money, I can pay for gas, I'll look for a job, we can live there, and I'll fix up the house little by little. But the insecurity was terrible—at kilometer 19.5 on the old highway to León, a lonely road, and so much insecurity during that first year after the elections, with the peace accords just signed, and Daniel Ortega pushing and announcing that Sandinistas were going to rule from the bottom up. Also, I had my two daughters who were young women, my elderly great-aunt, the housekeeper.... Conditions were not right for me to go out there to live, so I didn't move.

The second thing I got back from the Revolution was my former husband's Mercedes Benz that had been left at the U.S. Embassy and taken by State security. I drove around in elegant style, in a Mercedes Benz convertible selling fax paper! [Laughter.] I stayed in sales until I could find something else.

Getting back on my feet: University dean

In 1991, I was called by the Central American University [UCA], for which I am grateful. The current rector is my friend and former teacher, Mayra Luz Pérez Díaz. I was appointed chairperson of the Department of Arts and Letters and earned $300 a month, which was not a lot, but I could eat and maintain the household.

After about a year, Father Xabier Gorostiaga proposed that I become dean of the College of Humanities. I was not quite sure because of the struggle I discussed with you about writing poetry. I don't know if it is a justification of mine regarding literature, but I want to have more space to read and write, but at the same time, I need to work, and if it is a type of work that offers me possibilities to promote changes and make contributions, it is attractive to my personality. I consulted with friends. Michèle Najlis told me, "Think whether the appointment is going to bring you something or not; reflect on the issue of power"; she is very wise, very deep. I talked with Daisy Zamora, who was married to Óscar-René Vargas, a Marxist sociologist, and he said, "Of course, accept it right away! Don't you see that Daniel Ortega refused to appoint you vice-minister of Culture, and you can show him you are valued as a woman, because the Jesuits are choosing you as dean of the college!" Óscar-René always pushed Daisy and her friends; he challenged us and was a real supporter and friend to us. At first, he was in solidarity with Daisy and all of us, but later, he couldn't accept Daisy's intelligence and evolution; he began to compete with her, and it was terrible. That's machismo, no matter how intellectual some men may be. Not only did their marriage end, but also, the friendship we had was no longer the same. However, I recognize that at the time, he made me see an attractive side of the issue. I proposed that the appointment be made only after open competition. The procedures established by the Jesuits were followed; I was selected from the final candidates and began to gain a more solid footing.

That was an extraordinary experience, because while I was dean [1992-1996], Ileana Rodríguez returned to Nicaragua. She had been a university professor in the States, and I have always respected and admired her. We talked, and she said:

"Why do you think you and I get along so well?"

"Because we have objectives in common—equality and justice, and I like your direct approach, you don't sugar-coat your opinion, you are very analytical, you took the opportunity to get an education outside the country, you are very capable, and I respect your academic level." She has a doctorate in literature and has taught me a lot. She trusts me, and I trust her. I ask:

"What is happening at universities in the States?"

"University reform," she answers, in her precise style.

"Well, here too, reform is happening, and it is difficult. I find that the hope of many professors, especially those with long careers at their colleges, is to maintain the Revolution in this environment, but that will no longer be possible. I think the university should undergo reform, but we have to preserve humanist values. We must be open to new challenges and the advancement of contemporary knowledge."

I asked if she would serve as my consultant for reform at the College of Humanities, and she agreed and related something that had happened in her Spanish Department at a school in the States. A new chairperson took over who had been a manager at Nestlé. At the first department meeting, she put a clock on the table and said the meeting would last exactly one hour, and all the rest of the meetings would be the same, executive meetings. I think that's a reimposition of the market—"Time is Money!" Terrible!

We began to talk, and I said, "I think we are going to have to put in play the 'terrorist' act like we did before the shutdown of the Ministry of Culture." At the college, I had formed an Academic Council that included the chairperson of the Psychology Department, a very incisive Cuban professor, Gustavo Pineda, an intelligent, smart man, adored by his students, quite gifted, pleasant, and humorous. But he seemed to have reservations about me at first: "They bring in a poet as Humanities dean! Who knows whether she can 'connect her foot to the ball' in this arena!" His approach to psychology is very scientific, and the major is oriented exclusively toward clinical psychology. Besides Psychology, there was the Social Sciences Department, with concentrations both in sociology and social work, and Arts and Letters.

Ileana began to advise me, and the college did a reflection. I proposed an exercise to design a curriculum to combine our four majors into one transdisciplinary concentration. Of course, this provoked great fear, which hurt me deeply, but, on the one hand, there was the challenge of opening up to new possibilities, and on the other, the need to be attentive to the humanist aspects and try to avoid professors' losing their jobs. If the college costs a lot of money to maintain, if you reduce the size of the college—the great dilemma of universities, whether they are sustainable or not. Colleges of Humanities are generally not money-makers in market terms and are the first to have their budgets cut, though they are absolutely necessary. If all professionals had a solid humanist background, the world would not be so upside down, right?

How would we do this? It was an experiment, of course. I was coming from the Ministry of Culture that promoted all the cultural disciplines: dance, music, literature, plastic arts, etc. The College of Humanities was very rich in potential, and I thought of all the multicultural projects that could be undertaken. An exciting, new professional profile could be developed, but how could we motivate faculty members to participate?

Sociologists learn to use scientific instruments to analyze reality. Social work is a similar discipline, but these specialists cannot stop at diagnosis because they must intervene in given situations. How many times has a social worker needed the contextual analysis of the sociologist to deal with, for example, problems of alcoholism in communities, which can be treated by psychologists? How could we promote the benefits of doing interdisciplinary or transdisciplinary teamwork? Aspects of art and literature can be related to the defense of community identity and also to spiritual development. In a country like ours, I thought it was very important to work with young people to combat drug use and other unhealthy practices. What could I do to support an opening among professors so that they would break out of their compartments, their particular specialties, and try to work together?

I began to promote an interdisciplinary council and joint projects. Some funding existed for gender studies, an area that had been incorporated into a newly endowed chair called "Gender and Power." Instrumental in that was a very talented French woman, Ana Criquillon, who came with her Nicaraguan husband, Francisco Lacayo Parajón, in the 1970s and stayed on after they divorced. Ana is a gifted person, cofounder of Points of Encounter, an outstanding NGO working with women and young people. Ana's mentality is very European but also very Nican, and she has made solid contributions to gender studies in our country. Now, she has decided to become a lesbian and lives with U.S. filmmaker Amy Bank, and they are both very active and are focused on a project to support young women entrepreneurs. Ana was the first professor to hold the Gender and Power chair. She did not have a university degree but came with a wealth of knowledge and the necessary skills to advance the field of gender studies, which integrated gender theory, research, and social outreach. Some Norwegian funding was available for the gender studies chair in Sociology, later located in the Social Sciences Department when it was created. The Psychology Department was carrying out a project on sexuality with some limited funding that proved to be quite productive. Why couldn't these different approaches be forged into one and all the majors integrated within a gender-based perspective? That's what we did.

We established a first course for interested men and women professors from all the colleges, and some 50 teachers, more women than men, took the Interdisciplinary Course on Gender Studies. They came out of that course highly motivated, and we formed the Interdisciplinary Commission on Gender Studies (CIEG), to incorporate gender perspectives into all majors, even agricultural sciences, nutrition, business administration, law, communication.

University Rector Xabier Gorostiaga developed a relationship with the University of Chile, and colleagues from the National Women's Service-Chile, SERNAM, came to give a seminar, and out of that came the Interdisciplinary Program of Gender Studies, PIEG. Of course, there were internal conflicts, but the program was created and still exists. Professors who did not want to join stayed in the CIEG or went to other universities. The PIEG is available at the postgraduate level at the UCA, created from the seminar of which I was the executive coordinator, and the CIEG, of which I am an honorary member, functions as an outside interuniversity unit.

All that was part of needed changes and university reform, which generated very valuable studies. I met an outstanding sociology professor, Nelly Miranda, a young, eminent sociologist and academician, who later married poet Alejandro Bravo. I introduced them, they became friends, and got married. Alejandro is a lawyer, fiction writer, and fine poet. I told them, "Alejandro, you lack Nelly's discipline, and it would help you. And, Nelly, Alejandro's free child would benefit you, because you are very serious. You could be a great essayist if you add the grace of art and culture to your scientific rigor." They did an excellent joint project that was published by UCA's Institute of History in its *Cuadernos de Historia*, and that institute is doing very important work. The university, the academy, tends to be rigid in nature, because there are class schedules and defined course content. The institute can freely create interdisciplinary programs.

Later, when I left the university, I signed up for a postgraduate class on contemporary Nicaraguan painting at the Institute of History, where I did the study that I mentioned in homage to painter Leonel Vanegas, who had been with me in the cultural brigade in the war zones. I loved the class, which was taught by an excellent professor, Dolores "Lola" Torres. Ileana Rodríguez had mentioned that as part of the reform at her U.S. school, a Baroque Art specialist was retired and transferred to a foundation, where she could continue to work in her discipline and receive a dignified retirement income. I remember telling her, "Dolores is our great specialist, and I would want her to give only master classes. Too bad this country is so poor, because that sort of person deserves special treatment, support to live decently, do research, and develop postgraduate lecture series and presentations for the general public. She shouldn't be involved in this commotion of regular courses, just master classes." Dolores authored an important book on contemporary Nicaraguan painting, a precious tome, beautifully illustrated, useful, and well written. After the university reform, Lola embarked on interdisciplinary studies, such as an essay on trees in Nicaraguan painting, art and ecology, etc., new topics combining art and interesting new focuses.

In the same place and with the same people

When I went back to UCA as dean of Humanities, Ileana Rodríguez asked me, and Angelita Saballos did an interview with me, to explain how I felt during that period, in the early 1990s at the university. I said, "I can give you an answer. I feel like the Mexican *ranchera* song, 'in the same place and with the same people.' Why? Because I am again at the university where I studied and worked for many years. It's like the matrix from which I emerged to go out and work for the people, and now, I'm back." But back to what? It is true that we all were economically impoverished, but I belong to a social class and a family that have always offered some support. I am not adrift in the air. Yet here again I am an intermediary—dean of a college with very poor students, some of them working as maids. There was a girl from Boaco who went to Managua to work as a maid and, after work, studied at the university. The lady of the house told her she could no longer pay her wages, and the girl asked if she could at least pay her in kind, with food and a room to sleep, so she could continue her studies. But later, they said they couldn't even give her that. It was awful, and there were thousands of cases like hers—parents unemployed with children who wanted to study and had no way to pay for classes. It was terrible!

What did I need to do? The same as before—ask rich people for money to help poor people. Later, there was a big discussion about how university reform could help the financial aid issue. UCA defines itself as a private university dedicated to social service. As a member of the National Council of Universities, it receives a government stipend. Then I realize that after all that has happened, the tremendous changes, we are back at the same place, as if nothing had improved, with deepening disparities between rich and poor, trying to see how the rich can give to the poor—the same all over again.

We poets are right: Holistic view of reality

I am deeply committed to promoting inter and transdisciplinary research, study, and projects. As I understand the new reality theorists, the new theorists of contemporary world history, they are saying that we poets are right, because we have a holistic view of reality, and I agree with that. They say that we are beyond the mere rationalist method that has caused us to perceive reality as fragmented, when, in actuality, everything is interrelated. I strongly identify with inter and transdisciplinary focuses. In every place I have worked, I have tried to systematize mentally the new lessons and experiences. Once, Ileana asked me how I was feeling about the ongoing university reform, and I said, "Well, for me, university reform is also like a revolution. The great sociopolitical revolution we envisioned for the country could not be, but many advances can be made. There are two important realms: one is knowledge—we have to get up to date on innovations in knowledge, which are mind-boggling in the contemporary world, and university reform is part of that revolution. The second realm involves women's issues. I think that is the unfinished revolution that we must continue."

Democracy workshops with students from both sides

We had already held workshops on democracy. The Jesuit UCA embraced students of Sandinista and non-Sandinista parents, young people were returning to the country. Bilingual universities were being established, as well as others partnered with schools in the States, and some parents preferred to send their children there, or to private universities, like Catholic University. But some returning families sent their students to UCA, so you had parents and students from both sides, from the Revolution and from the counterrevolution. In addition, the Sandinista Front had, and still has, broad control over student leaders at public universities and at UCA. But UCA students had gained a certain level of autonomy from that party line, and in the College of Humanities we promoted democracy workshops in order to attempt to spark useful debate among the young people, discussion of ideas, and respect for different positions among ourselves, women and men, and with students.

We also contributed to electoral campaigns, first, in one of the 1996 national elections, when there were 23 participating political parties, and Arnold Alemán was eventually elected president. We joined other NGOs in a consortium to contribute to citizen preparedness. We drafted brochures to outline criteria for electing candidates, citizens' duties, voting responsibilities, etc. We offered workshops at the university and elsewhere using those materials. Martha Cabrera, a UCA psychologist, thought it was a good opportunity for us, because the university itself had experienced plenty of internal frictions—disagreements with some actions, with the leadership and with the reform, and we needed to seek discussion.

I left UCA's College of Humanities when I believed I had contributed everything that was within my power to reform. But, all in all, perhaps the Revolution was sufficient experience for me, and I had learned a lesson from the difficult and painful burial of the Revolution's cultural project. It had been a national project, but there were powers in play. I had to recognize that, in the end, I was a citizen who contributed, or attempted to contribute, to a project that was not exclusively mine, nor did I have the power to preserve it.

So, regarding university reform, I did not cling to it with utmost devotion, and I viewed it from a certain distance. When I believed we had established sufficient bases for the new direction of the college, the rector proposed that I take over the Office of Culture. Michèle Najlis was its director at the time, but she was diving ever more deeply into a theological project—just like her, nothing halfway, she does everything with great passion and dedication. I told her, "Really, they should name you UCA chaplain. That should be your area of responsibility." But the Jesuits' audacity doesn't stretch that far!

Michèle really wanted to focus on her theological project, but I didn't feel right taking over her position if it wasn't clear where she was going to go. I also realized that there were other forums for service, and an interesting one could be the ecumenical center whose founding director was inviting me to take charge of it. I understood, of course, that this meant again investing a lot of energy, because it was a question of reforming the vision and mission of an important center. I decided to talk with Father Uriel Molina to see what might be done there, because the Valdivieso Center still had enormous potential.

Committed women: New leaders at the Ecumenical Center

I spoke with Father Uriel Molina, and he was extraordinary. I want this testimony to appear in the book you are preparing, María, that Father Uriel Molina, a Franciscan priest, was the pioneer of ecumenism in Nicaragua. Also, he had the wisdom and willingness, which few can claim, to turn power over to a lay person, and a woman to boot. In that, I believe he was a visionary. He said to me:

"It will be good for you to take over leadership of the center. I've fought long and hard, and I'm tired. We have to see what the future of the center should be, and the best thing would be to have a woman in charge. You were a member of the founding assembly, and I ask you to please come." I replied:

"Obviously, Father, we've operated up to now with full and total identification with the Revolution and the Sandinista Front, but I believe we should put that behind us. If you think the membership will agree and will allow me to establish separation and autonomy from political parties, then I will consider it."

"Of course, you are totally free to establish separation and autonomy," he assured me. Above all, it was important to me that Uriel Molina, as the center's founding director, give me his support, independently from the other members who might not be so convinced. His support, knowing that he was expressing his unlimited confidence, was enough for me.

"I agree, then, and accept your nomination of me."

He proposed my appointment, the election process ensued, the assembly accepted me, a new group of governing directors was elected, and I became executive director [1997]. I invited Michèle Najlis and Martha Cabrera to join me. If I had been in charge of the organization of a new national project, my ideal team would have included Nelly Miranda and Martha Cabrera. Nelly is very speculative, gifted in pure reflection and abstract theory. Martha was one of the young professors I got to know as dean of the College of Humanities. She did a doctorate in psychology in Germany and was always questioning everything seeking truths. I was impressed with her work. She is a very active psychologist and works directly with people in settings like workshops and was interested in the possibilities of establishing new interventions through the Valdivieso Center.

I told them: "I am not sure how you feel and how satisfied you are at the university." To Michèle, I said: "If you want, come with me to the Valdivieso Center, and we'll see. You can continue your theological research even more reasonably there." Michèle had also been a member of the center's founding assembly. To Martha, I said: "Come, and let's see what we can all do together." She was courageous and accepted. We gave ourselves a vote of confidence and went to the center together. So I started as executive director with two very well-prepared, competent, talented women who were like a luxurious gift to the Valdivieso Center. I strongly believe in the intelligence of human beings and in women who assume a commitment. With Michèle and Martha at my side, I was not afraid to accept the challenge.

We revised everything, the vision, the mission, and set off in a new direction, which was not that simple and has taken until now to grow to maturity, under the leadership of Martha Cabrera. When I was still involved in the process, I promoted the renovation of a tradition at the center but without any party linkage. The center once again became a space for active citizen participation. People met to analyze real conditions and understand the new context, and an anticorruption movement was born from those meetings, Citizen Action against Corruption. We later joined the struggle against corruption to force Alemán, to give an accounting of his assets. We accomplished a lot.

I assumed the radicalism of the gospel

I was director of the Valdivieso Center in the 1990s, the revolutionary context had ended, a neoliberal system was being reimposed in Nicaragua and around the world, and we thought it necessary to seek meetings and dialogues with other sectors. I went to the presentation of a book by a former priest, Édgard Zúñiga, who had left the church, supported the struggle against the dictatorship, and later married—he didn't leave in order to get married; he left because the hierarchy was very rigid, and he had made a strong social commitment. After the end of the Revolution, he was still unsatisfied and felt marginalized but was a very progressive person. He wrote *The History of the Church in Nicaragua*, of the Catholic Church, that is—since I worked at an ecumenical center, I think we need to be clear. The Catholic Church is the largest church in the country, since it prevails on the Pacific Coast, which is more densely populated than the Caribbean Coast, where there are Moravian and Anglican Churches, in addition to indigenous religious beliefs.

The book was presented by a young priest, Father Rolando Álvarez, trained by the church hierarchy that did not support the Revolution. I wanted to hear what he had to say, because he was going to comment on the chapter about Friar Antonio de Valdivieso, the first martyred bishop in Latin America, who had forced the application of and obedience to Spain's colonial Laws of the Indies for indigenous people in the 1500s, and that bishop's attitude cannot be explained except by the radicalism of the gospel. Father Álvarez said that Valdivieso symbolized the radicalism of the gospel, which is not the same as extremism. I found this interesting and decided to invite him to the Valdivieso Center for a reflection.

When the book presentation was over, I thanked him for his lecture, which was very learned. You could tell he was a very knowledgeable priest. I respect intelligence, and even if I disagree with another position, I respect its being well grounded. I said to him, "Father, I direct the Antonio de Valdivieso Ecumenical Center, and I would like to invite you to come. I think an interesting topic to debate would be the difference between radicalism and extremism." He smiled and said he would come, but actually he didn't accept the invitation. A few days later, I sent him a formal written invitation that he never answered or even acknowledged.

The explanation for my own actions is that I assumed the radicalism of the gospel for personal coherence in what I faced. I don't claim to have been totally coherent in everything single thing, but I have tried. That is my own explanation, and when I talk about the attempt on my father's life, which killed him and was terrible for me, I speak about the importance of transcending it through faith. I lived through that agonizing moment, with much grief and intensity, to be sure, but always with an explanation of the events and a sense of transcendence.

When governments are irresponsible, you act: Hurricane Mitch, 1998

When Hurricane Mitch hit in October 1998, we made an emergency call from the Valdivieso Center to other NGOs to pool resources. These things happen in our lives—maybe you are immersed in a theoretical discussion, to see how to incorporate new currents of thought, and suddenly a tragedy like this strikes. Then what? Overnight, our Valdivieso Center auditorium, a place for theological reflection, study, and research, was turned into a warehouse, with rice, beans, plastic bags, all sorts of things that people need in an emergency. I felt enormous responsibility when Mitch hit. I am at the Valdivieso Center, a spiritual center, and we are seeking understanding, when suddenly a tragedy strikes. Donations poured in, containers full of supplies arrived, and the auditorium filled with sacks of food and other items.

There was a Women and the Community project in San Francisco Libre, a very poor community with lots of problems on the other side of the lake. Women at our center from that town could not return home because the only bridge had collapsed. Two days passed, and the rains continued. The water was rising, and we learned that the town center was flooded. The prognosis was dismal, because in the future, the water would rise again, and the town should be moved to higher ground. Imagine! I remembered that experience later, in 2005, when Katrina hit New Orleans, and had an idea of the magnitude of the tragedy.

The most urgent need was to send first aid. We went to a meeting convened by the Federation of NGOs, the FONG, to which we belonged, and made a special appeal to organizations with projects in San Francisco Libre. The goal was to unite all the entities and people in order to be more effective in providing support for the affected population. Later, out of that grew the Civil Coordinator for the Emergency and Reconstruction, but during those first days, the urgent need was to aid San Francisco Libre.

We needed to buy a boat, and for that, we had two allies: Reed, a British organization, and the Methodist Church, represented by its missionary, Nan McCurdy, and her husband, Miguel Mairena, who ran a women's support project in San Francisco Libre. I asked, "What can we do? We need a boat; there is no other way to reach San Francisco." They said they would extend us loans and gave us $12,000 between the Methodists and the British group, and we bought a boat. Since Miguel is from San Carlos and knew how to drive a boat, we went to the town with medicine and food. Michèle and Martha went too. Later, a firefighter visiting from the United States told Nan that we had saved lives because we were able to take action efficiently and quickly.

Some days later, I sent a message to all the agencies that were cooperating with us and reported on the situation. For me, the Internet with its marvelous e-mail is one of the most valuable conquests of our time! I sent the notice around the world and said we needed help, since we'd borrowed money to buy a boat and had to repay it. The Catholic Women of Austria, a very generous group that cooperates with us, gave me money, and I repaid the boat loan.

But we had to continue support efforts. I said, "Mine is a spirituality center, and we are not in a position to build homes and bridges. We know nothing about that." We were concerned because the Alemán government refused to respond or even acknowledge the gravity of the situation, and really, that was absurd. One of the criticisms of NGOs is that we should not supplement the State in its obligations, but when governments are irresponsible, you act. We kept meeting, and I said, "We have to do something. Who works on housing?" We divided up areas, and people took over their specialty, and we decided to contribute along with the mayor to develop a plan. But it is hard for people to work together and pool resources. I remember that Carlos Sáenz was there as dean of UCA's College of Agricultural Sciences, he also later went to work with me at the Valdivieso Center, and he had good relations at the university with people in Engineering. I put him under contract because at least, I thought, he is an imposing man who communicates well with people and has experience working with few resources and a lot of coordination. He trained as a veterinarian, like my husband, but was dedicated more to teaching than practicing, was a dean and also had a graduate degree in rural sociology. He was put in charge of coordinating the interinstitutional team, which was a job in itself.

"If you have an affair, bury yourself deep underground": Rejecting marital inequality

I told you that when I met Sergio Morazán after so many years and we danced, I liked his embrace, the physical contact with him, and also his extroverted, frank, sincere personality. I value directness, not double messages or ambiguity. I think women can establish stable relationships with other people. I have wonderful memories of my father; he was tender, responsible, rather quiet and reserved, not at all extroverted. But he always had a mistress, and I rejected that and refused to put up with infidelity. I programmed something different for myself.

Your generation too, at least, women with certain educational and life experiences rejected that unequal martial relationship.

Yes, and I imagine that is why I value so much a partner's frankness. I spoke with my first husband the same as with Sergio Morazán, who was my second stable partner, and I told each of them, "I prefer the truth. First, if you fall into temptation, and that's possible, because we are all human, I don't want to know about it. 'Eyes that see not, heart that hurts not.' If you're going to have an affair that cannot be avoided, you'd better bury yourself deep underground, because if I find out, I will not tolerate it. I don't like it, it makes me feel insecure, it bothers me, it affects my self-esteem, I do not want that in my life, and I prefer to end the relationship." I have been coherent and consistent in that, although sometimes we women say things and don't follow through. I know myself, and I know that this is how I am, and I have the strength and will to separate if I have to, because I do not want to live with an insecurity that will really bother me. Others react differently, like thousands of women in my country and throughout the world, right? They're in love with the man or are totally dependent, economically and emotionally. That's not for me.

Hooked up to a virtual oxygen tank: New love

I liked Sergio's extroverted, warm nature, and when we met again, his realistic, positive sense of life was very important. He had the energy that I needed, because like most people, when you're depressed, you lose energy, you can't work, you can't do anything. The symbolic figure, the metaphor that I have in my mind, is that Sergio was like my tank of oxygen—I hooked up to him, a virtual oxygen tank, and was revived.

An episode that I remember is that one of the days when we were going said, 'We are not in an era of changes, we are in a change of era.' What does this mean?"

We did a deep reflection and decided that between all of us we would have to develop a new method of analyzing reality that starts from a holistic, interdisciplinary, transdisciplinary view that embraces subjectivity and spirituality. New projects grow out of that analysis, that reflection. The construction of a new analytical method is being promoted, so you can find your place in the new international context and the world in which we live. Also promoted is a critical revision of our history.

Independent of political parties?

Totally autonomous. The different community leaders participate in workshops on, first, a new and objective analysis of reality, a new methodology, a new epistemology, shall we say. Second, a critical review of history, and this exercise is painful because a balance has to be made between achievements and errors. Thirdly, attention to people's health, and this comes from work done by Martha Cabrera, who is a therapist, so a review of your habits.

Martha's first sessions with the various groups were quite disconcerting to people. For example, units from the Communal Movement of Matagalpa were used to arriving at a workshop, and presenters come in, talk about organizational methodology or the law on citizen participation, which are concrete things. It's quite different when someone comes into the workshop and asks, "How many glasses of water do you drink a day? How do you feel?" In Martha's first report on the workshops, it turned out people were suffering from gastritis, backaches, and severe headaches, none of which was being treated. "Start with yourselves. What are your work schedules?" During the Revolution it was crazy—your workday never ended; days ran into nights. "No. You have to strike a balance in your day, take care of your family." And spirituality, Michèle Najlis worked on that dimension, and she begins by defining spirituality, clarifying that it does not imply the teaching of a specific religion but comes from something more basic and essential, such as finding the meaning of life—What meaning does your life have for you?

As you can see, what I am doing in my life, in all that I have been telling you, is making what I learn here in this place useful over there in that place. That is my charisma, my possibility, and what I try to do. That is what I introduced to the team I worked with at the Civil Coordinator and tried to gather others of like minds. There are many people with talents and natural aptitudes, and the key is to get them working on something very specific for which they have a true vocation. I really believe in this. I believe in the potential of people, and if they are truly motivated by what they are doing, the results can be marvelous.

I paid Carlos $500 a month from a donation that came from Holland. Regina Belli, a Nicaraguan zoologist-technician, was finishing her master's degree there; she felt moved by the tragedy in her homeland, called people to get support, and donated $7,000. With that funding, I contracted Carlos to coordinate the team and see what could be done in San Francisco Libre. He made an important contact with the postgraduate section in Architecture. If we or the mayor had tried to contract someone, it would have cost us a lot of money, but we were able to combine our resources with those of the university. Postgraduate students did a topographical study and mapped a new site that the city moved to. Nan McCurdy and her husband got a very large donation from the Methodist Church, some $900,000, for the construction of new housing and went to build houses for the people there.

This was a tremendous collaborative effort. Martha Cabrera and her team worked with people on emotional recovery. Michèle Najlis provided theological support. It was an intense experience, and out of those efforts came the directions that Martha proposed for the center, the formation of new leadership with a psychosocial focus. When the worst of the emergency was over, we tried to get back to normal business.

Nicaragua suffers from post-traumatic stress syndrome

At the Valdivieso Center in 1998, we were in the midst of searching for our post-Revolutionary direction, the hurricane hit, and we devoted our efforts to helping the victims. During this time, Martha Cabrera was developing a hypothesis that was dramatically confirmed after the hurricane—that Nicaragua suffers from post-traumatic stress syndrome, due to the series of unprocessed losses. Michèle Najlis was exploring a theology of hope, of resistance. Within that framework, I was committed to contributing to the reestablishment of the social fabric of a fragmented, divided society.

I was struck by the prize-winning essay on peace by journalist Carlos Powell. He said that peace accords in a country at war are signed in a relatively short period of time, because the situation of armed conflict gets to the point where both sides understand that it is preferable to reach even a minimal peace agreement in order to stabilize the country. Once there is willingness on both sides, it's a question of sitting down at the bargaining table and signing the corresponding documents and accords, but real peace is a much longer process. This is true because there are still wounds, distrust, and serious ruptures. Reconciliation must be based on justice, not injustice, and there are always reclamations.

That was the great topic for reflection: how can the reconciliation of the Nicaraguan people be achieved? I again felt as I had before regarding the

Revolution—that I joined not out of class resentment or hatred of the Guard. I was in a privileged psychological situation again, because I was able to reconcile with others and renew a dialogue. At the Valdivieso Center we spoke of reconciliation, but grounded in justice. How could it be achieved? We discussed the need for national reconciliation and rebuilding hope through development projects. That was when I became aware of the wide world of NGOs, non-governmental organizations, and the importance of funds channeled from developed countries toward social and economic projects in impoverished countries. The Valdivieso Center was a base for that type of support.

I work like a spider spinning a web:
Leading the Civil Coordinator, 2002-2005

Since the hurricane forced us to unite in order to respond to the emergency, and we soon saw the importance of remaining united, I realized that I had an enormous vocation for working like a spider spinning a web. María Amanda Rivas used that idea to dedicate a poem to me, because she too defines me as a spinning spider, and a friend of mine, Patricia Castro, a Baptist minister, also told me that was my working style. A relatively new organization called the Civil Coordinator was very attractive to me because it presented the possibility of articulating a holistic vision of reality, linking all society's interests and disciplines for practical purposes, and I agreed to be a candidate for one of the top two leadership positions. The FONG proposed me for the position of national liaison. The first liaison had been Ana Quirós, a Costa Rican nationalized Nicaraguan, and she did a great job. I served with her on the first governing board of the FONG. Work had to be done to reinforce cohesion and maintain better unity. The rule was established that two people would be elected to serve for three years as national liaisons, and I agreed to run, because I thought it was the right time to contribute through that organization. But when I went to the Civil Coordinator, within just a short time, I realized it was too stressful—the mammoth organization of over 300 NGOs was a totally untested endeavor for us and was too big, with too many diverse interests.

It had the attraction of being something new, challenging, and important but also implied enormous responsibility. My fellow liaison, Ricardo Zambrana Godoy, and I jumped from one topic to another, from the code on childhood and adolescence to the problematic of violence against women, or to the question of milk products, the Free Trade Agreement that was being announced, the concern among national producers…. So many issues!

"Maybe we have blundered into a trap," I thought

The Civil Coordinator got funding from external cooperation to do our strategic planning, determine our priorities, organize our work, and better channel resources and efforts. After a year and a half, however, I was very tired, so tired that I got sick. I had a problem with my eyes, which I had during the Revolution too, popularly called "weeping eye," severe conjunctivitis. Your eyes look like blood clots, and I couldn't read or watch TV or do anything and was ordered to stay home for two days to recover. That was when I became aware of my deep physical fatigue, and I realized that I was overextended and depressed. Do you know how I knew? Because of a very strange sensation. I suddenly thought, "Maybe we have blundered into a trap. What is the rich countries' objective in offering cooperation to our countries? Thousands of workshops are offered on governability, on citizenship, on topics placed on the world agenda by those countries' agencies and interests. But our country is not recovering, and there are still loads of problems. We could be caught in a huge conspiracy, a gigantic trap! They have us here involved in workshops, but this is going nowhere."

I felt wretched. "I do not want to do this. I cannot talk about hope. Truth is, I have no way to change this. I have no strength...." My mother called from the United States after my daughters, Karla and Vidaluz, urged her to, because they thought I didn't look well and couldn't understand my obsession with doing work that was making me sick. That's when I began to calm down. "Why am I here, since no one placed a gun to my head and forced me to get involved in something this complicated? No, I am leaving; tomorrow I will resign. I will have to think about what I am going to do, because I have to work to earn a living." I thought I could complete a really beautiful project that I had in mind, and there might be some financial support for it.

That night I suffered claustrophobia and had to get out of bed and leave the room. Morazán was very worried and asked what was wrong. "I feel severe anxiety and anguish, like the ceiling is going to fall on me, and I can't sleep." The next morning I decided to talk with Margarita Vannini, director of the UCA Institute of History, because I wanted to edit Pablo Antonio Cuadra's newspaper columns, which were very important for my generation. My university thesis involved an analysis of them, a guide for researchers, and that essay, with an index of themes, dates, and summaries of his 400 editorial columns, would help me with the editing. Pedro Joaquín Chamorro's widow and children created the Violeta Barrios de Chamorro Foundation which published an edition of his writings. Pablo Antonio worked with Pedro all his life; he was codirector at *La Prensa* and was in charge of the literary supplement, *La Prensa Literaria*, but he also wrote the Sunday editorial, which was a humanistic column of great importance. My project could be justified as a significant contribution to the history of ideas in Nicaragua. I felt better and called:

"Margarita, I would like to propose a project. You know that I am with the Civil Coordinator, but I am going to end my commitment soon. I would like to edit Pablo Antonio Cuadra's newspaper columns, 'Written on a Typewriter.' What do you think?"

"Great idea! Of course, let's do it. We will get funding from somewhere. I will talk with Cristiana Chamorro of Doña Violeta's foundation." Since Margarita was in favor of the project, I started looking forward to it and thinking how I was going to resign.

Just then, my coliaison, who was younger than I, suffered a severe attack of diabetes and had to leave the Coordinator. I abandoned my personal project and thought I would stay one more month. But then, perhaps because of the responsibility I felt, I gathered strength and decided to complete the rest of my three-year term, alongside the young leader Violeta Delgado, who took over for Ricardo. Besides, my project did not have funding at that point, and I could not go without a job. I calmed down and completed the final year and a half on the job in 2005. I can sum up my period of leadership as a contribution to a long process that must be supported—to work toward social cohesion, internal trust, and advancement in the building of citizenship. It's a middle- and long-range task, in which education is vital. The work advances and recedes. I think with the current government, we have lost the ground we had gained in the creation of institutions.

A change of era requiring holistic humanism

One of the Coordinator projects that continues is the Fortification of Participatory Capabilities, which in practical terms we call "The Toolbox," because we asked, what do people need? People need instruments with which they can contribute on their own behalf to public policy. Martha Cabrera was developing her own work on preparing new leaders, and we had many conversations about it. I told my colleagues at the Coordinator, "You know what I see? This organization's richness is its assembling of people from different disciplines—sociologists, social workers, agronomists. What people need is a base in humanistic values, at least that has been my experience, since I studied and worked at a Christian university with Jesuits. That is the meaning of a humanistic preparation, because one thing is the specific subject or discipline you take up, but another is values. Scientific challenges occur, and even if you have an excellent scientific education, if you lack humanistic principles, you won't care whether you build a machine to improve people's health or make a bomb or a weapon of destruction. As UCA Rector Father Xabier Gorostiaga around selling, we went into a store. I was watching him, because we didn't have any money, but he's capable of going in with no money and admiring things, eagerly looking at things that he likes or that could be useful. If I don't have money, I don't go in, because I think, why go in if I can't buy what I need? It's an entirely different attitude. But he goes in, and everyone would think he has money, and I was favorably surprised by this and considered it a positive force in his life. In this store, beautiful background music was playing, and immediately it sparked a deep sense of nostalgia in me. I don't know if it stirred up old feelings for me, but I was close to tears from the emotion caused by the music, and he didn't realize a thing. He goes up to the counter and says to me: "Look at this. As soon as I have enough money, I'm going to get this for you," and he shows me a set of tools for my car, not having the slightest idea that I am moved by the music and crying. That was so funny to me and erased my tears, because I see that this man expresses his tenderness this way—he's going to give me some practical tools so I won't be stuck on the side of the road if my car breaks down. [Laughter]

Another time, we had a lot of unemployed people dropping by the house. I was a little stunned by all that had happened, and the visits were part of what helped me, like therapy, talking and talking, like a catharsis of what had happened. People were out of work and looking for something to do to earn a living, like a friend down the road from us, Pepe Fierro, an Argentine who lost an arm in the war and stayed in Nicaragua, was nationalized, and ended up opening a restaurant. He was missing a hand but could still sing tangos with his wonderful voice and make really beautiful wooden crafts. Another friend would accompany him, a Salvadoran who also stayed in Nicaragua and would drop by. My poet friends who were out of work came by. With those friends and neighbors, we formed the Utopian Club, and the president was an architect who's in his seventies now, a very humorous man who was the only one of us employed at the time. When his company laid him off, he brought his last pay to me in a briefcase and said, "Take this and manage my last salary. We're going out tonight and spend it!" We went to three restaurants with all our friends. It was completely crazy. We named him president of the Utopian Club, and Ramiro, the Salvadoran who sings and plays guitar, composed an anthem for the club with beautiful music and lyrics.

We also got together with Ricardo Pasos Marciacq, another friend from before the Revolution, and his wife, Marta Terán. Ricardo was an agronomy engineer, a graduate of the Zamorano Agricultural University, and in the 1960s, he worked in the western area on cotton farms and later came to Managua to study philosophy, which he loved, and his adoring wife was a great support for him. They left their daughters with family members who had the means to take care of them and came to Managua, where I met them at the university bookstore. Ricardo was the store director, and I was his assistant. Afterwards, he left to earn a doctorate, and I stayed as director. We became close friends, a long friendship that has endured.

Ricardo had been the Revolution's ambassador to Sweden, then returned to Nicaragua, and in the 1990s, was unemployed. He taught some classes at the university, and at his home on the outskirts of the city, he started to raise rabbits and chickens. He told my husband one day that the rabbits had died from an infection, and he urgently needed to sell some chickens because he had no money. We didn't have much money either. I earned $300 a month at UCA, and Sergio treated some dogs and cats at his clinic set up in the house that we were building little by little. He told Ricardo, "Bring them to me." We bought some chickens for ourselves, sold others, and gave him the money. That is one of the things I admire in Sergio—he is a strong and very generous person. His way of responding is always very confident and assured. I told him, "You should be a congressman, because a lot of people call you, and you answer positively and with enthusiasm, even if we only have enough for tomorrow's breakfast; you always answer as if you are going to solve everyone's problems, although we don't have a way to do it."

A lot of people are fascinated by the house where we lived, because it is a very peculiar place, a handcrafted house, I call it. Sergio built it by hauling bricks and lumber in a pickup truck every day, like a little ant. With two carpenter helpers, he built different parts of the house as we needed them. Francisco Lacayo, the vice-minister of Culture whom I mentioned, later became a neighbor, and he used to visit us and say, "First, before I even say hello, I want to know which parts of the house are new today!" He had a great time saying, "Your house is so interesting; every time I come, you've added a new piece." And the architect president of the Utopian Club said, "This is called functional architecture, because the part you need is the part you build. Everything has a place."

The house where I lived before, the small place I had after the Revolution, was where the family went as they came back—my mother, my sister and her husband and children, and it became the return-from-exile home. My mother stayed in the house with Sergio and me for a while, but we were building the other place outside the city, where Sergio had his patients, and with the price of gas, it was expensive to go back and forth, so we moved out there. My daughter Vidaluz didn't want to go with me, because she didn't like my second partner, my older daughter didn't either, and she decided to stay with an aunt on her father's side while she finished at the university.

My girlfriends were scandalized, seeing how I left my small, but comfortable house and moved into a place with two dirt-floored rooms and an outhouse. The house was finished little by little, and we built two apartments to rent and a deck. Sergio cooks very well, and people were telling him he should open a restaurant, and he started thinking about it. I said, "Look, I don't want a restaurant with a lot of people coming into our home, but you could do something moderate and separate from the living areas." A deck terrace was perfect, because it preserved the privacy of the house, and I had my study, where I could work. He started an Italian restaurant open on Mondays and Fridays. I took advantage of that service, because when I worked at the Valdivieso Center and had delegations of visitors, we could organize dinners for them. They appreciated it, because it's outside the city, has a nice ambiance, and Sergio is an excellent host. He had an international menu with delicious, fresh salads and pasta dishes with sauce. He could handle groups and gave us a reduced price.

Besides being a veterinarian, Morazán is a devotee of history. His father was Francisco Morazán, a Honduran military officer who was in Guatemala when Jacobo Arbenz was president [1951-54]. He often spoke with his two small sons about history and geography, and Sergio is passionate about them, even as an adult. I gave him information on an intensive postgraduate course on Central American history, and he enjoyed it. He enrolled in a master's program, but he couldn't manage the studies on top of his work. He knows a lot and has a prodigious memory. I invited him to give presentations on Nicaraguan geography and history along with its fauna, which is his specialty. He gave talks for scholarship students from the Valdivieso Center who were studying different areas.

Women, the Revolution and feminism

Much has been said about women's advances during the Revolution. How did you experience that aspect of the Revolution? Did it empower women?

Yes. I have a thesis about my generation of Nicaraguan women, especially women writers. Michèle Najlis, Ana Ilce Gómez, and I are contemporaries; we are always cited together because we are roughly the same age and began to write around the same time. We are mentioned after Mariana Sansón and María Teresa Sánchez in the 1950s and 60s. In the 1970s, Gioconda Belli, Daisy Zamora, and, later, Rosario Murillo began to publish.

None of us had great feminist awareness, because the movement had not yet come to Nicaragua with much intensity. But women and men both assumed a social commitment, and for me, that was the vehicle for raising my awareness of feminism. At first, we women made a commitment as historical subjects—an important step for women, because tradition held that women did not get involved in politics, in public space, in social change, which were reserved for men. We worked for the Revolution and later realized in an assessment done by the Autonomous Women's Movement in Nicaragua that we had allowed the Revolution's priorities to prevail over our own. To a certain extent this is what happened to the Luisa Amanda Espinosa Association of Nicaraguan Women, the AMNLAE. Before the Revolution, I was in the Association of Women Facing the National Problematic, AMPRONAC. Many organizations formed to promote change, such as People United, which coordinated popular mobilization at the grassroots level, and AMPRONAC, which brought together middle and upper class women.

Feminism is sometimes unappealing

One of the many concerns in your life seems to have been, if not feminism per se, at least constant attention to the conditions and situations of women. You have played foundational roles in related organizations in Nicaragua and in the university gender studies that you mentioned.

Yes, that's true, both in women's organizations and in gender studies. When I began as dean of Humanities at UCA, Angelita Saballos asked me in an interview what I thought about feminism. I replied that it was a necessary extreme, with well-known martyrs. I think that the feminist movement, with its many currents and tendencies, in its most radical expression, is the sum of the pain, frustrations, and injustices suffered by women in a patriarchal system that oppresses them and treats them like a second class people. But a radical movement pays the price for its radicalism.

I believe in the couple. I believe, for example, that the alliance between the feminist and lesbian movements in order to transform a culture is legitimate, but those are two different movements. These are topics for a debate that will never end. In the 1980s when I was on a cultural tour in California, I met with an association of lesbians that invited me to lunch. They were very generous and made many contributions to the Revolution, especially books donated for libraries. At the luncheon, I said, "I have very competent, well-educated friends who are lesbians, though I am not, but I am interested in understanding you better, and I have a question: To what extent do you think many of you became lesbians out of frustration with emotional relationships with men? Or men mistreated you or did not understand you?" They admitted to me that there was a certain percentage for whom this was true, though not for all. Some women experience bad relationships and seek an emotional relationship with other women who understand and love them.

Feminism can appear unappealing at times. In Nicaragua, it is not spreading very quickly, and young men and women often reject it because statements by some feminists are full of anger, even though that anger might mask a lot of pain. The young women think, "Oh, oh! They don't want us to like men, and I am in love with this boy!" They don't find a way to reconcile the two things.

Do you consider yourself a feminist?

Yes, in the sense of wanting equality. I am committed to the struggle for justice and the establishment of new relations of power. I know that there are several tendencies in feminism, and I belong to the feminism of difference. I think that we women should learn from men's experience in the public space but not imitate their vices and errors. I just read María Eugenia López Brun's book of interviews with the first six women governors in Mexico. In their interventions, we can confirm what has been observed—that in practice, women have exceptional abilities for dialogue and agreement, invaluable qualities needed to forge that other possible world.

Women must have their own projects

You managed, as a married woman, to carry out your own projects. Is that the norm for women in Nicaragua?

No, and this is a topic of conversation among my friends—our advancement as women with respect to feminism. Now, in my mature years, I say to women—my daughters, my women friends, any woman with whom I have the opportunity to transmit some of my experience—that it is important for us to have our own personal projects, which has not been the custom. Women always marry and begin to operate in terms of the man's project, where he wants to practice his profession, and what he wants to do. I believe that in the male-female relationship there is a margin for negotiating interests so that favorable conditions are created for both.

Usually men have projects, whether professional, cultural, or of another type, and they develop and realize them, while the woman has to resign herself to staying on the side. She often becomes bored and, what's worse, stagnated. She becomes boring for the man. He evolves because he pursues his project but lives with a person who does not evolve, and many problems can ensue. What I recommend might sound scandalous. If the woman is not going to yield totally to the man's wishes, and he demands it, then that's the end of the marriage, because they want to accomplish different things. That's why I talk about negotiation. I believe that two fulfilled people are more likely to be successful. I recommend that we women always have our own personal project that we firmly believe in, because if you believe in it, you defend it and realize it. That allows you to grow as a person and to love someone else, not out of dependency and not totally absorbed in the other, but as two people, two developed, equal human beings who share a life in common of your own free will, not out of need, circumstances, or convention.

Would you say this recommendation is valid for women of all social classes?

Yes, but obviously the needs are different. I believe that all women have the right to a personal project, and the problem is the lack of equality. A woman in the country living in poverty can hardly aspire to realizing herself. But at a minimum, a poor rural or working woman can aspire to having help with the household duties and not being abused. Lack of physical abuse should be a basic condition, not an extraordinary exception. In the case of middle class working women, if they like their work and want to study, they should negotiate with their partners to share childcare, which is, after all, of common interest to both the man and the woman. They should share money, because perhaps enrolling in new classes might imply paying for a master's or special courses. Rich women, I think, have even more responsibility because they have more possibilities. Why should they be ignorant and bored? So yes, I think it applies at all levels.

Post-revolutionary Nicaragua: Neoliberalism and poverty

In what directions has the country gone since 1990, the year that marked the end of the Sandinista Revolutionary Government?

I would summarize the various neoliberal governments that we have had as follows.

Violeta Barrios de Chamorro, 1990-1997:
Pacification, ideals, mother figure

In synthesis, Doña Violeta's government meant: an important contribution to the pacification process, democratic opening, extreme poverty as a postwar consequence, application of International Monetary Fund measures, and privatization of the economy. The historical balance is generally favorable. I think she accomplished what she was given to do. Doña Violeta was a person without any political experience and was not prepared to lead a country. She was a good woman, faithful to her husband, and she incarnated the ideals of freedom of expression and civil liberties. The important role that she played was in the pacification of the country, taking us from war to peace and making both sides disarm. I believe that is a sufficient and very significant contribution. Are people saying there was corruption in her government? Undoubtedly there was, as well as corrupt processes of privatization, but in my opinion, that was not her responsibility.

A sociological analysis done in Nicaragua showed that Doña Violeta embodied the figure of the mother symbol in our culture in the context of the Virgin Mary, because we are devotees of the Virgin, a Marian people, and she represented mothers, who generally mediate and try to bring others to reconciliation. According to the Autonomous Women's Movement of Nicaragua, with her maternal attitude she even managed to put her own stamp as a woman on her official actions, and it is true that she broke with the rules of protocol and spoke from her presidential chair as if she were in her living room.

Some people ridiculed her way of communicating, lack of protocol, and maternal language. I remember in one of her televised interviews she was talking about the police force and said, "Oh, yes, the boys looked so handsome in their uniforms!" She spoke like a mother who had just bought them new uniforms and they had gone to school with pressed clothes and shined shoes. She kept the maternal tone too when she spoke with Pope John Paul II and said, "Oh, my son, you have to forgive the offense our people gave to you." She asked for forgiveness in the name of Nicaragua in her maternal, familiar language. But I think she accomplished the important task, which was not easy, of bringing peace to the country. I gave her, and will continue to give her, credit for that.

Doña Violeta's governing style was maternal, conciliatory, not feminist, but feminine, which was well-received, and until very recently, in surveys she was named as one of the most outstanding public figures. I believe that she gave notice that Latin America and the world are demanding "hand or command of a woman." The United States should open itself to candidates like Hillary Clinton.

Arnoldo Alemán, 1997-2002: Authoritarian, confrontational

Summarizing Alemán's government, it was authoritarian in style and confrontational. Viscerally anti-Sandinista, he promoted the political polarization of the country and closing of democratic spaces. Extreme poverty continued for the same reasons, worsened by the corruption of the president. Economic and social differences deepened.

Enrique Bolaños, 2002-2007: Oligarchic mindset, foreign support

Bolaños was a man with no political experience or ambitions and no interest in clinging eternally to power and following the tradition of strongman leaders. His moral principles are those of a right wing entrepreneur, and when I say that, I mean that he is a man of principles who is married, has a stable home and adult children, and I believe that he has been an honest person. The problem is that due to his class and concept of development, he stumbled into a mistake that traps so many political leaders, which is to favor specific groups. He favored a very small group of entrepreneurs and has an oligarchic mindset, which is another vice in our culture.

Since Bolaños was not a strong figure, the possibility arose to make the system more democratic, and civil society worked on that. But a big problem was not the president, but the legislators. The pact between Daniel Ortega, the leadership of the FSLN party, and former President Arnold Alemán, who was accused and found guilty of stealing from the State, closed the political system. President Bolaños, however, became an accomplice because he lacked the ability to take charge and establish alliances with the sector of the population that could have joined with him against the pactmakers. He felt secure because he was supported by the U.S. government, foreign entities, the Organization of American States—international organizations. He remained in power because those supporters kept him there, whereas he should have relied on the Nicaraguan people.

In summary, there was a democratic opening, similar to that of Doña Violeta's government, and exemplary organization of the macro-economy, but extreme poverty continued.

Daniel Ortega, 2007-: Clientelist policy, closure of democratic spaces

Daniel Ortega of the Sandinista party won the elections with the help of his pact with Alemán, which the prestigious late leader Reynaldo Antonio Téfel dubbed "the corruption pact," predicting that its consequences would be deeply harmful for the future of the country. He was right, because it devastated the fragile institutionalization that, despite everything, had continued to be forged. There were also important agreements with the hierarchy of the Roman Catholic Church on criminalization of therapeutic abortion.

The Ortega-Murillo government's first period, 2007-2011, can be summarized as: confrontational, authoritarian style that forced all State institutions to become partisan; closure of democratic spaces and physical aggression against the civil society that took to the streets with independent positions. The Ortega-Murillo government shares some of the characteristics of certain

Latin American leaders—populist and dedicated to a clientelist policies to get more votes. It consults with the party membership en masse and claims democratic approval for issues decided behind closed doors. It took ALBA funding provided by the Venezuelan government of Hugo Chávez, and uses it at will, with no transparency.

They could have won the November 2011 elections honestly, given the amount of "horse and house trading" covered by Venezuelan funds. Under previous governments, extreme poverty included over half the population living on two dollars a day, according to World Bank research. Despite that enormous advantage against an opposition divided on the Alemán-Ortega pact, they perpetrated extensive election fraud, in both the municipal and national elections, to obtain greater control over all the State entities.

In the second Ortega-Murillo period starting in 2011, the FSLN, which is no longer the party it was historically, has three characteristics that expert political analyst Emilio Álvarez Montalván says every party needs: charismatic leadership, which in the case of Ortega, I would call blind confidence among the party's militants, organization, and resources. In short, Ortega yields all the power to his wife, strengthens relations with the private sector, attacks civil society, and closes democratic spaces.

The government also issues laws that sound attractive, for example, that 50% of political power should be in the hands of women, but we'll have to wait for the results. The problem is that there is no internal democracy within the party, so members cannot present or develop initiatives not controlled by the presidential couple.

My priorities now are culture and education

Hurricane Katrina (2005) had a profound impact on me. First of all, because many members of my family live in New Orleans: my son, granddaughters, mother, siblings, aunts and uncles, and cousins. Ours, as I said in an article that I published at that time, "Reflection in Blue on New Orleans," is a family accustomed to disasters resulting from natural and social phenomena such as war and political exile. Once I knew my whole family was safe, I was shocked to see television images of how unprotected people were, blacks and whites alike. You could see lack of foresight or training in civil defense. Help was slow to arrive, as if the government remained unaware of the gravity of the situation. I also heard about the offers of help, medicine, and medical teams from Cuba and Venezuela, which were not accepted for political and ideological reasons. All of that made me write that article. I learned that poet Roberto Fernández Retamar, who knows about my family in the States, asked Ernesto Cardenal about us. Ernesto said all were OK and sent him my article, which he quoted in the section "Al pie de la letra" in the journal *CASA*.

After finishing my term as Civil Coordinator Liaison in 2005, I focused on the political party Sandinista Renovation Movement (MRS, Movimiento de Renovación Sandinista), and ran as its candidate for delegate to the Parlacen, the Central American Parliament, in 2006 and 2010, but with positions that made it difficult to get elected. MRS is a good party for the future; our positions are progressive, and the country's lack of development works against us in elections. Anyway, I believe I have more vocation for the social sector rather than politics, and I see that the country's only true strategic recourse is education. Right now, my priorities are culture and education.

The Nicaraguan Association of Women Writers (Asociación Nicaragüense de Escritoras) (ANIDE), of which I was the first executive president, operated for 10 years, thanks to funding by Holland's Cooperation Agency, HIVOS, to efficient executive leadership by the writer Isolda Hurtado, and to the magnificent integration of the entire membership, which made it possible to develop a strong program to promote literature written by women. ANIDE now holds national poetry and narrative contests each year for the "Mariana Sansón Argüello" and "María Teresa Sánchez" prizes, in addition to the "Rafaela Contreras" prize for Central America. ANIDE published 20 issues of the *Revista Anide* magazine, directed by Christian Santos and edited successively by Helena Ramos, Vilma de la Rocha, and Ángela Saballos. We organized two Congresses of Central American Women Writers, and at the first, formed a Federation of Central American Women Writers. We celebrated the second congress as a contribution to the peace process between our country and neighboring Costa Rica during a conflict surrounding the use of San Juan River, which belongs to Nicaragua and marks the southern border. Since the HIVOS financial support has come to an end, and lacking support from the State or private enterprise, the association has entered into a low intensity phase.

In 2011, I was named President of the Nicaraguan Writers Center (Centro Nicaragüense de Escritores, CNE), which faced the challenge of the end of financial support by the Embassy of Norway, which had lasted for 16 years and was eventually extended for three more years but with 40% less, and this will be the last period of support. We asked the National Assembly to include funding for the CNE in the General Budget of the Republic, as it does for other cultural organizations, but no funding was approved. As president, I am part of group projects with the board of directors composed of intellectuals Manuel Ortega Hegg, Margarita López Miranda, Guillermo Cortés Domínguez, Angelita Saballos, and the gifted young writer Ulises Juárez Polanco, who is editor of *El Hilo Azul (The Blue Thread)*, CNE's journal that is directed by Sergio Ramírez.

Cultural relations with the United States Embassy have been sporadic, although I have a good personal relationship with cultural attaché Valerie Wheat, who sponsored visits by Argentine American writer Luis Alberto Ambroggio to organize poetry workshops for young people in several cities. Last year an anthology of the young writers' works was published, and the book presentation was held at our headquarters.

The Revolution was not made by angels

1979, the first year after the triumph of the Revolution was difficult, because they jailed a lot of people, among them the caretaker at my parents' home outside Managua, a watchman, my mother's chauffeur, and the chauffeur of an uncle who was a general. All my parents' property was confiscated, and it didn't occur to me to protest. They confiscated the house outside Managua on the old road to León; they confiscated a rubber products factory in Jinotepe in which my father owned an interest; they confiscated a motel he and his brothers owned in Managua. Everything was confiscated, and it didn't occur to me to file a protest. My parents' home was turned into a military school and completely destroyed. It had been a very beautiful house with a swimming pool, and they ruined it. It was returned to me after the election loss in 1990, but in terrible shape.

The Revolution involved many trials and tribulations and the loss of privileges. Of course, that is a contradiction of the Revolution, because I realized, after I saw the abuses, that people who were combatants at a certain level ran to occupy the most luxurious houses. I, on the other hand, had turned over my larger house and moved to a smaller one, so I lowered my standard of living, while within the Revolution, many people improved their living standard or, at least, acquired things they had never had before.

I did not criticize them at the time, but I suffered the first year, because I wanted the Revolution to be impeccable. One day I even prayed and asked the Lord for humility, because I understood what I was probably doing—with my personal pride, I wanted to demonstrate to my family that my choice was the just and correct one. I remember my mother wrote me and said, "Our things will be enjoyed now by other people who didn't work to get them." That first year, I told her, "No, the confiscated houses are going to become museums, or schools, or public service offices," and some did, but not all. The Revolution was not made by angels, but by people. I realized that over time.

The new revolution is feminism for justice

Did you grow disillusioned with the Revolution, or are you still optimistic?

I think that the revolutionary project was essentially for justice, and we failed..., people failed..., but revolution never ends. I found that we women are the reserve strength to transform the world, and the new revolution is feminism, and women are going to bring about justice in the world.

At the end, I was not embittered, but I was left thinking that this type of society we have now is well-known to us. We have come back around to the same thing: a dependent country, a consumer society, neoliberalism, all the same; it's no novelty to me, this world of competition. Actually, a revolution, the possibility of a classless society, is a marvelous ideal that may never exist in reality, but we have to struggle for its existence. As a vital necessity for me, in order to live, I need to believe that a more just society is possible.

The conclusion I came to is that I believe in the personal quality of people more than in social classes. I like a phrase that is attributed to liberation theologian Gustavo Gutiérrez: "He who says that a poor person is good just because he is poor, has never come to my parish." I can identify with that. There are country people who are spiritual aristocrats. I have known men and women of very poor extraction, from a very poor class, with extraordinary spiritual refinement, attitudes, and human qualities. I also think it is more difficult for rich people, who have many vested interests, to be good and generous, although I have known people with vast economic resources who also showed great generosity and personal qualities. Extreme poverty can never be good, because it forces people into terrible levels of indignity with all the consequences, that's why I think it is a mistake to mythicize poor people and automatically consider them good. Not everyone can live their poverty with spiritual sanity or saintliness. I never was a Marxist-Leninist and never believed in class hatred. I believe that hate makes you sick and that you cannot generate positive things from negativity. I don't believe that hatred is the engine driving history, nor would I like it to be. I believe that love drives history, a purposeful attitude in favor of justice.

Love is the engine of history, not class struggle: Rebuilding family ties

I mentioned love as the engine driving history, and in that sense, for example, I never cut off relations with my family. We had no terrible ruptures, perhaps moments of tension or coldness, but nothing beyond that. I love my aunts and uncles a lot and owe a debt of gratitude to the former military uncle married to my mother's sister, Octavio Gutiérrez, because of all he did for my son Carlos and have tried to repay him in kind. For me, that is deeply important, because, as I mentioned to you, I was so worried that he would take a wrong path in the States, as you can imagine, a boy coming from the traumas of war, having been detained, his father against his mother in the Revolution. I was frightened that he could become a drug addict out of feelings of anguish about his life, or disillusionment, or not having a home. My aunt and uncle gave him that home.

What I tried to salvage always with my family was love. I told them, "I understand that you had to make many sacrifices and suffer losses, but that was what your generation faced, and you made your choices. I wanted to choose something different. That doesn't mean I don't love you." I tried to express my love for them. Fortunately, they had the same attitude, and for me, that was a consolation. In that, my mother was really extraordinary. Maybe this is more typical in Latin American cultures, because in Nicaragua there are several similar examples.

Christianity, poetry, revolution, and personal coherence

My mother is a very positive person, very upbeat, very practical. I have always had the theory that my mother is a poet who didn't write and opted for practicality, managing her life as well as possible. Although she is very different from me and is a mother with whom I have not shared deep and fundamental things, I recognize that she has helped me live, she has given me joy and love, and I think those are essential. She helped me so that my load was not as heavy for me. My mother is the one who has allowed me to feel a little less responsible for what's happening, because I felt responsible for my country, I felt responsible for everything.... The onus was on me, including during the Revolution, when my father had been assassinated, and almost all my family had left. Some of my siblings had married outside the country. Edmundo was with his family in Spain; Jairo went into exile in the States because he was married to Eunice, whose father was the other general I mentioned who was killed, Reynaldo Pérez Vega; my sister Meriulda married a man from Ecuador and ended up moving to South America. Some were already living outside the country, and the rest of the family went into exile—my mother and her two sisters, all three married to military officers.

I was left practically alone with my Great-Aunt Adelina, the one who stayed with me when she was very old, and all her brothers had died. My children started leaving because they did not like the Revolution. They were adolescents—the two older ones were around 14, the third left at age 12, and I had only Vidaluz with me. People remarked, "How strange that you opted for the total opposite." I thought, how strange that I know this is my place, despite the pain I feel from the separations. What I wanted was to live with my family in the Revolution, and above all else, I wanted my children with me.

How do you explain that you opted for something different than the rest of your family did? I think you spoke about this issue with Margaret Randall for her book, Sandino's Daughters Revisited: Feminism in Nicaragua.

Yes, well, based on one of the few syntheses, or clarities, that you come to in life, there are three things I have been unable to separate: my religious formation based on values of justice and deep equality, that is, Christianity; poetry, my way of apprehending the world, my way of living life and perceiving reality; and third, revolution, understood as permanent change, because for me, the Sandinista Revolution was a specific attempt during a specific historical period, but for me, revolution in the larger sense did not end. I began a revolution when I was a teenager and have not yet abandoned it. I believe we have to renew ourselves constantly and revolutionize ourselves, and I believe that there is work yet to be done in the world. Those three things I cannot separate; each one relates to the others, and all three are mutually included in the others.

Because of those values and the need for coherence that I felt…, I don't know, but I suppose that everyone in the world needs coherence. I believe that being coherent brings internal peace. I can tell you I have experienced very deep pain, difficult and heartrending ruptures, like the separation from my children that was so painful, but I accepted them in peace. In some poems, the epigraphs I use reflect evangelical radicalism, for example, where Jesus said, "I have not come to bring peace, but a sword"—war. There are some violent gospels! In another passage, Jesus said his brothers were not those of his blood, but those who shared the faith. That is how I understand it. I have had to accept certain things, because in life, I can change what is within my power and accept what is not, and that is the radicalism. That's how I have explained it to myself.

Did you learn that as a girl with the nuns at the Asunción School?

I think that, citing another gospel, the Word is sown and falls on fertile soil, on rocks, or among thorns that choke it. In life, the Word is there for everyone, but how you embrace it, that is the great mystery, and I embraced the Word. I don't mean by this that I was fertile ground and am a wonder. I simply mean this is how I interpret the gospel Word, and I have tried to be coherent.

II. VIDALUZ MENESES ON HER WORKS AND LITERATURE IN NICARAGUA

II. Vidaluz Meneses on Her Works and Literature in Nicaragua

Guarded Flame (1975)

Vidaluz, you have already mentioned several of your poems and the circumstances in which you wrote them. I would like to know more about your books and certain poems. In the interview with Margaret Randall about your first collection that came out in 1975, Guarded Flame, *you said that your husband paid for its publication.*

Yes, I had that support from him.

How did you come to publish your first book?

I was encouraged because my poems had been selected for publication in the major newspaper's weekly literary supplement, *La Prensa Literaria*, which meant that they had already been reviewed by certain readers. The supplement director, poet Pablo Antonio Cuadra, had approved them for publication, so I was sure they had at least some value. When I had enough, I thought it would be interesting to collect the poems in a book. I saw that several male writers of my generation had published books. I don't remember if Michèle Najlis had already published *El viento armado* [*Armed wind*], which was first published in Guatemala, but if her book was out by then, it would have been further encouragement for me.

Mario Selva, a writer and painter from a progressive intellectual group, ran Asel Typography, a printing operation named for his father, Adán Selva, a Nicaraguan intellectual and politician. Mario was known to offer reasonable prices for writers to publish their books with his press. I asked him to prepare a proposal, and my husband, who had a good income as a lawyer, paid for the printing, and that's how *Guarded Flame* came into being.

Fernando Silva suggested the book title to me. I always have trouble finding titles for my poems and collections. Since it was lyrical poetry, Fernando liked that title, and I thought he knew me well, since he was my children's pediatrician and now is the father of my grandchildren's pediatrician, Fernando Antonio Silva, also a poet. Besides, Fernando and I belonged to a group of Christian poets, along with Luis Rocha and others, and we often met with Father Ángel Martínez. We both participated in a circle of Christian friends who agreed on the need for changes in Nicaragua.

Fernando Silva understood my first poetry, which I consider much more intimate. I think I have never stopped being lyrical, but that book is more hermetic. It has more images than my later books, where the language is more open, in the exteriorist style. He also suggested a stanza from a poem by Father Martínez, a Spanish Jesuit priest, to explain the title:

When will I give myself to this life
with the song of the soul that I carry?
Always bursting from the soul,
always staying inside.

I thought these lines from Father Martínez's poem "¿Cuándo?" [When?] reflected the meaning of my poetry. The ordering of the poems to create a certain thematic unity was determined by my dear friend Fanor Téllez, now married to Karla Sánchez, a poet from a younger generation. I appreciated Fanor's fraternal support, and it was a wonderful experience.

Fanor wrote the first penetrating and insightful analysis of the book, published in the National University's journal *Cuadernos Universitarios*. The United Nations declared 1975 as the International Year of Women, and Fanor edited issue number 15 of *Cuadernos Universitarios* in honor of Nicaraguan women. He included a small anthology of women poets: Michèle Najlis, Ana Ilce Gómez, Gioconda Belli, Daisy Zamora, Carlota Molieri, and myself. Fanor did a brief review of works by each of us, and I liked what he wrote about my poetry, because it was clear that he appreciated the type of poetry I was writing and understood the meaning of my poems.

Was your first collection warmly received?

No, not especially. I remember a nice note from poet Napoleón Fuentes, welcoming the book. Honestly, I think that at the time, Michèle Najlis was writing strong, passionate, combative poetry, and Ana Ilce Gómez was considered the more mature and polished voice. In a historical approach to poetry, I am linked generationally with these two excellent poets, and we are considered part of the novel phenomenon of women poets publishing books. Much later, Ligia Guillén of my generation published books, but her sister, Adriana Guillén, with the *nom de plume* "Carla Rodríguez," did not. *Guarded Flame* was certainly not a best-seller! But at that time and in a country with a high level of illiteracy, poetry often languished on bookstore shelves. After the triumph of the Revolution, I donated hundreds of unsold copies to the national library system.

The poem "Alfonso" appears in this first collection with the epigraph: "A patch of blue is more intense / than the whole sky...."

Those are the first two lines of a poem by Alfonso Cortés, a postmodern Nicaraguan poet. The original title of the poem was "Un detalle" [A detail], but it came to be known as "Ventana" [Window].

I wonder, then, if you would agree with Danielle Raquidel's interpretation of your poems, and if you would attribute something similar to Alfonso Cortés. Danielle identifies as a constant in your poetry the union of the imagination with terrestrial and cosmic space. She describes this space as welcoming and not hostile to humanity, though it has become a target for destruction by humans wanting to destroy the cosmos.

I deeply admire Alfonso Cortés, but I believe that other poets have had stronger influence on me. Nevertheless, I think the mystery of poetry consists in what others perceive in an author's words.

One of your most frequently cited poems, "When I Married," has been interpreted as a form of protest. Nydia Palacios says that in this and other poems, Vidaluz Meneses "subverts and reconstructs Biblical and Greek myths... and shows the need to construct a new image, a self-image, a self-portrait, and redefine oneself beyond patriarchy." Was this one of your purposes in writing the poem?

That poem corresponds to a period when my feminism was unconscious. But yes, it was written with a mixture of irony and resignation.

In the beautiful poem "Bonanza" that you dedicate to your Great-Aunt and Uncle, Virginia and Leslie, you include a Miskito song.

I don't have the literal translation, but the general sense is that it's about a loved one who leaves. It means: "My love, where have you gone?" It's a nostalgic love song about a woman abandoned by her beloved, or vice versa.

Air that Calls Me (1982)

Your second poetry collection, Air that Calls Me (1982), *appeared some seven years after* Guarded Flame.

Yes, the second book was published during the years of the Revolution. The title, "Air that Calls Me," is a kind of play on words. Poet Luis Rocha helped me find the title, which comes from a poem by Joaquín Pasos:

> This is not her, it's the wind,
> it's the air that calls her;
> it's her place, it's her empty space
> calling out for her.

I liked the title because, first, it was a play with "llama," which means "flame" in Spanish, but also is a form of the verb "to call." So *Llama guardada, Guarded Flame*, had the noun form, "flame," and this book title, *El aire que me llama, Air that Calls Me*, had the same word, but as a verb, so I was playing with the words. The title also made sense, because "Air that Calls Me" refers to the changes in the air, the winds of liberation, which was the prevalent ambiance in the revolutionary decade, during which, as I mentioned on a personal level, I felt I came into my maturity as a person and as a woman. I was in control of my life and of myself. From age 35 on, I think I began to be myself, to know who I was, what I wanted to do in life, and to act in accordance with my beliefs. I thought it was a good title, because it reflected that moment in my life and my poetry. I also included some poems written before, along with others that I had just written, which were poems of the Revolution.

Poetry as denunciation

In this second book indigenous themes appear in "Cakchiquel Woman."

Yes, the poem is from a visit we made to Guatemala. My father was ambassador to Guatemala at the time, and I went on vacation with my children, my husband, and his mother. We visited markets and historical sites. I enjoyed traveling with the family, but my critical conscience tormented me as I recalled history and thought of present-day injustices.

Teresa Anta San Pedro highlights a historical point of view in this poem, which she interprets as evidence that your commitment as "a subject in History" is not limited to present reality. She calls your indigenous figure "a great Amerindian hero," a woman-subject, not the woman-object implicit in the term "heroine." She considers her "one of America's forgotten Penelopes ... condemned to abort the life engendered in her being with the same brutal force with which it was conceived."

Fundamentally, it is a song of solidarity and a denunciation of injustice. I appreciate Teresa's concept of women heroes, because indigenous women are anonymous heroes on a daily basis.

Nydia Palacios, citing your poem "Compañera," perceives in your work a legacy that is extended to all the women in Nicaragua who, "previously anonymous, are the invisible columns in the construction of a better future, and [Meneses] turns them into heroines and makes them pass through the great door of Nicaraguan history." What special sensitivity does a woman poet bring to the political reality around her when she considers herself capable of operating as an agent of change?

I am so glad that Nydia perceives my poem in that way. As the musicologist Salvador Cardenal observed, "There are poet-producers and poet-consumers." I think that literature contributes to the development of human beings, and, therefore, women are particularly receptive to poetry written by women.

Perhaps we could draw parallels between your poetic expression of History's woman-subject in "Cakchiquel Woman" and attempts by Central American novelists to reinscribe women as active agents in the evolution of History. I am thinking of your compatriot Rosario Aguilar, and of Panamanian-Nicaraguan Gloria Guardia and Chilean-Costa Rican Tatiana Lobo, for example.

I believe that just making women more visible is a contribution to the recovery of history. As today's feminists say, "history" has already been written, it is known to us, and now we have to understand and write "herstory."

For you, what is the meaning of the last line of the poem, "tradition made woman"?

For me, "woman" has been the eternal grand educator, the transmitter of customs and values; in particular, women who make products by hand pass on their art, which is of ancient origin.

Do you make any conscious connection between this poem "Cakchiquel Woman" written in 1978, and "Familiar April," from 1975, also published in this collection?

No, not a conscious connection, but undoubtedly the backdrop is the same—social concern and a denunciation of the marginality of people living in the countryside. In 1977, when I was studying library sciences, I had to do a paper for a research methodologies class, and I wrote it on the causes of oppression of rural women.

Speaking of poetry as denunciation, there is exteriorist poetry, which says everything as clearly as possible, but other poetry does not. This poem of yours from the 1970s that I just mentioned, "Familiar April," says:

April, familiar and sun-drenched
—death by water—
The seers foresee unanimous.
And it might rain fire from heaven
Already fire rains in the hills.
Not even the screams of childbirth reach us.
But the city is deadly quiet.
And in the morning only a slash of
parched, hoarse wind sliced the sky in two.
They say from on high they fly them.

That "sliced the sky in two" refers to a helicopter. Those were the stories that we heard, that they were throwing poor rural people out of helicopters high in the air.

Did everyone understand what the verses meant? I saw Kathryn Peters's translation of your line, "Dicen que desde arriba los vuelan," which is literally, "They say that from above they fly them," and her translation said that bodies or live people were being thrown out of helicopters. Did readers have to know the code to understand it?

You're right, it was a sort of code, and "they fly them" meant that. Some people would not understand, but many did.

Do you consider it one of your more hermetic poems?

Yes, and poet-critic Helena Ramos told me, "You know, I have been studying this poem, and I think there is a possible intertexuality with T. S. Eliot's *The Wasteland*." It could be, I don't know where I got the lines, "—death by water— / The seers foresee unanimous." I had read U.S. poetry, because my poet boyfriend had given me the *Antología de la poesía norteamericana* [Anthology of U.S. poetry] translated by José Coronel Urtecho and Ernesto Cardenal. I ended up losing it, because I loaned it to everyone I knew, and someone did not return it. I'm sorry because it is an irreplaceable book with a very personal dedication.

The poem says something that might seem contradictory:

—death by water—
The seers foresee unanimous.
And it might rain fire from heaven.

Here we are talking about water, and I come out with rain made of fire. But this was an image to reflect the guerrilla struggle in the mountain. "Already fire rains in the hills. / Not even the screams of childbirth reach us." That's a reference to Ernesto Cardenal's poem about the rape of rural women and a woman who aborted while seated, which Carlos Mejía Godoy turned into a popular song, "The Women from Cuá." "Already fire rains in the hills. / Not even the screams of childbirth reach us." Yes, those are short, powerful verses about a terrible reality people had to try to survive. I was deeply affected by the reports, knowing that women were raped, and then they aborted, that people in the country were being murdered and hurled out of helicopters. "They say from on high they fly them." I had to say something, and I said it in that hermetic way.

And people understood.

Oh, yes.

Pilar Moyano, in her insightful study, "'Raíces que rompen el tiesto…" [Roots that break the pot…], states that you would probably agree "with those critical positions that affirm that social structures cannot be separated from linguistic structures, and poetry, as a subversion of the codes and clichés of ordinary language, is necessary for social transformation." Does your poetry of denunciation follow this concept of poetry as a weapon to achieve the transformation of society?

Undoubedly, yes, but this would be valid, I think, for all social poetry written in Latin America and throughout the world.

Feminist and postfeminist poetry

Pilar Moyano says that your poetry is "to a great extent, a question—What does it mean to be a woman?" She states that an important number of your poems constitute an investigation, in poetry, of the tensions women experience when they face socially imposed imperatives. Do you believe that you consciously propose to answer this question—What does it mean to be a woman?

I believe that this is the great challenge for feminism, and I also think that this grand question is one of the main reasons why there are so many divergent feminist tendencies.

Teresa Anta San Pedro, in her subtle and incisive analysis, "El callado feminismo en la poesía de Vidaluz Meneses" [Quiet feminism in poetry by Vidaluz Meneses], which I cited earlier, expresses surprise at the 1980 poem "All in All," whose theme is the end of a great love:

*I'll not say I was
your next plaything,
a chess piece,
a timely justification.
[...]
I shall gather the ashes, tangible proof
of the authenticity of my fire:
it will be humus, hope, golden shaft of grain,
in and for better fields.*

She believes that your concept of no-longer-requited love as a fertilizing element for the future anticipates by many years the postfeminist period, "something that is inconceivable in Spanish America in the year in which the poem was written, 1980." Postfeminism no longer focuses on denunciations of the marginalization of women or the struggle to eliminate the injustices, barriers, and prejudices that victimize women. "The woman in that poem no longer feels like a victim or guilty or inferior to men. She knows very well what she wants, and she is determined to achieve it. She has gone from object to subject. It's no longer about the field that the man sows and tends when he wishes. She will sow and tend her own field with her own seeds and fertilizer." How did you first conceptualize that very self-affirming way of overcoming and channeling pain?

I wrote that poem when I accepted that my married life with Carlos was over. I think the context of the Revolution greatly helped me deal with that rupture. I had to recognize the end of the individual love for my partner, but at the same time, I was opening myself to a great love for my people. In an autobiographic essay I wrote a few years later, "Heart in the Open," I say that the Revolution "exploded with fireworks in my country and in my heart; I passionately surrendered myself to it." In other words, I immediately had a substitute passion.

The "discrete silence" that both Álvaro Urtecho and Teresa Anta San Pedro find in your poetic works, does it respond to a conscious decision on your part to avoid what Urtecho calls "the scream of the ovaries, the mise-en-scène of brazen, resentful femininity"?

I think it's a question of personality. People express emotions according to their temperament and character.

In examining your poems, "My Aunt Adelina," "Mother," "Daughter," and "Looking at Her Photograph," Cristina Guzzo perceives the transfer of a sense of rootedness from woman to woman, a chain of heredity, a dialogue between generations. She observes: "This poetry offers a feminism with domestic roots; generational succession is what grounds Meneses's feminism."

Yes, I think that is an accurate observation. There is an invisible linking thread in matriarchy.

Flame in the Wind (1990)

Your third book, Flame in the Wind (1990), *reprints some of your previous poetry.*

In 1990, I am approaching 50, arriving at an age where you have to derive a synthesis of your life and your work, and I thought it would be a good idea to include some, but not all, of the poems from the other two books. I chose ones that I thought had some larger significance, and, perhaps, a certain level of quality. If we looked only at quality, people would think I had written just two poems before then, the ones that were always reprinted and cited: "When I Married" from *Guarded Flame*, and "Last Message to My Father" from *Air that Calls Me*. I omitted poems that I thought were merely circumstantial, such as the playful poems for my children. Poems I wrote at the end of the Revolution appeared as a section in *Flame in the Wind* with the title of the poem "On the Side Most Fragile" about my Great-Uncle Leslie, who was the grandfather figure of my childhood. I also included a section of new poems about the Revolution dedicated to my youngest child, Mariano Edmundo. Since he did not want to share the experience of the Revolution to the end with me and left when he was 12, I wanted him to have something as a legacy from that historical experience.

Flame in the Wind has three sections. It begins with an anthology in two sections that are clearly marked as coming from your first and second books. The third section titled "On the Side Most Fragile," has three parts: the first with no title, the second called "With the Same Hands," and then a third part, "To Future Men and Women." Does this three-part third section contain only new poems?

Yes. I didn't put a title on the first new part because it was a compilation of diverse themes. The poems all have a similar treatment as lyrical poetry, which is what I normally write, but there is a lot of variety in the portraits of people and references to the Revolution. In the second part I wanted to collect poems that had a certain correspondence to poetry by Roberto Fernández Retamar. I had a close literary and personal relationship with the Cuban poet, and he taught me a lot and enriched me as a poet and as a person committed to the Revolution. The third part I wanted to dedicate, especially as an explanation, maybe as a historical testimony, incarnated in my own youngest son, Mariano Edmundo. I had dreamed he would be with me throughout the Revolution, like my daughter Vidaluz, the only one of my four children who shared the fullness of that experience. I wanted to leave those poems as a legacy for him and for the generation of young people who lived the Revolution, as well as those who did not. That's why I call the section, "To Future Men and Women."

Álvaro Urtecho's prologue to Flame in the Wind *is very rich in allusions.*

It is. I invited him to write it because he is one of two younger Nicaraguan writers whom I greatly admire, and the other is Julio Valle-Castillo. Both were colleagues at work; I was their boss at the Culture Ministry in the Office of Art Promotion. Julio loves me like an older sister, but he says he has a conflict with me like he does with his mother. He wrote a very beautiful poem on Pope John Paul II's visit to Nicaragua, a visit that caused a worldwide scandal! It's true that the Pope was disrespected, but he displayed a very authoritarian attitude. Julio wrote a poem and dedicated it to his mother and to me. He is very talented and strict in his poetic preferences, and although I think he believes in my poetry, I have the impression he prefers other writers. I did not want to ask him to write a prologue for my book if he didn't think it was extraordinary poetry. Álvaro, my other essayist friend, is a philosopher and poet with a broad philosophical background, and I like his approach to literature. Álvaro knew me well, knew my poetry, and had a respectful opinion of it. I didn't think I was putting him on the spot by inviting him to write the prologue.

I think it is an excellent introduction because it draws attention to key aspects of your poetry, for example, its lyrical tone, the warm and intimate world, intelligent perception of the word, rejection of exhibitionist and narcissistic verbalism, concern for clarifying the meaning of human relations, exaltation of feminine sovereignty, and love in its personal, concrete, historical sense.

Well, with that comment, you're telling me I was right!

You have made clarifying comments on several of the new poems in Flame in the Wind. *Do you consider the poem "Woman, 1950s," dedicated to Irma Prego, a denunciation of social hypocrisy and of the impossibility for a woman of the wealthy class to define her own life?*

Yes. I opened the flood gates of the rage I found in Irma, who lived the drama of many women: she dedicated her time, intelligence, and talents to her husband, and then when they were older, he dumped her for a young secretary at the international organization he represented. She never forgave him for that, and she never forgave herself for the concessions she made to him, always postponing her personal project. I think Irma would have become a talented and delightful narrator. The sample that she left proves it.

Flame in the Wind *ends with the 1990 poem "Wailing Wall," a work of great emotional impact.*

Yes, great impact. I totally opened up in that poem. Normally, I am a person who tries to keep her emotions under control. I am authentic and sincere, but in general, I try to keep an even-keeled attitude toward life. One of the characteristics often attributed to me is that I am sensible, which implies a certain emotional balance. But for this poem, I had to recognize that the loss of the Revolution, the deaths of so many people, the sacrifices, the ruptures, and everything implied by those things, was a great tragedy.

In all the years of the Revolution, among the people with whom I shared ideas and conversations were two friends who joined me at the Culture Ministry at the beginning and were also with me at the UCA College of Humanities—Antonina Vivas, who played guitar and sang, and Adilia Moncada, an insightful historian and great reader. They said to me, "You know what's the matter with you? You can say to us, 'Oh, my father died' and then 'Oh, I bought a pair of shoes.' You say important things in the same tone as insignificant ones."

You must give things the meaning they deserve, and I wrote that poem giving free rein to my frustration, anger, and pain, everything wrapped up together. I thought it was appropriate to use an Old Testament Biblical motif, because spirituality, my Christian convictions, helped me deal with pain.

Cristina Guzzo refers to your "writing of mourning...what has been lost, what remains, what has been newly conquered." She considers Wailing Wall" almost a poetic testament, "an ellipsis where Meneses's mysticism is condensed"—the valley of tears, orphanhood, life beyond.

I believe this is true. I recognize that it is written from the deepest place within my being.

All is the Same and Different (Poems 1992-2001) (2002)

Your last collection came out in 2002 with a title that must be charged with meaning, All is the Same and Different. *Are these new poems?*

Yes, it contains 30 poems that I wrote during the 1990s, and the title is related to an anecdote from an interview with Angelita Saballos, who asked me, "How do you feel?" and I answered, "Like the Mexican ranchera song, 'in the same place and with the same people." Why? Because I felt that the 1990s were a return to the past, and the situation in the country was difficult again. There was no dictatorship, but once again, and still, differences deepened, and there were many problems and a lot of accumulated pain. When people returned from exile, the country underwent a reorganization. For me, many things were like experiencing the same all over again, but it was not exactly the same. The title of this collection means that during the 1990s, "everything is the same and different." Who could believe it? What was the purpose of so much sacrifice, such a drastic change, just to return to the same situation? But it's not the same, so "all is the same and different," as the title says.

The poem "Questions" from this last book has fascinated me since I first read it. I imagine there is a story behind it.

Yes, it attempts to unite the pain of many women—women who have committed suicide, women who endure violence and are unable to denounce it because they are so deeply destroyed, they lack the strength to make accusations, women who are abused in the middle of the night and not even their cries are heard. Or the woman who fearfully huddles like a child in her bed. Or the woman who puts on her makeup and pretends she is in control of the situation but is in pain because her life is a difficult challenge. Those are the questions posed to society in that poem: Who understands her? Who helps her? Who rescues that woman from her suffering? That is the sense of the questioning.

Would you explain the context for writing the poem "Jurassic Evocation"?

Well, that reflects the debut of my new life with a veterinarian! As I mentioned, after the end of the Revolution, Sergio Morazán and I moved outside the city, and the scenery brought me memories of Bonanza, where I had spent so many happy days in my childhood. It did me a lot of good to recover the mountains and trees, and when it rained, the grey mist. That poem is about my partner, a large, strong, stout man who is very dynamic in his clinic, prescribing medicines, treating his animal patients.

In that poem and others in this last collection, I note a certain playful tone, a sense of humor that is less evident in previous poems. Do you too feel that there was a turning in this direction?

You know? You are right. Sometimes critics can help writers become aware of what we are doing. I think something else was happening there that you will find interesting as a literary critic. Margarita López Miranda mentions that the quality of this collection is reflected in its linguistic forms and structures, and that in this more recent poetry, verbal experimentation is a notable characteristic. She attributes to me a control over my writing that allows me to take certain liberties to play with humorous and experimental forms. This could be, and I think two things converge—a level of development in the writing of poetry and a more evolved psychological attitude anchored in greater maturity. My life has been charged with strong emotions, some very beautiful ones but also other very painful ones, and very strong in every sense of the word. I am arriving at an age when I would like life to be gentler, and I believe that psychologically it helps me to play a little and develop a more carefree dimension in art and poetry.

Did you intend in All is the Same and Different *to craft the reaffirmation of a feminine subject and reflexive maturity that Margarita López Miranda also talks about?*

Yes, now I fully assume an awareness of my gender, and nothing is innocent, much less unconscious.

Pilar Moyano has observed that your poems posit the transgression of sociocultural conventions and thereby attempt to imbue patriarchal traditions with new meanings, for example, in "Alive Are We." *The writers you mention there—Virginia Woolf, Sylvia Plath, Alfonsina Storni—succumbed, but they are rescued and survive when later poets like you consider them your precursors as writers.*

Well, perhaps I am pretentious, but I believe I give meaning to their lives and their deaths. The transcendence of their timely works should be enough, but I think they should also be recovered as individual persons, as pioneers in the liberation of women.

"That Woman Is Crazy" is another poem that I consider very significant.

Yes, that is a social poem based on an actual incident after, as I said, we came back around to the same thing. One day I was headed into the Valdivieso Center, and I noticed a thin woman carrying a bag who walked up to me and appeared to be disoriented. She asked me for help, and I gave her bus money but was left with the image of her. Well, I thought, that's part of the drama of everything being the same but different. We are back to poverty and tragedy. I thought of that poor woman, penniless, lost in the street, and I also thought of the development of the world, of humanity. I have access to Internet and e-mail, and human beings communicate more than ever, but that woman probably came from a small town—the rest is imagination—she is trying to mail a letter, to find signs of what she had known. I thought, if she is from the country, she must feel totally lost, when I live in the city and have trouble myself assimilating changes. Here she comes, and even the post office is not the same. Almost no one uses mail these days, we all send quick messages. I put that together with the alienation that often assails people who lack access to innovations brought by development. That poem is the portrait of an alienated, impoverished woman.

And like her, many?

The standard of living dropped drastically in Nicaragua in the 1990s, and the demoralizing statistics said 70% of the population lived on two dollars a day. You can imagine what it's like, then, when unemployment is terribly high, and 800,000 children have no access to education, not even primary school. That gives you an idea of the number of people who find themselves in this situation. The poem denounces that, and it is an intentional denunciation.

The next-to-last poem in the book is "Journey toward the Interior."

Yes, that poem aspires to express a sense of transcendence. The theme of life and death runs through a lot of my work. I am just now realizing this.

In that poem, you talk about seeking and searching, then conclude with:

—Such desire to order the chaos!
And what if I decide to stay quiet
like a surfboard loose
on the ebb and flow of the waves?

Are you saying, therefore do nothing?

You know, I had a doubt about this poem, because Álvaro Urtecho, with his philosophical background, thought it started out with a deep, transcendental theme but the end doesn't fit the rest of the poem, at least that's what I understood him to say. I thought that might be true, and I wondered whether to revise the poem, rework it and not publish this version. It might have been a little irresponsible of me to include it in the book, because he could be right; the ending is not proportional to the approach at the beginning; the ending is almost irresponsible, insignificant, laissez faire, and lacking the intensity of the beginning.

Is it only because of the surfboard? I wonder, if it were a more traditional image to suggest remaining inert, doing nothing, would that be more acceptable? Perhaps according to poetic strictures of other times a modern metaphor cannot be used to express deep existential concern. Maybe you have anticipated the incorporation of new images, like those of younger poets who will use modern images taken from their own worlds including, no doubt, surfboards.

Well, yes, you could be right. Your explanation is convincing, and that is precisely what startled my friend.

The images from nature that you have at the beginning of this poem, do they relate for you to your stays in Bonanza as a child?

I have begun the journey to the center of myself,
the necessary return to elemental things:
a river and its bed of smooth, white stones,
wildflowers —cup of honey for butterflies—
and afternoons buzzing with cicadas.

Yes, but from my whole childhood, in Las Segovias as well as Bonanza. For me, river settings were very important. I didn't see the sea until I was 14. My childhood memory is full of rivers, dirt paths, wooded areas. Like in the silence here, where you and I are talking today, in the country you can hear the cicadas. Then I talk about returning to the womb. After all, babies live in liquid before birth, so returning to the matrix is what people always want—to return to the mother, to security. The poem is linked to the Big Bang theory and references to cosmic poetry that Ernesto Cardenal introduced in Nicaraguan literature. This is being debated in the contemporary world—the first explosion of life, how life first begins, the whole question of abortion, when a life begins, whether you are really ending a life by abortion, or not, because it's something that is just being formed. I think, this is a rich life—daughters came out of me, others came out of my daughters, and I am prolonging myself, my blood, my cells, in others.

That is one of the recurring themes in your poetry too, a focus on your descendants.

I mention my children because they have given me strength. I also have the figure in a poem where children are like part of the roots that anchor you. At the end of the search in this poem, after so much life, so much effort, so much work, "—Such desire to order the chaos!" Also, the reference to chaos relates to some contemporary readings, because people from later generations, like Martha Cabrera, open me up to new books, new theories. A book that I reread and consult frequently is *The Seven Life Lessons of Chaos*. I thought, how curious, when we studied at school, when they teach you religion and speak of spirituality, when you read the Bible, chaos is always a symbol of disorder, of what is not correct and has to be put in order. God is the principal provider of order.

That is why, in the poem dedicated to women poets who committed suicide, "Alive Are We," I say, "prophetess of the androgynous orderer / of chaos," because chaos is disorder. But now, it turns out that chaos has its own laws that end up giving it order. This is fascinating to me for two reasons. First, as a poet, I believe that we should always be open to what is new; routine is the worst possibility; we must always be open to things that are different from what we know. Second, as a Gemini, I like change and novelty. I was pleasantly surprised that chaos has its own laws and ends up ordering itself. Why are we humans so worried about bringing order to chaos, if it has its own laws and the universe can be ordered? Instead, I say, "Let it be."

In talking about chaos are you consciously referring to the Revolution?

I think so, because somehow, I am becoming convinced that my generation attempted to bring about a transcendental change in our reality, but apparently we just stirred things up, and now we're back to the same, but it's not the same. And we urgently need to see where this is going to lead, but we will not necessarily see it, because our physical life will end. But I believe that the seed of change remains and will bear fruit, though my generation may not see it.

Afro-Caribbean themes

A poem richly imbued with Caribbean motifs, and one that I love, is "Mayaya June Beer" from Flame in the Wind.

I'm glad you like it, because I think it has meaning and a good poetic pulse. When I read it at your literary events at Howard University, I thought it had a special meaning for your students. June Beer was a painter from Bluefields in the Nicaraguan South Caribbean area and was a friend of mine. When I was in charge of libraries at the Culture Ministry, we named her director of the public library in Bluefields. For me, the most important thing was not that she direct and manage the whole library, but that she do what she did very effectively—animate the children's reading room as a primitivist painter. When June died, I wanted to write her a poem of homage, using songs of the Caribbean Coast, where she was originally from.

I begin the poem by mentioning two outstanding Caribbean poets. David Macfield has been a friend of mine since the 1960s. He lived in Managua and was a university professor for many years before the Revolution, then served as the Revolution's ambassador to Angola, Congo, and Mozambique. Carlos Rigby, another friend, is an extraordinary poet and actor. He has been invited for performances in Great Britain and is very versatile, plays trombone, and writes heavily rhythmic poetry. He has not yet published a book and used to walk around with a roll of manuscript poems tucked under his arm. I would scold him and keep his poems safe at the bookstore. We held May Pole celebrations with him in Managua. I put my Caribbean friends together in this poem. In "Mayaya June Beer" I use words from songs, because May Pole songs often introduce people's names.

"May Lullaby" in All is the Same and Different *takes up Afro-Caribbean themes first presented in "Mayaya June Beer".*

When I read the poem recently for you to film and use on a web site about my poetry, I was glad the recording went well, because I cannot always read my poems. I have to be "in the mood." That poem always makes me happy, because I wrote it when my first grandson was born, Alejandro Carlos, and I was delighted that his other grandmother was from Corn Island in the Nicaraguan Caribbean, an area that I love.

I never imagined a daughter of mine would marry someone from a Corn Island family. I like the island's May Pole tradition, which came from Jamaica, along with Afro-Caribbean music and its unique rhythm. The May Pole is the tree with ribbons at the top that is danced around, and it's a fertility rite in the month of May. A grandchild's arrival is the fertility of the family. The figure of the tree with the woven family that I mention in the poem, "and the endless family woven / into a luxuriant May Pole," is the image of the dancers who weave the ribbons together around the May Pole. I used that figure and verses from May Pole songs.

As you say in "May Lullaby," May is "a good time to be born."

Yes, and that grandson was like a birthday present for me, because he was born almost on my birthday, May 28; he came on the 31st. It just so happens that this date is very important in May Pole festivities in Nicaragua's South Caribbean area, which are begun precisely on that day. That was a happy coincidence.

Was Alejandro Carlos the first grandson?

Yes, he's my older daughter Karla's son. My oldest grandchild is Carlos's daughter, Esther María. I wrote a poem for her during the Revolution. She was born outside the country, and you can tell that she was far away. I called it "Looking at Her Photograph" and used a stanza from a poem by Ernesto Mejía Sánchez as an epigraph.

The poem has some references in English in the original, for example, "Miss Edith lost the keys." I imagine there is a story behind this.

Yes. I used some verses from May Pole songs, and one of them is very nice, "Maya ya la sin ki" or "Mayaya las 'im key," and one of the well-known popular translations is "Mary lost the key." A recent article by Humberto Peralta in *El Nuevo Diario* will serve as a reference for this poem, because Peralta cites someone I liked very much from the Atlantic Coast, Donovan Brautigam Beer, whom I saw when I was at the university but not afterwards. He left during the revolutionary decade but did important research on African legacies such as the marimba and May Pole. Peralta cites Donovan and gives a different sense of the song's lyrics.

I used the phrase in the way it is popularly known. My cograndmother is Edith Jackson, and on Corn Island, she is called "Miss Edith." My daughter and son-in-law asked us to be on the alert at Miss Edith's house because they were going to let us know when my daughter was about to deliver. The phone was in a room that somehow got locked, and when they called, it rang and rang, but we couldn't open the door, and Miss Edith and I ran around searching for the keys! This is a true story that I remembered when I wrote the poem, so I said, "Miss Edith lost the keys!" There is also a lovely part of a song I heard poet Carlos Rigby sing that goes, "Rikiting ting ting," an onomatopoeic sound that could be a telephone, and I incorporated those words. The grandson is on the way! The grandmothers are so excited! And we can't go to the hospital because we can't find the keys, and the phone is ringing and ringing, "Rikiting ting ting." It was interesting when a teacher asked my grandson to recite a poem, he chose that one about him.

Who is the monarchical grandfather figure? "The rushing grandson arrives at daybreak / looking like his monarchical great-grandfather."

Well, that's humorous, because my cograndmother's father arrived from Jamaica to Corn Island, and, as I understand it, became a very powerful man. The British Crown colonized those islands, and the manner of Jamaicans and other Caribbean people is often regal or monarchical. It's a product of my imagination, because when a child is born, you always ask, "Who does she or he look like?" I thought he looked like the Jackson family, and I invented the part about him looking like a monarchical great-grandfather.

And Uncle Simon? "Welcome, Alejandro Carlos, / Uncle Simon sings to you: / Sin saima si ma ló...!"

That is something that Humberto Peralta also mentions. There is another Caribbean song that says, "Sin saima si ma ló," which is popularly thought to be a form of the English "Sing, Simon, sing my love," and that's the sense in which I use it. But Peralta says, citing Donovan Brautigam Beer, "According to the notes I have at hand from the coastal folklore researcher, 'Sin saima sima ló,' is evidently a phonetic corruption of 'Simp Simón simoleón' and not of 'sing, Simon, sing my love.' 'Simón Simplón' [Simple Simon] is a popular character in universal folklore. 'Simoleón,' meaning dollar in slang, was a term introduced by U.S. southerners in the nineteenth century and is a more rhythmic word."

Well, that would give it an entirely different interpretation.

Yes, that is a different interpretation, but for my poem, the popular interpretation is the one I used, "Sing Simon, sing my love," and I talk about an Uncle Simon from the Afro-Caribbean song that I had heard. It's like what I said about "Maya ya la sin ki," that I used in its popular version, "Mary lost the key." Peralta says, "The month of May in the Christian universe is associated with fervor related to the Virgin Mary, which is why 'Mayaya las 'im key' is the inaugural song of the festivities and also coincides with the name of the Virgin Mary, 'Mayaya,' the queen of May." There's no problem with that, because I say it is "Mary lost the keys." Donovan Brautigam Beer agrees that Mayaya is Mary, the Virgin Mary, who is important in the Pacific side of Nicaragua. The Atlantic is more a Protestant, evangelical world. I think they venerate Mary as the Mother of God, but not necessarily as the Virgin Mary, and the difference is the subject of theological debate. But in the case of Simon, Donovan has a different explanation.

Yes, an explanation based on folklore, and without that explanation of the context, a reader might not understand the origin of the references.

I believe that a poem can be admired, accepted, or rejected, like any aesthetic work. The aesthetic effect speaks to the mind and the spirit, but if you understand everything there is, your experience can be enriched. That is an important role played by literary and art critics. One of my projects during the Revolution was to prepare true critics who could help evaluate a work. In our countries writers normally undertook the task and became very refined, intellectual, and cultured, because their own efforts gave them an understanding of a specific aesthetic category.

In the contemporary world now there is much art appreciation theory, and I think it is beneficial to utilize its instruments to evaluate a work. My own preparation was technical, not literary. I studied general culture at the UCA College of Humanities, with a concentration in library sciences and prepared for library work, but I was not educated in literature. During the Revolution, we organized symposia on Latin American and Caribbean literature that attracted a large number of prestigious critics, and I learned certain things, for example, about intertextuality. I said to my writer friends, "Well, if we recall when we were in school, if you copied a writer's line, that was literary plagiarism." Of course, it still is, if you copied and stole the line. The explanation I understood of intertextuality is that you can literally copy a line or paragraph, with no quotation marks or footnotes citing the reference, but only if you change the meaning of the quote into something different. This is what I attempt to do in poetry, and my incorporation of lines from Afro-Caribbean songs in a poem can be seen as a modality of intertextuality.

In other poems you used verses from Darío, for example.

Yes, exactly. Sometimes I put quotations marks, but after I learned about intertextuality, I didn't worry about it any more.

"Because it is nude the star twinkles...," from your "Mistress of Her Song," belongs to Darío.

Yes, but actually in that poem, it is a quote of another quote. Fernández Retamar, the Cuban poet who nurtured me culturally and literarily, is a great expert on Darío. He won the Rubén Darío International Poetry Prize and used that verse in one of his poems. I remembered it from his use, it's a quote of a quote.

The poems about the Caribbean are very musical.

I always feel like getting up and dancing! I'm glad you are asking me to read these poems to film, because they make me happy. Others bring me sadness, and people, especially youngsters, should be read joyous, rhythmic pieces.

Poets: Prophets who denounced and announced

For you as a poet, what is the function of art in public life, in the politics or life of a nation?

There have been different moments in my life and the life of my nation when art has fulfilled different functions. Obviously, as we said at the beginning, I belong to a generation that lived an era of extraordinary worldwide changes, not only in Nicaragua. This is true throughout Latin America. Nicaragua had a system of military dictatorships, and principally young people, the students of my generation, voiced the need for changes. Poetry became a vehicle for denunciation, and it is often said in our countries, particularly in Nicaragua, where there are many poets, that poets became prophets who denounced injustices and announced the good news of another possible and better world. I believe that poetry, to a great extent, still has this function. At the present time, we cannot talk about local revolutions, but we can talk about the necessity for a world revolution which, I believe, is gestating.

Despite the globalization or Americanization of culture?

Globalization is a subject for much discussion, even in Latin America, and my country is no exception. Social movements are joining antiglobalization efforts, and other voices have been heard also, including those of liberation theologians who, for me, continue to be an inspiration and guide when they speak of globalizing solidarity and justice. Instead of aspiring to extend markets to allow rich countries to crush or absorb poor ones and destroy their culture and richness, let's have worldwide enrichment.

I think, and I said this in the 1980s in California, when I visited the United States on a cultural tour, that when revolution triumphs in the world, we will witness the exchange of the best from each culture. The synthesis of true revolution will be when human beings are capable of sharing the best that human intelligence has offered. As a woman, I can see that the U.S. has contributed important inventions for daily life. Houses are cleaned more easily in that country, dishes are washed in a machine, and that creates more free time. The ideal would be for us to recapture what the Ancient Greeks called creative leisure, not leisure for idleness, self-destruction, and self-degradation as human beings, but the use of free time by women, men, children, and youths to create, to create beauty.

Perhaps through poetry? You have said that poetry is a different way of apprehending, grasping, and understanding the world.

I have read with interest that new theorists of history and culture indicate we poets have been right all along. When I was dean of the College of Humanities at the Jesuit university UCA in the 1990s, the rector, Father Xabier Gorostiaga, a theologian and economist, spoke to us often and cogently alerted us, "We are not in an era of change, but in a change of era." Many studies and essays coming out now claim that the planet itself is demanding a new type of relationship between humans and natural resources. Our vision cannot be myopic and limited to the place where we live. Reality demands from us a planetary vision, a cosmic conception of the world. And I say that poets have an advantage and privilege, because we see reality integrally, not fragmentedly.

Intuitively?

One of the reflections I have made as an adult is about people's different ways of understanding. The biggest advantage of university studies is the systematization of knowledge, but the methodical process is not my way of grasping something. I can spend days and days reading a theory and not understand it. I can listen to explanations and nothing. Then suddenly, something like a spark flashes, and I assimilate absolutely everything all at once, so intuition must play an important role in the process. When I review my life and my perceptions of the world, apprehension through poetry is what has led me to work toward articulating diverse endeavors, and as a citizen in a dependent, developing country, to try to articulate all the reflections on the best type of development for us. At this point, we are exhausting the planet's resources, and developed countries face a great dilemma: we were wrong, we cannot stimulate the same sort of development and similar use of resources throughout the planet, because we will exhaust them in days, hours, minutes.

Besides, the more general question is whether that type of development has brought more happiness to people, and then we start to talk about quality of life. Human happiness is not guaranteed by having the biggest advances and all the money in the world. We must see if we haven't betrayed a more humane vision of a more habitable world that we should have built. Poetry helps you see not fragmented reality but the global scenario, where we humans should aspire to live in happiness and equality.

Speaking of poetic knowledge and its acquisition, I wonder if you would agree with Teresa Anta San Pedro who describes your poetry as gnoseological in its search for knowledge, understanding, and illumination—poetry as a tool, an instrument in the search for knowledge, rather than just an expressive vehicle for the known.

It's possible. I greatly admire intelligence and knowledge, and I think that is why I am more full of questions than of answers, and much less, of consummate certainties.

Poetry Vanguard in Nicaragua (1930-1950)

In your poetry, you mention a number of writers who were part of the Vanguard literary movement in Nicaragua. What characteristics of that movement do you consider significant for contemporary poetry?

One of the most important achievements of the Vanguard movement was its break with the Rubén Darío model. At first, there was a necessary step that psychologists define as patricide—killing off the father. Darío was too powerful, and it was difficult to get out from under his influence; everyone wanted to be created in the same image and cast in the same mold. The Vanguard poets established a rupture with Darío, *ex profeso* as irreverent youth, only to recover him in their maturity. They strove to found a national literature and promote autochthonous cultural themes. José Coronel Urtecho was decisive in terms of experimentation and the search for new forms and is called a man of eternally experimental and free poetry. He and Luis Alberto Cabrales were our bridge to universal culture. Cabrales returned from France and Coronel from the United States, and they arrived with other readings, other landscapes, other universes and founded the Vanguard movement. Both were major contributors to its richness. Cabrales was more of an ideologue and more interested in politics. Coronel's work was also political, but he was essentially a poet; his political mistakes and changes, for which he is ferociously attacked by some, were precisely because he was not a politician. He was fundamentally a poet in search of truth, harmony, beauty, novelty, and, above all, freedom.

For me, Coronel Urtecho was personally important, because during the Revolution I had the opportunity to spend many days in his company. Ernesto Cardenal used to travel a lot outside the country, and Coronel was very sociable, pleasant, and open to everything. When Ernesto was gone, I would to say to him, "Come with me, because Ernesto is traveling. You were awarded the Rubén Darío Order of Cultural Independence, and you can rightfully represent the Ministry of Culture." We would go out and inaugurate Rubén Darío Day celebrations, or we would go to small towns to give public readings, and Coronel was always open to young poets and everyone else who came to talk with him. He spoke with eloquence and was a great conversationalist. Julio Valle-Castillo's book, *Conversaciones con Coronel* [*Conversations with Coronel*], prepared with the help of Ernesto's assistant, Luz Marina Acosta, is very useful, because Coronel's conversations deserved to be recorded.

What political errors and changes by Coronel Urtecho invited attacks on him?

Most of the Vanguard poets had been students at Catholic schools in Nicaragua and educated by priests or Christian brothers, some from France and Italy but most from Spain. Francoism had enormous influence, Catholicism was very strong, and at one point, some Vanguard writers declared themselves "blue shirts," Franco supporters. In Nicaragua, they rejected Yankee imperialism and recognized Sandino as a patriot, but at the same time, they accepted Somoza's intervention to bring peace and stability to the country. As young men, they came to believe, especially Coronel, that a peacemaker was needed, a strong figure, a *caudillo* like Franco. Later, they regretted it, and all turned against Somoza. Coronel joined the Sandinista Revolution, but when some intellectuals of the left and extreme left refer to him, they bring up his former position. One even called him and Pablo Antonio Cuadra, whom he mentored, "fascist, right wing ideologues." They are rough on them.

Is it impossible to separate literature and politics?

Yes, but I think politicians tend to be more calculating, and we poets are idealists and can be mistaken. Frankly, I do not attack the Vanguard members. Obviously, I am not a person brought up with a leftist ideology either, and for me it is easier to understand them because I am a Christian, and I give them a vote of confidence—that they were very talented people embarked on a search, and they tried to be coherent with themselves at each moment.

Carlos Martínez Rivas

In several poems you mention Carlos Martínez Rivas, a well-known Nicaraguan poet. What does he represent for you?

Carlos Martínez Rivas is considered an important poet in Nicaraguan literature. Even his contemporary, Ernesto Cardenal, considers him the best poet since Rubén Darío; he is considered to be at that level as a poet. My generation had as a reference what we called "The Three Ernestos": Carlos Ernesto Martínez Rivas, Ernesto Cardenal, and Ernesto Mejía Sánchez. Mejía Sánchez was not as well-known as the others because he lived much of his life in Mexico, but all three were excellent poets.

Carlos lived an extremely tormented life, considered himself a *poète maudit*, a misunderstood and outcast artist, and cultivated that attitude toward life. As a person, he was highly complex and controversial, and as a poet, he was very important. I maintained a long friendship with him but at a certain distance. I knew him from when I published my first book and sent it to him in Costa Rica. He responded with his commentary in a letter. Unfortunately that letter, which I treasured for many years along with two others, was stolen from my car. When he lived in Managua, we would meet at different events and talk. I was always interested in listening to him because he was quite expressive. He wrote me when he lived in Granada and even when he lived in Managua, and I have several beautiful, unpublished letters from him that I will include in my memoirs, because their content is interesting.

We once had a public spat, because I wrote an essay on Nicaraguan women in art and culture. I wanted to leave a record of the great number of women who, before and during the Revolution, were outstanding in different artistic disciplines. In one of the citations, talking about the painter Mercedes Graham, I was fascinated by a phrase from an essay by Julio Valle-Castillo, "the diaphanous eye of terra firma." I quoted the phrase attributing it to Julio, not noticing that Julio had forgotten to put it in quotation marks and also not noticing that it was a quote, as indicated in the footnote, from Carlos Martínez. I published the essay in a newspaper, and Carlos sent me a public letter published in the *La Prensa Literaria* asking why I had robbed him of authorship of the phrase and attributed it to Julio. He was harsh, angry with me and insulting to Julio, and I was shocked. Also, he said that I said he had used the word "artisanal" which did not exist, according to the Spanish Academy's *Dictionary of the Spanish Language*. I was surprised, but I consulted the latest edition of the dictionary, and there it was.

First, I expressed a public apology, as he demanded, in the newspaper. But I also informed him that regarding his second complaint, he was wrong, and I gave him all the information just as he liked it, with quotations and page references, all the t's crossed and the i's dotted. I sent the letter to him personally and said it would appear on Monday in the paper, as he stipulated. He responded in a public letter with great gallantry, thanking me for correcting his mistake and politely telling me that it was honorable to lose to a lady. It was a debate that started out acrimoniously but turned into a charming exchange, and people encouraged me to continue the public debate with him, but I did not.

Carlos Martínez Rivas hated errors. He was furious if his poem was published with the slightest change, even a letter, and he was right about that. Everyone is irritated if your text is changed, but he would raise a ruckus. If he sent a poem to the *Cultural Supplement*, he practically wanted them to photocopy it as it was. He had a typewriter at home, and he could fit the poem, his signature, initials, year and place of composition in the exact size of the square, like a linotype box. If anything was changed, he was bothered.

When he won the Rubén Darío Latin American Poetry Prize in 1984, with his book *Infierno de cielo y antes y después* [*Hell of heaven and before and after*], I was working in the department of Art Promotion at the Ministry of Culture, and he would not turn over the manuscript for us to publish. Vice-Minister Francisco Lacayo told me, "Ask the poet for the manuscript, because we have to comply with the contest rules and publish it." Knowing him, I wrote a letter and said that we begged him to collaborate and allow us to fulfill our duty, as established by the rules of the competition. I knew that he suffered when there were printing errors, and we promised that he would oversee the edition throughout and correct it down to the last galleys to guarantee the book would be totally correct.

He indignantly answered my letter saying, "Vida Luz, luz de mi vida, no me amenaces," which is a line from a *ranchera* song, playing on my name—Vida-Life and Luz-Light—to say, Life Light, light of my life, don't threaten me." He continued, "I received your sentencing—the publication of my book. Among the conspirators you mention the name of *compañero* poet Francisco Lacayo, vice-minister of Culture—'Tu quoque fili mi'"—quoting Julius Caesar's question to Brutus, "You too are against me?" —Even he has risen up against me? You are always in my rancorous thoughts. I will never forgive you." And he continued on in the same vein. His letters were very original, full of historical figures and quotations. That was his psychology, but really Carlos was a master, and his poetry will always be a paradigm for future generations.

Is his style known by any particular name?

No. His poetry was hermetic, very cultured, with many coded images that characterized it. He made constant allusions to his readings, and his poetry is not easy to follow. You have to know the sources that he read in order to understand fully his poetry.

Álvaro Urtecho mentions that your "poetry of psychological analysis and introspection has enriched…the paths opened by Ernesto Mejía Sánchez and Carlos Martínez Rivas in the 1940s," as did the poetry of Ana Ilce Gómez and Daisy Zamora. Do you consider Mejía Sánchez and Martínez Rivas models for aspects of your poetic production?

Yes, but I would not talk about a direct influence, though I recognize my admiration for them. On the other hand, my exteriorist poetry I definitely owe to Cardenal.

Claribel Alegría

Claribel Alegría is a recognized poet who now lives in Managua and is part of the panorama of poetry in Nicaragua. She was elected as the first president of the Federation of Central American Women Writers founded in Managua in 2002.

Claribel is a writer whom I greatly esteem. I am proud to have her as a friend. It was wonderful to get to know her in the 1980s, and she ended up living nearby with her husband, Darwin Flakoll. They were a warm, engaging couple, and since I was losing my family during the Revolution, they represented for me the image of a beloved U.S. man and his wife, like my great-uncle and aunt. Claribel and Bud were like older siblings to me. They were strictly disciplined as writers and ended their work day at five in the afternoon, when they opened their home for visits. I used to go over to converse with them and enjoy an extra dry rum with lemon and water. We talked a lot about everything.

In their home, I felt like the doors of the world were opened to me. They talked about their trips, the places where they lived. The three of us would talk honestly, lovingly, respectfully. Claribel tells me I am like Maya, one of her daughters. I felt comfortable, and they were like family to me. It was a great lesson for me, because Claribel is a vanguard woman for Central and Latin America. As Angelita Saballos would say to me, "It's a shame that we still don't recognize what it means to have Claribel Alegría living in Nicaragua. She is a person of trajectory and substance, like literary giants Julio Cortázar Mario Benedetti, Eduardo Galeano, and we have the privilege of having her with us."

She seems to be well-respected around the world. Is her work sufficiently appreciated in Nicaragua?

Her poetry is well-received in Nicaragua. It is published in cultural supplements, and the anthology of her work that came out in 2003 sold. It was launched at a beautiful presentation with a video. There are interviews on the radio, because Claribel has had such an interesting life and was a personal friend of all the figures of the Latin American literary boom. Her experience should be recorded, and a Nicaraguan intellectual, José Argüello, did radio programs with her. She is recognized internationally, because we see that at every symposium and congress, Claribel's work will be present, and many studies have been done on her. Claribel has a life style that is admirable at her age. She imposes firm discipline on herself and has great physical and mental stamina. She continues to travel for presentations at universities and other centers throughout the world, and those trips can be exhausting for anyone.

She and her husband served a valuable function as observers of their times. They recorded the testimonies of thousands of people who died in the struggle for justice for their people. The role they chose is a humble one. She did not just focus on her own work as an individual. She and her husband dedicated part of their energies to recording for history events that are important for the future.

Their testimonial texts are used in many university courses on literature, culture, sociology, and political science. Also, her creative work has won an international reading public for Claribel Alegría.

Her work is a legacy that will be valued more and more in Nicaragua as time goes on. Perhaps only later will we realize all that she is doing for our nation. At this point in time, there is no clear awareness of what Claribel does and represents. She is not only a great poet and writer, but also a really marvelous and committed person.

Death is part of life

You told me that you didn't know anything about death as a young person, yet one of the first themes in your poetry is death.

I wrote a poem on death when I was an adolescent. Carmen Centeno Gómez interviewed me for a radio program she had with journalist Gabry Rivas. She said it was unusual that at my age, 14, I would write about death.

I am struck by a parallel to Gabriela Mistral, the great Chilean poet and Nobel Laureate, who won her first poetic prize in the Floral Games of 1914 with her Sonnets on Death.

Possibly it was due to the melancholic personality I had as an adolescent. My adolescence was difficult, maybe that's why I wrote about death at that time.

Didn't you write love poems?

One of my favorite poets at the time was Rubén Darío, of course. Darío has a little bit of everything, I mean, it surprises and amazes me to find so many people now who are experts on Darío and to discover, even as an adult, all the richness of his works. I myself can find a poem for each occasion, for each moment in my life, so he is a poet of universal dimension. Also, his changes in style, from rhymed poetry—which I think is wonderful for children, especially; rhymed poetry has a special charm, and its musicality helps children approach poetry—to free verse, with all his writing skill and vast culture. My father would often recite Darío's "The Rawí's Head" to us and get into character and declaim the poem with a special voice. His father also loved poetry and often recited to us grandkids when we would visit. I also read Amado Nervo, and I especially remember his "Pensive Ship." And Gustavo Adolfo Bécquer. Darío, Nervo, and Bécquer were the poets of my adolescence. Later, the poet who was my first boyfriend gave me Neruda's *Twenty Love Poems and A Desperate Song,* which fascinated me.

By the 1970s, I think I was operating on a broader spectrum. I have always been a romantic, in love with someone, and fell so deeply in love with that first boyfriend, but I had concerns about social issues and focused on the spirituality encouraged at school. Perhaps I was already processing the potential conflict of my opting for a change in Nicaragua. I imagine that this sort of internal process inspired me to write about topics like death.

Your first book, Guarded Flame, *ends with "Triptych on Death" which gives a great sense of transcendence. Has anyone studied the theme of death in poetry by Vidaluz Meneses?*

No. Well, I have always been interested in death, and maybe it is part of the life of the spirit, of our temporality on earth, according to my Christian beliefs. Now that I am older and more mature, I read advanced theology books, new theories, and I have enjoyed *Search for Truth* by the Benedictine priest Willigis Jäger. His whole reflection is ecumenical, because he has learned from Buddhism, oriental philosophies, and other churches. He has a chapter on medical ethics, and almost everything these days points to the conclusion that, in effect, something we should have known all along but never accept, death is part of life. I think I have internalized that concept.

Did you ever make a mental comparison between the death of your father, the basis for "Last Message to My Father, General Meneses," and the impending death of your Great-Uncle Leslie Hoey in "On the Side Most Fragile"?

No, I never compared them. I wrote the second poem in 1987, when my uncle was gravely ill. He apparently had a cerebral hemorrhage, and his hand was paralyzed. They called me saying he was close to death. For me, it was terribly sad. That day, I was scheduled to go to a formal luncheon at the French Embassy, because the ambassador was going to offer us generous scholarships, and as acting vice-minister of Culture, I needed to be in attendance, though I was quite sad on my way there. But, well, I shook it off and went to the luncheon, and everything was going along all right. When dessert comes… [tears], apple pie! That's why it appears in the poem. It's true that poetry is hermetic, because those are images a person experiences by herself, that's why the poem begins:

End of the formal luncheon,
finally arriving at dessert.
The smooth, even eloquent,
after-dinner conversation
stumbles at the final course
—apple pie—
and the dizzying wheel of time turns
to stop at the side most fragile of my childhood.

The apple pie suddenly took me back to my childhood. When I got home, I wrote that poem for Uncle Leslie, with what I remembered of him, of my childhood with him in Bonanza. They thought he was going to die that day or the next, but actually, he lived three more years. When he died, I was not at his side, and he went very quickly. I was informed after his death, so it was different, and I imagine that I had already assimilated his death. So, no, it never occurred to me to make a comparison because the experiences were very different for me. The poem to my great-uncle was written from a certain distance, while I was at my father's side when he died.

Poetry needs spiritual space

Have there been times when you were able to write more poetry or write more easily? You have held many professional positions that are time- and energy-intensive.

Poems have come to me pretty much throughout my life, but I am not very prolific. Since my last book published in 2002, I have just a few poems: one I wrote on the occasion of my 60th birthday, one for Pablo Antonio Cuadra, and others in draft form that I am working on. One is on my ancestors, inspired by aunts and uncles with whom I lived in Somoto, and with it, Luis A. Jiménez's observation that my works are palimpsests will become a reality. Another is on the nature of marriage, the routine that is partly comfortable security and partly a great challenge for couples. A third is on a theme that obsesses me, about people who commit suicide.

At times in my life I've thought I am not going to write again, but suddenly a few poems come to me. When I have enough, I start thinking about putting them together in a book.

You have no regular work routine, like Monday, Wednesday, Friday, six a.m. to noon?

No, I tried that just now, when I was attempting to write fiction, and confirmed my experience that narration is a premeditated, intentional act, and fiction writers all tell you the same thing: you need to establish a routine, sit down, and write every morning. Not for poetry. Poetry needs more of a spiritual space. My work for the Civil Coordinator totally saturated me, and now I have to empty myself of everything I did to make space for poetry. Possibly I'll go into a cycle when I'll write more poetry. That could be. I plan to review some thoughts and notes, and I may write more.

I have heard comments from friends, like David Pezzullo today, asking, "Why do you insist on being a novelist? You're not a novelist, you're a poet." What's with me, then? On the one hand, my own narrative writing bores me, when I am the first person who should be interested in what I want to relate. I assume that someone writes an interesting story or novel, because he or she enjoys the writing and the story, because the first person who has to be interested is the writer. But life for me has been and is so intense that I'm not interested in writing fiction.

Nevertheless, in poetry you have to condense so much, and I feel that I have lived with such intensity that I have a lot of things to say, so I am going to write narrative, because the space is too limited in a poem. I tried to turn my biography into a novel, using my life as the narrative thread, but with the narrative voice of my Great-Aunt Adelina, who lived to age 102, to try to establish emotional distance. I wrote 70 pages, showed them to distinguished writer friends, and they pointed out the challenges they thought I would have to overcome. They tried to encourage me, but I ended up discouraged. Two poets recommended that I put the pages away and use them sometime later to write some interesting family portraits or stories. Maybe that 70-page text, "Ballad for Adelina," will never become a narration, but I might take some of its themes and write poetry with that material. I put the narrative manuscript aside and began reworking the notes in my campaign journal from when I went with the Leonel Rugama Cultural Brigade into the war zones in 1983. Anamá Publishers in Managua published it in 2006 with the title, *Struggle is the Highest Song* [*La lucha es el más alto de los cantos*], a line of poetry by Fernando Gordillo. This testimony is my first incursion into narrative.

Lately, I have written less poetry but am working on my memoirs. Talking with Ernesto Cardenal about my frustrated experience as a fiction writer, he said, "Don't write a novel. Write your memoirs, like I am doing. I am telling things as I remember them, and maybe that's not exactly how they happened, so you end up writing fiction." And I decided to write my memoirs. Ernesto makes everything simple and doesn't complicate your life. I took up the idea of writing my memoirs, remembering that Daisy Zamora once told me, "Write them, because what our generation experienced, no one will ever live through again." So, I started again and have about 200 pages, some of which will probably stay as they are, but most of them I'll have to rework putting more of myself into the text. Apparently, my inclination is more toward describing other people and their situations and less toward my own emotions or personal experience. I'm more of a chronicler when I write narrative, and I've been advised to give more emphasis to my feelings and experience.

Our generation was a vanguard, but we paid a price

Vidaluz, you have spoken of the first achievement of Nicaraguan women in art and culture as the decision to express themselves. You were in what we could call the first generation of women poets in Nicaragua, a miniboom that includes your contemporaries Ana Ilce Gómez and Michèle Najlis, as well as those who follow shortly afterwards—Daisy Zamora, Rosario Murillo, Gioconda Belli. You were not the first women poets in Nicaragua, because before you came Piedad Medrano Matus, María Teresa Sánchez, and Mariana Sansón Argüello. But as a "critical mass," as a generation, why at that particular time, and not before, did there appear what Nydia Palacios calls "an uncommon group of women's voices of great quality"?

It seems true, as far as we know, that we were the first generation of women poets rather than just isolated figures, but not enough research has been done to see if this theory is sustainable. Helena Ramos discovered that many women before us published their writings, especially in local newspapers, and were unfairly excluded from critical attention. I think we are the poets of modernity. In the case of Mariana Sansón Argüello [1918-2002], we have to remember that she began publishing late in life, practically in the 1960s. I think she is perceived as a precursor mainly because of her age, because she is more or less a contemporary of María Teresa Sánchez [1918-1994]. In any event, more and deeper research is needed on the works of the many women writing before the 1960s in order to establish a definite judgement on this issue. It is also true that my generation is the product of a university education—Najlis, Gómez, all of us went to the university.

When I was in Managua for the founding of the Federation of Central American Women Writers in 2002, I was astounded by the number of new women writers and the exceptional quality of their works read during recitals that Helena Ramos organized. I walked around asking why there were so many, and such good, poets in Nicaragua and got varied answers citing the influence of Darío, the lack of a "time is money" culture, the tradition of oral literature, a general custom of poetry recitations in diverse settings, and poet Blanca Castellón even ascribed it to your volcanic surroundings and lava flows. Do you have a theory about this?

My response is Darío. Perhaps that's a bit sociological, but I believe he was the great paradigm. I compare it this way: When the Revolution triumphed in 1979, 52% of the population was illiterate; it is true that during Darío's adolescence, let's say in 1881, there was less population, but proportionately I don't think the level of illiteracy could have been lower, and suddenly, he emerged—a person who didn't even finish his secondary school studies, never got a high school diploma, was able to renovate the language of the conquistadors! He thoroughly accomplished the motto of the Spanish Royal

Academy—to bring brilliance and splendor to the language!

Obviously, the model your generation gave, as well as its support for new writers, has favored the flowering of excellent poetry among women. Looking back, I wonder if you would agree with an observation Daisy Zamora made to Pilar Moyano—that you were women of transition; that your generation was crippled by a history from which you could not entirely liberate yourselves.

Yes, undoubtedly. The experience of the Revolution marked us all.

In several of your poems Alba Fabiola Aragón finds a special, unique presentation of motherhood, which you achieve by emphasizing certain aspects ignored in traditional culture: daily worry about your children, the solitude implied in that worry, the mutual need of mother and children in contrast to the abstract heroine mother or the Pietà who sacrifices everything for her children. As she points out, not just the children, but the mother too is consoled by the idea of a return to the watery cave.

I am quite surprised when certain strongly maternal characteristics are attributed to me, and, more than anything, it embarrasses me to think that I may have been a "lamp in the street, darkness at home," as the saying goes. Remember that I belong to the generation of the Revolution, specifically mentioned in the resentments of daughters and sons whose needs were postponed due to the social and military actions the process required. Without a doubt, I have been fully aware of my responsibility as a mother, but I think that in practice, I paid more attention to the macro dimension of the context than to the daily care of my own sons and daughters. Perhaps belonging to a generation that broke with the old model gives us a new way of being a woman or being human, as Rosario Castellanos said. Remember that line of hers that I inserted intertextually into the poem "That Woman"—"The mother orphaned of offspring." Ruptures also create fear. I think our generation was a vanguard, but we paid a price. Writing about our vulnerability is also part of our strength. That is the paradox.

When you were speaking about your work in the cultural brigade, you mentioned the constant worry about your children, the anguish you felt as a mother. And you expressed that sense of orphanhood when three of your four children left you in order to escape from the Revolution. Do you think that anxiety marked your poetry in any way?

Oh, yes. My only source of consolation was the gospels. There are several passages that refer to parents and siblings or other relatives; for example, when Jesus goes missing at age 12, and they find him preaching in the temple, He says He is in the house of His Father. Another passage from St. Luke is one that I cite in a *prosema*: "Our brothers and sisters are not those of our blood, but those of our faith."

For me, the radical Christian option was the Revolution, social change, and opting for the poor, and that required an immense sacrifice. Another terrible passage in the Old Testament is when the mother of the Maccabees sends her children one by one to their deaths because they insisted on affirming their Christian faith. I couldn't have gone that far, because if my boys were not in agreement with the Revolution and were approaching the age for obligatory Patriotic Military Service, I might have tried to send them away or leave and take them with me. I would not allow them to be forced to risk death for something they did not believe in or feel was their struggle.

Are you aware of the international projection of your work? Cristina Guzzo believes that Vidaluz Meneses's poetry "is multiplied in many others and links itself to a collective production far beyond Central American borders and the concrete historical experience in which her poems are produced."

I don't think my case is unique. To the extent that I am aware of translations and international publications in which my poems appear, my belief is confirmed that we women publishing in the 1960s, 1970s, and later, after the Revolution, have achieved an international audience. Undoubtedly, our voices resonate with those of other Latin American women poets who lived through similar social experiences.

III. POEMS IN SPANISH AND ENGLISH

Llama guardada (1975)

*A Carlos Rodolfo
A mis hijos*

*¿Cuándo me daré a esta vida
que el canto del alma llevo?
Siempre brotando del alma
y siempre se queda dentro.*

–Ángel

Guarded Flame (1975)

*To Carlos Rodolfo**
To my children

*When will I give myself to this life
with the song of the soul that I carry?
Always bursting from the soul,
always staying inside.*

–Ángel

---

* Carlos Rodolfo Icaza Espinosa: Meneses's husband when this first poetry collection was published.
Ángel Martínez Baigorri, S.J. (Navarra, Spain 1899-Managua 1971): Spanish priest, religious and mystic poet, teacher at the secondary school Colegio Centroamérica in Granada, Nicaragua, and at the Central American University in Managua; mentor to important figures in contemporary poetry. He described himself as "born in Spain and born again in Nicaragua."

I. Del acontecer cotidiano

Del acontecer cotidiano

    I

Contra tu propia voluntad
las cosas te envuelven
lenta e irremisiblemente
en el transcurrir del día:
        la soga circundando
        el cuello de tus sueños
        (hasta que sutilmente los ahorca).

    II

Como una presa de agua
inundándose ocasionalmente
(me gusta pensar las cosas en grande)
—ahora no me digas que soy la gota que te colma.

    III

No importa donde me ubique,
sé que además del pequeño escritorio
de la estrecha oficina
o el rincón más íntimo de mi cuarto
siempre hallaré un lugar donde tejer un sueño.

I. On Everyday Events

On Everyday Events

    I

Against your own will
things wrap round you
slowly, steadily
in the course of the day:
       the rope encircling
       the neck of your dreams
       (until it subtly hangs them).

    II

Like a water dam
flooding occasionally
(I like to think things big)
—don't tell me now I am the drop running you over.

    III

No matter where I go,
I know that besides the small desk
in the narrow office,
or the most intimate corner in my room,
I will always find a place to weave a dream.

Llama guardada

A mis padres

Venga el sol a purificarlo todo:
Hierva el agua en su cauce
y revivan los pétalos de la flor.

Que al hombre, el sol que lleva dentro
le baste.

1973

Solitario transeúnte de la noche

Solitario transeúnte de la noche
¿Has visto acaso el tímido anhelo
que delataban sus ojos?

Yo fuí también una muchacha
que cifró su esperanza
en el tránsito fugaz de una estrella.

1972

Guarded Flame

To my parents

Let the sun come to purify it all:
Boil water in its channel
and revive the flower's petals.

For humans, may the sun they carry inside
be enough.

1973

Solitary Passerby in the Night

Solitary passerby in the night,
did you see, perhaps, the timid longing
revealed in those eyes?

I too was a young girl
who pinned her hopes
on the fleeting path of a star.

1972

[Included in *Flame in the Wind**]

---

* *Flame in the Wind* (1990) begins with an anthology selected by Meneses of poems from her first and second books. She believes they reflect a certain quality.

Paradoja

A Rosa y Valeria

Esta noche y la plática banal
que mi hermana y la empleada pueblerina
sostienen en el cuarto:

> "En mi pueblo las visitas son hasta las nueve
> si no critican..."

(Por eso las doncellas conciben
a la orilla de los ríos).

1968

Inventario de un hombre moderno

Cuenta en el Banco,
seguro de vejez,
standard de vida
acorde a las circunstancias,
sedante oportuno en pastillas
o en terapéutica calistenia
y las ganas de repente
de mandar todo al diablo.

1973

Paradox

*To Rosa and Valeria**

Tonight and the banal conversation
between my sister and the country maid
in the bedroom:

> "In my village visits go only 'til nine,
> otherwise, they criticize…"

(That's why maidens conceive
on river banks).

1968

Inventory of A Modern Man

Bank account,
retirement security,
standard of living
in keeping with his circumstances,
ready tranquilizer in pills
or therapeutic calisthenics,
and the urge, suddenly,
to send it all to hell.

1973

[Included in *Flame in the Wind*]
[Translation by Kathryn Peters and María Roof]

---

* Rosa: Daughter of Valeria, a woman who worked in the household of Meneses's great-aunts after she was taken in by the Valle family as a child.

La trampa

Fuertes e inquebrantables cánones
ciñen nuestra supervivencia
y el íntimo temor de asomarnos
algunas veces, como una rata,
por el agujero de la trampa.

1973

"Quien tenga oídos"

Durante el día:
No más allá del cerco
que quedó en pie,
el panorama es el mismo.
Fijamos la atención
en curiosos episodios cotidianos
como el acecho del garrobo
y su hurto furtivo del higo madurado.

Por la noche:
Una fina y nebulosa cortina de lluvia nos aísla
y, sin embargo, gota a gota
el mudo mensaje de la ciudad se cuela.
Porque escrito está en las ruinas
lo temporal de nuestro paso
y en el polvo de los escombros
nuestro retorno.

The Trap

Tough, unbreakable canons
cinch our survival
and the intimate fear of peering
on occasion, like a rat,
out the hole of the trap.

1973

"He Who Has Ears to Hear"*

By day:
Just beyond the wall
still left standing
the panorama is the same.
We fix our attention
on curious everyday episodes
like the garrobo iguana stalking
and his furtive theft of a ripe fig.

By night:
A fine, misty curtain of rain isolates us,
and yet, drop by drop,
the city's mute message trickles through.
Because written in the ruins
is the impermanence of our passage
and in the dust of the rubble,
our return.

---

* [Included in *Flame in the Wind*]
 [Translation by Kathryn Peters and María Roof]
 Matthew 13:9 and Luke 8.8: "He who has ears to hear, let him hear."

Ahora deambulamos solos

Aquí amé los campos con Zhivago
donde la nieve nos penetraba
            hasta quemarnos.
Aquí tomados de la mano
me habló de su terrible pasión por Lara.

Y su sed de libertad y pan
fue mi sed de libertad y pan,
        porque su poesía nos traspasó
como espada fundida
por sus sueños y los míos.
Ahora deambulamos solos
perdidos en las grises calles
de cualquier ciudad rusa.

(1968)

Alfonso

*Un trozo azul tiene mayor
intensidad que todo el cielo...*
        —*Alfonso Cortés*

En las constelaciones celestes
allí donde tu Ventana infinita
te revela el paisaje que añoraste.

En el lugar donde estuviste siempre
y que ahora con mayor integridad habitas,
donde nuestra estatura jamás logró alcanzarte,
allí, Alfonso, tu cabeza
blanca, como una luna nueva.

(1969)

Now We Wander Alone

Here, I loved the fields with Zhivago*,
where the snow penetrated us
      until it burned.
Here, hand-in-hand,
he spoke to me of his terrible passion for Lara.

And his thirst for freedom and bread
was my thirst for freedom and bread,
      because his poetry pierced us
like a sword forged
from his dreams and mine.
Now we wander alone,
lost in the gray streets
of any Russian city.

(1968)

Alfonso†

> *A patch of blue is more intense*
> *than the whole sky…*
>   *—Alfonso Cortés*

There in the celestial constellations,
where your infinite Window
reveals your longed-for landscape.

In the place where you always were
but now inhabit with more integrity,
where our stature never rose to yours
there, Alfonso, your head,
white like a new moon.

(1969)

---

* Zhivago and Lara: Characters in a love triangle in Boris Pasternak's novel, *Dr. Zhivago*, made into a film of the same name by David Lean in 1965

† Alfonso Cortés (León 1893-1969): Nicaraguan metaphysical poet, victim of periodic madness after age 30. One of his best known poems, "A Detail," is popularly called "Window" (see Meneses's comments in Chapter II).

Tú dijiste

Un ángel es terrible, Rilke,
y nunca es más cierta tu aseveración
que cuando el ángel de ellos y mío se rebela.

Un ángel es ciertamente terrible
y duro como a ti ya me ha herido;
por eso tu canción es el intento de mi canto
porque el peso de la noche es más intenso
cuando el cielo se nos siembra por la espalda.

Fiero sable aún goteante,
aleteo mortal,
un ángel es terrible.

1965

Intuyo

Intuyo certera mano
en puñalada trapera.
No es hora de cantar el jazmín
que penetró su olor por la ventana.
Bajo mullida grama
espinas hay al acecho.

1973

You Said

An angel is terrfying, Rilke*,
and your assertion is never more true
than when their and my angel rebels.

An angel is truly terrifying
and cruelly, as it did you, has wounded me;
so, your song is the intent of my verse
because the weight of night is more intense
when heaven is sown on our backs.

Fierce saber, still dripping,
mortal beating of wings,
an angel is terrifying.

1965

I Intuit

I intuit a skilled hand
feigning a thrust.
It's not time to sing of the jasmine
penetrating its smell through the window.
Beneath the plush lawn are
thorns watching and waiting.

1973

---

* Rilke, Rainer María (1875-1926): Poet born in Prague (then, Austria), who says in his *Duino Elegies* that angels are terrible and terrifying (see References).

Escarnio

No en la plácida rutina del tejido
a la que adecuadamente estáis llegando,
ni en la recomendable revisión de vuestras vidas,
ni en el ejemplo, ni en el consejo sabio,
ni en la sana costumbre de ir enterrando
uno a uno los rencores,
sino certeramente, como finos estiletes,
dignísimas y hermosísimas señoras
váis en la carne de vuestros amigos.

1970

Ellos reirán de vuestra hambre

Ellos reirán de vuestra hambre
y se burlarán de vuestra buena fe
e intenciones.

Porque no será el hombre y su valor
sino su precio
y éste fijado por sus necesidades.

Por eso, cuando la angustia te asalte
calla,
y si el momento te apremia,
espera,
pero no envilezcas tus lágrimas
aunque todo parezca perdido
algo queda.

1974

Contempt

Not in the placid routine of knitting
at which you are appropriately arriving,
nor in the recommendable review of your lives,
nor as example, nor wise counsel,
nor in the healthy habit of burying,
one by one, your grudges,
but rather, unerringly, like fine stilettos,
most dignified and beautiful ladies,
you pierce the flesh of your friends.

1970
[Included in *Flame in the Wind*]
[Translation by Kathryn Peters and María Roof]

They Will Laugh at Your Hunger

They will laugh at your hunger,
mock your good faith
and intentions.

Because it won't be about man and his value
but his price,
set by his needs.

So, when you are assaulted by anguish,
be silent,
and if rushed by the moment,
wait,
but don't dismiss your tears,
though all seems lost,
something remains.

1974

A Pavel

Todos han puesto como consigna el pueblo
pero Ojo por Ojo
y Diente por Diente.

Sin embargo tú y yo,
identificándonos en la plática casual,
palpándonos número en la auténtica lucha
en que ni carne de cañón
ni borregamente enfilados
entonaremos al final
la verdadera canción de amor de los hermanos.

1973

To Pavel*

Everyone has taken "the people" as their motto,
but Eye for an Eye
and Tooth for a Tooth.†

However, you and I,
defining ourselves in casual conversation,
sensing ourselves involved in the authentic struggle,
in which neither as cannon fodder
nor lined up like sheep
will we sing in the end
the true song of brotherly love.

1973

---

* Pavel: Hero son of narrador Pelagea in the novel *Mother* (1907) by Maxim Gorky (1868-1936), Russian playwright and novelist, founder of Soviet Socialist Realism.

† "But if there is serious injury, you are to take ... eye for eye, tooth for tooth...": Old Testament reference regarding appropriate punishment for an offense (Exodus 21:24).

He visto

He visto en tu ojo
la muerte redonda aproximarse.
¡Ah ribera de sombra
que encauza mi agonía en esta hora!

Quiero morir de espaldas a la noche
para que el cielo siembre su cosecha de estrellas
en mi dorso desnudo.

He mojado con mi llanto
la camisa ensangrentada
de los muertos en Viet Nam
y el dolor de las bombas que mi era engendró
para desintegrar el cosmos.

Pequeña es al fin y al cabo mi melancolía
ante el dolor supremo de mi gran hermandad.

Por eso es esta muerte poco a poco
   como una bomba de tiempo
       que no llega a estallar.

1974

I Have Seen

I have seen in your eye
the circle of death approaching.
Oh, river bank of shadow that
channels my agony at this hour!

I want to die turned from the night
so the sky can sow its starry harvest
on my naked back.

My tears have soaked
the blood-stained shirts
of the Vietnam* dead
and the pain of bombs
birthed by my era
to disintegrate the cosmos.

Small, in the end, is my melancholy
alongside the supreme suffering
of my great human family.

That's why this slow death is
       like a time bomb
              not yet exploding.

1974

[Included in *Flame in the Wind*]

---

* Vietnam: Asian country bordering Cambodia, Thailand, Laos and China; French colony 1859-1945; war of separation from France 1946-1954; divided into two parts 1954. "Vietnam War", 1954-1975, conflict between North Vietnam and South Vietnam that also involved the U.S.S.R., China, and the United States.

Poema para sobrevivir

Cuando tenemos necesidades de creer
y no encontramos a qué aferrarnos.

Cuando la vida se nos vuelve
como una película
       (en la que nunca se sabe
       quiénes son los buenos y
       quiénes los malos).

Cuando día a día
vas palpando el crecimiento de tus hijos
y su cercanía a enfrentarse a la lucha.
Cuando aún crees en el amor y su fuerza
y tu boca aún no ha dicho mentira.

Cuando compruebas que el hombre es pez
       (y por su boca muere).
Entonces, rabiosamente esperamos
       ese Otro Día
sin la certeza que lo poseeremos.

1970

Poem for Survival

When we feel the need to believe
and find nothing to latch onto.

When life becomes for us
like a film
      (in which you never know
      who are the good guys and
      who are the bad).

When day to day
you sense the growth of your children
and their closeness to facing the struggle.
When you still believe in love and its power
and your mouth has not yet said a lie.

When you verify that humans are fish
      (and die by their mouths).
Then, we furiously hope for
      that Other Day
without the certainty that we will attain it.

1970

Bonanza

A Leslie y Virginia

El continuo y sordo sonido
de la mezcladora,
las paladas de piedra
de los hombres trabajando,
recuerdo así el afectuoso grito del viejo Hoey
al negro: ¡Hi, Mike! y éste contestando
con su risa blanca: ¡Hallo, Mr. Hoey!

Ahora ya Mike tamborilea
en el seno de la tierra su mískita canción:

> Amor la twan kira
> Anira Kama ki
> Pura payaska valvia kaka
> Anira kama ki.

Y el viejo Hoey casi a los 30 años
se despidió de trabajar en la mina
para marchar con su vieja a los EE.UU.

Ahora sí, mi descanso prescrito es un hecho
pues el continuo y sordo rumor a plantel de mina
es mi mejor sedante.

1972

Bonanza*

To Leslie and Virginia

Non-stop deafening noise
of the mixer,
shovelfuls of rocks
of the men working,
I remember old Hoey's affectionate greeting
to the black man: "Hi, Mike!" and he answering
with his white laugh: "Hallo, Mr. Hoey!"

Now Mike drums
deep inside the earth's bosom his Miskito song:

> Amor la twan kira
> Anira Kama ki
> Pura payaska valvia kaka
> Anira kama ki.

And old Hoey after almost 30 years
bid farewell to his work in the mine
to return with his wife to the U.S.

And now, my prescribed rest is real,
for the non-stop deafening noise of the mine
is my best sedative.

1972

[Included in *Flame in the Wind*]

---

* Bonanza: Mining town in northern Nicaragua, where Meneses spent vacations as a child with her maternal Great-Aunt Virginia, married to the U.S. miner Leslie N. Hoey (see References).
"Amor … ki": Song sung by the indigenous Miskitos about a loved one who has gone away.

Abuela

A Clementina S. de Espinosa

La regresión se ha consumado
y como una pequeña y quieta niña
en su silla perenne se ha quedado la abuela.

Su laboriosidad de antaño
la pregona su mano derecha que aún domina
la otra, en justo descanso,
se le ha quedado dormida.

Para cumplir su cometido de abuelita
entre los rastros de su belleza
su pelo encaneció en el tiempo preciso.
Abuela:
        en tu mirada muchas veces ausente
        y en tu sonrisa infantil
        la ternura se hizo eterna.
Toma aquí mi canto como un rosario de nietos.

1968

Hoy

Hoy las hojas me invitan
el césped me atrae a retozar en él.
Mi hechura terrestre está latente.

1968

Grandmother

*To Clementina S. de Espinosa**

Regression is complete,
and like a small, shy girl
grandmother sits in her perennial chair.

Her old laboriousness
revealed in the right hand she still moves,
the other, in well-deserved rest,
has fallen asleep.

To fulfill her grandmotherly duties
among the traces of her beauty
her hair turned gray at just the right moment.
Grandmother:
        in your often absent gaze
        and in your childlike smile
        tenderness became eternal.
Take this, my song, as a rosary of grandchildren.

1968

Today

Today the leaves invite me,
the lawn lures me to frolic on it.
My earthly origin is patent.

1968

[Included in *Flame in the Wind*]

---

* Clementina Sotomayor de Espinosa: Paternal grandmother of Meneses's children.

Rama

      I

Licor, sexo, calor.
Y el Siquia, el Mico y el Rama
arrastrando ramas,
      juntándose
           y jugando al "Escondido"

      II

Calor, amor, techo, cuarto pequeño.
Rama a esta hora es una sola siesta.

Rama, 1970

Llueve

Llueve en la tarde
y en el alma, como en tierra lavada
afloran a la superficie viejos cantos.

1970

Rama*

I

Drink, sex, heat.
And the Siquia, Mico and Rama
dragging branches,
        joining
                and playing "Escondido"—hide and seek.

II

Heat, love, ceiling, tiny room.
Rama at this hour is one big siesta.

Rama, 1970

[Included in *Flame in the Wind*]
[Translation by Kathryn Peters and María Roof]

It Rains

It rains in the afternoon
and, in the soul, as in washed earth
flowering to the surface come old songs.

1970

---

* Rama: City and river in Nicaragua's Caribbean Coast region.
Siquia, Mico and Rama: Rivers that form the Escondido River.
"branches": Play on words. In Spanish, "branch" is rama, like the name of the city and town.
"Escondido": Another play on words. "Escondido" is the name of the river formed by the Siquia, the Mico and the Rama. "Jugar al escondido" is Spanish for playing hide and seek.

Hoy no soy más

Hoy no soy más
que un manojo de hojas secas
queriendo lanzar
la aridez de su armonía al viento.

1964

Encontrar los amigos

Encontrar los amigos
con la íntima satisfacción
con que desempolvamos viejos libros
celosamente guardados.

Recorrer palmo a palmo el idéntico lugar
y sentirte cada vez más distinta.

Atisbar en los pequeños momentos de soledad
hasta tu último sentimiento
y descubrir al fin, mínima y sencilla mujer,
que el corazón te vence.

1972

Today I Am Nothing More

Today I am nothing more
than a bunch of dry leaves
wanting to toss
the aridness of their harmony to the wind.

1964

Meeting with Friends

Meeting with friends
with the same intimate satisfaction
as dusting off old,
zealously-guarded books.

Crossing inch-by-inch the identical place
and each time feeling yourself a different woman.

Glimpsing in brief moments of solitude
your deepest feelings
and discovering in the end, small and simple woman,
that your heart has won out.

1972

[Included in *Flame in the Wind*]

II. Instantáneas

High life en tres movimientos

I

De todas las culturas trató de asimilar
un poco en la Magna Europa
lo que ignoran los demás
es que de lo que menos sabe es de ella misma.

II

Temblorosa como una hoja
avanzó bajo las inquisitivas miradas
de la más "escogida" sociedad
mientras su amantísimo padre
la exponía como un trofeo de caza mayor.

III

Había que ensayar la manera más moderna de conquista;
por eso las entregas (tuvieron que ser varias)
se realizaron al calor de los High balls
y en la penumbra de los Night Clubs.
En consecuencia, el epílogo fue también
de la manera más moderna:
       el de una meretriz de lujo.

1968

II. Snapshots

High Life in Three Movements

I

From all cultures she tried to assimilate
a little in Great Europe;
others fail to grasp that
what she knows least is herself.

II

Shaking like a leaf
she emerged under the inquisitive eyes
of the most "select" society,
while her very loving father
exhibited her like a big game trophy.

III

The most modern form of conquest had to be used;
so the submissions (which were several)
came in the warmth of high balls
and in the shadows of night clubs.
As a result, the epilogue was also
one most modern:
      that of a high class, kept woman.

1968

Advertencias

No le hagas mal a nadie
el bien, cuando esté al alcance:
la medida es el largo de tu brazo.

Porque categóricamente te comprobarán
que "el que se mete a Redentor
            crucificado termina"
y al fin y al cabo, en estos tiempos
el plato de lentejas viene bien condimentado
y al alcance de todo Contadorcillo bien pagado
de C$3,000.00 para arriba.
Arriba: Gerente con Post graduado de INCAE
                        Stanford o Yale.
Experto en producir el ciento por uno
        (sin alusión bíblica por supuesto).
Y conste, con formación integral.

No descuidando la bonificación anual al empleado
porque el lomo es más explotable
sobándolo a su tiempo
—psicología industrial-comercial aplicada—.

Por eso no hay que divagar, ni teorizar
prohibido idealizar, es pasado de moda o peligroso.

Marcha a tu meta
        ser un "buen partido"
            una fiel réplica humana de eficiente IBM
un "big shot"
un envidiado miembro del "jet set"
una aristocrática minoría
un Ministro sin obligaciones.

Al final sólo te recomiendo unas potentes orejeras:
Preferible no oigas tu autocondena:
                a lo mejor todavía te afecte.

1971

Warnings

Do harm to no one,
good, when it's within reach:
the measure is the length of your arm.

For they will prove to you categorically
that "he who aspires to be Savior
        ends up crucified,"
and in the end, these days,
a well spiced plate of beans is
within the reach of any accountant
paid $3,000 córdobas* and up.
Up: Manager with a post graduate from INCAE[†],
        Stanford or Yale[‡].
Expert at producing a hundred from one
        (no Biblical allusion, of course).
And clearly with complete training.

Not overlooking annual bonuses to employees,
because backs are more exploitable
if greased at the proper moment
—applied industrial-commercial psychology.

So no digressing or theorizing,
idealizing prohibited, it's old fashioned or dangerous.

March toward your goal
        be a "good catch"
            a faithful human replica of an efficient IBM
a "big shot"
an envied member of the "jet set"
an aristocratic minority
a Minister without duties.

In the end, I only recommend powerful earguards:
Preferable not to hear your self-condemnation:
        it just might still affect you.

1971
___

* Córdobas: Nicaragua's monetary unit; the amount is roughly $400, a good salary at the time.
† INCAE: Acronym for Instituto Nicaragüense de Comercio y Administración de Empresas, the Nicaraguan Institute of Business and Business Administration, associated with Harvard Business School.
‡ Stanford, Yale: Prestigious U.S. universities.

Instantánea conyugal

No tocaron ningún tema; todos afectaban drásticamente su unión. Iniciaron un largo viaje por Europa y Medio Oriente queriendo restituir todo lo perdido. Los paisajes pasaron por las ventanillas de metros y de buses como fugaces postales. Las veladas de clubs nocturnos fueron artificioso preámbulo a forzadas noches de amor en hoteles de lujo.

Al regreso, un muro de silencio se levantó entre los dos, con la sutileza de lo ya esperado.

Por las mañanas, él se afeita con la vaga expresión del ejecutivo accionista que presidirá largas mesas de sesiones durante el día; y ella sale de la cama con la pesada melancolía escondida entre los pliegues de su bata vaporosa.

1972

Snapshot of a Marriage

They discussed not one issue, though all drastically affected their union. They began a long trip through Europe and the Middle East, hoping to restore all that was lost. Landscapes streamed by subway and bus windows like speeding postcards. Club soirées were crafted preambles to nights of forced lovemaking in luxury hotels.

On their return, a wall of silence rose between them, with the subtlety of the expected.

Each morning he shaves with the vague expression of a shareholding executive who will preside over long conferences during the day; and she leaves bed with heavy melancholy hidden in the folds of her sheer gown.

1972

[Translation by María Roof. Kathryn Peters published her translation, "Instant Marriage," in *Harvard Review* 9 (Fall 1995): 97.]

III. Páginas de una nueva desposada

Cuando yo me casé

Cuando yo me casé
la Capilla era chiquita
y Monseñor recitó los salmos de rigor:

> "Que sea hacendosa como Martha,
> prudente como Raquel,
> de larga vida y prolífera como Sarah".

Y heme aquí tenue sombra de Martha,
martillando la máquina de escribir en la oficina
después de los afanes del hogar,
callando la protesta fútil "silenciosa Raquel"
transcurriendo mi vida interminable como un río
para completar a Sarah.

1967

III. Pages of a New Bride

When I Married

When I married,
the chapel was tiny,
Monsignor recited the traditional psalms:

> "May you be diligent like Martha,
> prudent like Rachel,
> of long and prolific life, like Sarah."

And here I am, pale shadow of Martha
hammering at the office typewriter
after housework at home,
muffling my futile protest, "silent Rachel,"
my life flowing like an endless river
to become Sarah*.

1967

[Included in *Flame in the Wind*]
[Translation by María Roof. Nora Wieser published a different version in *Open to the Sun* (116-117).]

---

*Martha, Rachel, Sarah: Biblical models for proper married women's behavior.

En el llano

No diré la palabra suave
sino la fuerza de tu amor
poseyéndolo todo.

Aquí a llano abierto
donde solos, el campisto y su mujer
trabajan la tierra y el amor.

Aquí, amado, un mundo nuevo,
en la sinfonía perenne
del viento entre la espiga.

1973

Pequeño canto de la buenaesperanza

Porque llenará con su llanto
mis silencios
mi esperanza está plena.

1967

On the Plain

I'll speak not the soft word
but the power of your love
possessing all.

Here, on the open plain
where, alone, the farmer and his wife
work the land and their love.

Here, beloved, a new world,
in the perennial symphony
of the wind among the grain.

1973

Short Song of Good Hope

Because she* will fill with her crying
my silences,
my hope is complete.

1967

---

* "Because she": The subject of the verb "will fill" is not indicated and could be "he," "she," or "it." Since Meneses's daughter Karla was born in 1967, "she" was selected.

Apuntes para una primeriza

Al principio, como nerviosa pepesca
que pellizca la migaja de pan que cayó al agua
para largarse después a vagar
       en las tranquilas aguas.
Luego como aleteo de pájaro aprisionado.

Preparad nombre después
que en correntadas de agua,
el hijo del hombre se desliza a la vida.

1972

Pájaro en tres cantos

      I

Pájaro que se remonta
y en picada regresa
flecha de vértigo y sonido
soy.

      II

Nido hecho, trabajado
con la paja del amor
no es deshecho.

      III

Gusanitos y piedritas
a mis retoños doy
pájara Karla, pájaro Carlos
es la hora de mangiare!

1969

Notes for Her, A First-timer

At first, like a nervous pepesca fish that
pinches the bread crumb fallen into the water
then leaves to roam
        in still waters.
Later, like wing beats of a caged bird.

Prepare a name afterwards,
for in waves of water,
the son of man glides into life.

1972

Bird in Three Songs

       I

Bird that soars on high
and dives back down,
arrow of vertigo and sound
am I.

       II

A nest created, worked
with the straw of love,
is not undone.

       III

Little worms and tiny grit
I give to my babies.
Karla bird, Carlos bird*,
it's time to mangiare!

1969

---

* Karla, Carlos: Meneses's two children born before the date of the poem.
mangiare: Eat in Italian.

Ninguna campesina madre crea

Ninguna campesina madre crea
que la risa de mi niña
ahogó el eco del llanto de su hijo.

Hasta aquí inmersa en el bullicio
................de la ciudad
mi postura de madre es solidaria a la suya.

Porque en sus manecitas hemos escrito
la bondad de su estrella
y en su boca dibujado
........el grito de la esperanza.

Porque el mismo llanto nos desvela
en lo profundo de la noche
y el mismo anhelo nos alienta
en la alborada.

1969

Let No *Campesina** Mother Believe

Let no *campesina* mother believe
that the laughter of my daughter
drowned the echo of her child's cries.

Even here, immersed in the hustle and bustle
                of the city,
my position as mother is in solidarity with hers.

For in their little hands we have written
the kindness of their star
and in their mouths drawn
        the cry of hope.

For the same cry wakes us
in the deep of night
and the same longing inspires us
at the dawn of day.

1969

---

* *Campesina*: Frequently translated "peasant," referring to a rural, usually poor, woman farmer.

Pequeña muerte

*A María Bíblica, a quien a diferencia de Martha,
la hacendosa, le fue permitido sólo cantar.*

Solidariamente.

Abres los ojos
y encuentras el momento que te sepulta.
Ahora cuando todo se ha vuelto irrevocable
y ya las soledades ensayadas no te pertenecen,
porque son solamente momento de fuga,
"mecanismo de defensa".

Cuando tu tajante inutilidad en las pequeñas cosas
te limita, te bloquea,
Entonces te toca saborear minuto a minuto
                            tu Pequeña Muerte.

1970

Small Death

*To the Biblical Mary, who, unlike industrious Martha,
was permitted only to sing.*

In solidarity.

You open your eyes
and find the moment that buries you.
Now, when all has become irrevocable
and the usual solitudes can no longer be yours,
because they're just moments of escape,
      "defense mechanism."

When your categorical uselessness for little things
limits you, blocks you,
then you must savor minute by minute
      your Small Death.

1970

[Included in *Flame in the Wind*]
[Translation by Kathryn Peters and María Roof]

Yo amanezco persiguiendo un canto

El día se tiene que resolver
y yo amanezco persiguiendo un canto.
La humedad de hoy no me sugiere
precisamente "Dry Cleaning".
La grama no clama por su corte periódico
sino por mis pies hundidos en ella.

El patio me llama en el mango enano,
en la caña, en el plátano,
y en el incipiente heliotropo
que ya asoma.

Hoy no será el lienzo
en los vidrios empolvados
sino la promesa de liberación
que es una ventana.

Un avión atraviesa las nubes
con la vertiginosa potencia de su máquina
pero ya antes los pájaros
tomaron posesión del cielo.

No escucharé la radio que me recuerda
el tiempo de los relojes,
haré mi día sin horas
porque hay que resolverlo todo
y he salido temprano en busca de un canto.

1971

I Awake Chasing A Song

The day must be organized
and I awake chasing a song.
Today's humidity doesn't suggest
"Dry Cleaning" exactly.
The lawn clamors not for its regular trim
but for my feet sunken in it.

The patio calls to me in the dwarf mango tree,
in sugar cane and plantain,
in the budding heliotrope
already peeping out.

Today there will be no rag upon
dusty panes,
but the promise of liberation
that is a window.

A plane pierces clouds,
with its engines' vertiginous power,
but earlier, birds had
already claimed the sky.

I'll not listen to the radio
reminding me of clock time,
I'll make my day without hours
because everything must be organized,
and I left early in search of a song.

1971

[Included in *Flame in the Wind*]

Sol en la playa

Sol en la playa de mar
con rokonola de fondo en mediodía
o—
sol en patio casero
con fondo de televisión
—la canción popular—
el palmoteo alegre de los niños
y la prudente voz de la abuela
a la expectativa.

Yo, como una ostra aletargada
en su concha,
y el hastío vital que al menos matiza
la espontánea sonrisa de un hijo.

1971

Mujer estéril

—¿Dónde reflejarás la diáfana
belleza de tus ojos
flor que no fijará raíces
agua que no abrirá surco?

1971

Sun on the Sand

Sun on midday ocean sand
jukebox music in the background
or
sunlit patio at home
with the TV going
—pop music—
children clapping gleefully
and grandmother's prudent voice
supervising.

I, like a oyster lethargic
in its shell,
life's tedium somewhat softened by
the spontaneous smile of my child.

1971

[Included in *Flame in the Wind*]

Barren Woman

Where will you reflect the diaphanous
beauty of your eyes,
flower that will set no roots,
water that will cut no furrow?

1971

Ahora poseo el tiempo

Ahora poseo el tiempo
y a lo largo de la tarde
increíblemente mía
viejas palabras escritas reviven su
momento.

Otro eco, sin embargo, borra mis soledades
y pequeñas voces infantiles
pueblan mis horas.

Como un árbol, descubro entonces,
que mis raíces han proliferado
y que mi tronco enhiesto ya nada lo abate.

1974

Acto de fe

Abierta a todas las creencias,
acucioso oído a la esperanza de cada uno,
muriendo íntimamente para dar palabra viva,
he de heredarles un mundo ancho y generoso,
y que tras mi recuerdo ni se diga
que mi tiempo fue inútil.

1974

Now I Have Time

Now I have time
and throughout the afternoon,
incredibly mine,
old words written relive their
moment.

Another echo, however, erases my loneliness
and small children's voices
populate my hours.

Like a tree, I discover then
that my roots have spread,
and nothing can fell my towering trunk.

1974

Act of Faith

Open to all beliefs,
attentive ear to the hope of each being,
dying intimately to give the living word,
I shall bequeath to them a broad and generous world,
and, as a memory of me, let no one say
my time was wasted.

1974

Alguna noche insomne

Alguna noche insomne,
sentada al borde de la cama
los pies en mullidas zapatillas
y la tristeza enroscando
como un gato su cola en mis tobillos,
contemplo su tranquilo descanso,
su confiado sueño,
como si aún flotaran
en la acuosa seguridad de mis entrañas.

1974

On A Sleepless Night

On a sleepless night
seated on the edge of the bed
my feet in furry slippers
and sadness coiling
like a cat tail round my ankles,
I watch their peaceful sleep,
their trustful dreaming,
as if they floated still
in the aqueous security of my womb.

1974

[Included in *Flame in the Wind*]

IV. Oficina

Oficina

El viento se cuela
por las paredes altas
de la oficina.

Un ambiente de máquinas y papeles
me sepulta
y soy incapaz de atrapar
mi propio canto en esta hora.

Estoy pensando en Ha Ta Shte
la secretaria del primer ministro Japonés
(la de los pies exóticos) que el Sr. Ministro
conoce muy bien,
y en Peggy Lee la dulce mecanógrafa
que Mr. Wells sienta en sus rodillas.

Todo esto me descubre que en las oficinas
hay muchas cosas archivadas.

Pero lo que me duele
son mis manos atadas
y un sueño revoloteando solitario.

1965

IV. The Office

The Office

The wind seeps through
the high walls
in the office.

An ambiance of machines and papers
buries me,
and I am unable to catch
my own song in this hour.

I think of Ha Ta Shte,
secretary to the Japanese prime minister
(she of the exotic feet), whom Mr. Minister
knows quite well,
and of Peggy Lee*, the sweet typist
Mr. Wells sits on his knees.

All this reveals to me that in offices
many things are filed away.

But hurting me
are my tied hands and
a dream fluttering alone.

1965

---

* "Ha Ta Shte," "Peggy Lee," "Mr. Wells": Names invented by the poet to sound typical of the nationalities of the figures. She clarifies: "For me, the developed world meant offices where bosses and secretaries had affairs, and this influenced our countries. My father did not want me to work after I graduated from high school with a secretarial degree, because he thought I was too young for that environment. Nevertheless, I got my first job at age 19 with the mortgage firm Inmobiliaria de Ahorro y Préstamo, S.A. I later went back and got an academic diploma so that I could do university studies."

Fugaces, intermitentes

Fugaces, intermitentes,
las luces de los automóviles
me deslumbran
a través de la ventanilla del pequeño bus
que nos transporta de la oficina.

Recorremos Managua de noche,
unas veces atravesando
silenciosos barrios residenciales
y otras, bordeando el Mercado Boer,
que semeja un campamento gitano
con sus lonas y sus fuegos bajo el sereno.

A esta hora recuerdo
cómo se le humedecen los ojos a mi madre
cuando lee mi poema,
a esta hora, madre yo también,
ansiosa de estrechar a mis hijos
retorno al hogar.

1969

Fleeting, Intermittent

Fleeting, intermittent,
automobile lights
blind me
through the window of the minibus
transporting us from the office.

We cross Managua by night,
through quiet residential neighborhoods
or alongside Boer Market
looking like a gypsy camp,
with its tents and fires under the evening dew.

At this hour, I remember
how my mother's eyes grow damp
when she reads my poem,
at this hour, I, a mother too,
eager to embrace my children
when I'm back home.

1969

Siento el suave rumor

       Siento el suave rumor del nuevo pájaro
       en el árbol vecino a mi oficina.

En esta quietud que sólo rompía
el teclear de las máquinas de escribir
o el ineludible y vano:
       —¿Cómo se llama?
       —¿Ya llenó el censo?
       —¿Trae sus documentos?
de todos los días.

En este momento ya es un eco muerto.

Pero es agradable disfrutar
de escribir un poema sobre la montaña
de papeles de mi escritorio,
mientras que para esta hora
pienso que la pájaro-madre
ya dio de comer una hermosa lombriz
              a su retoño.

1968

I Sense the Soft Murmur

I sense the soft murmur of the new bird
      in the tree outside my office.

In this stillness broken only by
keystrokes on typewriters,
or the inevitable, empty
      —Your name?
      —Did you fill out the form?
      —Did you bring your papers?
of every day.

At this moment it's already a dead echo.

But it's pleasant to write
a poem on top of the mountain
of papers on my desk,
while at this time
I think that the mother bird
has given a beautiful worm
      to her baby.

1968

Es la vida

Esta tarde que habla del tedio
de las máquinas en la oficina
y de las secretarias,
yo maquinalmente tecleando (casi otra máquina)
siento que la normalísima monotonía
de esta oficina me ahoga.

Afuera, ahí abajo, la gente y los carros
teclean su vertiginosa, inútil premura
y yo dentro, aquí arriba, ajena a todo ruido
como un ángel delegado ante las naciones diz que unidas
y así el mundo va pasando
y su camino redondo nadie lo entorpece.

Pero hay otra faz de la tierra que dejamos,
que añoramos secretamente
cuando nos vamos alejando dentro del ruido
y comenzamos a teclear desesperadamente.

Entonces el espíritu erosiona y amontona su arrastre
de barro, piedras y hojas secas.
Todo está ahí como lo hemos dejado;
pero ahora es tarde y lo que nos importa
es la valentía de enfrentarse al mañana,
es la fuerza de encararse a un nuevo día:
es la vertiginosa marcha que envuelve
y lleva y revuelca lo estático.

1966

That's Life

This afternoon that speaks of the tedium
of office machines and
secretaries,
I, mechanically typing (almost another machine),
feel the well-known monotony
of this office suffocating me.

Outside, down below, people and cars
type their useless, dizzying haste,
and I'm up here inside, away from all noise
like an angel delegate to the so-called united nations,
and thus the world goes by, and
no one blocks its round path.

But the earth has another face we left behind
and secretly long for,
when we escape within the noise
and begin to type desperately.

Then, our spirit erodes and heaps up
its sludge of mud, stones and dry leaves.
Everything is there as we left it;
but now it's late and what matters to us
is the courage to confront tomorrow,
is the strength to face a new day,
is the dizzying march that envelops
and drags and overturns what's static.

1966

[Included in *Flame in the Wind*]
[Translation by Kathryn Peters and María Roof]

Abandono, adrede y concientemente

Abandono, adrede y concientemente
el ojo avizor de ejecutivo oficinesco
y me sumo en el sopor
del ronroneo de la mezcladora
—"reminiscencia del mimo de la niñez"—
dictaminarán doctos los psicólogos.

Altamente recomendable
ese mecanismo de defensa
retorno por ello al ruido
de plantel de mina
de la Bonanza de mi infancia.

1973

Todos los días

Todos los días haces inventario del tiempo:
La ruta rutinaria
el saludo oficinesco
y el tableteo de la máquina de escribir
como una metralleta domesticada.
El aire acondicionado condicionando
con su confort las mentes y los cuerpos.
Los límites de la miope reflexión
marcando el día en el calendario,
programando los pagos,
superando las propias marcas de venta.
El camino al carro y a la casa
y el peligroso convencimiento
de que en el país de los ciegos
el tuerto es rey.

1974

I Abandon, Purposely and Consciously

I abandon, purposely and consciously,
my watchful, office executive eye
and plunge myself into the drowsiness
of the rock mixer's purr,
"reminiscence of childhood doting,"
wise psychologists will diagnose.

Highly recommendable
that defense mechanism,
so I return to the noise
of mining operations
in the Bonanza* of my childhood.

1973

Every Day

Every day you take an inventory of time:
the routine route
office "hello"
and typewriters clattering
like domesticated machine guns.
Air conditioner conditioning
with its comfort minds and bodies.
The limits of near-sighted reflection
marking the day on the calendar,
scheduling pay outs,
surpassing personal sales records.
To the car and home again
and the dangerous conviction
that in the land of the blind
the one-eyed man is king.

1974

[Included in *Flame in the Wind*]
[Translation by Kathryn Peters and María Roof]

---

* Bonanza: Mining city where Meneses spent vacations with her Great-Aunt Virginia (see References).

V. Tríptico de la muerte

I

Tan simple como los viejos tíos
que te escriben y dicen:
>"la casa que si terminamos de pagar
>le quedará a los hijos
>y si nos morimos antes
>pagamos menos".

Así de resumida la vida
a la inevitable condición de la muerte.
Allí empieza tu prisa
de economizar los minutos
y de revivir en el calendario
la hoja del día inútil que arrancaste
y el considerar que el tiempo
no es más que otro invento del hombre
y que las pequeñas metas alcanzadas
no son más que un comienzo,
y tienes afán de construir
y muchas veces destruyes
a pesar de que siempre
>"Hay tiempo para todo bajo el sol".

Y esa máxima es tu asidero
porque si no, naufragas y se acabó tu historia
hombre-pez que viene y al agua va.

Así de simple y sin copla
como río que se va a la mar.

V. Triptych on Death

    I

As simple as your old aunt and uncle
who write you and say:
    "If we pay off the house,
    it will go to the kids,
    and if we die first,
    we pay less*".

Thus life is summed up
to the inevitable condition of death.
There begins your rush
to save minutes
and revive on the calendar
the useless day's sheet you tore off
and deem that time
is no more than another human invention
and the little accomplishments
are only a beginning,
and you long to build
and often you destroy
although always
    "There is time for everything under the sun."
And this maxim is your handhold,
otherwise, you drown and your story ends,
man-fish who comes from and to the water returns.

As simple as that, without fanfare,
like a river flowing to the sea.

---

*"pagamos menos/we pay less": Verse revised by Meneses in May 2005.

II

Graba tu afán de eternidad
en la piedra, hijo mío,
porque ave de paso es el hombre
y el tiempo a su hechura.

III

¿Brotó al fin el sueño de los muertos
en el árbol que cobijó sus tumbas?
Me parece que al amanecer
alguien susurró entre las hojas
una canción.

1972

II

Engrave your wish for eternity
in stone, my son,
because man is a migrating bird
and time is made in his image.

III

Did the dream of the dead finally bud
on the tree shading their graves?
I think at dawn
someone murmured among the leaves
      a song.

1972

[Translation by Kathryn Peters and María Roof]

El aire que me llama (1982)

Esta no es ella, es el viento
es el aire que la llama;
es su lugar, es su hueco
vacío que la reclama.

—Joaquín Pasos

***Air that Calls Me* (1982)**

*This is not her, it's the wind,
it's the air that calls her;
it's her place, it's her empty space
calling out for her.*

—Joaquín Pasos*

---

* Joaquín Pasos (1914-1947): Nicaraguan Vanguard poet (see References).

I. De ineludible memoria y otros poemas

Apunte

Allá en El Jícaro, localidad rural de Las Segovias, paisaje rocoso y seco en el verano y hermosamente verde y terriblemente lodoso en el invierno, a todo lo largo del Coco que lo baña; donde al atravesar la plaza me quedaba la pequeña y bulliciosa escuela pública de aceras altas y ladrillos de barro, donde al comienzo de las clases se canta el Himno y se persigna, allí, donde mi buena maestra regordeta y ojos claros, impartía su clase al Tercer Grado.

Cuando a la orilla de mi casa las carretas pasaban con la lenta mansedumbre de sus bueyes, yo corría tras ellas y montaba con Edmundo y Meriulda, mis pequeños hermanos, hasta bajarnos a la salida, a Los Planes, meta de miel y de guarapo.

Y en los paseos al río, a mí, la menor del grupo entre los amigos de mis padres, me tocaba en suerte un burro como medio de transporte (figura indispensable y toque de gracia de las calles del pueblo), y siempre era yo el punto final de la caravana, víctima de la terquedad del animal. Cuando mi padre lo azotaba para hacerlo caminar, sólo conseguíamos que se doblara como una herradura, la caminata se convertía entonces en horas de impaciencia contenida o de resignada tolerancia, hasta que al fin, ya en la ribera del río, montábamos rústicas balsas de cepas de guineo y marchábamos con la fuerza de la corriente, río abajo.

1968

I. On Inescapable Memory and Other Poems

Sketch

In El Jícaro*, a rural town in Las Segovias, rocky, dry countryside in summer, beautifully green and terribly muddy in winter, all along the Coco River that bathes it. Crossing the square, I would go to the bustling little public school, with high walkways and mud bricks, where classes began with the singing of the National Anthem and crossing yourself, and my good teacher, plump and light-eyed, taught Third Grade.

When carts passed next to my house, with the slow gentleness of their oxen, I'd run after them and jump on with my little brother Edmundo and sister Meriulda and off at the edge of town at Los Planes, known for its honey and sugar cane juice.

On outings to the river, I was the youngest in the group of my parents' friends, so for transport, I got the burro (indispensable figure and amusing touch on the town streets) and was always the last one in the caravan, victim of the animal's stubbornness. When my father gave it a swat to make it walk, we only got it to bend like a horseshoe. The excursion turned into hours of contained impatience or resigned tolerance, until at last, at the river bank, we made rustic boats of banana trunks and floated with the current's force downstream.

1968

---

* El Jícaro: Town in Las Segovias, a region of five northern provinces —Matagalpa, Jinotega, Estela, Madriz, and New Segovia— where Meneses lived as a young girl. Las Segovias was the area where Sandino engaged the U.S. marines in battle.
summer, winter: The two seasons in tropical climes, dry (in Nicaragua, January to April) and rainy (May to December).

Las niñas Valle

¡Cómo me hacían feliz las pequeñas cosas!

Aquella vieja cómoda de la tía Adelina llenita de santos.

Aquel baúl donde con visión múltiple descubría vestidos doblados, novenas, rosarios, regalos aún sin desempacar, y en algún lugar semioculto aquella vieja foto amarilla dedicada amorosamente a Elvira.

Y las venidas de la tía Toya (infatigable maestra rural) con sus invariables hijas de crianza, de cachetes rosados, caderas redondas y el frescor de la brisa de la montaña aún latente.

Las tres tías tan queridas, niñas viejas, Hermanas del Santísimo, Terciarias, Hijas de María.

1969

The Valle Girls*

Small things made me so happy!

That old dresser of Aunt Adelina's, covered with saints.

That trunk where my multiple vision discovered folded dresses, prayer books, rosaries, gifts not yet opened, and in some half-hidden place, that old, yellowed photo lovingly dedicated to Elvira.

And the comings and goings of Aunt Toya (energetic country school-teacher) with her constant girls taken under wing, with their rosy cheeks, round hips and still sharp freshness of the mountain breeze.

Three beloved aunts, elderly girls, Sisters of the Most Holy, Tertiaries, Daughters of Mary.

1969

---

* Valle girls: Unmarried maternal great-aunts, renowned for their beauty, with whom the young Meneses spent time in the northern town of Matagalpa (see References).
Sisters of the Most Holy, Tertiaries, Daughters of Mary: Religious societies to which women could belong.

Verano

I

Salobre la ola, revienta el recuerdo sobre la paciente arena. Días santos aquellos, en que las tres niñas Valle, ahora dos sin Elvira, que ya alcanzó su blanca palma, entraban y salían del atrio al altar, del altar al atrio en un efectivo trabajo de indulgencias del cual darán cuenta no pocas ánimas agradecidas.

II

Rosadas conchas, ensortijados caracoles, deposita con la peligrosa raya y entre las nerviosas carreras de los cangrejos, la rebelde palmada de la ola, mientras la Valeria ausculta de reojo y desde su vejez mi lacónica actitud de observar y escribir.

1975

Summer[*]

I

Salty wave, memory breaks on the patient sand. Blessed days those, when the three Valle girls —now two without Elvira, who has already grasped the white palm- went to and fro, atrium to altar, altar to atrium, in a fruitful labor for indulgences, which more than a few grateful souls will acknowledge.

II

Rosy shells, spiraled snails deposits the rebellious slap of the wave near the dangerous stingray and crabs' nervous capers, while Valeria[†] examines from the corner of her eye and her old age my laconic attitude of observing and writing.

1975

[Included in *Flame in the Wind*]

Invierno
---

[*] Summer: Dry season, January to April in Nicaragua.
Valle girls: Great-aunts of Vidaluz (see notes to previous poem and References).

[†] Valeria: A woman who worked in the Valle household, taken in by the family as a child.

Invierno

La lluvia revolvió todo anoche y la mañana amanece como si nada. Rescata la mano de la madre los tallos azotados, los entablilla, los cuida con celo. El vecindario está poblado de camisones y de pantuflas. Es como si los hombres hubiésemos retoñado. Don Tulipán —quise decir— barre su acera exento de todo machismo. Doña Acacia, diligente maneja su pala desterrando las cunetas.

Mañanas de desayunos calientes —imagino los del mercado Oriental— con chilero y amor, la mirada lasciva del cargador a la comidera.

De sabia escuela naturalista recojo el gesto simple de la vendedora alargando el nacatamal al hijo, que a la vista y paciencia de la abuela, el rápido chavalo lo engulle.

Se desbordaron los cauces, pero el pueblo sobre los elementos, como sobre otras cosas, hormiguea entre los lotos de lodo amanecidos.

1975

Pax

Bandera blanca desde la barricada:
pieza número 18 del hospital,
tropa cansada quiere rendirse,
duda de poder enviar
próximo teletipo. Stop.
Duermo o leo.

1972

Winter*

Rain stirred up everything last night, and morning dawns as if nothing had happened. The mother's hand rescues beaten stems, ties them to splints, zealously cares for them. The neighborhood is populated by nightgowns and slippers. It's as if we humans had just resprouted. Mr. Tulip, I meant to say, sweeps his walk free of machismo. Diligent Mrs. Acacia wields her shovel to clear the drains.

Mornings of warm breakfasts —I imagine those at the Eastern Market— with hot pepper and love, the deliveryman's lascivious gaze at the cook.

From the wise naturalist school I record the simple gesture of the market woman passing the nacatamal to her son, a quick boy who swallows it under grandmother's patient eye.

River banks overflowed, but the town —upon the elements, as upon other things— works like ants among the morning's lotuses of mud.

1975

Pax†

White flag from the barricade:
hospital room number 18,
fatigued troop wants to surrender,
doubt can send
another teletype. Stop.
I'll sleep or read.

1972

---

*Winter: Rainy season, May to December in Nicaragua.
† Clarification by Meneses: This poem was written during hospitalization for recovery from domestic abuse.

Bajamar

I

El ojo abierto
que ya no duerme para no soñar,
el ojo vigilante de lo evidente
frío y estático
como pequeño pez disecado.

II

Naturaleza muerta
reunió en ovalado azafate
días ruinosos, improductivos.
—Ni siquiera con el acre sabor
del fruto fermentado—.

Hacia el pleamar

Sobre el gozo pleno, individual,
la culpa.
El pequeño bienamado momento
que no fue compartido.

Pleamar

No ahogaré este fermento que me
recorre
y que no pocas mañanas me
incomoda.
Como pequeños caracoles
anidé en cada cavidad un sueño;
vendrá la ola inmensa
portadora de vida o de muerte,
sobrevivirá de la sirena el canto.

1975

Ebb Tide

    I

The eye opened
that no longer sleeps
so as not to dream,
the eye watchful of the obvious
cold and static
like a small, dried fish.

    II

Still life
gathered in an oval basket
ruinous, unproductive days.
—Not even with the bitter taste
of fermented fruit.

Almost High Tide

Over sheer, individual delight,
guilt.
The small cherished moment
that was not shared.

High Tide

I will not drown this ferment
that rushes through me,
and not just a few mornings
discomforts me.
Like small shells
I nested in each hollow a dream;
the immense wave will come,
bearer of life or of death,
of the siren, the song will survive.

1975

[Included in *Flame in the Wind*]
[Translation by Kathryn Peters and María Roof]

Mayo Nicaragua

Mayo significó hace tiempo
mi debut en el mundo,
rojas primaveras florecieron
en los cercos de Matagalpa,
El Jícaro y Ocotal.
Atrás había quedado
la umbrosa selva de Bonanza,
paradisíaco mundo infantil.

Muchas lluvias han lavado
desde entonces el recuerdo.
Cada vez más escasa, el agua,
como marea que se retira para
siempre,
desnuda la aridez de arena y rocas.
Busco en la ligera brisa,
lluvia tímida de este mayo,
un principio de vida
para esta madre que se nos muere
—sangre por los cuatro costados—
Muerte de madre en cruz,
madero florecido en mayo.

1978

May in Nicaragua

May used to mean
my debut in the world,
red primroses flowered
in the gardens of Matagalpa*,
El Jícaro and Ocotal.
Left behind was the
dark rain forest of Bonanza,
heavenly childhood world.

Many rains have since washed
the memory.
Ever more scarce, the water,
like a tide ebbing
forever,
reveals the aridness of sand and rocks.
I search in the gentle breeze,
for this May's timid rains,
a beginning of life
for this, our dying mother
—blood in all four sides—
mother's death on a cross,
wood flowering in May.

1978

[Included in *Flame in the Wind*]

---

* Matagalpa: Birthplace of Meneses, a city in the Dariense mountain range.
El Jícaro: Rural town in Las Segovias where Meneses lived as a child.
Ocotal: Northern city in the Dipilto mountain range.
Bonanza: Northern mining town where Meneses spent vacations as a child (see References).

Madre

Yo compartí contigo
el dolor desde sus orígenes
y conocí en tu risa
la alegría de la primavera,
y te heredé esos largos silencios
donde se nutren los sueños,
este corazón de caracol sonoro
que me hermanó a todos los
hombres.

1978

Epitafio

Te recordamos maestro rural
o inspector de escuelas
cambiando tu regla
por el trago apurado en el estanco
de Muy Muy o Esquipulas,
gastándote el ultimo sueldo,
a costa de los anteojos, de la
dentadura postiza,
para anochecer con guitarra
cantando
y amanecer tres días después
nítido, de traje blanco y corbata
—inspector de escuelas—
matagalpino Montemar Valle.

1981

Mother

I shared with you
pain at its origin,
and learned in your laughter
the joy of springtime,
and inherited from you those long silences
where dreams are nourished,
this heart of a sonorous sea shell
that bound me to all of
humanity.

1978

[Included in *Flame in the Wind*]
[Translation by Kathryn Peters and María Roof. Amanda Hopkinson's version appears in *Lovers and Comrades*.]

Epitaph

We remember you, rural teacher
or school inspector,
exchanging your ruler
for a hurried drink at the shop
in Muy Muy or Esquipulas*,
spending your last paycheck,
at the cost of eyeglasses and
false teeth,
to spend the night with a guitar
singing
and arise three days later
bright and shining, in white suit and tie,
—school inspector—
Matagalpa's Montemar Valle.

1981

---

* Muy Muy, Esquipulas: Towns in Matagalpa Department, Nicaragua.
Montemar Valle: Brother of the Valle great-aunts (see References under Valle).

II. Hijos-juegos

Karla Dolores

Karla Dolores es un poema japonés.
Sus ojos fueron hechos de palabras rasgadas.
Y su piel, de finísima porcelana,
fue robada a Lin Fu, el alfarero.

Karla Dolores, el mejor poema
que tu madre no escribió:
tú te hiciste.

Karla Dolores es un poema japonés
que en su pequeñez mueve
inmensidades.

1967

II. Children-Games

Karla Dolores

Karla Dolores* is a Japanese poem.
Her eyes were made from slanted words.
And her skin, of the finest porcelain,
was stolen from Lin Fu†, the potter.

Karla Dolores, the best poem
your mother did not write:
you made yourself.

Karla Dolores is a Japanese poem
who in her smallness moves
immensities.

1967

---

*   Karla Dolores: First of Meneses's four children.
†   Lin Fu: Name invented by the poet.

Hijos

Karla Dolores

Con la suavidad de la geisha
frágiles rodillas al suelo
la guitarra sobre el pecho
y los mínimos dedos arrancando
Barrio de Pescadores entre las
cuerdas.

Carlos Rodolfo

Indolente, casero garrobito socarrón,
soñador de selvático Tarzán
o sofocado corredor
del equipo camiseta azul.

Vidaluz

¿Qué aconteció hoy en el pueblo,
doña Socorrita y doña Soledad?
agita colochona cabeza,
manos de mariposa,
lleva y trae la risa
el cuento fantasioso de Chilotesán.

Mariano Edmundo

Nuestro pequeño corderito
anunciado por cometa,
visitado por blanca paloma de la paz
en primario Moisés.
Anunciador, ojalá
de Buena Nueva.

1974

Children

Karla Dolores

With the geisha's softness
fragile knees on the ground
guitar to her chest,
and tiny fingers pulling
"Fishermen's Wharf" from the
strings.

Carlos Rodolfo

Indolent, cunning little house iguana,
dreamer of Tarzan of the Jungle
or out-of-breath runner
for the blue-shirt team.

Vidaluz

"What happened in town today,
Mrs. Help and Mrs. Solitude?"
shakes her curly head,
butterfly hands,
bringing laughter time and again from
the fanciful story of Chilotesán.

Mariano Edmundo

Our small little lamb,
announced by a comet,
visited by the white dove of peace
as a primary Moses.
Messenger, we hope,
of the Good News.

1974

Canto para un invierno que no comienza

A Luis Rocha, Poeta

No es la esperanza trunca
del árbol sediento,
ni la agonía prematura
del viejo riachuelo,
ni el solaz del garrobo,
ni la melancolía de la tortuga,
sino la ansiosa espera
de estos pequeños locos
que como el hijo del poeta aguardan
para aprender gozosos una palabra
nueva:

Lluvia, lluvia, lluvia.

1970

Song for a Winter* that Does Not Begin

To Luis Rocha†, Poet

It is not the truncated hope
of the thirsty tree,
nor premature death throes
of the old brook,
nor the iguana's stillness,
nor the turtle's melancholy,
but the anxious waiting
of these tiny fools
who, like the poet's son, wait
to happily learn a new
word:

Rain, rain, rain.

1970

---

* winter: Rainy season, May to December in Nicaragua.
† Luis Rocha (1942): Nicaraguan poet (see References).

Fauna nica

Tortuga Casera

Introvertida, se recoge
en sabio silencio la tortuga,
el amor y el calor solar la fecundan.

Siembra su maternidad
en el nido telúrico
y en el invierno,
cuando las primeras lloviznas caen,
emerge con mansa alegría
a saludar el agua y la vida.

Garrobo

Orgullo ancestral
en grisácea piel.
Ojo avizor sobre la tapia.
Bebedor de sol en pleno mediodía.

Guapote

En roca firme
fija su residencia bajo el agua
o en transparente orilla pedregosa
de lago o río.

Pequeños, aprendices de vida,
son herbívoros.

Mayores, capaces y audaces
carnívoros rapaces.

1980

Nican Fauna

Box Turtle

Introverted, the turtle pulls back
in wise silence,
love and the sun's warmth fertilize her.

She sows her motherhood
in the telluric nest,
and in winter,
when the first drizzles fall,
emerges with calm joy
to greet water and life.

Garrobo Iguana

Ancestral pride
in greyish skin.
Alert eye on the wall.
Sun drinker at full midday.

Guapote Fish

On firm rock
it establishes residence under water
or in the transparent pebbly edge
of a lake or river.

Young, life apprentices,
they are herbivores.

Older, efficacious and audacious,
carnivores rapacious.

1980

Hubo una vez

Hubo una vez una mujer feliz de tener un secreto para ella sola, guardado, aprisionado, escondido en lo más íntimo de su ser, y fue su razón de vivir el conservarlo íntegro, hasta que el colmo de su dicha fue morirse sin habérselo revelado a nadie.

1973

Once There Was

Once there was a woman happy to have a secret all to herself, guarded, imprisoned, hidden in the most intimate part of her being, and her reason for living was to conserve it intact, and the height of her pleasure was to die without ever revealing it to anyone.

1973

Notas de viaje

I

Que si mágicas monedas
tiradas a dos manos al río Moscova
o el paseo nocturno a la sombra
de los abedules bordeando el Ukraína
después de vertiginoso tránsito del metro
Boris Klimenko, soñando costas
del Mar Negro y diciendo con ojos
encendidos
los versos de Ana Ajmátova,
la poeta cuya alma de mujer
decís que comprendiste.

Todo eso es suficiente para llenar
mi sola y nueva pequeña habitación.
Ese momento compartido en otro
tiempo, otro lugar y sin embargo
hoy tan cercano.

II

En el amable Plovdiv
divisamos sobre los tejados
la plácida estación de una cigüeña.
Es mediodía en Nicaragua
y aquí de noche, atravesado el
meridiano
pero —a causa de las estaciones—
son las nueve con la claridad
de las cinco de la tarde,
hora de los poetas, recordable
en "Los Viejos Oficios", rincón latinoamericano
con mojito cubano y la presencia
de Nikolai, Amelia y Stoyan, el plovdense.

1981

III. Travel Notes

Travel Notes

I
Magical coins
tossed by two hands into the Moscow River,
or the evening walk in the shade
of birch trees flanking The Ukraine*
after the dizzying ride on the metro
Boris Klimenko†, dreaming of
Black Sea coasts and reciting with eyes
aglow
verses by Anna Akhmatova‡,
the poet whose woman's soul
you say you understood.

All that is sufficient to fill
my lone, new, small room.
That moment shared in another
time, another place, and yet
today so near.

II
In charming Plovdiv§
we spied atop tiled roofs
the placid stance of a stork.
It's midday in Nicaragua
and night here,
the meridian crossed,
but —due to season—
it's nine with the light
of five in the afternoon,
poets' hour, memorable
at "Los Viejos Oficios," a Latin American corner,
with a Cuban mojito¶ and the company
of Nikolai, Amelia and Stoyan, the Plovdivite.

1981
[Included in *Flame in the Wind*] [Translation by Kathryn Peters and María Roof]

---

* The Ukraine: Hotel in Moscow on the Moscow River.
† Boris Klimenko: Russian journalist. Also mentioned in "Inquiries," *All is the Same and Different.*
‡ Anna Akhmatova (Odessa 1889-Moscow 1966): Pseudonym of Anna Andréievna Gorenko, Soviet poet associated with St. Petersburg/Leningrad, who abandoned her early poetry on feminine intimacy to link her own tragedy to that of Russia. Also mentioned in "Inquiries," *All is the Same and Different,* and "Heart in the Open," not published in a collection.
§ Plovdiv: City in Bulgaria, on the banks of the Marica River.
¶ Cuban *mojito*: Drink made of rum, lemon juice, mint, sugar, water or club soda, and ice.

Mujer cachikel

I

He palpado los surcos de los siglos
en tus mejillas, mujer cachikel.
La desconfiada ceremonia
comercial del regateo,
tu impasible posición de tejedora,
Gandhianas rodillas contra el suelo
y las manos como rápidas ardillas
entrecruzando los hilos del mantel,
del delantal o la alfombra
que hablarán de vos,
morena Penélope, en otras latitudes.

II

Silente compañera que tejiste los cabellos del amado
bajo la luna que aullando
quisieron atrapar los viejos lobos.
Vientre preñado que abortó rubios hijos de conquistadores.
Diligente sombra-símbolo,
tradición hecha mujer.

1978

Cakchiquel Woman

I

I have touched the furrows of centuries
in your cheeks, Cakchiquel* woman.
The distrustful business ceremony
of bargaining,
your impassive weaver pose,
Gandhian† knees against the ground
and your hands like swift squirrels
weaving the threads of a tablecloth,
apron or rug
that will speak of you,
dark Penelope‡, in other latitudes.

II

Silent partner, you wove the hair of your lover
under the moon that ancient wolves howling
tried to trap.
Pregnant belly that aborted blond children of conquistadors.
Diligent shadow-symbol,
tradition made woman.

1978

[Included in *Flame in the Wind*]
[Translation by Maria Roof. David Volpendesta's version appears in *Volcán*.]

---

* Cakchiquel: Person, people, and language of Mayan heritage in Guatemala. Its spelling varies: Cachikel, Cakchiquel, Kaqchikel, Kaqchiquel.
† Gandhi, Mohandas, "Mahātmā" (Porbandar 1869-Delhi 1948): Nationalist Hindu religious leader of India; proponent of the doctrine of passive resistance, non-violence and civil disobedience in India's struggle for independence from Great Britain.
‡ Penelope: In Greek mythology, a weaver and symbol of wifely faithfulness (see References).

Antigua

Estrechas calles empedradas
—Calle de las Ánimas—
me avivan el recuerdo de letanías y rosarios
dichas en coro por las niñas Valle.
Mañaneras misas bajo las brisas
del norte de Nicaragua
o melancólicos atardeceres
sobre cementerios de pueblo.

Me inquieta el sueño petrificado de una monja.
La simbólica figura de antiguos éxtasis.
Las mínimas celdas con la sola
apertura al mundo de una ventana.

Subterráneos túneles guardadores
de viejas pasiones en su telúrico seno.
Severo guía con voz grave atestigua
el entierro de tiernos fetos.

Literatura turística oralmente bien dicha
no evita que al mencionar

> "la nostalgia de los españoles
> expresada en los pequeños
> leones de atrios y campanarios"

un eco rebelde cachikel nos grite
allá en el fondo: ¡No llamen a la dominación, nostalgia!

1978

Antigua[*]

Narrow cobbled streets
—Street of the Spirits—
spark my memory of litanies and rosaries
said in unison by the Valle girls[†].
Morning masses under breezes
in northern Nicaragua
or melancholic sunsets
over small town cemeteries.

I am disturbed by a nun's petrified sleep.
The symbolic figure of ancient ecstasies.
Tiny cells with the lone
opening to the world in a window.

Underground tunnels, guardians
of old passions in their telluric bosom.
Grim guide with his grave voice attests to
the burial of young fetuses.

Tourist literature orally well-recited
cannot prevent, after noting

> "the Spaniards' nostalgia
> expressed in the small
> lions in the atria and bell towers"

a rebellious Cakchiquel[‡] echo that shouts to us
from the depths: Do not call domination "nostalgia"!

1978

---

[*] Antigua: Original capital of Guatemala, with a rich group of Spanish Baroque colonial buildings: the cathedral, Mercy Convent, St. Peter and St. Francis churches, town hall, university (now a colonial museum). Declared World Humanity Heritage Site in 1979.

[†] Valle girls: Great-aunts of Meneses (see References).

[‡] Cakchiquel: Person, people, and language of Mayan heritage in Guatemala.

IV. Sobrevida

Nosotros los sobrevivientes,
¿A quiénes debemos la sobrevida?
¿Quién se murió por mí en la ergástula?
¿Quién recibió la bala mía,
La para mí, en su corazón?
   —Roberto Fernández Retamar

Golpeas impotente la puerta de la Nochebuena

Golpeas impotente la puerta de la Nochebuena
para que entren todos
y de verdad sea buena,
porque para ser cierta
tiene que ser completa;
aunque tus puños firmes y sangrantes
contra la hermética madera se estrellen,
incansable y fallida irredenta
que aún retornas a la fe de que con todo y sequía
María y José no verán agonizar su niño
que nacerá al hambre,
a una mesa vacía.

1972

IV. Survival

We, the survivors,
To whom do we owe our survival?
Who died for me in the dank prison?
Who took my bullet,
The one for me, in his heart?
  —*Roberto Fernández Retamar*[*]

Helpless, You Knock on Christmas Eve's Door

Helpless, you knock on Christmas Eve's door
so that all can enter
and it might truly be good[†],
for to be so,
it must be complete;
though your firm, bloody fists
smash against the hermetic wood,
tireless, failed, unredeeming[‡] woman
who still returns to the faith that with the drought and all else,
Mary and Joseph will not see their son in death's agony,
he will be born to hunger,
to an empty table.

1972

---

[*] Roberto Fernández Retamar (1930): Cuban essayist and poet committed to the Cuban Revolution (see References).

[†] good: The word for Christmas eve in Spanish is "la Nochebuena," literally "the Good Night."

[‡] unredeeming: The poet clarified that she meant to imply her failure in attempts to redeem others.

Abril casero

Abril casero y soleado
—Muerte por agua—
Vaticinan unánimes los videntes.
Y parece que va a llover fuego del cielo
Ya llueve fuego en la montaña.
Ni los gritos de parto nos llegan.
Pero la ciudad tiene la quietud de la muerte
Y por la mañana sólo un corte de viento
seco y ronco partió el cielo en dos.
Dicen que desde arriba los vuelan.

1975

Familiar April

April, familiar and sun-drenched
—death by water—*
The seers foresee unanimous.
And it might rain fire from heaven
Already fire rains in the hills.
Not even the screams of childbirth reach us.†
But the city is deadly quiet.
And in the morning only a slash of
parched, hoarse wind sliced the sky in two.
They say from on high they fly them‡.

1975

[Included in *Flame in the Wind*]
[Translation by Kathryn Peters and María Roof]

---

* "death by water": One of the predictions in the Tarot.
† "Not even screams of childbirth reach us": Intertextuality with poems by Ernesto Cardenal on the resistance by rural women of Cuá, who refused to reveal guerrilla fighters' locations to National Guard soldiers. In "The Peasant Women from Cuá," Cardenal calls their cries under torture "cries of women like pangs of birth" and "wails from the homeland like pangs of birth" (Cardenal, *Flights of Victory*; trans. Edward Baker). Carlos Mejía Godoy created a song based on this poem that became very popular.
‡ "They say from on high they fly them": This is a literal translation of the line, in order to reflect the original's precise, conversational words. But, as Meneses explained, this expression was understood by most readers to refer to the National Guard's practice in rural areas of rounding up suspected sympathizers or collaborators with the FSLN, loading them into helicopters, and flinging them to their deaths from high in the sky (see other comments in Chapter II). Compare Meneses's hermetic expression to Cardenal's more direct allusion in "The Peasant Women from Cuá" (11):
> the patrols came and went with prisoners
> They sent Esteban up in a helicopter
> and soon after returned without him…

and in his *Flights* poem, "On the Lake": "They hurl peasants from helicopters".

La falda nueva

La falda nueva, el gesto vago
cigarrillo en mano,
la inversión cotidiana del tiempo
intrascendente;
su vacío señalándonos,
haciéndonos sentir parásitos,
araña tejedora de una tela inútil
que nos envuelve y asfixia.

1975

Los que no han muerto

Los vientos de noviembre
le trajeron los días del hijo muerto.
Diciembre repicará en sus campanas
su ruidosa soledad.
Sol en un enero
anunciará la buena nueva.
De los hijos sembrados
se está nutriendo el pueblo,
fuertes se levantarán sus brazos
y sonora su voz.

1975

The New Skirt

The new skirt, the vague gesture
cigarette in hand,
the daily investment of time
intranscendental;
its emptiness pointing at us,
making us feel like parasites,
spider spinning a useless web
that encircles and asphyxiates us.

1975

[Included in *Flame in the Wind*]

Those Who Have Not Died

November's winds
brought the days of their dead son.
December will echo in its bells
their noisy solitude.
Sun in January
will announce the good news.
From our children sown
the people nourish themselves,
strong shall their arms rise
and resounding their voice.

1975

Comerciales

I

La poseyeron porque se creyó
la Toña o la Victoria.

II

Digo que los hombres muy hombres
no tomaron Ron Plata
un día abrieron los ojos
y se fueron a cazar el sol
para su pueblo.

III

Sin vaso, sin agua, sin tierras,
con esperanza, Phillips,
harán un mundo nuevo.

1977

Commercials

I

They possessed her because she thought she was
Toña or Victoria.*

II†

I say that men, real men,
didn't drink Plata Rum;
one day they opened their eyes
and went off to capture the sun
for their people.

III

No glass, no water, no land,
with hope, Phillips‡,
they will build a new world§.

1977

---

* Toña y Victoria: Brands of Nicaraguan beers. Meneses explains: "There was an ad that showed a blonde girl in a bikini next to a bubbling bottle of beer, and a voice said: 'Enjoy the blonde,' referring to the color of the beer but also with a double meaning. This is an epigram based on that ad, where I try to sensitize young women, so they will not let themselves be exploited for commercial purposes."

† II: Meneses: "This is based on another commercial that was broadcast during baseball games and said: 'Only men who are real men drink Plata Rum.' When I say, 'real men … went off,' I am referring to the young men who joined the clandestine struggle."

‡ Phillips: An analgesic like Alka Seltzer that was advertised as requiring no glass or water to take.

§ "they will build a new world": Meneses: "An allusion to the poor who would one day bring about the Revolution. I published this type of political epigrams in 1977 in *La Prensa Literaria* to increase social awareness."

Mínimo homenaje

Con la producción en el suelo.
Sin escritorios ni máquinas de
escribir suficientes,
asumimos el reto
de la segunda etapa de tu obra, Carlos,
y es como cuando vos te enmontañaste
con pocos compañeros, mínimas
armas y una bandera.

1980

En el nuevo país

El dolor ha sido reto
y el porvenir esperanza,
construimos como escribiendo un poema
creando, borrando y volviendo a escribir.

1980

Small Homage

With production ground to a halt.
Not enough desks
or typewriters,
we accept the challenge
of the second stage of your work, Carlos*,
and it's like when you took to the hills
with a few *compañeros*†, some
arms and a flag.

1980

[Included in *Flame in the Wind*.]
[Translation by María Roof. Other versions appear in Amanda Hopkinson's *Lovers and Comrades* and in Marc Zimmerman's *Nicaragua in Reconstruction and at War*.]

In the New Country

Pain has been a challenge
and the future, our hope,
we build like we write a poem:
creating, erasing and writing again.

1980

[Included in *Flame in the Wind*]
[Translation by Kathryn Peters and María Roof. Amanda Hopkinson's version appeared in *Lovers and Comrades* and was reprinted in *Women and Revolution in Nicaragua*. Marc Zimmerman's translation is in his *Nicaragua in Reconstruction and at War*.]

---

* Carlos Fonseca Amador (1936-1976): One of the three founders of the Sandinista National Liberation Front (FSLN) in 1961; poet and combatant against the Somoza regimes (see References).

† *compañero*: Does not have a good equivalent in English. It was used in Cuba after the triumph of the Revolution and among Sandinista supporters to signal equality, democratic treatment, and respect for fellow citizens. Sometimes translated as "comrade" in English, but this gives it a false Soviet resonance.

El vuelo

A Claudia Ashby

Hay que entrar en la onda,
desprenderse como vos, Claudia,
desde hace mucho tiempo.
Pero tu libertad de pájaro
no todos la poseemos
y en la nutrida bandada
algún lugar vamos tomando
—aunque sea en la retaguardia—
porque este vuelo de la revolución es infinito
y unos presienten que caerán en picada,
pero otros confiamos que en el
trayecto
nos crecerán las alas.

1980

Epístola

Ahora envío cartas a la madre
con esas palabras que puente y
abismo nos unen y desunen.

1979

Flight

To Claudia Ashby[*]

We have to get in sync,
break away like you did, Claudia,
long ago.
But your bird-like freedom
we don't all possess,
and in the large flock
we're taking a place
—even if only rearguard—,
because this flight of the revolution is infinite,
and some foresee they will plummet,
but others trust that,
along the way,
we will sprout wings.

1980

[Included in *Flame in the Wind*]

Epistle[†]

Now, I send letters to my mother
with words that, bridge and
abyss, unite and divide us.

1979

[Included in *Flame in the Wind*]

---

[*] Claudia Ashby: Cultural activist with a hippie lifestyle; friend to Meneses and other poets.

[†] Context: Meneses's mother, sisters, and other relatives, almost her entire immediate family, left Nicaragua and moved to the United States just before or after the triumph of the Sandinista Revolution in 1979 (see her comments in Chapters I and II).

A los técnicos

Yo les pediría que ajustaran
sus máquinas IBM,
sus sistemas Fortran IV
y sus computadoras
a la medida de nuestro pueblo.

Que las rectas intenciones
de rédito y los excedentes
incluyeran en sus aceradas y exactas cifras
los mls. cúbicos del sudor de nuestros trabajadores.

Que la libertad fuera medida
con los parámetros del hambre crónica
y no con las vacaciones anuales programadas.

1980

La tierra recobrada

Esta es la tierra recobrada
donde ahora entonamos nuevos cantos.
Me despierta una lluvia nocturna
que habla de renovaciones,
de la nueva hierba que crece
verde, dándole fondo de esperanza
a cada gota que cae.

Esta es la nueva canción
que he querido que entonemos juntos.

Raudo es el vuelo, sí,
y enterrar la muerte
ha sido rescatar la vida
darle su nuevo colorido.

1980

To the Technical Experts

I would ask that you adapt
your IBM machines,
your Fortran IV systems
and your computers
to the measure of our people.

That the righteous intentions
of interest and profits
include in their steeled, exact calculations
the cubic milliliters of our workers' sweat.

That freedom be measured
in parameters of chronic hunger
and not scheduled annual leave.

1980

Land Recovered*

This is the land recovered,
where we now begin to sing new songs.
A night rain awakens me
speaks of renewals,
of the new grass that grows
green, giving space for hope
with each drop that falls.

This is the new song
I wanted us to sing together.

Swift is the flight, yes,
and burying death
has meant rescuing life,
giving it new color.

1980

---

* Zoë Anglesey's quite different translation titled "The Earth Recovered" appears in her wonderful anthology of Central American poetry for peace by women authors, *Ixok Amar·Go.*]

La Primera Dama

No supo tentar al fauno.
Extranjera a su propio pueblo,
con criterio de inversionista en "países en bruto"
y socialmente motivada como un filantrópico turista.

Disfrutó de las tácticas maneras tuyas
para servir el "whisky on the rocks"
y el análisis freudiano de sus domésticos malestares.

Te envió oportunas colonias "for men"
y anotó cuidadosamente los cumpleaños de tus hijitas
en primoroso libro de "my favorite birthdays".

Me pregunto: ¿Aún se interesa por tu destino
desde su confortable exilio?

1980

First Lady[*]

She knew not how to tempt the faun.
Foreign to her own people,
with the criteria of an investor in "gross countries"
and socially motivated like a philanthropic tourist.

She enjoyed those tactical ways of yours
to serve whiskey on the rocks and
your Freudian analysis of her domestic malaise.

She sent you timely bottles of cologne "for men"
and carefully noted your daughters' birthdays
in her neat book of My Favorite Birthdays.

I ask myself, does she still wonder about your fate
from her comfortable exile?

1980

---

[*] First Lady: Esperanza "Hope" Portocarrero de Somoza, wife of General Anastasio Somoza Debayle, overthrown by the Sandinista National Liberation Front in 1979. "Doña Hope," as she was called, went with her family into exile in Miami (see comments on this poem in Chapter II).

Diciembre 7

Aquí me atrapa la solitaria insurrección del poeta.
Domingo siete asonado
por cohetes, bombas y triquitracas,
la recámara y su fondo de bolero radial.

Te volvés la muchacha de Cartagena
un rato, porque halaga ser llamada
solamente por sí misma.

Recogés el canto, el sueño pleno,
lo imaginado y concretado
en esta noche asonada,
en plena revolución de 80,
revolucionándote toda por dentro,
pariendo esa otra mujer
que ama y teme su nueva libertad.

1980

December 7th [*]

Here, the poet's solitary insurrection[†] overtakes me.
Sunday the seventh, shaken
by rockets, bombs and firecrackers,
the bedroom and its radio-ballad background.

You become the girl from Cartagena[‡]
for a while, because it's flattering
to be called simply as yourself.

You pick up the song, the full dream,
imagined and made concrete
on this loud night,
in full revolution of '80
revolutionizing your whole self,
birthing that other woman
who loves and fears her new freedom.

1980

[Included in *Flame in the Wind*]
[Translation by Alba Fabiola Aragón]

---

[*] December 7: The eve of the Day of the Immaculate Conception, occasion for fireworks and a religious procession. Margaret Randall describes the celebration of the "Purísima," the Most Pure, as: "the celebration of the Virgin Mary that takes place from November 30 through December 8. It is a popular tradition in Nicaragua, where families and institutions construct elaborate altars in honor of the Virgin, often outside or in the doorways of homes. People circulate, singing special songs, and the hosts offer fruit, pieces of sugarcane, and other sweets. After the Sandinistas came to power, some altars began to incorporate a revolutionary theme; the Virgin became symbolic of freedom and solidarity" (*Sandino's Daughters Revisited* 145 n. 2).

[†] "solitary insurrection": Allusion to the title of a collection by Postvanguard poet Carlos Martínez Rivas (1924-1998), who rebelled against the bourgeois spirit (see References).

[‡] "You become the girl from Cartagena": An intertextual reference to a poem by Carlos Martínez Rivas about a girl from Cartagena who was his muse, according to Meneses.

Advertencia

Sólo te diré
que manos con manos
edifican la esperanza
y que a tu escepticismo
antepongo mi sueño
con la certeza que lo vence.

1981

Compañera

Sacudís con firmeza las cadenas
y su atronadora caída
no te estremece.
Vas al encuentro
de tu destino infinito de persona.
Hacés propio tu nombre
y lo sembrás como bandera
en territorio liberado.
Ya nada te detiene.
Ya vos misma reconocés
tu propio paso.
Dueña de tu camino.
Consciente de la porción de historia
que te corresponde, compañera.

1981

Notice

I will only tell you
hands with hands
build hope,
and against your skepticism
I place my dream,
certain it will prevail.

1981

Compañera[*]

You firmly shake off the chains
and their thundering fall
leaves you undefeated.
You set out to meet
your infinite destiny as a person.
Making your name your own
and planting it like a flag
in liberated territory.
Nothing stops you now.
Now, you recognize
your own way.
Owning your path.
Aware of the portion of history
that belongs to you, compañera.

1981

[Included in *Flame in the Wind*]
[Translation by Alba Fabiola Aragón. Marc Zimmerman has a version in his *Nicaragua in Reconstruction and at War*.]

---

* *compañera*, female form of *compañero*: Does not have a good equivalent in English. It was used in Cuba after the triumph of the Revolution and among Sandinista supporters to signal equality, democratic treatment, and respect among fellow citizens. Sometimes translated as "comrade" in English, but this gives it a false Soviet resonance.

Nota para Ángela

En la tarde larga e ineludible
del domingo, te escribo.
Quiero pensar que gastás estas horas
revisando telex o monitoreando,
a la expectativa de cada palabra
que acecha a nuestra Revolución.
O que has tenido unas horas disponibles
y has buscado apartamento
para regresar por tus hijos.

En el tiempo de encontrarte con vos misma
te deseo que tengas las fuerzas que compartimos
cuando decidimos, cada una en su tiempo, ser
no la mujer de Lot, atada a su pasado,
sino dejar todo lo que no pudo acompañarnos
y seguir con dolor y amor
sobre el camino de la historia.

1980

Note for Angela*

On this unavoidable long Sunday afternoon,
I write to you.
I'd like to think that you're spending these hours
reading telexes or monitoring
each and every word that
threatens our Revolution.
Or, maybe you had some hours
and found an apartment so you could
come back for your children.

When you find time for yourself
I hope you have the strength that we shared
when we decided, each on her own, not to be
Lot's wife†, tied to her past,
but to leave behind all that could not go with us
and continue with pain and love
on the road of history.‡

1980

[Included in *Flame in the Wind*]
[Marc Zimmerman's rendition is in his *Nicaragua in Reconstruction and at War*.]

---

* Ángela Saballos: Friend of Meneses from adolescence. In 1980 she held a Sandinista diplomatic post in the United Status.
† Lot's wife: Biblical figure (Genesis 19.26) who, while escaping the destruction of the city of Sodom, ignored God's warning, looked backwards, and was turned into a pillar of salt.
‡ (Comment by Meneses, May 2005: "And the personal insurrection continues!")

Pedro: Ahora he estado recordando...

Pedro: Ahora he estado recordando cuando conversamos hace años en la Librería de la Universidad. Me dijiste que eras obrero, miembro de la directiva del Partido, que tenías deseos de mejorar tus escritos y yo te regalé un Curso de Redacción de Vivaldi.

Varios días después regresaste para entregarme un libro dentro de una bolsa de papel y me dijiste: —Escriba como Mayakovski. Vano intento, no he podido prestarle su voz. Yo que he escalado tanto las palabras, me quedé sin ellas, hoy 1ro. de Mayo, cuando hubiese querido escribir un homenaje, pensando sobre todo en vos, Pedro.

1982

Hija

Hoy me duele la historia de cada objeto.
Tu ropa de adolescente
colgada con displicencia.
Tu corazón dividido.
El vacío de tu maleta verde de tortuguitas.
Tus confidencias y dudas.
Nuestro pequeño puente de palabras yendo y viniendo.
Mi amor de pájara
enseñándote a volar,
mostrándote el horizonte
y el reto infinito de ser.

1982

Pedro: Just Now, I Have Been Remembering…

Pedro: Just now, I have been remembering when we talked years ago at the University Bookstore. You told me you were a worker, a member of the Party Directorate and wanted to improve your writings, and as a gift I gave you Vivaldi's Writing Course.

Several days later you returned with a book for me in a paper bag and said, "Write like Mayakovsky."* Vain attempt; I have been unable to assume his voice. I who so often let words flow, found myself without them today, the first of May, when I wanted to write a homage, thinking mainly of you, Pedro.

1982

Daughter

Today the history of every object hurts me.
Your teenage clothing
hung with indifference.
Your divided heart.
The emptiness of your green little turtle bag.
Your confidences and doubts.
Our small bridge of words going and coming.
My love like a mother bird's
teaching you to fly,
showing you the horizon
and the infinite challenge of being.

1982

[Included in *Flame in the Wind*]

---

* Mayakovsky, Vladimir (Georgia 1893-Moscow 1930): Soviet futurist poet and dramatist who praised the Russian Revolution of 1917 but satirized the new regime. Also mentioned by Meneses in the poem "Inquiries" in *All is the Same and Different* and in the uncollected essay, "Heart in the Open."

Última postal a mi padre, General Meneses

Debiste haber cumplido años hoy
y ya no estás, para tu bien.
Guardo tus palabras
y tu postrera ansiedad por mi destino,
porque la historia no te permitió
vislumbrar este momento,
muchos menos comprenderlo.
El juicio ya fue dado.
Te cuento que conservo para mí sola
tu amor generoso.
Tu mano en la cuchara
dándole el último desayuno al nieto,
haciendo más ligera
la pesada atmósfera de la despedida.
Cada uno en su lado,
como dos caballeros antiguos y nobles
abrazándose, antes del duelo final, fatal.

1980

Last Message* to My Father, General Meneses

You would have been a year older today
but now you're gone, better for you.†
I remember your words
and your parting anxiety about my future,
for history did not allow you to
glimpse this moment,
much less understand it.
Judgment has been made.‡
I'll tell you I keep for myself alone
your generous love.
Your hand on the spoon
giving the last breakfast to your grandson,
lightening the heavy atmosphere of farewell.
Each on our chosen side,
like two ancient noble knights
embracing each other before the final, deadly duel.

1980§

[Included in *Flame in the Wind*]
[Margaret Randall's version is in her *Sandino's Daughters Revisited*. The note to Amanda Hopkinson's translation in *Lovers and Comrades* contains unfortunate errors regarding the circumstances of General Meneses's death.

---

* "Last Message": Spanish American poetry has a tradition of using "postal" in the title of brief poems. In other translations into English, the title of this poem is "Last Postcard....," which is a literal version of the Spanish word. In conversations with the poet, however, it became clear that "message" was more in keeping with her original intention.

† "better for you": According to the poet, "better" in the sense that he was not in jail awaiting trial for any actions as a National Guard officer, and after the assassination attempt against him in September 1978 in Guatemala, he died instead of surviving in a paralyzed state, which would have been difficult for the active man he was.

‡ "Judgment has been made": The triumph of the Revolution meant death for those judged to be murderers.

§ This is one of the best known poems by Meneses, written on December 6, 1980 (see her other comments on it in Chapter II).

V. Porque amor no es aureola

Y porque amor no es aureola
ni cándida moraleja...
—Mario Benedetti

La propia insurrección

Resistirme a ser reducida
por mínimos detalles al ojal,
al agigantamiento de los objetos perdidos
emergiendo de su ausencia
y armándose como invencibles fantasmas,
invadiendo la difícil paz en el hogar.

Luchar contra lo que no tiene rostro
ni pista capaz de detectar
su fatídico paso.

Desenmarañar la selvática interioridad
de ese otro, que ahora y siempre se transforma
y te juega a la zancadilla
y te pretende —perrito cirquero— desconcertar
cuando te desvía el aro en llamas
de la prueba fatal.

1979

V. Because Love is Not a Halo

And because love is not a halo
or candid moral lesson...
     —Mario Benedetti*

Private Insurrection

Resisting my being reduced
by minute details to a buttonhole,
to the exaggeration of lost objects
emerging from their absence
and evolving like invincible ghosts
invading the strained peace of our home.

Fighting against what lacks a face
or trace to detect
its ominous step.

Unraveling the wild interior
of that other, who now and forever changes
and trips you up
and tries to trick you, little circus dog,
when he shifts the flaming hoop
of the fatal act.

1979

[Included in *Flame in the Wind*]

---

* Mario Benedetti (Uruguay 1920-2009): Poet, essayist, short story writer, novelist, and playwright.

Inmersa en las multitudes

Inmersa en las multitudes
en esos brazos-abrazos compartidos
de agrietadas epidermis
que trasladan tu tersura
a la otra orilla de la vida,
a esa mitad de noche de los que van
        recuperando amaneceres.

Allí donde muy a pesar tuyo
te soy cada vez más cercana,
donde me creés compartida y casi
diluída allí me tenés plena.

Mujer capaz de abrasarte
con el fuego más certero y perenne.

Si te dejaras alcanzar
por la llama más frágil de mi mano
¡incendiaríamos la noche!

1980

Immersed in the Multitudes

Immersed in the multitudes am I,
in those shared arms and embraces
of cracked skins
that shift your smoothness
to the other shore of life,
to the half night of those
      recovering the dawn.

There, where much to your sorrow,
I am ever closer to you,
where you find me shared and almost
diluted, there you have me most fully.

Woman able to inflame you
with the surest and most everlasting fire.

If you allowed yourself to be touched
by the slightest flame of my hand,
we would set the night afire!

1980

A fin de cuentas

No diré que fuí
tu juguete de turno,
la pieza de ajedrez,
la justificación a tiempo.

La presta actitud de recogerte
en la caída de bruces.
La prudente advertencia
a la orilla del abismo,
la paterna advertencia desechada:

"lo volcánico, como se enciende
se apaga".

No volveré a ver atrás
en el fatal designio de Lot.

Recogeré las cenizas, prueba palpable
de la autenticidad de mi fuego:
será abono, esperanza, espiga dorada
en y para mejores campos.

1980

All in All

I'll not say I was
your next plaything,
a chess piece,
a timely justification.

Ready and willing to catch you
in your headlong fall.
The prudent warning
at the edge of the abyss,
paternal warning discarded:

"The volcanic, as it ignites,
so does it die."

I'll not look back again
as in the fatal design for Lot*.

I shall gather the ashes, tangible proof
of the authenticity of my fire:
it will be humus, hope, golden shaft of grain,
in and for better fields.

1980

[Included in *Flame in the Wind*.]

---

* Lot: Biblical figure who fled with his family from the destruction of Sodom. His wife disobeyed God's warning to not look back and was turned into a pillar of salt (Genesis 19.26).

Encontrarte en el momento adecuado

Encontrarte en el momento adecuado
cuando el azar nos propicia
en el marco del juego de luces y de música
la circunstancia del "crimen perfecto".

Donde en tus brazos me sentí
como en puerto seguro
y tus palabras eran como olas
golpeando impetuosas y apremiantes
las costas de mis tímidos gestos.

Mi balbuceante, atemorizado
sentimiento de mujer entera sojuzgada,
renunciada a la ternura,
al ideal compartido en plenitud,
negada a ese mágico momento
donde lo que menos importa es la continuidad:
sólo el instante y lo que lo torne
trascendente.

Aún repaso mansamente cada
palabra tuya y tu gesto,
los entrecruzo, los labro como madera preciosa
y construyo una balsa.

1981

Finding You at the Right Time

Finding you at the right time,
when chance provides us
framed by the play of lights and music
circumstances for the "perfect crime."

Where in your arms I found myself
as in a safe port,
and your words were like waves
breaking swift and urgent against
the coastlines of my timid gestures.

My stammering, frightened
sentiment as a woman wholely subjugated,
renounced to tenderness,
to the ideal fully shared,
given to that magical moment
where nothing means less than continuity,
only the instant and what can turn it
transcendent.

I still calmly recall
your every word and gesture,
mix them, carve them like precious wood
and build a raft.

1981

He ido creciendo

He ido creciendo
hasta tu encuentro.

Midiéndome en el tiempo
donde tu cautela me acerca.

Donde mi fuego próximo y temerario
preparó el incendio de la noche.
La hoguera capaz de alumbrar
días postreros.

El gozo de apartar todo atisbo
de ceniza
donde aún en la distancia
guardemos el calor.

1981

I Have Been Growing

I have been growing
toward your encounter.

Measuring myself in the time
where your caution nears me.

Where my fire, close and bold,
prepared the night conflagration.
The bonfire capable of lighting
later days.

Joy at eluding any sign
of ash
where even at a distance
we'll retain the warmth.

1981

Canción de amor para vos

       I
Ahora en la distancia,
quiero hacerte llegar palabras nuevas
recién estrenadas para vos
en quien todo ha sido renovado.
Quiero decirte que ya estabas en mí
antes de tu llegada,
que tus manos y pecho no me han
sido extraños caminos,
que tu voz es campana
para la que soy toda eco.

      II
¿Qué te diré, vasija de hermoso barro moldeado,
manos largas para dibujarme en el cuerpo
sueños infinitos,
voz llamándome desde siempre?

1982

Las palabras nos precedieron

El río Neva bajo el puente urbano.
La llama guardada que veríamos arder
presentida en un país lejano
—Avenida Nevsky de Leningrado—
en el brazo de la mongola en su rubio,
las manos del azerbaiyano y su moscovita
(descifrado el poema, como el
enigma de nuestro encuentro),
el incendio del trópico
en plena noche blanca de San Petersburgo
deslumbrando con su fuego
al "espectador perpetuo,
al indeseado solitario",
al poeta en su soledad esperando algo.

1982

Love Song for You

I

Now, at a distance,
I want to send you new words
just debuted for you,
in whom everything is renewed.
I want to tell you you were already in me
before you arrived,
your hands and chest not
unknown paths for me,
your voice a bell
for which I am pure echo.

II

What shall I say to you, vessel of beautiful molded clay,
long hands to draw upon my body
infinite dreams,
voice calling me since forever?

1982

Words Preceded Us

Neva River* under the city bridge.
The guarded flame we would see burning,
sensed before in a faraway country
—Nevsky Avenue in Leningrad—
in the arm of the Asian woman in her blond man's†
the Azerbaijan's hands and his Moscow lady
(the poem deciphered, like the
enigma of our meeting),
tropical burning‡
in the full white night of Saint Petersburg
blinding with its fire
the "perpetual spectator,§
the undesired solitary man,"
the poet in his solitude, waiting for something.

1982
[Included in *Flame in the Wind*]

---

* Neva River, Nevsky Avenue, Leningrad: References to the Russian port city Saint Petersburg, known from 1924 to 1991 as Leningrad.
† "in the arm of the Asian woman in her blond man's": Intertextual reference to poem by Roberto Fernández Retamar (1930), Cuban essayist and poet (see References).
‡ "tropical burning … Saint Petersburg": Intertextual reference to poem by Carlos Perezalonso (León, 1943), Nicaraguan poet.
§ "the 'perpetual spectator … solitary man'": Quotation of verses by Fernández Retamar.

Llama en el aire (1990)

I. Selección de poesías de *Llama guardada*

II. Selección de poesías de *El aire que me llama*

III. En el costado más frágil

Me acerco y me retiro:
¿quién, sino yo, hallar puedo
a la ausencia en los ojos
la presencia en lo lejos?
    —Sor Juana Inés de la Cruz

Flame in the Wind (1990)

I. Selected Poems from *Guarded Flame*

II. Selected Poems from *Air that Calls Me*

III. On the Side Most Fragile

I approach and I withdraw,
Who, if not I, can find
absence in the eyes
as presence in the distance?
—*Sor Juana Inés de la Cruz**

---

* Sor Juana Inés de la Cruz (Juana Inés de Asbaje 1648-1695): Mexican nun, poet, and playwright; one of the greatest Baroque figures of Hispanic letters; considered the grandmother of contemporary feminism for her defense of women's education and freedom from limited roles as wives and mothers. These verses are from her "Dirge II: Which Explains A Witty Sense of Absence and Disdain."

Eva de siempre

Virgen es la dueña
de su propio cuerpo.
(Sabiduría antigua)
      o en otras palabras:
           El hombre propone
           y la mujer dispone
           (Refrán popular)

Sucede que en una de esas vueltas que da la vida
te convertís en don apetecido.

De pronto te empiezan a descubrir
una bella cabeza de Nefertiti egipcia o de Coré griega.

Gustan de tu sonrisa
o de tu forma de hablar
entre ponderada y profana.

Se trata también de que perciben
tu cuerpo y lo que en él destaca.

Sabido esto advertirás a tiempo
la intención de quien te acecha,
dueña y señora de tu libertad
que define el día y la hora, o nunca.

1987

Forever Eve[*]

The virgin is mistress
of her own body.
(Ancient wisdom)
           or in other words:
                  Man proposes,
                  woman disposes.
                  (Popular saying)

It happens that in one of life's twists and turns
you become a desired gift.

Suddenly, they begin to discover
your beautiful head of Egyptian Nefertiti[†] or Greek Cora[‡].

They love your smile
or the way you talk,
between profound and profane.

They begin to notice too
your body and all its wondrous parts.

Knowing this, you will perceive in time
your pursuer's intentions,
you, mistress of your freedom,
who decides the day and the time, or never.

1987

---

[*] In the selection from *Air that Calls Me* in the second section of *Flame in the Wind* this poem mistakenly appears after "All in All" and before "Words Preceded Us." It should have been included here, in the section of new poems.

[†] Nefertiti: Queen of Egypt in the 14th century B.C., known for her extraordinary beauty.

[‡] Cora: In Greek mythology, she was kidnapped by Hades/Pluto and wed to him, becoming a goddess and queen of the underworld. Allowed to return to the surface of the earth for part of the year, she is the personification of spring and symbol of virginity. Also know as Core, Kore, Persephone, and Proserpina.

Mi tía Adelina

Observo tu deslizar de sombra,
sutil presencia con que habitabas
la vieja casona.
El comienzo del día con un baño
en las frías madrugadas
cuando las campanas
de la iglesia de Molagüina
rebotaban su eco en nuestro sueño.
El inicio solemne del mismo ritual
ahora que ya nadie te espera,
más que las cartas de tu hermana
o la lectura del diario en el sofá
sumergiéndote artificiosamente
en un mundo que apenas ya transitás.
Es curioso, hemos unido soledades
y aún recuerdo cuando te dormías
mentón en pecho y manos en el regazo
sin terminar el cuento infantil.
Ahora cuando nuestros diálogos
se vuelven infinitos y sobre el mismo tema,
porque diariamente te sorprende
el tamaño y la edad de mis hijos
y me relatás como nuevo acontecimiento
la crónica de la muerte de tu hermano.
Sentarnos y compartir el silencio
o explicarte la revolución Sandinista
tu nivelación salarial de maestra jubilada
el primer año del triunfo,
por qué las mujeres hacemos oficialía,
el uniforme de las milicias
y tantas cosas nuevas
que intentarás comprender
antes de tener que abandonarlas.

-1982

My Aunt Adelina[*]

I watch you glide like a shadow
your subtle presence inhabiting
the old home.
Beginning your days with a bath
in the cold dawns
when the Molagüina[†] church bells
echoed in our sleep.
The solemn beginning of the same ritual
though no one awaits you now,
only your sister's letters
or reading the newspaper on the sofa
artfully submerging yourself in a world
you barely travel now.
It's strange, we've joined solitudes
and I still remember when you dozed off,
chin on chest, hands in lap,
without finishing our children's story.
Now, when our dialogues
are infinitely about the same topic,
because each day you're surprised
at the size and age of my children,
and you tell me as a new event
the story of your brother's death.
To sit and share the silence
or explain to you the Sandinista Revolution
your increased pension as a retired teacher[‡]
the first year of the triumph,
why we women work overnight,
the militia's uniform
and so many new things
you'll try to understand
before you have to leave them.

-1982

[Margaret Randall's version appears in *Risking a Somersault* (53-54)]

---

[*] Aunt Adelina: One of Vidaluz's great-aunts, a Valle girl (see References).

[†] Molagüina: Name of a colonial church in the city of Matagalpa.

[‡] "increased pension": Increase in teachers' pay authorized by the Sandinista government, for example, from a monthly 300 córdobas ($43) to 1,200 ($170).

Salomón

Salomón parece un árabe.
Tiene los ojos negros, la barba cerrada
y el color moreno aceitunado en su piel.
Cuando saluda, casi es una reverencia
a Alá y cuando me viene a reportar
que la puerta de alguna oficina quedó abierta
o el aire acondicionado encendido
adquiere una expresión de misterio y complicidad
como si me trajera un racimo de uvas
o un plato de maná robado en la tienda del vecino.

Salomón no tiene turbante, ni túnica, ni sandalias,
ni puñal, ni daga, pero dentro de su uniforme de CPF
podría ser un fedayín internacionalista,
siendo de León de Nicaragua.

1985

Salomón

Salomón looks Arabic
with his black eyes, thick beard,
and dark olive-colored skin.
When he greets you, it's almost a reverence
to Allah, and when he comes to report
that some office door was left open
or an air-conditioner running,
he acquires an expression of mystery and complicity,
as if bringing me a cluster of grapes
or a plate of manna stolen from a neighboring tent.

Salomón has no turban, or tunic, or sandals,
or sword, or dagger, but in his CPF* uniform,
he could be an internationalist Fedayin†,
though he's from León, Nicaragua.

1985

---

* CPF: Physical Protection Corps, general name given to watchmen or guards of public and private places.
† Fedayin: Palestianian guerrilla combatant(s). The term is sometimes used generically for any Islamic combatant.

Poeta o ángel terrible

A mis hermanos poetas

Tener un poeta en la casa
      es cosa terrible.
Todo lo pone de cabeza.
Saca la vida familiar a la calle,
le da sonido al silencio,
habla con la boca cerrada,
los detalles no le pasan inadvertidos
sino que los agiganta;
dialoga directo con los muertos
y con el inconsciente de los vivos,
desata el nudo de la realidad
tejida con imaginación.

Pone las estrellas de cielo raso
e ilumina la casa con la luna llena,
acelera el ritmo lento de los mayores
y aquieta a niños y adolescentes.

Cuando está ya se ha ido
Y cuando se va aún permanece.

Es terrible como los ángeles de Rilke
con todo y el olor de santidad
con que impregna lo que toca,
convencido de que lo carnal
      es sobrenatural.

1987

Poet, or Terrible Angel

To my fellow poets

Having a poet in the house
      is a terrible thing.
He stands everything on its head.
Puts family life out on the street,
turns silence into sound,
speaks with his mouth closed,
details don't go unnoticed,
rather he exaggerates them;
he speaks directly with the dead
and with the subconscious of the living,
unties the knot of reality
woven with imagination.

He sets stars in the open air
and lights the house with a full moon,
hurries the slow rhythm of elders
and calms children and adolescents.

When he's present, he's already gone
and when he leaves, he yet remains.

He is terrible like Rilke's* angels
with all this and the odor of sanctity
that pervades all he touches,
convinced that the carnal
      is supernatural.

1987

[*Lovers and Comrades* has a significantly different translation, "Poet or Avenging Angel".]

---

* Rilke, Rainer María (1875-1926): Poet born in Prague (then, Austria), who says in his *Duino Elegies* that angels are terrible and terrifying (see References).

Si no es por un polvazal de los Barrios Orientales

A Hans Gutiérrez

Si no es por un polvazal de los Barrios Orientales
no caigo en la increíble realidad de tu muerte.

¿Qué hiciste en tus últimos instantes?
¿Te aferraste a los brazos del asiento
buscando acaso la SALIDA DE EMERGENCIA?
¿De qué compañero, de qué mano te agarraste?
¿Perdiste el sentido cuando todo se viró
o se vino a pique vertiginosamente?

Quizá la espiral de polvo es tu respuesta
en el tremendo silencio del mediodía.

1985

If Not for A Dust Whirl in the Eastern Neighborhoods

*To Hans Gutiérrez**

If not for a dust whirl in the Eastern Neighborhoods
I could not accept the incredible reality of your death.

What did you do in your last moments?
Did you latch onto the arms of the seat,
searching maybe for the EMERGENCY EXIT?
What companion, what hand did you grasp?
Did you faint when everything began to spin
or went into a dizzying nosedive?

Perhaps the spiral of dust is your answer
in the grand silence of noon.

1985

---

* Hans Gutiérrez: Nicaraguan sociologist and revolutionary combatant; head of communications for the Sandinistas, later director of an aluminum factory; died in 1985 in a Cuban Airlines plane crash on his way back from a conference in Havana.

Niño de siempre

Al poeta José Coronel Urtecho

Pol-la d'ananta katanta paranta.
Abuelo juguetón, niño de siempre.

A través de vueltas y revueltas
en rápido tránsito por el río
nos hacés recuperar la infancia
jugar con la Petenera,
escondernos detrás del sillón, Don Chón.

Maestro insurrecto de bastón y boina
apuntalando con el índice
la afirmación o la advertencia.

Ojos de eterna curiosidad y asombro
escudriñando el mundo.
Enlazador de palabras como juegos de abalorios.
Mago sacando fila de vocablos del sombrero.
Hacedor de laberintos donde el lenguaje
termina mordiéndose la cola.
Por muchas vueltas y revueltas
llegamos con vos a tus ochenta años
que es regresar a los ocho, dieciocho
veintiocho, pero no más José,
porque no sé cuántos serán después.

1986

Always a Child

*To the poet José Coronel Urtecho**

Pol-la d'ananta katanta paranta.†
Playful grandfather, always a child.

By spinning and turning
in rapid transit on the river‡
you make us recover our childhood
play with Petenera,§
hide behind the armchair,⁋ Mistair Fair.

Insurrectional teacher with a cane and beret
index finger marking
an affirmation or warning.

Eyes of eternal curiosity and amazement
scrutinizing the world.
Stringer of words like sets of beads.
Magician pulling a streamer of words from a hat.
Maker of labyrinths where language
ends up biting its own tail.
By much spinning and turning
we arrive with you at your eighty years
which is to return to eight, eighteen,
twenty-eight, but no more, José,
for I know not how many there will be later.

1986

---

* José Coronel Urtecho (1906-1994): Cofounder with Luis Alberto Cabrales of the Vanguard Movement. One of the great Vanguard poets, known for his word play (see References).

† *Pol-la d'ananta katanta paranta* is the title in Greek, taken from epic poet Homer's *The Illiad* (7th century B.C.), of the first collection of poems and translations by José Coronel Urtecho, compiled by Jorge Eduardo Arellano and published in 1970. The title indicates that "no matter how many turns and spins we do, we always end up with things." The version used by Coronel was: "no matter how many risings and fallings, turns and spins they do, they find things." Steven White's *Modern Nicaraguan Poets* cites Richmond Lattimore's translation of *The Iliad*: "They went many ways, uphill, downhill, sidehill and slantwise" (147-48).

‡ "in rapid transit on the river": "Rapid Transit (to the U.S. Beat)" (1953) is José Coronel Urtecho's chronicle of his life in the United States, with reflections on Nicaraguan history and, especially, on the department of Río San Juan—San Juan River.

§ Petenera: Name of a dove, character in Coronel Urtecho's comedy *The Petenera*, considered an example of theater of the absurd.

⁋ "hide behind the armchair, Mistair Fair": Meneses says that her triply rhyming phrase, "sillón, Don Chón," was meant to reflect the type of word play and playful rhyming that were common among Nicaragua's Vanguard poets. Any words that rhyme with "armchair," then, could be substituted for "Fair": Care, Stair, etc., even if, like "Chón," it is not an actual dictionary word: Mistair Bair, Nair….

Mujer, años 50

> *A Irma Prego, Musa de C.M.R.*
> *(Ella me contó este poema)*

"Cuando ya no me quieras",
repite transfigurada la musa
los versos dedicados en los días
en que se empinaba a la vida
sobre los vacilantes tacones de adolescente.

> "Se pone pantalones con portañuela y se sienta
> a fumar en la cuneta, sólo le chifla el poeta
> y la desvergonzada corre a montarse en el coche".

Erigía como arco triunfal
los puñales del vecindario,
para marchar desafiante
hasta la costa del lago
donde izaba su libertad
como barrilete asido por un hilo
        infinito.

Pero la casaron con las yardas de tul
que había decidido su madre.
Cazada, como cervatillo en red de nylon,
con el que tuvo fachada de príncipe consorte
y nada cercano a vate en bicicleta.

La encasillaron, madona, en las formalidades
        de su rol,
hizo mil cosas sin querer
dejó de escandalizar a las vecinas
y se puso a decorar con primor
lo que hoy con dolorosa ironía identifica:
Una familia como foto de la revista *Life*,
de impecable producto de fábrica, nítidamente falsa.

1986

Woman, 1950s

To Irma Prego*, Muse to C.M.R†.
(She told me this poem)

"When you no longer love me,"
the transfigured muse repeats
verses dedicated in the days
when she stood up to life
on shaky adolescent high heels.

> "She wears pants with a fly and sits on the curb
> to smoke. The poet just whistles and
> the shameless hussy runs to jump in his car."

She built the neighbors' daggers
into a triumphal arch,
to march defiantly
to the lake's shoreline,
where she raised her freedom
like a kite tied to an infinite
        string.

But they married her off in yards of tulle
chosen by her mother.
Trapped, like a baby fawn in nylon netting,
with a man who had a prince consort façade
and nothing like a bard on a bicycle.

Madonna‡, they molded her to the formalities
        of her role,
she did a thousand things she never wanted to,
stopped scandalizing the neighbor ladies
and began elegantly decorating
what she identifies with painful irony today:
A family like a *Life* magazine photo,
an impeccable factory product, clearly false.

1986

---

* Irma Prego (Granada 1933-San José, Costa Rica 2000): Fiction writer whose works denounced machismo and its effects on women. She is considered "Muse of the Happy Years of the Generation of 1940," a group of poets that included Ernesto Cardenal, Carlos Martínez Rivas, and Ernesto Mejía Sánchez. Flaunting 1950s' restraints on women's behavior in public, Prego wore pants outside, smoked, and talked with men, thereby scandalizing the proper ladies. She married Costa Rican journalist Julio Suñol and lived in Costa Rica after 1956, though she later separated from him. She is the muse of the beautiful poem by Martínez Rivas, "She Who is Placed in the Tomb."

† C.M.R.: Carlos Martínez Rivas, one of the best-known poets in Nicaragua (see References). Irma Prego's first serious boyfriend.

‡ Madonna: Italian for "my lady," madame.

Mayaya la June Beer

Que el Poeta Macfield haga retumbar
los ancestrales tambores del Congo,
        Angola y Mozambique.

Y Rigby con su trombón deshipotecado
para siempre, como Nicaragua,
toque una serenata de soul
para esta reina de bata larga y floreada
que nos dejó con una conversación inconclusa.

En Mayo estuvimos con lo que une y reúne
Maya ya la sin ki:

        Con los viejitos del Zinica
        y los niños de la Biblioteca Raití,
        a los que ella hizo dibujar cocoteros,
        casitas de tambo asomando los corredores al río,
        monos jugando a cazar mariposas de colores,
guiados por sus ojazos brillantes que nunca va a cerrar
porque se han quedado mirándonos desde sus paisajes
en la luna de Pointeen, Beholden y Old Bank.

Sin Saima si ma lo
Cantá Simón, cantá mi amor
para esta reina, June Beer.
Desde la large noche del Walagallo
te hemos estado esperando para cantar con vos:
Maya ya la June Beer, Maya ya oh!

-1986

Mayaya* June Beer

Let Poet Macfield† beat thunder from
ancestral drums of the Congo,
        Angola and Mozambique.

And may Rigby,‡ with his trombone out of hock
for good, like Nicaragua,
play a soul serenade
for this queen in the long, flowery robe
who left us an unfinished conversation.

In May, we were there with what unites and reunites
"Maya ya la sin ki": §

    With old folks from Zinica¶
    and children at Raití** library
    taught by her to draw coconut palms,
    little shacks stretching walkways to the river,
    monkeys playing to catch bright butterflies,
guided by great shining eyes that she will never close
as they watch us still from moonlit landscapes
in Pointeen,†† Beholden and Old Bank.

"Sin saima si ma lo,"‡‡
Sing, Simon, sing my love
for this queen, June Beer.
Since the long night of the Walagallo§§
we've been waiting to sing with you:
"Maya ya la June Beer, Maya ya oh!"

---

* Mayaya: May Pole festival called in Spanish "Maya ya," "Mayaya," and "Mayo ya."
June Beer (Bluefields 1935-1986): Afro-Nicaraguan poet and painter, promoter of culture and Sandinism in the Atlantic Coast area.

† Macfield, David (Rama City 1938): Afro-Nicaraguan poet, composer, and musician, author of three poetry collections, university professor, Sandinista government ambassador to several African countries.

‡ Rigby, Carlos (Pearl Lagoon 1945): Afro-Nicaraguan poet, trombonist, and radio host who introduced May Pole festivities in Managua.

§ "Maya ya la sin ki": Song that begins May Pole festival activities. One explanation of its origin is the English verse, "Mary lost the key." Meneses talks about her use of this verse in Chapter II.

¶ Zinica: Town and river in the North Atlantic region.

** Raití: Town in the North Atlantic region.

†† Pointeen, Beholden, Old Bank: Neighborhoods in Bluefields, the oldest city on Nicaragua's Atlantic Coast, an area explored by the English and Dutch, populated by indigenous and African-descended peoples, including Garífunas and Jamaicans.

‡‡ "Sin Saima si ma lo": Some scholars of Afro-Caribbean Nicaragua believe that this verse derives from the English, "Sing, Simon, sing my love." Meneses talks about her use of it in Chapter II.

§§ Walagallo: Dance of the rooster; a three-day ritual with prayer, dance, drumming, and food practiced by the Garífunas for the recovery of a sick person or his "good death" and the salvation of his soul.

Evocaciones de Mayo ya/86

I

Brooks hace el amor en cayucos
entre redada y redada de ostiones frescos
mientras la casa de tambo, los remos sueltos
y la luna de Mayo, tiemblan en el espejo de
 agua en Old Bank.

II

Collar de coral negro
o pulsera y anillo de filigrana o carey
para unas manos suaves como las uvas.

1987

Evocations of May Day/86

I

Brooks* makes love in dugout canoes
between one haul and another of fresh oysters,
while the wooden shack, loose oars
and May moon shimmer in the water mirror
    at Old Bank†.

II

Necklace of black coral
or bracelet and ring of filigree or tortoiseshell
for hands soft as grapes.

1987

---

* Brooks Saldaña, Ronald (Bluefields 1943-2001): Afro-Nicaraguan poet, professor, translator, historian of the Atlantic Coast, and consummate fisherman; political prisoner under Somoza.
†Old Bank: A neighborhood in the old Atlantic Coast city of Bluefields, Nicaragua.

Mirando su fotografía

A Esther María, mi primera nieta.

Niña de mis ojos, fervor
de carne más querido, más
antiguo, más alto que su
misma inocencia.
                —Ernesto Mejía Sánchez

Más alto que su misma inocencia
rosa húmeda en mi tallo familiar.
Más cercano al rasgo, la expresión
de mi propio hijo cuando él a su vez
fue la bienvenida criatura.
El sello materno, del hoyuelo en la barbilla.

Ateridas manos empuñadas
al contacto del agua en la bañera.
(Nada que sustituya la tibia
cavidad acuosa original).
Para siempre enfrentada
la órbita atónita al orbe.

Mirando su fotografía, mar de por medio
donde he escuchado misteriosamente
lejanos graznidos de ánades,
también le he puesto oído a mi sangre
palpitando con fuerza en ese pequeño caracol
renovándose en el inexorable ciclo de la vida.

1987

Looking at Her Photograph

For Esther María, my first granddaughter*

Apple of my eye, fervor
of flesh more beloved, more
ancient, more lofty than her
own innocence.
           —Ernesto Mejía Sánchez†

More lofty than her own innocence
dewy rose on my family stem.
More like the features, the expression
of my own son when he at his turn
was the welcomed newborn.
Maternal stamp, the dimple in the chin.

Freezing fists clenched
on contact with the bath water.
(Nothing can replace the original
warm, aqueous cavity.)
Forever facing the world,
her surprised orbit fixed.

Looking at her photograph, an ocean apart,
where I mysteriously heard
distant calls of mallards,
I also pressed my ear to my own blood
beating inside this tiny sea shell
renewing itself in the inexorable cycle of life.

1987

---
* Esther María: United States-born daughter of the poet's older son, Carlos Rodolfo Icaza Meneses.
† Ernesto Mejía Sánchez (1923-1985): Great Nicaraguan Vanguard poet (see References).

Evasión

A un lado el informe
—Proyecto para bajar costos
en economía de guerra—
en rápido tránsito me sumerjo y escapo,
recurro al paliativo del Canto a mí mismo
o acompaño en una banca
del Bosque de Chapultepec al Poeta
viviendo su soledad compartida
con la camella semejante a la zancona muchacha.
Me atrapan al fin los ruidos de la noche:
la sirena de la película de policías
en el canal de TV, el radio del vecino insomne,
uno que otro traquetear del zinc
enfriándose con el sereno,
el silbido ocasional de los celadores
y los ladridos de los perros contestándoles.
Para remate, vos no estás.

1987

Evasion

On one side, the report,
"Project to Lower Costs in the
War Economy,"
in rapid transit*, I submerge and escape,
resort to the sedative of "Song of Myself"†
or accompany the Poet on a bench at
Chapultepec Zoo,‡
living his solitude shared
with the camel similar to the long-legged girl.
Night noises finally trap me:
police sirens from the film on TV,
the sleepless neighbor's radio,
one and another crack of the zinc roof
cooling under the night dew,
the occasional whistles of watchmen
and responding barks of dogs.
All that, and you are not here.

1987

---

* "in rapid transit": Intertextuality with "Rapid Transit (to the U.S. Beat)" by José Coronel Urtecho, a chronicle of his experiences in the U.S. and reflections on the history of Nicaragua, published in 1953 (see Coronel Urtecho in References).
† "Song of Myself": Title of a poem published in *Leaves of Grass* (1855) by U.S. poet Walt Whitman (West Hills, NY 1819-Camden, NJ 1892).
‡ "or accompany the Poet on a bench at / Chapultepec Zoo": Allusion to Carlos Martínez Rivas and his 1963 poetic narrative *A Flame in Chapultepec Wood* (see References).

Evocación de Ernesto

Al poeta Ernesto Gutiérrez

Fácil es adivinar tu deseo de haber sido
evocación viviente de Quintus Horatius Flaccus,
de quien anotaste, riguroso profesor,
datos biográficos y académicos:

>Nacido en Venusia en 65,
>estudiante en Roma
>en la escuela de Orbilio,
>perfecciona su educación ateniense
>¡Ah, los *Temas de la Hélade*!
>Allí escribe sus primeros versos en griego
>y toma las armas de tribuno militar
>en el ejército de Bruto
>como te armaste de pluma detrás de *Barricada*
>siendo consecuente con su *Epístola a los Pisones*,
>el *ars poética* de armonizar lo útil con el deleite,
>que es lo mismo que escribir con Rugama:
>"los poetas también socan".

Cuarto de los Ernestos, el Flaco
y el segundo en marchar hacia el Olimpo,
donde yaces sobre el cerro de Esquilino
a la par del poderoso Mecenas
en el incomparable atardecer
sobre el Lago de Nicaragua.

abril 1988

Evocation of Ernesto

To the poet Ernesto Gutiérrez[*]

Easy it is to sense your desire to be
a living evocation of Quintus Horatius Flaccus[†],
whose biographical and academic data
you imparted, meticulous professor:

> Born in Venusia in 65,
> student in Rome at
> Orbilius's school,
> he perfects his education in Athens.
> Oh, *Themes from the Helade*![‡]
> There, he writes his first verses in Greek
> takes up arms as a military tribune
> in the army of Brutus,
> like you armed yourself with a pen for *Barricada*,[§]
> consistent with his *Letter to the Pisos*,[¶]
> the *ars poetica* to harmonize utility and pleasure,
> the same as writing with Rugama,[**]
> "poets can get down too."

Fourth of the Ernests,[††] the Skinny One
and the second to march toward Olympus,[‡‡]
where you lie on Esquiline Hill[§§]
alongside powerful Maecenas[¶¶]
in the incomparable sunset
over Lake Nicaragua.

April 1988

---

[*] Ernesto Gutiérrez (Granada 1929-Havana 1988): Poet, essayist, translator, engineer, director of the University Press and the journal *Cuadernos Universitarios* of the National Autonomous University of Nicaragua in León; Sandinista ambassador to Brasil and UNESCO in Paris.
[†] Quintus Horatius Flaccus: Horace (65-8 B.C.): Italian lyrical poet, model of the classic virtues of balance and moderation, propagated especially in his *Letter to the Pisos*. He penned the phrase "aurea mediocritas" — "the golden mean of moderation," which Meneses uses in her last poem in this collection, "Wailing Wall," as "—golden mean smashed to bits." Another of Horace's famous phrases is "carpe diem"— "seize the day" or "gather ye rosebuds while ye may."
[‡] *Themes from the Helade*: Collection of poems (1973) by Ernesto Gutiérrez. "The Helade" was another name for Ancient Greece.
[§] *Barricada*: Official newspaper of the Sandinista National Liberation Front.
[¶] *Letter to the Pisos*, also known as Horace's *Ars Poetica*, or theory of art, recommends unity in literary works, the imitation of Greek models, and mixture of utility and pleasure in order to "sweeten the medicine," "edify and entertain," for "pleasure and profit"; it represents the unity of ethics and aesthetics.
[**] Rugama, Leonel (1949-1970): Poet and Sandinista fighter who died in combat (see References).
[††] "Fourth of the Ernests": Meneses adds Ernesto Gutiérrez's name to the traditionally recognized "Three Ernests," teachers to her generation of poets: Ernesto Mejías Sánchez (1923-1985), Carlos Ernesto Martínez Rivas (1924-1998), and Ernesto Cardenal (1925).
[‡‡] Olympus: A mountain in Greece considered the home of the gods.
[§§] Esquiline Hill: The highest of the seven hills on which Rome was built. In its cemetery Horace and Maecenas are buried.
[¶¶] Maecenas, Gaius: Patron to Horace and other Ancient Roman poets.

Esa mujer

A Rosario Castellanos

Esa mujer que ha desviado la mirada
del pájaro en la ventana
para atender el doblez uniforme
de sábanas y manteles
y levantar impecables hileras
de ropa planchada guardada con naftalina,
tuvo el sobresalto de inexperta primeriza
verificando el peso de la criatura
antes y después de amamantarla
dudosa de la fuerza de sus pequeños pechos
de su frágil humanidad expuesta al parto
cuando aún no se había terminado de parir a sí misma.

La madre huérfana de prole.
La incendiaria que dinamitó su casa
construida sobre arena
para edificar sobre roca firme.

La que supo dar brazos y manos extendidos
desde el fondo de los siglos
y no preguntó sino que confió.

Esa mujer que avanza iluminada
bajo el sol de su terca certidumbre
la agónica, la siempreviva,
la que muere y renace cada mañana
arrebatada en la cauda luminosa de un astro.

1989

That Woman

To Rosario Castellanos[*]

That woman who turned her glance
from the bird at the window
to attend the uniform folding
of sheets and tablecloths
and lift impeccable stacks
of ironed clothes stored in mothballs,
was frightened by her inexperience as a new mother,
verifying the weight of her infant
before and after nursing,
doubtful of the power of her small breasts,
of her fragile humanity exposed to childbirth
when she had not yet finished birthing herself.

The mother orphaned of offspring.[†]
The incendiary who dynamited her house
built on sand
to reconstruct on solid rock.

She who extended arms and hands
from the depths of the centuries,
and questioned not but trusted.

That woman who advances enlightened
under the sun of her obstinate certainty,
the suffering, the ever-alive,
who dies and is reborn each morning,
caught in the brilliant wake of a star.

1989

---

[*] Rosario Castellanos (1925-1974): Mexican writer (see References).
[†] "The mother orphaned of offspring": Allusion to a verse by Castellanos (see Meneses's comments on this poem in Chapters I and II).

Monet en el almanaque

La suerte echada en el tiempo
herradura en el calendario.
La mano impresionista en el mes de turno
trae el campo de amapolas
con sus corolas de adormidera.
Las siluetas azules podrían ser mujeres
con motetes en la cabeza
conversando en la planicie
y detrás acarreadoras, recolectoras
sosteniendo el saco y oteando en el horizonte
de montañas azuladas bajo el cielo gris.
Podría ser la aurora, prefiero pensar que es el atardecer.

Mayo/90

Monet* on the Calendar

Luck cast in time
horseshoe on the calendar.
This month's impressionist hand
brings a field of red flowers
with corollas of poppies.
The blue silhouettes could be women
with baskets on their heads
chatting in the clearing
and behind, women gatherers
carrying sacks and scanning the horizon
of azure mountains under a grey sky.
It could be dawn; I prefer to think it sunset.

May 1990

---

* Monet, Claude (Paris 1840-Giverny 1926): French Impressionist painter.

En el costado más frágil

A Cecilia

Fin del almuerzo protocolario
para llegar con alivio al postre.
La plática fluida, hasta elocuente
se tropieza con la sobremesa
—pastel de manzana—
y la rueda del tiempo gira vertiginosa
para hacer alto en el costado más frágil de mi niñez.

Imagino inertes tus poderosas manos de minero
fundidor de pesados lingotes de oro,
manos capaces de la mayor ternura:
quizás una de ellas te sirva
para hacer vagas señales
a la hija, a las hijas-sobrinas
asomándose expectantes a tu palidez
desde el borde de la cama de hospital.

      Good night sweetheart
      Good night honey

Recuerdo las películas de vaqueros,
Roy Rogers en la pantalla,
los chiflidos al cortarse la cinta,
los chiclets aventados en la luneta,
el triunfo del chavalo y the end.
El regreso a la casa en el jeep Willys trotón
y el pastel de manzana esperando.

Leslie N. Hoey, de ancestros irlandeses con hermano Bill en Peoria. Llegado en los años veinte de Estados Unidos a Matagalpa, Nicaragua, donde se casa con la señorita Virginia Valle y se convierte así en abuelo de nietos y sobrina-nietas como yo, de sus preferidas, quien lo evoca:

Amoroso padre mayor,
a quien ya se te comenzó a apagar el día,
a quien ya desde el fondo de la noche
otras voces queridas te llaman:

      Good night sweetheart, Good night honey.

1987

On the Side Most Fragile

To Cecilia

End of the formal luncheon,
finally arriving at dessert.
The smooth, even eloquent,
after-dinner conversation
stumbles at the final course
—apple pie—
and the dizzying wheel of time turns
to stop at the side most fragile of my childhood.

I imagine inert your powerful miner hands of a
smelter of heavy gold ingots,
hands capable of utmost tenderness;
perhaps one of them serves
to make vague gestures
to your daughter, your niece-daughters,
gazing anxiously on your pale face
from beside the hospital bed.

>   Good night, sweetheart
>   Good night, honey

I remember cowboy movies,
Roy Rogers on the screen,
loud whistles when the film broke,
bubble gum blowing in the balcony,
triumph of the good guy, and "The End."
Return home in the galloping Willys jeep
and apple pie waiting.

Leslie N. Hoey, of Irish ancestry, with his brother Bill in Peoria. Arrived from the United States, 1920's, in Matagalpa, Nicaragua, where he marries Miss Virginia Valle and becomes the grandfather of grandchildren and of grandnieces like myself, one of his favorites, who now evokes him:

Loving older father,
for whom the day now begins to darken,
and to whom from the night's depths
other beloved voices now call to you:

Good night, sweetheart, Good night, honey.

1987

IV. Con las mismas manos

Con las mismas manos de acariciarte estoy
construyendo una escuela.
—Roberto Fernández Retamar

Vigilia

Leo tus cartas en horas de oficialía
entre llamadas telefónicas y reportes
de entrada y salida.

El pueblo armado de Sandino
ha puesto la paz en pie de guerra.
Vos que en mí, decís
que volvés a vivir tu propia historia.

Inmersos en el pueblo
somos dos gotas de aguas juntas
en medio del océano
o una lengua de fuego
nuestras almas saliendo
por la ventana de una casa incendiada.

Convencidos desde el agua y desde el fuego,
desde la tierra para siempre recobrada
desde el amor indetenible,
desde siempre y para siempre
¡Que jamás pasarán!

1982

IV. With the Same Hands

With the same hands* that caress you
I am building a school.
　　　—Roberto Fernández Retamar

Night Duty

I read your letters on overnight duty
between phone calls and reports
on comings and goings.

Sandino's armed people†
have put peace on a war footing.
In me, you say
you relive your own history.

Immersed in the people,
we are two drops of water together
in the middle of the ocean
or a flicker of fire
our souls leaving
out the window of a burning house.

Convinced from the water and from the fire,
from the land forever recovered
from love unstoppable,
from always and for always, that
They shall never pass!‡

1982

[The poem in Spanish published by Zoë Anglesey in *Ixok Amar·Go* was apparently later revised for inclusion in Meneses's *Llama en el aire*. Nancy Esposito's translation there, "I Read Your Letters" (345), reflects that earlier version.]

---

* "With the Same Hands": Title poem in an anthology by Roberto Fernández Retamar (1930), Cuban poet, professor, and essayist (see References).

† "Sandino's armed people": The epigraph to "Scenes from Jalapa," later in this collection, quotes Sandino: "We are not soldiers. / We are the people, / We are armed citizens."

‡ "They shall never pass!": A revolutionary phrase used in several countries to signal the intention to defend a position to the death against an enemy's advance.

Te escribo ahora

Te escribo ahora pensando que
a la par del inevitable sarro que corroe
en el devenir cotidiano hay algo imperecedero.
Un trasfondo de costumbre,
de cálido atardecer que neutraliza
la inevitable nostalgia de anochecer sola.

Quiero creer que el amor es la suma
de amores compartidos,
más allá de nuestro pequeño mundo
colmado de ansiedades y de sueños.
El amor galáctico fundiendo
en su plateada luz energía positiva.
El lugar propicio para expandir
este sentimiento sin que destruya lo que toca
y más bien se agigante.
Donde se equilibre el universo.
Te invito y me invito
a habitar ese paraíso, a reposar en la estrella
donde el mismo amor está más allá de nosotros
innombrable, indefinible, siendo.

1982

I Write to You Now

I write to you now thinking that
alongside inevitable rust that corrodes,
in daily life exists something imperishable.
A backdrop of habit,
of a warm evening that neutralizes
the inevitable nostalgia of a night alone.

I want to believe that love is the summation
of shared loves,
beyond our small world
filled with anxieties and dreams.
Galactic love smelting
positive energy in its silvery light.
The proper place to expand
this feeling without destroying what it touches
and, rather, growing immense.
Where the universe is balanced.
I invite you and I invite myself
to inhabit that paradise, to recline on the star
where love itself is beyond us,
unnamable, indefinable, being.

1982

[The poem in Spanish published by Zoë Anglesey in *Ixok Amar·Go* was apparently later revised for inclusion in Meneses's *Llama en el aire*, and Nancy Esposito's untitled translation in *Ixok* reflects that earlier version.]

Recuento

> *Matamos lo que amamos.*
> —Rosario Castellanos

I

¿Con qué palabras, amor, voy a contestar tu carta?
Es un mes y han sido siglos
en los que he retornado a unos versos íngrimos
escritos en el corredor de la casa paterna.

Alba mañana de nupcias raramente
mezclándose el cortejo de la nave eclesial
con el desamparo del cordero
rumbo a la piedra de sacrificio.

El regreso a crepusculares habitaciones
donde sublimaba, mujer del siglo veinte,
el sometimiento:

Marta, la hacendosa
Raquel, la prudente
Sarah, la de vientre florecido en el ocaso.

Días y noches tejiendo y destejiendo el sueño.
—Y no era la esperanza de Penélope—
No era más que el inútil devenir.
Chispas acaso en el tiempo del desamor.

II

El sordo rumor del volcán
que un día emergió para lanzarlo todo,
el sereno recuento de lo destruido.
Trozos dispersos que reuní
para identificar las manos cálidas,
las miradas que trascendieran el horizonte,
el abrazo mortal que sellara para siempre
el encuentro fortuito.

—¿Cómo no salir maltrecha
y ofrecerte entre los despojos
un intacto corazón?

1983

Reckoning

> *We kill what we love.*
> *—Rosario Castellanos*[*]

I

With what words, love, shall I answer your letter?
It's been a month, and it's been centuries
when I returned to solitary verses
written in the halls of my father's house.

Pure white nuptial dawn strangely
mixing the church nave procession
with the helplessness of the lamb
on its way to the sacrificial stone.

The return to crepuscular rooms
where I sublimated, twentieth-century woman,
the submission:

> Martha, the industrious
> Rachel, the prudent
> Sarah, of the flowering womb at sunset.[†]

Days and nights weaving and unweaving the dream.
And it wasn't the hope of Penelope.[‡]
Nothing more than useless change.
Sparks, perhaps, in the time of disaffection.

II

The quiet murmur of the volcano[§]
that one day burst to spew everything,
the serene reckoning of what was destroyed.
Scattered bits that I gathered
to identify warm hands,
gazes that transcended the horizon,
the mortal embrace that forever sealed
the fortuitous encounter.

How could I not emerge battered
and offer you out of the rubble
a heart intact?

1983

---

[*] Rosario Castellanos (1925-1974): Mexican writer (see References). The epigraph is from her poem, "Destiny."

[†] "Martha...Rachel...Sarah": A reference to her 1967 poem, "When I Married" (see her comments on the earlier poem in Chapter II).

[‡] "the hope of Penelope": The hope that, like Penelope in Greek mythology, she could weave by day and unravel by night a cloth that symbolized her intention to remain faithful to her absent husband (see References).

[§] "The quiet murmur of the volcano / that one day burst to spew everything": Compare the verses in "All in All" from 1980: "The volcanic, as it ignites, / so does it die."

Sorprendido, feliz

Desde que bajo la luminaria de la esquina de los Robles
te dejé ir como bala trazadora
mi escueta declaración de amor
y vos superando segundos de desconcierto me besaste,
porque lo deseabas desde hacía tiempo como yo,
aún sin saber con la plena conciencia
que había llegado tu hora y mi momento, es que deduje
que todo es bíblico y marxista, pues si

>"Hay un tiempo para cada cosa
>y un momento para hacerla bajo el sol",
>es lo mismo que decir:
>"cuando las condiciones están dadas".

1984

Nuestro amigo Semionov

Nuestro amigo Semionov, el oso polar que piensa como pájaro
y que salía del ascensor del hotel
inaugurando el día con una sonrisa
cuando nos encontraba en el vestíbulo
mirándonos y conversando infinitamente
conocedor de nuestro secreto a voces
del tiempo que no dejamos escapar para decir que nos queremos,
en plenas jornadas anti imperialistas,
en los congresos de paz por nuestros pueblos,
de proclamas, de llamadas al cierre de filas con nuestra lucha;
un día nos dijo el oso: los invitaré a Krimea
y así don Quijote y Dulcinea deambularán como siempre
en su propio espacio, íngrimos en la multitud,
recorriendo y haciendo la historia cotidiana,
viviendo plenamente este sueño de locos,
        que no acabará jamás.

1984

Surprised, Happy[*]

Since that time under a corner streetlight in Los Robles[†] when
I sent you, like a tracer bullet,
my unadorned declaration of love,
and you, overcoming disconcerted seconds, kissed me,
because you had desired it for a time, like me,
even without knowing with full awareness
that your hour and my moment had arrived, that's when I deduced
that everything is Biblical and Marxist, for if:

> "To every thing there is a season,
> and a time to every purpose under the sun,"[‡]
> it's the same as saying:
> "When conditions are ready."

1984

Our Friend Semionov[§]

Our friend Semionov, polar bear that thinks like a bird
and emerged from the hotel elevator
inaugurating the day with a smile
when he met us in the lobby
watching us and talking endlessly,
knower of our open secret,
of the time we didn't waste in saying we love each other,
in the middle of anti-imperialist meetings,
peace conferences for our peoples,
proclamations, and calls to close ranks with our struggle;
one day the bear told us: I will invite you to Crimea,
so Don Quijote and Dulcinea[¶] can stroll as always
in their own space, alone in the multitude,
walking and making everyday history,
living fully this mad dream,
       that will never, ever end.

1984

---

[*] "Surprised, Happy": "Surprised, Happy, Worried" is the title of a 1972 poem by Cuban author Roberto Fernández Retamar (see References).
[†] Los Robles: A residential neighborhood in Managua.
[‡] "To every thing...": A version of the Biblical verse, Ecclesiastes 3.1.
[§] Semionov: Contemporary Russian writer.
[¶] Don Quijote and Dulcinea: The protagonist and the object of his love in the novel, *Don Quijote de la Mancha* (1605; 1615) by the Spaniard Miguel de Cervantes (Alcalá de Henares 1547-Madrid 1616).

Ciclo fatal

La cuenta se me vuelve regresiva,
dieciséis, quince, catorce… hasta llegar el día,
la hora cero, en que te diviso bajando del avión,
infinitos flash back como un relato de Proust,
repetidas escenas que no corrige ningún Director.

El montón de gente en fila avanzando
y la mirada expectante atravesando
como rayo láser la pecera,
haciendo camino para encontrarnos,
conteniendo la mutua intensidad en el saludo protocolario.
El borbotón de palabras que apenas dicen algo
cuando te abrazo con alegría y congoja
porque partirás y comenzaré a inventarte otra vez
agotando los detalles en la memoria.
Tratando de ignorar el tiempo que transcurre sin vos
hasta el próximo aviso de llegada
hasta que el ciclo fatal comienza su cuenta regresiva.

1984

Fatal Cycle

The count turns backwards on me,
sixteen, fifteen, fourteen… until the day arrives,
zero hour, when I spot you exiting the plane,
infinite flashbacks like a Proust story,
repeated scenes uncut by a director.

The lined-up crowd moving closer
and the expectant look crossing
the fishbowl like a laser beam,
making our way to meet,
containing our mutual intensity in the official greeting.
The torrent of words that barely say anything
when I embrace you with joy and grief
because you will leave and I'll start to invent you again
exhausting memory's details.
Trying to ignore time passing without you
until the next arrival notice
until the fatal cycle begins its backward count.

1984

Sueño submarino

Es tan breve el tiempo del que disponemos
que no he acabado de verte y ya se nos quedan
cosas por decirnos.

      Una vez quedó la ventana
hacia la avenida donde pasa la mulata
con su amor.

          Otra vez fue un balcón
hacia el mar, que se estrella contra el dique,
agitado por el viento de La Habana.
Al marcharte, no habías desaparecido,
sino que abrazados nos sumergimos
hasta tocar la quieta caracola,
desatando tormentas en el cielo submarino
cruzado por fugaces anguilas,
pero el trote de los caballos de mar y la ola
nos arrojó a la costa como náufragos somnolientos
hasta romper el sueño de esta mujer que sola,
extiende la sábana como quien iza velas
contra el filo del amanecer.

1985

Underwater Dream

The time we have is so brief
that I've just seen you and already things
have gone unsaid.

      Once it was the window
onto the avenue where the mulatto woman passes
with her love.

         Another time it was a balcony
on the sea, that crashes against the breakwater,
stirred by the Havana wind.
When you left, you hadn't disappeared,
and we submerged embracing
and touched the still conch,
unleashing storms in the underwater sky
crossed by fleeting eels,
but sea horses' trotting and the wave
hurled us upon the beach like drowsy castaways,
breaking the dream of this lone woman who
spreads the sheet like someone hoisting sails
to catch the dawn wind.

1985

[Translation by Kathryn Peters and María Roof]

Nombres

Fui el encanto, la fantasía
de los nombres inventados.
¡Jamás la leve cojera!,
sino "albatrosa":
      la pájara torpe caminando
        sobre la cubierta de los barcos.
"Albat Rosa", Penélope
que hilaba redes y lanzaba
mensajes cifrados de amor
al Mar Caribe.

"Mochín", la monja china
que abrió sus hábitos
para entregar el loto,
la flor, su estrella.

"María Cisne", la que hoy escribe
sobre versos alados su protesta de amor.

1985

Names

I was the enchantment, the fantasy
of invented names.
Never the slight limp!
But "albatross":
       the awkward bird walking
        on ship decks.
"Albat Rosa," Penelope*
who wove nets and tossed
coded messages of love
into the Caribbean Sea.

"Mochín," the Chinese nun
who opened her habits
to surrender the lotus,
the flower, her star.

"Maria Swan," who today writes
on winged verses her protestation of love.

1985

---

* Penelope: In Greek mythology, a weaver and symbol of wifely faithfulness (see References).

Baraja

El espejo en la memoria.
Lluviosos son estos días
y no hay calor de alero
donde guarecerse.
Se empaca entonces el alma
en papel de celofán
para divisar desde su transparencia el agua.
Imagino lluviosa también La Habana.
Más vigorosas las olas contra el malecón.
Más fuertes las manos en las manos.

El espejo persiste en la memoria
reclinada en él, una fresca postal
impregnada más que de palabras.

El esfuerzo de imágenes superpuestas
para que triunfe el olvido,
bálsamo para la herida abierta.
Consulta a la dama del oráculo,
semejante a voluptuosa gata angora
anunciando: "la luna sobre la fuerza,
pero al final usted vence:
      sol, estrella, emperatriz.
Basta que esté convencida".

1986

Tarot

The mirror in memory.
Rainy are these days
and no warmth of eaves
to find shelter.
The soul wraps itself then
in cellophane
to watch through its transparency the water.
I imagine Havana also rainy.
Harder the waves pounding the sea wall.
Tighter the hands holding hands.

The mirror persists in memory
leaned against it, a fresh postcard
imbued with more than words.

The effort of superimposed images
to allow oblivion to triumph,
salve for the open wound.
Consultation with the fortuneteller,
like a voluptuous angora cat
announcing: "The moon occults the power,
but in the end you will prevail:
      sun, star, empress.
You just must believe."

1986

Vista Casablanca con ojos nuevos

El tiempo detenido en un atardecer de la antigua ciudad; en su costado el embarcadero, el incesante trajín de la lancha hacia y desde Casablanca, donde recorrimos sus calles oscuras igual que camino a Beholden en la noche húmeda de Mayo Ya.

    Colgada de tu brazo y confiada en tu larga figura de ciprés era un pájaro nocturno que en tus ramas se ponía a cantar prescindiendo de la inútil mentira de la perpetuidad. Subiendo y bajando escalinatas de hierro salitrosas, al borde de la bahía llena de grandes barcos flanqueando el barrio que transitamos solitarios: observando escenas familiares frente al televisor, al pie de la biblioteca divisada por una ventana, en ruedas de mesas de juego o en balancines y butacas de corredor, donde éramos simplemente un hombre y una mujer que pasan, como todo lo que sin ser espectacular aspira a ser verdadero.

1986

Casablanca Viewed with New Eyes

Time stands still in the twilight of the old city; on one side, the wharf, the non-stop bustle of the ferry to and from Casablanca, where we walk the streets, dark like the road to Beholden* on the humid night of Mayo Ya.†

    Leaning on your arm and trusting your long cypress figure, I was a nocturnal bird that in your branches began to sing, casting aside the useless lie of "forever and ever." Climbing and descending salt-gnawed iron stairs, along the bay filled with huge ships flanking this neighborhood that we cross alone: observing family scenes before television sets, next to the bookshelf seen through a window, around card tables or in porch swings and gliders, where we were simply a man and a woman passing by, like everything that, without being spectacular, aspires to be true.

1986

[Translation by Kathryn Peters and María Roof]

---

* Beholden: Neighborhood in the old Atlantic Coast city of Bluefields, Nicaragua.
† Mayo Ya: One of the names for the May Pole festival.

Paseo en otoño

Cierro los ojos y evoco el camino umbroso,
una que otra pisada haciendo crujir la tarde
sobre la tostada alfombra de azafrán.
Piedras que se erigen sobre el sueño.
Tu mano larga con su temblor antiguo
alcanzando mi hombro y desviándome
hacia la tumba de Brecht y su compañera
—difícil imaginarlos inertes
después de tanto objeto vivo observado—.
Las múltiples mesas de trabajo de Bértolt.
La vajilla azul con diseño exclusivo.
Las distintas habitaciones de la pareja.
El amor y el desamor que han ido de la mano.
La vida y la muerte omnipresente entre dos.

1989

Autumn Stroll

I close my eyes and evoke the shady path,
footsteps that rustle the afternoon
on the toasted saffron carpet.
Rocks piling up on the dream.
Your long hand with its old tremor
reaching my shoulder, turning me
toward the tomb of Brecht* and his companion
—hard to imagine them inert
after so many live objects observed.
Bertolt's many worktables.
Blue china with its exclusive design.
The couple's different rooms.
Love and disaffection that went hand-in-hand.
Life and death omnipresent between two.

1989

---

* Brecht, Bertolt (1898-1956): German playwright, poet, and fiction writer. The companion buried with him is his wife, Austrian actress Helene Weigel. Also mentioned in the next section of this book and in Meneses' "Inquiries," in *All is the Same and Different*.

V. A los hombres futuros

A Mariano Edmundo

Y sin embargo sabíamos
que también el odio contra la bajeza
desfigura la cara.
También la ira contra la injusticia
pone ronca la voz. Desgraciadamente, nosotros,
que deberíamos preparar el camino para la amabilidad,
no pudimos ser amables.
—Bertolt Brecht

Del revolucionario y algunas de sus debilidades

El próximo mayo cumpliré cuarenta años, tengo cuatro hijos, amo a un poeta; he sido de la clase acomodada, voy a las brigadas de corte de algodón y de café y también a las culturales; aprobé el primer curso de Milicias.

En el corte soy lenta y torpe, me distraen el color y dimensión de las bolitas de los cafetos (se supone que me pasa por tener una visión poética del mundo). Cortando algodón se me van las horas limpiando las motas que recojo del suelo (porque "algodón que pisas son divisas"). En las brigadas culturales, lamento no saber escrito grandes poemas épicos y no poseer una hermosa voz a la altura del heroísmo de nuestros guardafronteras. Rompí el carnet de Milicias que me había firmado Caín, como le llama nuestro pueblo.

Leí en San Lucas lo que más tarde supe que había dicho el Che Guevara: "Los hermanos no son los de la sangre, sino los que comparten le fe"... revolucionaria, agrega el Che.

Che Comandante dice también que "todos tenemos derecho a cansarnos, pero no a ser hombres de vanguardia". Confieso que con frecuencia me declaro eficiente retaguardia; lo importante, sí, es que nunca dejaré de aspirar, aunque sea de última en la fila, a llegar con los hermanos obreros y campesinos hasta el final.

1983

V. To Future Men and Women

To Mariano Edmundo**

And yet we know:
Hatred, even of baseness,
Distorts the features.
Anger, even against injustice,
Makes the voice grow hoarse. Oh, we
Who wished to lay the foundations of human kindness
Could not ourselves be kind.
　　　—Bertolt Brecht †

About the Revolutionary and Some of His Weaknesses

This May I'll turn forty years old. I have four children and am in love with a poet. I came from the privileged class; I join brigades to pick coffee and cotton and cultural ones as well; I passed the first Militia course.

Picking coffee I am slow and awkward; the shape and color of the shrubs' beans distract me (supposedly because I have a poetic view of the world). Picking cotton, I spend hours cleaning the balls I retrieve from the ground (because "cotton tossed is money lost"). In cultural brigades I lament not knowing how to write great epic poems or possessing a beautiful voice equal to the level of the heroism of our border guards. I ripped up my Militia ID card signed by Cain‡, as our people call him.

I read in St. Luke what I later learned Che Guevara§ had said: "Our brothers and sisters are not those of our blood, but those of our faith"… revolutionary faith, Che adds.

Commander Che also says that "we all have the right to work ourselves to exhaustion but not to be members of the vanguard." I admit that I frequently declare myself an efficient member of the rearguard; what's important is that I will never stop aspiring, though I may be the very last in line, to reach the final goal beside my brother and sister workers and farmers.

1983
[Margaret Randall's version appears in *Sandino's Daughters Revisited*. The rhyming "cotton tossed is money lost" is her clever rendering of the literal, "the cotton you trod upon is foreign trade income."]

---

* Mariano Edmundo Icaza Meneses: The youngest of Meneses's four children.
† Bertolt Brecht (1898-1956): German playwright, poet, and fiction writer. These verses are from one of his best known poems, "To Those Born Later" ("An die Nachgeborenen," 1938), published in English in *Poems in Exile* (1944) and often performed to music. Also mentioned by Meneses in the previous poem and in "Inquiries," *All is the Same and Different*.
‡ Cain: Edén Pastor, a FSLN officer, headed the National Militia under the Sandinista government and signed its members' ID cards. When he abandoned the Sandinistas in 1982 and joined the counterrevolutionary forces, many Militia members showed their anger by publicly burning their cards.
§ Ernesto "Che" Guevara (1928-1967): Argentine revolutionary who was instrumental in the triumph of the Cuban Revolution and held ministerial positions in the new government. In an attempt to spark revolution in Bolivia, he was captured and killed.

Postal para Alba Azucena

A principios de enero recibí tu tarjeta
con trineos sobre nieve.
Pienso en las calles y aleros de Juigalpa
sustituidos por las amplísimas avenidas de Moscú.

Habría que imaginar la estatua del admirado Pushkin
orlados la cabeza y los hombros de blanco,
el río Moscova congelado y estático
y las cúpulas de los edificios
levantándose como sobre algodón
con la pesada arquitectura de antiguas catedrales,
Lenin guardado del frío en el calor de su pueblo.

Y vos, en tu piso de la Komnata 91,
intentando acercar Nicaragua a Voronezh,
haciendo de la muerte de Ahmed
un motivo más para afirmarte
en el amor a la comunidad.

1983

Message for Alba Azucena*

The beginning of January I received your card
with sleighs in the snow.
I think of Juigalpa's† streets and overhanging eaves
replaced by Moscow's broad avenues.

I imagine the admirable Pushkin's‡ statue
head and shoulders trimmed in white,
the Moscow River frozen and still
and building domes
rising up out of cotton
with the heavy architecture of ancient cathedrals,
Lenin§ guarded from the cold by the warmth of his people.

And you, in your flat at Komnata 91,
attempting to bring Nicaragua close to Voronezh,¶
turning Ahmed's** death into
one more reason to affirm yourself
in love for your community.

1983

---

* Alba Azucena Torres (Juigalpa 1959): Poet who studied in the Soviet Union and resides there since 1982; author of two poetry collections.
† Juigalpa: Capital of Chontales Department.
‡ Pushkin, Alexander (1799-1837): Great Russian writer; child poet prodigy; founder of the Russian novel with his *Eugene Onegin*. Also mentioned by Meneses in "Inquiries," *All is the Same and Different*.
§ Lenin, Vladimir (born Vladimir Ilich Ulyanov,1870-1924): Russian politician and Marxist theorist; proponent of the conception of a centralized, revolutionary party, led by a professional cadre; Bolshevik director of the 1917 Revolution; first premier of the Soviet Union. Also mentioned by Meneses in "Inquiries," *All is the Same and Different*.
¶ Voronezh: City and region in south central Russia..
** Ahmed Campos (1956-1982): Poet contemporary to Alba Azucena, author of a poetry collection, who was murdered.

Estampas de Jalapa (La Limonera)

Nosotros no somos militares.
Somos del pueblo,
somos ciudadanos armados.
        —Sandino

I

La cuchara en la bolsa
como una pluma fuente,
el salto en el charco
frente a la pipa
lavándose los dientes,
llenando la cantimplora
rutina atenta a la campana
de alarma de ataque aéreo o terrestre
de incendio en el área
de formación para abordaje
de emergencia a los camiones
para el relevo de heroicos guardafronteras.

II

Cuando te pregunté
qué hacía uno
a la hora de tener miedo
en el combate, vos me contestaste:
"No hay que acordarse
de los momentos felices,
¡que te valga verga todo!
Pero la verdad es que
cuando le pongo mente
me digo: Si dió su vida
un Carlos Fonseca, fundador
de la vanguardia,
un Germán Pomares, un Leonel Rugama,
¿quién soy yo para no dar la mía?".

1983

Scenes from Jalapa (La Limonera Military Unit)

We are not soldiers.
We are the people,
we are armed citizens.
    —Sandino

    I

The spoon in your pocket
like a fountain pen,
the jump over the puddle
from the water barrel,
brushing your teeth,
filling the canteen
routine alert to the bell
warning attack by air or land
fire in the area
formation for emergency
boarding into trucks
to relieve the heroic border guards.

    II

When I asked you
what one can do
with fear felt
in the midst of combat, you answered:
"You can't remember
the happy times,
all that can't mean a damn!
But the truth is,
when I think about it,
I tell myself: If a Carlos Fonseca,
founder of the vanguard,
gave his life,
a Germán Pomares, a Leonel Rugama*,
who am I not to give mine?"

1983

---

* Carlos Fonseca, Germán Pomares, Leonel Rugama: Heroes of the Revolution who died in combat before the triumph (see References).

Trabajo voluntario

Dejamos los escritorios,
los memorandums y los informes
para marchar a los cafetales.

Las mujeres recordamos los meses de embarazo
cuando nos amarramos las canastas a la cintura
y aumentamos paulatinamente su peso
en la recogida del café.

Disfrutamos la naturaleza,
cortando de arbustos agobiados
bolitas rojas y brillantes parecidas a cerezas;
otras oscurecidas con la maduración
adquieren el tono de las uvas
y hasta su roce con las yemas de los dedos
tienta la imaginación.
Los sazones amarillos o verdosos, ovalados o redondos
como peras y tomates diminutos.
En los surcos de repela
quedan dispersos los granos.
Unos negros y arrugados como pasas
y otros duros calcinados como semillas.

En ese paraíso frutal,
se desliza verde sobre la rama verde
el temible chichicaste.
Cuando te ataca, el dolor es como de inyección de aceite.
La sabiduría del campo descubrió que en él
están la vida y la muerte,
que su excremento verde, intenso,
se vierte sobre el piquete
para quitar el dolor y evitar la fiebre.

Recoger café como algodón
es regresar a nuestras raíces
cuando nuestros primeros padres
cosecharon el cacao.

El café y el algodón son nuestra moneda ahora.

1983

Voluntary Labor

We abandon desks,
memoranda and reports
to head for coffee fields.

We women recall months of pregnancy
as we tie baskets to our waists
and gradually increase their weight
in the coffee harvest.

We take pleasure in nature
picking from heavy bushes
small, cherry-like, brilliant red balls;
others darkened by ripeness
acquire the hue of grapes,
and even their touch on fingertips
tempts the imagination.
Beans yellow or greenish, oval or round,
like tiny pears and tomatoes.
In the discard troughs
grains are scattered.
Some blackened, wrinkled like raisins,
others hard and calcified like seeds.

In that fruited paradise
the feared chichicaste caterpillar creeps green
on the green branch.
When it attacks you, the pain stings like a shot of oil.
Country wisdom discovered it holds
life and death,
its bright green excrement
pressed on the wound
to relieve pain and ward off fever.

Gathering coffee and cotton
is a return to our roots
when our first parents
harvested cacao.

Coffee and cotton are our coin now.

1983

[*Poets of the Nicaraguan Revolution* has Dinah Livingstone's version.]

A mis hijos, Carlos y Karla, en su autoexilio

No piensen que vine a
la tierra a traer la paz;
no vine a traer la paz
sino la espada.
        Mateo X, 34

I

Trastabillando siempre, vacilante y dudosa
merodeando el corazón sin encontrar cómo hablarles
sin resignarme a darlo todo por perdido.

A tu hermana la encuentro más alta, espigada
florecida en sus dieciséis años
amorosa y distante por lo que nos une y nos separa.

Y a vos, mi muchachón de quince años
parido en la época supersónica,
mi niño ronco de manos hábiles, ansioso armador
y desarmador de objetos electrónicos
infatigable buceador del fondo de las cosas.

Ignoro si es en vano que espero
a que regresés con tu hermana
y se den cuenta que irse
sólo servía para lograr perspectiva
como remontarse en un avión y poder divisar
la geografía de la patria, sus maltratadas fronteras,
el pueblo fiero y armado de dignidad hasta los dientes
al que vale la pena sumarse.

To My Children, Carlos and Karla*, in their Self-exile

> *Do not suppose that I have come*
> *to bring peace to earth.*
> *I did not come to bring peace,*
> *but a sword.*
>   Matthew 10:34.

I

Stumbling always, vacillating and doubtful,
searching my heart but not finding how to speak to you
without resigning myself to accept that all is lost.

I find your sister taller, willowy,
blossoming at age sixteen,
loving and distant, for what unites and separates us.

And you, my big fifteen-year-old,
birthed in the supersonic age,
my husky-voiced child with skillful hands, eager assembler
and disassembler of electronic objects,
indefatigable diver to the depths of things.

I know not if in vain I hope
that you will return with your sister
and realize that leaving
only served to gain perspective,
like soaring in a plane and perceiving
the geography of the homeland, its violated borders,
the people brave and armed to the teeth with dignity,
worthy of joining.

---

* Carlos and Karla: The first two of Meneses's three children who left Nicaragua during the Sandinista decade to live in the U.S. (see Chapter II).

II

A Vidaluz, Ximena y Dorel
que unidas a muchos hermanos
hacen posible el futuro.

Hemos ganado otro día y no hay que bajar la guardia.
Nos han dado un receso las reuniones,
los círculos de estudio y los informes.
Hay tiempo para hablar con las hijas adolescentes
incorporadas ya a la Juventud Sandinista,
estrenando su revolución como juguete nuevo
y aprendiendo a ser, a encontrarse a sí mismas
en la vida de su pueblo.

Es la hora también del cansancio acumulado.
De necesitar un pecho donde recostar la cabeza.
La hora de leer y releer la última carta o telegrama
llevada en la cartera como la licencia de conducir.
Como baluarte imprescindible, talismán al alcance de la mano,
convocación del símbolo que nos hace reposar sobre la esperanza.

Mujeres al fin con el amor a cuestas
como el canasto de café o el saco de algodón
asumiendo el parto colectivo de la revolución,
hija predilecta de la historia,
guardando a la criatura del mal parto,
del acecho, del mal de ojos,
mimándola para que crezca y desarrolle
para que como mujer fértil se reproduzca
a lo largo y ancho de América.

1985

II

To Vidaluz*, Ximena† and Dorel‡
who, side-by-side with many sisters and brothers
make the future possible.

We have won a new day but can't lower our guard.
The meetings, study groups and reports
have given us a recess.
There is time to talk with adolescent daughters
already members of the Sandinista Youth,§
enjoying the revolution like a new toy
yet learning to be, to find themselves
in the life of their people.

It is also time of accumulated fatigue.
Of needing a chest on which to lay your head.
Time to read and reread the last letter or telegram
carried in the wallet like a driver's license.
Like an indispensable bastion, talisman at hand's reach,
drawing upon the symbol that lets us rest on hope.

Women finally carrying their love on high
like a basket of coffee or bag of cotton
giving collective birth to the revolution,
history's preferred daughter,
guarding the baby against miscarriage,
abduction, evil eye,
pampering her so she will grow and develop
into a fertile woman and reproduce throughout
the length and breadth of America.

1985

---

* Vidaluz: Meneses's third-born child, the only one of her four who lived in Nicaragua during the entire revolutionary decade.
† Ximena Matamoros: Meneses's godchild, daughter of her longtime friend, Ángela Saballos.
‡ Dorel Ramírez: Youngest daughter of Sergio Ramírez, writer, member of the governing junta (1979-1984) and vice-president (1984-1990).
§ Sandinista Youth: Organization of militant youths in the Sandinista National Liberation Front (FSLN).

**Reportaje de una brigada de cortadores de café
(Cosecha de 1984-1985)**

Al llegar al Complejo "Los Milagros"
(Unidad de Producción Estatal "Porfirio Sobalvarro")
la planificación urbana se había realizado:
Ciudad Sandino, en la loma,
con divisiones de tablas y piso de tambo.
Bello Horizonte, frente a la Rotonda
como correspondía, covachas, con camarotes.
Acahualinca, al borde del guindo
transitada por chanchos, piso de tierra,
Las Colinas, albergue de servicios médicos,
recámaras separadas por biombos,
corredor espacioso, puerta de entrada
con dintel en semicírculo,
iluminación de una bujía y ladrillo de cemento.

Margarito confiaba orgulloso
su experiencia de quince años
palmeando tortillas como L.P.
y su ingenio haciendo variaciones
sobre un mismo menú, que solía anunciar
eufemista y con voz entre gangosa y aguda:
"¡medio pollo, medio pollo! ¡cena, cena!"
La montaña nos esperaba de pie todas las mañanas.

Los de la brigada "Cornelio Monjarrez",
trabajadores de once instituciones estatales,
ascendíamos el cerro vertical de "Los Milagros"
bajo la llovizna y en un lodo
entre liso y pegajoso, donde ¡chocoplós!
se nos hundían las botas hasta el borde
y los varones caían pesadamente
con los sacos de café a cuestas.
Yo siempre he tenido problemas
para ser vanguardia, pero el asma
de la Chilo De Nueda, el vértigo de la Moncada

Report of a Coffee Brigade (1984-1985 Harvest)

Arriving at the Los Milagros Complex
(Porfirio Sobalvarro State Production Unit),
urban planning had materialized:
Sandino City on the hilltop, *
with wood partitions and plank floors.
Bello Horizonte facing the roundabout,
as it should, huts with bunks.
Acahualinca, on the edge of the steep slope,
crossed by pigs, dirt floors.
Las Colinas, medical services dispensary,
rooms separated by screens,
spacious hall, entrance door
with a semicircular lintel,
single light bulb and cement blocks.

Margarito proudly confided
his fifteen years experience
palming tortillas like L.P. records,
and his cleverness at making variations
on the same menu, as he announced
euphemistically in his high-pitched, nasal voice:
"Half a chicken, half a chicken! Dinner! Dinner!"
The mountain stood awaiting us each morning.

The Cornelio Monjarrez Brigade,
workers from eleven state agencies,
climbed the vertical Los Milagros slope
in the drizzle and in the
slippery, sticky mud, where slurp!
our boots sank up to the tops,
and the men fell heavily
with sacks of coffee beans on their backs.
I've always had problems
being in the vanguard, but
Chilo† De Nueda's asthma, Moncada's‡ vertigo,

---
* Sandino City, Bello Horizonte, Acahualinca, Las Colinas: Names of neighborhoods in Managua.
† "Chilo" (Auxiliadora) De Nueda: Director of Art Schools, Ministry of Culture.
‡ Adilia Moncada: National Archive Director.

y la presión alta de la Cony
me empujaban en la retaguardia.
(Omar: La montaña también es una
           inmensa caja de resonancia.
           Todo ruido se vuelve importante
           y alguno hasta majestuoso
           como el sonido de pleamar
           cuando el viento remueve
           los flancos del bosque.)
En las laderas empinadas como cuerda floja
envidié a los cirqueros y los bailarines.
Patricia, Alejandro, Isaac, cortaban el café
en equilibrio sobre las puntas de las botas
o con las piernas abiertas en ángulo de 45o.
No era chiche cortar en esos guindos,
pero la escuadra de "Los gansos salvajes",
antihéroes, terroristas verbales, irreverentes,
cortaron 7 latas diarias de rojito;
las dos Socorros hacían 9 ½ cada una
y las brigadas de choque se perdían de vista:
19 ó 25 latas de café por persona.
A 3 kms. de nosotros la contrarrevolución
pegó fuego y se corrió
y reforzamos entonces el orden militar
y hasta el último lugar de la retaguardia
y hasta la lata de café y el puño, lata y polvo,
se llevaron con una altura y verticalidad
sólo parecida a "Los Milagros".

1986

and Cony's* high blood pressure
pushed me into the rearguard.
(Omar:† The mountain is also an
    immense sound box.
    Every noise becomes important
    and some, even majestic
    like the sound at high tide,
    when the wind stirs
    the forest's flanks.)
On inclines steep like tightropes,
I envied the circus performers and dancers.
Patricia,‡ Alejandro§, Isaac¶ picked coffee
balanced on the toes of their boots
or with legs spread at 45-degree angles.
It was no easy trick picking coffee on those vertical slopes,
but the Wild Geese Squadron,
irreverent antiheroes and verbal terrorists,
picked 7 cans of good coffee beans a day;
the two Socorros** did 9-1/2 each,
and the shock brigades were out of sight:
19 or 25 cans per person.
Three kms. from us the counterrevolutionaries
set a fire and ran,
and we reinforced military order,
and even the last place in the rearguard
and even the coffee can and fist, can and powder,
were raised with a height and verticality
only akin to Los Milagros itself.

1986

---

* Cony Pérez: Reference librarian, National Library.
† Omar Cabezas (León 1950): Leader in the Sandinista National Liberation Front. Here, the verses "Omar: The mountain is also an / immense sound box" allude to his 1982 award-winning testimonial narrative of his experiences as a guerrilla fighter in the 1970s, whose title is literally, "The mountain is something more than an immense green steppe." Its translation by Kathleen Weaver as *Fire from the Mountain: The Making of A Sandinista* (1985) was a best-seller in the U.S., and film director Deborah Shaffer made a highly-praised documentary of the same name (1987).
‡ Patricia López: Member of the Contemporary Dance Group.
§ Alejandro Cuadra: Founding director of the Folkloric Dance Group "Macehuatl" and promoter of Popular Culture Centers.
¶ Isaac Carballo: Folkloric composer and singer.
** two Socorros: National Library and Archive employees.

El sexto signo

> *Esos son los que han salido de*
> *la gran persecución, han lavado*
> *y blanqueado sus vestiduras*
> *con la sangre del Cordero.*
> *Apocalipsis 7, 14*

Vemos la fotografía
y no es el ordenamiento
sacerdotal del grupo.

Vano intento de verdugos
en ahogar sus voces contra el suelo.

Todos de bruces.
Consumación de la entrega
cuerpo a tierra elegida.

La sangre corriendo como poderosos afluentes
hacia el río de los mártires
rugiendo en la profética voz de Ellacuría,
arrollándonos para siempre
con la silenciosa fuerza de Amando
activo y fiel como su nombre.

Juan Ramón, Segundo, Ignacio, Joaquín,
la humilde mujer que cayó arrullando
a la primogénita adolescente
y tantos otros mártires que nos han precedido
valientes, generosos, y con fe en la utopía del Reino
por quienes estamos seguros de la victoria final.

The Sixth Seal *

> *These are they who have come out of*
> *the great tribulation; they have washed*
> *their robes and made them white*
> *in the blood of the Lamb.*
> *Revelation 7:14.*

We see the photograph
and it is not the priestly ordination
of the group.

Vain attempt by executioners
to smother their voices against the ground.

All face down.
Consummation of surrendering
the body to the chosen earth.

Blood flowing like powerful tributaries
toward the river of martyrs
roaring with the prophetic voice of Ellacuría,
pulling us along forever
with the quiet strength of Amando
active and faithful like his name.†

Juan Ramón, Segundo, Ignacio, Joaquín,
the poor woman who fell cradling
her adolescent firstborn daughter,
and so many other martyrs who preceded us
bold, generous, trusting in the utopia of the Kingdom
through whom we are assured of the final victory.

---

* Context: The murder at the Central American University (UCA) in San Salvador on November 16, 1989, of six Jesuit professors and administrators, known as the "Martyrs of UCA," and of their housekeeper and her daughter. Killed were Spaniard Fathers Ignacio Ellacuría, Amando López, Juan Ramón Moreno, Segundo Montes, and Ignacio Martín-Baró; Salvadoran Father Joaquín López y López; and Julia Elba Ramos and Celina Marisetta Ramos.

† "active and faithful like his name": The name "Amando" in Spanish is the gerund form of the verb "amar"—loving .

Tríptico para recordar

> *La muerte de cualquier hombre me disminuye, porque estoy ligado a la humanidad; y por consiguiente, nunca hagas preguntar por quién doblan las campanas; doblan por ti.*
> *—John Donne*

I
A mamá.

El padre yace para siempre inerte
y todavía alguien cumple la diligencia
de levantar la sábana y tomarle fotos
para el expediente de archivo
que rotulará en letras gruesas:

CASO CERRADO

II
A Graciela y Alvaro Avilés.

Veinte años y parece que está dormido.
La mano de la madre entre las suyas
en afán de permanencia inútil,
el porte y aspecto que le sacó la montaña.
Los brazos, el pecho de esta criatura grande
crecido a la altura de su ideal.

III
A J. M.

A la Sociedad de los poetas muertos.

Y como había leído:
    "...donde quiera que haya una injusticia..."
tomó su mochila y se marchó hacia el sur.

Ese cuerpo informe de la fotografía
y estas noticias armadas como rompecabezas
hacen su historia.

1970

Triptych to Remember

> *Any man's death diminishes me,*
> *because I am linked to humankind;*
> *therefore, ask not for whom*
> *the bells toll; they toll for thee.*
> —John Donne[*]

I
To Mother

Father lies forever still
and yet, someone follows the order
to lift the sheet and take pictures
for the file report
that he will stamp in big letters:

CASE CLOSED

II
To Graciela and Álvaro Avilés[†]

Twenty years old, and he seems to be sleeping.
His mother's hand in his
vainly wishing for permanence,
the bearing and appearance the mountain brought out.
Arms, chest of this big child
grown as high as his ideal.

III
To J. M.[‡]

To To the Dead Poets Society.[§]

And since he had read:
   "… wherever there is an injustice…"[¶]
he grabbed his backpack and headed south.

That formless body in the photograph
and these bits of news pieced together like a puzzle
tell his story.

1970

---

[*] John Donne (1572-1631): British poet and priest, author of metaphysical poetry.
[†] Graciela y Álvaro Avilés: Parents of Álvaro Avilés Cevasco, son of Nicaraguan medical doctor Álvaro Avilés Gallo and his Peruvian wife, Graciela Cevasco, members of a prayer group with Meneses. He died at age 20 during his Patriotic Military Service.
[‡] J. M.: José ("Chepe") Mendoza: Member of the Sandinista military, son of a Nicaraguan father and Argentine mother killed in action outside Nicaragua (see References).
[§] "Dead Poets Society": Popular 1989 film by director Peter Weir that presents a paean to the enjoyment of poetry and to *carpe diem*—"seize the day."
[¶] "… wherever there is an injustice…": Quotation of Ernesto "Che" Guevara (1928-1967): Argentine revolutionary who was instrumental in the triumph of the Cuban Revolution and held ministerial positions in the new government. During his attempt to spark revolution in Bolivia, he was captured and killed. This quotation reflects his commitment to carry revolution beyond national boundaries.

Muro de lamentaciones

Esta vez no ahogaré la memoria,
asumiré los muertos y la separación de los amantes
que es otra forma de morir.
No deambularé esquizofrénica por el mundo
sino con el estandarte del holocausto vivido,
no ahogaré sus voces que claman por el reino que
no hemos podido construir,
no ignoraré la sangre en el barro,
el alarido del fondo de las entrañas,
el rugido de la multitud acumulado en el pecho,
la furia de los impotentes,
el mal gusto de gritar en una calle contra las
impecables paredes,
la punzada directa en el corazón
al detenernos en un semáforo.
No pondré diques al llanto
ni pesaré las palabras en el fiel de la balanza
—la mediocrita áurea hecha trizas,
la mesura apartada por inútil—
sin tributos ni mayores concesiones a la vida.
Hay un tiempo de llorar que debe ser cumplido
hasta el hundimiento total, Valle de lágrimas,
Muro de lamentaciones,
rasgadura de velos para que salga el ánima
y se exponga en la piedra de sacrificio,
hora en que el náufrago suelte su asidero de vida,
hora del despliegue de la orfandad ante el final
más allá de lo visto y vivido, más allá.

1990

Wailing Wall

This time I'll not stifle memory,
I will claim the dead and the separation of lovers
which is another form of death.
I'll not wander the world schizophrenic
but with the banner of the holocaust lived,
I'll not stifle their voices clamoring for the kingdom
we were unable to build,
I'll not ignore the blood in the dirt,
the scream from the bottom of the gut,
the masses' roar packed into the chest,
the fury of the powerless,
the discarded scream in a street against
spotless walls,
the direct stab in the heart
as we stop at a traffic light.
I'll not dam this flood of tears
nor weigh words in the balance scale
—golden mean smashed to bits,
restraint abandoned as useless—
no tributes or great concessions to life.
There is a time to weep that must be fulfilled
to the utter depths, Valley of Tears,
Wailing Wall,
rending of veils, so the soul can appear
and offer itself on the sacrificial stone,
hour for the shipwrecked to loosen his hold on life,
hour for unfurling orphanhood given the end
beyond all we have seen and lived, far beyond.

1990

[Margaret Randall gives a partial translation in *Sandino's Daughters Revisited* and Dinah Livingstone an interpretive one in *Poets of the Nicaraguan Revolution*]

Todo es igual y distinto

(Poemas 1992-2001) (2002)

All Is The Same And Different

(Poems 1992-2001) (2002)

Neoliberalismo

Neoliberalismo: Acomodarse
A cómo darse.

¿Dónde estás?

Redescubriéndote
Realmente oculta
Redes, cubriéndote.

Neoliberalism*

Neoliberalism: Adjust yourself
Add just your self (-price).

Where Are You?†

Rediscovering yourself
Really hidden
Nets, covering you.

---

* In contrast to Meneses's previous collections, *All is the Same and Different* omits the date of the poems. The editor has added it when it appears in the manuscript copy in her possession.

Note: This poem's play on words is difficult to transpose into English. "Neoliberalism" is equated with "acomodarse"—"adjust yourself, get used to, conform, get comfortable." But "acomodarse" separated into groups of syllables gives a quite different meaning: "at what price to sell oneself?" Another version could be "Neoliberalism: feel fine / For a feel fine price."

† Note: This poem is a play on words that does not work in English in the literal meaning, as given above. To see the structure, compare the following versions, if "redis" or "reun" in English meant "nets" or "netting."

Rediscovering you.	Reuncovering you.
Really hidden	Really hidden
Redis, covering you.	Reun, covering you.

Another version could be: "Rediscovering you / Really hidden / Redish nets covering you."

Oficinistas

Recréanse en revistas Vanidades o Cosmopolitan
y en frases que definen al hombre favorito:
"mitad caballo, mitad cordero"
es decir, fuerte y delicado.

Pueblan con risas nerviosas y voces cantarinas
el ámbito oficinesco.
Gatunamente el Contador da vuelta
en su silla giratoria y pasando inspección
a las piernas descubiertas por las minifaldas
exclama: —Todo está word perfect!

Síntesis del encuentro

A Sergio

Hemos desandado el camino
hasta un vago recuerdo de niñez en bicicleta,
de paseos en el parque.
Luego la juventud y los efímeros reinados.
Los casuales encuentros, los años, los hijos,
el tumultuoso tiempo de revolución,
la apasionada entrega, el día sin horas
el tiempo lleno de contenido.
Nos desbordamos de vida hasta asfixiarnos
hasta encontrarnos maltrechos,
—Jodidos, pero contentos!
Esgrimiendo el resto de ilusión que aún nos queda
y que atesoramos en este abrazo de náufragos.

Office Girls

They delight in Vanidades or Cosmopolitan magazines
and in phrases that define their favorite kind of man:
"half horse, half lamb,"
that is, strong and delicate.

They fill the office space
with nervous laughter and lilting voices.
Like a cat, the Accountant swivels
in his chair and inspecting
legs exposed by miniskirts
exclaims: "Everything is word perfect!"

Synthesis of the Encounter

To Sergio

We have retraced our steps
to a vague memory of childhood on bicycles,
and walks in the park.
Later, youth and ephemeral reigns.
Casual encounters, the years, children,
tumultuous time of the revolution,
passionate commitment, endless days,
time full of content.
We were flooded with life until we drowned,
until we found each other tattered and torn,
-down, but happy!
brandishing the scrap of illusion that we retain
and treasure in our embrace of those shipwrecked.

Evocación Jurásica

Las montañas, el risco.
La lluvia que al final dejará
gris nostalgia de neblina
ventana por donde diviso
el mismo paisaje interior
que llevo desde la infancia.

Tu figura grande, vital
el silbido con que soltás
invisibles volutas al aire,
mientras afanado ordenás
suero, vitaminas, analgésico
y revisás las pupilas enrojecidas
del paciente de la mañana,
el solemne y quieto adviento
de la parturienta,
el lisiado en accidente,
mientras la agradecida lengua
de la convaleciente te lame
el envés de la mano
y todo lo observa
el ojo hipnótico de la lora,
la mirada lánguida de la vaca parida
y mi voz animal murmurando
desde ese remoto origen telúrico
del que surgimos.

Jurassic Evocation

The mountains, the cliff.
The rain that will leave
fog's grey nostalgia,
window through which I glimpse
the same internal landscape
I've carried since my infancy.

Your large figure, full-of-life,
the whistle with which you release
invisible spirals into the air,
while you hurriedly order
serum, vitamins, analgesics
and check the reddened pupils
of the morning patient,
the solemn and quiet advent
of the birthing mother,
the accident-injured,
while the grateful tongue
of a convalescent licks
the back of your hand,
and observing everything is
the hypnotic eye of the lady parrot,
the languid look of the cow that has calved
and my animal voice murmuring
from that remote telluric origin
from which we emerged.

Amor en cualquier tiempo, I

(Versión libre)

Hemos dado cauce a la audacia del amor
cuando el brillo gris
se ha instalado como aura en tu cabeza
y en el entorno de mis ojos y labios
los años han puesto su huella incipiente.

Hace tiempo que no sos el esbelto muchacho karateca
ni yo la espigada reina estudiantil
desplazándose inalcanzable por su efímero reino.

Ya no pudimos encontrarnos en la timidez
y el leve temblor adolescente,
ni con la llama que envuelve con voracidad
los cuerpos encendidos.

Algo de todo sin embargo, quedó sedimentado
que fluye entre los dos cuando fundidos somos uno
entregándonos sin triunfos ni derrotas al amor
jugando a ganarle la partida al tiempo.

1995

Love at Any Time, I

(Free Verse Version)

We yield ground to the audacity of love
when a grey shine has settled
like an aura round your head,
and on my eyes and lips
years have left their incipient mark.

For some time, you've not been the slim karate kid,
nor I the willowy student queen
gliding untouchable in her ephemeral kingdom.

We could not find each other in
adolescent shyness and trembling,
nor in the flame that voraciously envelops
bodies on fire.

Yet, some of all this remained
and flows between us when, fused, we are one,
surrendering ourselves to love without triumphs or defeats
trying to win the game against time.

1995

Amor en cualquier tiempo, II

(Versión en soneto)

Hemos dado cauce al amor audaz
cuando en el entorno de tus ojos
el tiempo ha hollado a su antojo
y un aura gris corona tu faz.

Ya no sos el muchacho vigoroso
ni yo la reina estudiantil
dejando atrás su edad infantil
para soñar el porvenir hermoso.

Ya no nos encontramos en timidez
de adolescente temblor y mudez
ni en las llamas que envuelven voraces.

Algo de todo en nuestro abrazo fluye
cuando palpamos que el dolor huye
de este amor del que somos capaces.

Love at Any Time, II

(Sonnet Version)

To audacious love we've given way,
though round your eyes, shining still,
time has trod, marching on at will,
and crowning your face is an aura of grey.

You're no longer the vigorous boy
nor I the student queen
leaving behind her years as a teen
to dream a future of joy.

We meet not in timid hesitance
of adolescent trembling and silence
nor in flames that envelop, voracious.

Yet some of this in our embrace flows
when pain flees from us and goes
far from this love amply spacious.

[The translation is meant to be a humorous version. Certain liberties were taken to make rhythms and rhymes, all in keeping with the tenor of the poem.]

Confidencia

A los tres años de edad
dije que me había caído en una zanja,
que por eso cojeaba,
mi madre, casi una adolescente,
no relacionó mi repentina cojera
con las recientes fiebres
que había sufrido y de cuyo delirio
me sacaban con oraciones al Niño de Praga
tías abuelas devotas
rezando en coro a la orilla de mi cama.

A los once años, en la frontera
de la definición de los sexos
jugaba con mi primo César
echándonos a quien corría más
entre chavalas y chavalos del barrio
y yo era una gacela sobre mis dos pies
desiguales asentando la planta del pie izquierdo
y apoyándome en la punta del derecho
como bastón auxiliar para completar el paso.

Enfrenté el desafío de la patineta, de la bicicleta
y aún más de los dos patines
que desarrollaron mi pierna derecha
más delgada que la izquierda.
Adolescente, el rock and roll volvió a retarme
y me incorporé a los frenéticos movimientos
de mis compañeros de fiesta,
disimulando los desequilibrios con la gracia
de la juventud
en oportunas volteretas.

Confiding A Secret

At three years of age
I said I had fallen in a ditch,
that's why I was limping,
my mother, almost still adolescent,
didn't relate my sudden limp
to recent fevers
I had suffered and the delirium from which
my devout great-aunts rescued me
with pleas to the Child of Prague
praying in unison around my bed.

At eleven, at the edge
of sexual definition
I played with my cousin César
betting who could run farthest
among neighborhood girls and boys,
and I was a gazelle on my two uneven feet,
planting the sole of my left foot and
leaning on the toe of my right
like a helpful crutch to finish the stride.

I faced the challenge of the scooter, the bicycle,
even worse, roller skates
that developed my right leg,
thinner than the left one.
As an adolescent, rock and roll challenged me again,
I joined in all the frenetic movements
of my fellow partygoers,
hiding my imbalances with
youth's gracefulness and
timely spins.

Años más tarde
una compañera de estudios me confesó
que hacía denodados esfuerzos por caminar
de esa forma particular como lo hacía yo
ignorando el supremo empeño de mi parte
por no cojear, por aparentar el natural balanceo
de una modelo en la pasarela.

No todos los pasos de los bailes folklóricos
puedo imitar
los tendones de mi pie derecho
carecen de la elasticidad para asentar la
planta,
y el talón se levanta inmisericorde
convirtiéndome la pierna en bastón.

Los avances de la ciencia
me aseguran corrección completa
y a estas alturas ya la pienso dos veces,
ya convivo con mi pierna-bastón,
con mi andar de albatrosa,
navegando en la vida cotidiana
como velero, cabeceando levemente su proa,
llegando de cualquier manera a todo lugar.

1996

Years later
a classmate confessed to me that
she made determined attempts to walk in the
unusual way I did,
ignorant of the supreme effort on my part
to not limp, to show the natural swing
of a model on the runway.

Not all the steps of folkloric dances
can I manage;
the tendons in my right foot
lack elasticity for putting
sole to the ground,
heel rising mercilessly,
turning my leg into a walking stick.

The advances of science
assure me total correction,
but at this point, I hesitate,
I get along now with my cane-leg,
with my albatross walk,
navigating through daily life
like a sailboat, dipping slightly in the bow,
arriving, one way or another, everywhere.

1996

[Child of Prague: Meneses explains that some families decide to offer devotion to certain saints because their story is interesting or exemplary. Among her great-aunts, the Child of Prague was one of their favorites.]

Dueña del canto

A mis hijas Karla y Vidaluz

Que yo recuerde, no tuve
esa vigorosa actitud de mi hija a los 18 años
mucho menos a los catorce,
sino la confusa adolescencia
deambulando por las habitaciones,
incapaz de responder con eficiencia
a los insignificantes requerimientos
cotidianos de pasamanos:
        pasar la ropa,
        pasar las tijeras
        llevar el sombrero colgado
        detrás de la puerta.

Todos los objetos jugando al cero escondido
y yo, a la gallina ciega, palpando al mundo,
rodeada de aparente perfección,
calles delineadas, señales precisas,
altos, mucho altos:
        por ahí no.
        A esa hora no
        cuidado con la oscuridad!,
        mucho menos si musitan a tu oído:
"de desnuda que está brilla la estrella".

Las veredas derechas eran falsas
las izquierdas prohibidas
mi cuerpo, un enajenado territorio.
Mi voz, inaudible.
Mi nombre, diluido.

Cuánto camino hubo que recorrer
para llegar a ser lo que soy:
Mujer que mira orgullosa tercera generación
de su descendencia
y se reconoce mojón, punto de partida
puerto para zarpar con velas indoblegables.

Dueña y señora de su canto.

Mistress of Her Song

To my daughters, Karla and Vidaluz

As I recall, I didn't have
that vigorous attitude of my daughter at eighteen,
much less at fourteen,
but rather, confused adolescence,
wandering through rooms,
incapable of responding efficiently
to the most insignificant daily tasks
as passer-of-things:
        pass the clothes
        pass the scissors
        bring the hat hung
        behind the door.

All objects playing hide-and-seek
and I, blindfolded, feeling the world,
surrounded by apparent perfection,
straight streets, precise signals,
stop signs, many stop signs:
        Don't go there.
        Not at that hour
        be careful in the dark!,
        especially if they whisper in your ear:
"because it is nude the star twinkles."*

The paths on the right were false
those on the left, forbidden,
my body, an alienated territory.
My voice, inaudible.
My name, diffused.

What a long road to travel
to become what I am:
Woman looking proudly at the third generation
of her descendance,
recognizing herself as touchstone, departure point,
port to set off under unbending sails.

Mistress and owner of her song.

---

* "because it is nude the star twinkles.": Verse by the great Nicaraguan Modernist poet, Rubén Darío, from his poem "I Am He Who Just Yesterday Would Say," in his 1905 collection, *Songs of Life and Hope* (see References).

Canción de cuna de mayo

Mayo es ya, Alejandro!
buen tiempo para nacer
la lluvia hace germinar el verde
el Palo de Mayo ya floreció.

Buen tiempo para nacer,
pero Miss Edith lost the keys!
buscan las abuelas con qué abrir,
el corazón palpitando y el teléfono
Ring, ring, ring
Rikiting ting ting.

El nieto acelerado llega al amanecer
con la pinta del monárquico bisabuelo
saluda el último día de Mayaya Oh!
y a la interminable familia trenzada
en un frondoso May Pole.

Bienvenido Alejandro Carlos
te canta el tío Simón:

Sin saima si ma ló…!

May Lullaby

May is here, Alejandro!*
A good time to be born
rain brings out green foliage
the May Pole has bloomed.

A good time to be born,
but Miss Edith lost the keys!†
Grandmothers search to unlock the door
their hearts aflutter and the phone
Ring, ring, ring
Rikiting, ting. ting.

The rushing grandson arrives at daybreak
looking like his monarchical great-grandfather
greets the last day of Mayaya Oh!‡
and the endless family woven
into a luxuriant May Pole.

Welcome, Alejandro Carlos,
Uncle Simon sings to you:

Sin saima si ma ló…!§

---

* Alejandro Carlos: Meneses's grandchild, son of her daughter, Karla Icaza, born in her birth month of May (see other comments on this poem in Chapter II).
† "Miss Edith lost the keys!": In English in original. The mother of Meneses's son-in-law is Edith Jackson, from English-speaking Corn Island, Nicaragua.
‡ Mayaya Oh: One of the names for the May Pole festival celebrated on the Atlantic Coast.
§ "Sin saima si ma ló": Generally believed to be a phonetic transcription of the English verse, "Sing, Simon, sing, my love."

Canción interior

A mi sobrino, Moisés Alvarado Meneses

Cuando naciste, te imaginé en tu cuna
recorriendo los detalles del nuevo entorno
al que fuiste lanzado y acogido brevemente
por los brazos de tu madre.

A los pocos días, ella, enferma,
te dejó en otros regazos amorosos,
pero sé que percibiste el vacío.

A su regreso, no hubo gesto de sobresalto
al jubiloso portazo,
ni atención al chischil
ni al tintineo de campanas.

Aún no he aprendido
ese lenguaje de palomas revoloteando
con el que te comunicás ahora,
pero advierto la música interior
que llevás en el pecho.

Moisés, salvado de los ruidos de este mundo
para escuchar mejor la suprema sinfonía del Universo.

Internal Song

To my nephew, Moisés Alvarado Meneses

When you were born, I imagined you in your crib
examining the details of the new surroundings
you were thrown into and embraced briefly
by the arms of your mother.

A few days later, she, sick,
left you in other loving laps,
but I know you perceived the emptiness.

When she returned, there was no start
at the joyful bang of the door,
no attention to the rattle
or the ringing of bells.

I still have not learned
that language of fluttering doves
you communicate with now,
but I notice the internal music
you carry in your chest.

Moisés, saved from the noises of this world
to better hear the supreme symphony of the Universe.

Evocación

A Dolores Cantarero de Meneses
In memoriam

Esta casa fue eficiente
gracias a la mujer que hoy se ha marchado.
En este zaguán queda su sombra
menuda y diligente.
Aquí vendió la mantequilla escurrida
y la lecha de vaca recién ordeñada.
Esa mujer fuerte procuró el abrigo
de diez hijos logrados en catorce partos
y los reunió a todos a la hora del Ángelus
para agradecer la vida.
Se levantó al alba y en horno de leña
hizo marquesotes y pan de maíz
que precavida almacenó para el invierno.
En sus manos confió el corazón de su marido.
Dejémosla dormir, que por primera vez
hijos y nietos la vemos en reposo
aunque extrañemos su quietud
y su aparente indiferencia ante nuestra cercanía
acomodando los ramos de flores
de quienes la conocieron
aprendamos una nueva forma de tenerla entre nosotros.
Apaguémosle la luz para que continúe el sueño.

Jinotega, Enero 27, 1998

Evocation

To Dolores Cantarero de Meneses*
In memoriam

This house was efficient
thanks to the woman who departed today.
In this entry hall her shadow remains,
small and diligent.
Here she sold strained butter
and recently drawn cow's milk.
This strong woman managed to raise
ten children from fourteen births
and gathered them all at the hour of the Angelus
to give thanks for life.
She rose at dawn and in a wood stove
made marquesote cakes and corn bread
she prudently stored for winter.
In her hands she entrusted her husband's heart.
Let's allow her to sleep, for the first time
we children and grandchildren see her at rest
though we are surprised by her stillness
and apparent indifference to our nearness
arranging the flower bouquets from
people who knew her
let's learn a new way to have her among us.
Let's extinguish the light so the dream can continue.

Jinotega, January 27, 1998

---

* Dolores Cantarero de Meneses: Meneses's paternal grandmother.

Paco

Al Teniente Coronel Francisco Morazán Elvir
en sus hijos, Danilo y Sergio

Al imitar la gesta morazánica
soñaste con ser el Bolívar centroamericano
y hasta tuviste tu Manuelita,
fiel campeona de la retaguardia
sin quien ninguna de tus empresas
hubiese sido acertada
porque aún con tu don de mando
te fue ingobernable tu insurrecto corazón,
prendido de la cabellera caoba
o de la falda abierta como al descuido
el fatal aleteo de los años treinta
o el sensual robacorazón de los cincuenta.
Todo fue soportado por la estoica segoviana,
hasta que previendo como siempre,
que se marcharía antes,
dió las últimas recomendaciones al primogénito
para que los achaques de la vejez te fueran leves.

Vano el amoroso intento que no pudo liberarte
del temblor que se te pegó en el cuerpo
al quedarte solo.
Desde entonces, frenético te dedicaste

Paco[*]

To Lieutenant Colonel Francisco Morazán Elvir[†]
in his sons, Danilo and Sergio Morazán

Imitating the Morazanic epic[‡]
you dreamed of being Central America's Bolívar,[§]
you even had your own Manuelita[¶],
loyal champion of the rearguard
without whom none of your deeds
would have succeeded
because even with your gift for leadership
you never could govern your insurgent heart
captivated by mahogany hair or
a casually parted skirt
the fatal flutter of eyelids in the thirties
or the sensual heartbreaker of the fifties.
All was tolerated by the stoic Segovian woman
until, prescient as always, she knew
she would go first and
gave final recommendations to her firstborn
so that your old age ailments would be lighter.

Futile was the loving intent that could not relieve
the tremor overtaking your body
once you were left alone.
Frenetic, you began to dedicate yourself

---

[*] Paco: Common nickname in Spanish for Francisco.
[†] Lieutenant Colonel Francisco Morazán Elvir: Honduran military officer who supported Jacobo Arbenz in Guatemala when he was elected president in 1951 and overthrown in a 1954 coup by forces supported by the U.S. Like Sandino, Arbenz posed a challenge to U.S. hegemony in Central America. Morazán Elvir was the father of Meneses's husband, Sergio Morazán.
[‡] "Imitating the Morazanic epic": Reference to Honduran politician Francisco Morazán Quezada (1792-1842), president of Honduras, of the United Provinces of Central America, and later, of El Salvador.
[§] Bolívar, Simón (Caracas, Venezuela 1783-Santa Marta, Colombia 1830): "The Liberator" who fought against Spain in the War for the Independence of South America; proponent of continental union and not the constitution of separate nations.
[¶] Manuelita Sáenz (Quito, Ecuador 1793-Paita, Perú 1859): "Liberator of the Liberator," Simón Bolívar's companion.

a escribir tus memorias
que recitabas en voz alta con la marcial dignidad
con que marchaste con Arbenz al poder
y en cincuenticuatro al exilio;
con la pasión de protagonista
de la legión del Caribe
o el eco de los diálogos interminables
con los revolucionarios de América
que ya nunca te dejaron en paz
y con su sueño a cuestas recorriste alucinado
los corredores de tu casa en largas madrugadas
para que al fin decidieras convocar
a la poca familia que te quedaba,
pusieras tus relaciones en orden
y te despidieras gentilmente
no sin antes conocerme y confiar
parte de lo que he contado,
porque supiste que al comprenderte
te liberaba de culpas,
escuchando esas confidencias que sólo se dicen
cuando ya no se espera más de la vida
que la misericordia de abandonarla en paz.

to writing your memoirs
reciting them aloud with the same martial dignity
of your march with Arbenz into power
and, in 54, into exile;
with the passion of protagonist
of the Caribbean Legion
or the echo of interminable dialogues
with the revolutionaries of America
who never again left you alone
and with their dream on your shoulders, you roamed excitedly
through the halls of your home on long mornings
until finally deciding to summon
the small family you had left,
to put your affairs in order
and gracefully bid farewell
not without first meeting me and confiding
part of what I have related,
for you knew that by understanding you,
I would release you from guilt,
listening to those confidences revealed only
when nothing is expected from life
but the mercy of leaving it in peace.

Vida con vida

A don José y doña María
In memoriam

Primero fue María quien se diluyó en el río
y ahora Don José con ella haciéndose uno.

Una sola corriente hacia el caudal sereno
al fin el uno restituyendo al otro
la vida del otro que vivía
y ya tiene cada cual la vida que tenía
otra vez en el otro como suya.

Convidados al fin y para siempre por el río
a fluir en la eternidad vida con vida.

Life with Life

*To Don José and Doña María**
In memoriam

First was María who dissolved in the river
and now don José becoming one with her.

A lone current toward the serene sea
finally the one restoring to the other
the life the other lived †
and now they have the lives they had
again in the other as their own.

Invited at last and forever by the river‡
to flow into eternity life with life.

---

* José Coronel Urtecho, great Nicaragua poet, and his wife, María Kautz (see more on him in References).
† one/other/other; life, lived, lives, invited: Imitation of Coronel Urtecho's poetic style, with varying words from a common root.
‡ "forever by the river": Reference to their permanent residence in the San Juan River area.

Esquelas mortuorias que corona la fama

Empiezo a recibir Convocatorias
en las que mis amigos ya son nombres de Concurso:
Jaime Sabines, por ejemplo, y yo recordándolo tan vivo
en casa de Efraín Huerta y su Telmanagua, en México, D.F.
con otros escritores alrededor de una mesa de trabajo
y entre los papeles con suficiente sitio para el ron.

Campeando el ingenio mexicano en el juego de palabras,
aunque ya ni sé si fui yo la protagonista
de una conversación que a lo mejor he imaginado
observando la foto en que aparece Efraín
con un parche en la garganta.
Tal vez nunca estuve en su mesa con él y Efraín Huerta
pero sí con Telma y su poesía
suficiente para acercarme a la de sus amigos,
además de las crónicas literarias
y etílicas de Julio Valle,
bebiéndose en su primera juventud
las reglas de juego dictadas por Mejía Sánchez
y la docta Rosario Castellanos desplazándose
como la describe Julio, sobria y sabia
vestida de traje sastre, rostro severo
de cejas impecables, una legítima Maestra,
también convertido su nombre y ya quizás el de Mejía
en Convocatoria de Concurso.

Death Notices Crowned by Fame

I begin to receive announcements of literary events
in which my friends are now names of contests.
Jaime Sabines,[*] for example, and I remember him so alive
at the home of Efraín Huerta[†] and his Telmanagua, in Mexico City,
with other writers around a worktable
and between the papers, sufficient room for rum.

Celebrating Mexican ingenuity with plays on words,
though I no longer know if I was the protagonist
in a conversation I may have imagined
observing the photo of Efraín
with a patch on his throat.
Perhaps I never was at his table with him and Efraín Huerta
but I was with Telma[‡] and his poetry
enough to approach that of his friends,
besides Julio Valle's[§]
literary and spirituous chronicles,
drinking in his first youth
the rules of the game dictated by Mejía Sánchez[¶]
and the learned Rosario Castellanos[**] walking around,
as Julio describes her, sober and sage
dressed in a fitted suit, severe face
with impeccable eyebrows, a legitimate Teacher,
her name now also converted, perhaps Mejía's too,
into an Announcement of Literary Contest.

---

[*] Jaime Sabines (1926-1999): Renowned Mexican poet.
[†] Efraín Huerta (1914-1982): Renowned Mexican poet.
[‡] Telma Nava: Efraín Huerta's wife. Her Nicaraguan friends recognize her support and soldarity by fondly calling her "Telmanagua." She cofounded in Mexico the pro-Sandinista movement "Hands Off Nicaragua."
[§] Julio Valle-Castillo (Masaya 1952): Nicaraguan writer, poet, novelist, essayist, art and literary critic, anthologist and historian of literature, who was mentored in Mexico by Ernesto Mejía Sánchez and wrote chronicles for Nicaraguan newspapers on his contacts with literary groups in the Mexican capital.
[¶] Mejía Sánchez, Ernesto (1923-1985): One of the great poets of the Nicaraguan Vanguard movement, who resided in Mexico City. Professor, poet and critic (see References).
[**] Rosario Castellanos (1925-1974): Renowned Mexican writer (see References).

Homenaje

Al Maestro CMR, en sus 70 años

Lo imagino solitario e iracundo
contra el mundo bofo.
Envuelta la total desnudez
en bata tomada al azar y con desgano.

Arribando, ya en la cúspide a sus setenta.
En permanente desafío a los eternos principiantes
enrostrándonos novísimos términos del léxico
registrados por la Real Academia de la Lengua.

Tomándonos del cuello y estampándonos
de nariz contra las páginas
para bucear el verbo, la palabra precisa
con que deberá contar este homenaje
para estar a la altura de quien en vida
ha ido escribiendo su propia, única forma
de danzar hasta el final,
como su alter ego Baudelaire,
conociendo el grado exacto de prensilidad
de la muerte encarnada
de la carne descarnada
de un esqueleto escarlata,
con el que se abrazará en el acto nutricio y supremo
que lo devolverá a su origen.

1994

Homage

To Master Teacher CMR*, on his 70th

I imagine him solitary raging irate
against the farcical world.
His absolute nakedness wrapped
in a robe grabbed by chance and reluctantly.

Arriving, now at the summit, to his seventies.
In permanent challenge to eternal beginners
reproaching our use of the newest lexical terms[†]
approved by the Royal Academy of Language.[‡]

Grabbing us by the nape of the neck and slamming
our noses against the pages
to dive for the verb, the exact word
that this homage should have
to be at the level of someone who in life
has written his own, unique form of
dancing to the end,
like his alter ego Baudelaire,[§]
knowing the exact degree of prehensility[¶]
of death in the flesh
of flesh unfleshed
of a scarlet skeleton,
that he will embrace in a supreme nourishing act
that will return him to his origin.

1994

---

* CMR: Carlos Martínez Rivas (1924-1998): One of the greatest Nicaraguan poets, exemplar for the generations of poets that included Meneses (see References).
† "reproaching our use of the newest lexical terms / approved by the Royal Academy of Language." In Chapter II Meneses relates perceptions about CMR surrounding an incident of public rebukes by him.
‡ Royal Academy of Language: A highly select Spanish honorary society founded in the 17th century. Its dictionary specifies words officially accepted as legitimate in the Spanish language. Since 1871 Latin American members have expanded the range of accepted terms.
§ Baudelaire, Charles (1821-1867): French poet who spoke of the tragic sense of life and explored occult relationships in the world.
¶ "knowing the exact degree of prehensility / of death in the flesh / of flesh unfleshed / of a scarlet skeleton": Intertextual reference and echo of CMR's plays on words.

Aquí estarías

Aquí estarías aborreciendo la estulticia
con que tantos expresan su cotidiano vivir.
Invitando a la amiga que pasa y se posa
en tu puerta infranqueable.
Reservada la entrada a tu casa
sólo a quien tu soberana voluntad decidiera.
Solicitando al pasante que te lleve,
con la urgencia de un moribundo,
a comprar una leche, un pan, una semilla de jícaro.
Deteniéndolo luego angustioso
en la vuelta de la rotonda para mirar a la putita,
musa predilecta de tus versos, estrella, cáliz de plata.
Lamento recogido en lo profundo de la tarde.
Herida abierta por nadie suturada
habitante nocturna de tu pecho en la alta noche.

2001

Here You Would Be *

Here you would be abhorring the stultification
with which so many express their daily life.
Inviting the girlfriend who passes and poses
at your unyielding door.
Admission to your house reserved
only for whomever your sovereign volition might deign.
Requesting the passerby to take you,
with the urgency of a dying man,
to buy a bottle of milk, a bread, a calabash seed.
Stopping him later anxiously
in the middle of the traffic circle to look at the little prostitute,
favorite muse of your verses, star, silver chalice.
Lament captured in the afternoon deep.
Open wound by no one sutured
nocturnal inhabitant of your chest in the middle of night.

2001

---

* Meneses clarified that the "you" addressed in the poem is the great teacher of her generation, Carlos Martínez Rivas (see previous poem and References).

Indagaciones

      I

¿Dónde estará, me pregunto, Igor Martínez,
mesero del hotel Praga e improvisado intérprete,
hijo de inmigrante hispano y madre soviética?
¿Y los traductores y guías Boris Klimenko y Ala?
¿Quiénes circulan ahora
por los largos pasillos del hotel Ukraína
levantado con imponente arquitectura catedralicia
a las orillas del río Moscova?
Y en el Kremlin,
¿continuará la infinita fila de recién casados
depositando sus ramos de bodas
sobre la tumba del soldado desconocido?

¿A qué hora salen los trenes hacia la cosmopolita
Leningrado, perdón, San Petersburgo
que espera con sus hileras de abedules,
iluminados en el mes de julio
por el sol de sus noches blancas,
la avenida Nevsky y el sereno curso del Neva,
la multifacética población que atraviesa el arco
hacia la plaza del Ermitage,
al Palacio de invierno de Catalina II,
o el vertiginoso Batiskav que se desplaza
hacia las quince fuentes del imponente Petrogodost

Inquiries

I

Where is, I wonder, Igor Martínez,
Praga Hotel waiter and improvised interpreter,
son of a Hispanic immigrant and Soviet mother?
And guide-translators Boris Klimenko and Ala?
Who walks now
down the Ukraine Hotel's long halls
built with imposing cathedral architecture
on the banks of the Moscow River?
And in the Kremlin,*
does an endless line of newlyweds still
place their wedding bouquets
on the tomb of the unknown soldier?

At what time do trains leave for the cosmopolitan
Leningrad,† sorry, Saint Petersburg
that awaits with its rows of birch trees,
lit in the month of July
by the sun of its white nights,
Nevsky Avenue and the calm flow of the Neva,
the multifaceted population that crosses under the arch
toward Hermitage Plaza,‡
the winter palace of Catherine II,§
or the swift Batiskav that moves
toward the fifteen fountains of the stately Petrogodost¶

---

* Kremlin: A self-contained city in the center of Moscow, on the banks of the Moscow River, with palaces, armories, churches, and a medieval fortress; former residence of the tsars; home of the Soviet government 1918-1991 and of the Russian government since 1991; declared World Heritage Site in 1990.
† Leningrad, Saint Petersburg, Nevsky Avenue Neva River: References to the port city of St. Petersburg, built by Peter the Great on the Gulf of Finland and the capital of Russia 1710-1918; called Petrograd from 1914 to 1924, and Leningrad from 1924 to 1991.
‡ Hermitage Museum, St. Petersburg: World's largest museum of art, with some three million works on exhibit, housing the art collections of Peter the Great and Catherine the Great and more modern acquisitions.
§ Catherine II, the Great (1729-1796): "Empress of All the Russias" (1762-1796), of the Romanov family dynasty; known as the epitome of the "enlightened despot" or "philosopher on the throne"; stimulated one of the most prosperous periods of the Russian Empire; patron of arts, literature, and education in contact with the French encyclopedists; commissioned the Hermitage Museum.
¶ Petrogodost, also, Petrodvorets, Peterhof: Peter's Palace, a major palace and park complex in the suburbs of St. Petersburg founded by Peter the Great in the early

del sagaz Pedro I, el hábil Zar de manos artesanas
y corazón imperial?

He soñado las voces
de Mayakovsky, de Pushkin y de Ana Ajmátova
levantándose inmortales como la presencia
de los millones que abonan infinitos rosales.

      II

Recuerdo a Velusheva, la funcionaria
de vacaciones en el Mar Negro.
Bulgaria tiene su forma graciosa de ser
y la conservará.
Veneran al poeta Jristo Botev
y a los gemelos Okiriul y Metodii,
creadores del alfabeto esclavo.
Igual que a Lenin en Moscú,
la guardia de honor custodiaba a Jorge Dimitrov.

of the wise Peter I,* talented Tsar with a craftman's hands
and imperial heart?

I have dreamed the voices
of Mayakovsky,† Pushkin‡ and Anna Akhmátova§
rising immortal like the presence
of the millions who nurture infinite rose bushes.

II

I remember Velusheva, the government worker
on vacation in the Black Sea.
Bulgaria has an a humorous way of being
that it will conserve.
They venerate poet Hristo Botev¶
and twins Cyril and Methodius, **
creators of the Slavic alphabet.
Like for Lenin†† in Moscow,
the honor guard watched over Georgi Dimitrov.‡‡

1700s, with stately parks, plentiful fountains, beautiful cascades, gilt and marble statues of gods and heroes, and exuberant decoration of the palaces to symbolize the grandeur of Russia.

* Peter I, the Great (1672-1725): Russian tsar (1682-1725) and emperor (1721-1725) of the Romanov family dynasty; known for the modernization and westernization of Russia; made St. Petersburg the capital (1710).

† Mayakovsky, Vladimir (1893-1930): Soviet futurist poet and dramatist who praised the Russian Revolution of 1917 but satirized the new regime. Also mentioned by Meneses in "Pedro: Just Now, I Have Been Remembering" in *Air that Calls Me*.

‡ Pushkin, Alexander (1799-1837): Great Russian writer; poetic child prodigy; founder of the Russian novel with his *Eugene Onegin*. Also mentioned by Meneses in "Message for Alba Azucena," *Flame in the Wind*.

§ Anna Akhmátova (1889-1966): Pseudonym of Anna Andréievna Gorenko, Soviet poet associated with St. Petersburg/Leningrad, who abandoned her early poetry on love and feminine intimacy to link her own tragedy to that of Russia. Also mentioned by Meneses in "Travel Notes," *Air that Calls Me*.

¶ Hristo Botev (1848-1876): Bulgarian writer and patriot, philosopher of materialism, known for his nationalist and revolutionary poems; died in combat against the Ottoman Turks.

** Cyril and Methodius: Catholic saints who evangelized the Slavs in the 9th century; brothers born in Salonika, Greece, died in Rome; translators of the Bible and liturgical texts into Slavic; Cyril created a Slavic alphabet that was later simplified and called the Cyrillic alphabet.

†† Lenin, Vladimir (born Vladimir Ilich Ulyanov 1870-1924): Russian politician and Marxist theorist; proponent of the conception of a centralized, revolutionary party, led by a professional cadre; Bolshevik director of the 1917 Revolution; first premier of the Soviet Union.

‡‡ Georgi Dimitrov (1882-1949): Bulgarian politician; general secretary of Third

Me pregunto, ¿Y en una avenida
de la moderna, industrializada Sofía,
estarán aún los dos ancianos fotógrafos
bajo el tapado negro, haciéndoles daguerrotipo
a los transeúntes?

III

En Potsdam se distribuyeron Alemania
que había producido a Hitler y al fascismo,
pero también a Carlos Marx y a Rosa Luxemburgo,
a Kant, a Hegel y a Engels,
a Beethoven y a Juan Sebastián Bach,

I wonder, on an avenue in
modern, industrialized Sofia,*
are the two ancient photographers still
under the black hood, taking daguerrotypes
of passersby?

III

In Potsdam† they divided up the Germany
that had produced Hitler‡ and fascism,§
but also Karl Marx¶ and Rosa Luxemburg,**
Kant,†† Hegel,‡‡ and Engels,§§
Beethoven¶¶ and Johann Sebastian Bach,***

Communist International (1934-1943); Bulgarian prime minister (1946-1949).
* Sofia: Capital of Bulgaria.
† Potsdam: German city southwest of Berlin. The Potsdam Conference at the end of World War II (July-August 1945) defined the occupation of Germany and Austria by the victors: Great Britain, Russia, and the United States.
‡ Hitler, Adolf (1889-1945): German political leader; developer of the racist, ultranationalist, anti-Semitic doctrine of Nazism, National Socialism; German chancellor in 1933, later president and Führer at the head of a dictatorial state that attempted to annex large sections of neighboring countries and exterminate Jewish populations; defeated in 1945, ending World War II.
§ fascism: Hierarchical, nationalist, totalitarian political system with one party, severe censorship and repression of liberties, cult of the leader, predominance of police and military power; associated with Hitler in Germany and Mussolini in Italy from the 1920s to the defeat of Germany in 1945.
¶ Karl Marx (1818-1883): German philosopher, economist, and politician; theorized historical materialism, which prioritizes material changes as the motor of history, based in part on Hegel; proposed class struggle as a liberating principal, especially that of the proletariat against exploitative capitalists.
** Rosa Luxemburg (1870-1919): Marxist theoretician, philosopher, politician, and revolutionary; author of several analyses of capital and of trade unions.
†† Kant, Immanuel (1724-1804): German philosopher who defined the parameters of knowledge accessible through reason and the moral obligation or "categorical imperative," based on the autonomy of human free will.
‡‡ Hegel, Friedrich (1770-1831): German philosopher who systematized the dialectical method of inquiry that proceeds by overcoming contradictory theses.
§§ Engels, Friedrich (1820-1895): German theoretician and politician; Marx's collaborator for several foundational texts on socialism as a superior socioeconomic stage to that of capitalism; proponent of historical and dialectical materialism.
¶¶ Beethoven, Ludwig van (1770-1827): German composer, child prodigy, precursor of German romanticism.
*** Johann Sebastian Bach (1685-1750): German composer of vocal, instrumental, and religious music.

a Goethe y a Brecht,
a Wilhelm von Humboldt y a Beckenbauer,
para nombrar desde la filosofía al football.

¿Estará vivo mi amigo, Wolfgang Hoffman,
viejo obrero que en la revolución
estudió para historiador y traductor,
fino tallador de figuras de madera
los quiebranueces con cara de monarcas,
princesas y leñadores que encarnaron la historia?
¿Y su esposa, maestra jubilada
que sustituyó las agujas de tejer
que alteraban los nervios de la pareja
con su clic, clic, clic
y se dedicó a pintar en radiantes colores
las colecciones de muñecos quiebranueces?

¿Le habrán publicado al viejo
los lindos cuentos para sus nietos
que me leyó sentados en una banca
de la plaza Carlos Marx?
Pienso que por sus ojos habrán pasado
vertiginosos los días,
protagonistas de la generación del asalto al cielo.
Lo imagino ahora, atónito ciudadano
asomado al impredecible fin de siglo.

Octubre 1995

Goethe* and Brecht,†
Wilhelm von Humboldt‡ and Beckenbauer, §
to name names from philosophy to soccer.

Is my friend alive, Wolfgang Hoffman,
an old worker who during the revolution
studied to be a historian and translator,
fine sculptor of wooden figures,
nutcrackers with the faces of monarchs,
princesses and woodsmen that incarnated history?
And his wife, retired teacher
who put down her knitting needles that
got on the couple's nerves
with their click, click, click
and began to paint in bright colors
the collection of nutcracker dolls?

Will they have published the old man's
lovely stories for his grandchildren
that he read to me seated on a bench
in Karl Marx Square?
I think that passing before his eyes
were vertiginous days,
protagonists of the generation of the assault on heaven.
I imagine him now, amazed citizen
at the edge of the unpredictable end of the century.

October 1995

---

* Goethe, Johann Wolfgang von (1749-1832): German writer and natural philosopher; principal figure of the 18th-century Storm and Stress Movement (*The Sorrows of Young Werther,* 1774); later evolved toward more classical tendencies (*Faust* 1808; 1832).
† Brecht, Bertolt (1898-1956): German playwright, poet and fiction writer; proponent of distanced criticism and non-identification with characters in a work of art. Also mentioned by Meneses in "Autumn Stroll" and "To Future Men and Women," *Flame in the Wind.*
‡ Wilhelm von Humboldt (Potsdam 1767-Tegel 1835): German linguist and politician who attempted to find commonalities between language, thought, and cultures. His brother, Alexander von Humboldt (Berlin 1769-Potsdam 1859), was a naturalist and geographer who studied the flora and fauna in Spain, Canary Islands, Spanish America, and Asia.
§ Beckenbauer, Franz (Munich 1945): German soccer player, captain of the West German team that won the World Cup in 1974.

Itinerario/97

I

Me anunciaron Ginebra aséptica
como un quirófano.
Me sorprendió el silencio
en calles y autobuses,
pero aún más, el osado muchacho
que saltó al tren con su guitarra
y comenzó a entonar una canción.

II

Recorrí Berlín unificado de noche
de nuevo, en su costado este,
me encontré a Carlos Marx y a Engels
tallados en poderosa escultura oscura.
Marx sentado y Engels de pie
observando el desmontaje del escenario
que realiza poderosa maquinaria
borrando la antigua faz de la ciudad.
En la penumbra, erecta,
la torre de Alexanderplatz
el reloj mundial de la solidaridad
que no ha detenido su marcha
imperturbable, ante la caída del muro.

III

Viena, sobria e imperial
con sus Palacios Reales y jardines
no queda exenta
de los bluejeans y zapatos tenis
en el corre, corre
de trenes y autobuses.

Itinerary/97

I

They warned me of a Geneva as sterile
as an operating room.
The silence of streets and buses
surprised me,
but even more, the daring young man
who leapt onto the train with his guitar
and began singing a song.

II

I roamed united Berlin by night
again, on its eastern side,
I found Karl Marx and Engels*
carved in a powerful dark statue.
Marx seated and Engels standing
observing the striking of the set
powerful machinery accomplishes,
erasing the ancient face of the city.
In the twilight, erect,
Alexanderplatz tower
the world clock of solidarity which
has not stopped ticking
unperturbed, with the fall of the wall.

III

Vienna, sober and imperial
with its Royal Palaces and gardens
not free from
blue jeans and tennis shoes
in the hustle and bustle
of trains and buses.

---

* Karl Marx, Engels: German socialist theoreticians of the 19th century (see notes to previous poem).

IV

En el monumento más alto de Londres
honran al Almirante Lord Nelson
la explicación de la altura
es porque así divisa el mar.
Pocos saben que la frágil
y llorosa Rafaela Herrera
con sábanas incendiadas
incineró sus naves
en nuestro Río San Juan.

V

En Estocolmo, mi prima Ivania
y mi amiga Ritva
viven en Bromma,
pero toman la vida en serio.

Julio 1997

IV

In the highest monument in London
they honor Admiral Lord Nelson,*
the explication for the height is
so he can see the sea.
Few know that the fragile
and tearful Rafaela Herrera†
with sheets set ablaze
torched his ships
on our San Juan River.‡

V

In Stockholm, my cousin Ivania
and my friend Ritva
live in Bromma,§
but they take life seriously.

Julio 1997

---

* Lord Nelson (1758-1805): British admiral, served in India, conquered Malta, defeated the French-Spanish fleet in battle off the Cape of Trafalgar in Spain, and died in that battle.

† Rafaela Herrera: Symbol of the bravery and patriotism of Nicaraguan youths and women. The British Crown, seeking an interoceanic waterway, sent a naval contingent to invade Nicaragua in 1762 along the San Juan River and demand surrender of the Immaculate Conception Castle. Given the cowardice of the fort's leaders, Rafaela Herrera, a 19-year-old woman "tearful" after the recent death of her father, the fort commander, shot a cannon blast that wreaked havoc on the English vessels. She then soaked sheets in alcohol, lit them, and sent them floating toward the enemy fleet, which retreated.

‡ San Juan River: Southern river that divides Nicaragua and Costa Rica, considered at various historical times as the best route for the construction of an interoceanic canal.

§ Bromma: The Spanish word for joke, humorous act, or comment is "broma."

Hoja de diario

Aún guardo el olor-sabor de Isla Negra,
las empanadas chilenas y el vino,
la terraza de la casa de Carmen,
la grama verde, la bañera sembrada de flores
y la montaña de la poderosa cordillera de los Andes
al alcance de la mano.
Sobre ella, el desplazamiento del ovni
visto por María José y por mí.

Aún percibo la tibieza de las sábanas
en mi habitación de Reina de Saba.
El cerro de Santa Lucía coronado de identidad
con hierbas medicinales, chalecos bordados a mano
y las tristísimas notas de la flauta andina.

El derroche milenario de piedras preciosas y semi preciosas
—lapislázuli y malaquita— exhibidas en el mercado
que recorrimos con Cecilia Leblanc.
El calor de Santiago que me hizo recordar Managua.
Y el regreso al atardecer como a mi casa,
donde Morazán me espera con el caldo al jerez,
como ustedes lo hicieron, cálidas hermanas.

Diciembre 1996

Diary Page

I still preserve the smell-taste of Isla Negra,[*]
Chilean empanadas and wine,
the terrace at Carmen's house,[†]
green grass, tub sown with flowers
and the mountain of the powerful Andes range
an arm's length away.
Above it, the passing of a UFO
seen by María José[‡] and me.

I still feel the warmth of the sheets
in my Queen of Sheba room.[§]
Santa Lucía[¶] hill crowned by identity
with medicinal herbs, hand-embroidered vests,
and the most sad notes of the Andean flute.

The millenary extravagance of precious and semiprecious stones
—lapis lazuli and malachite— on display in the market
we visited with Cecilia Leblanc.[**]
The warmth of Santiago made me remember Managua.
And the afternoon return to my home,
where Morazán[††] awaits me with a bowl of broth-with-sherry,
as did you, warm sisters.

December 1996

---

[*] Isla Negra: Home of the Chilean Nobel laureate, Pablo Neruda (1904-1973).
[†] Carmen Waugh: Chilean art collector and gallery founder; organizer in Managua, under the Sandinista Ministry of Culture, of the Julio Cortázar Museum of Contemporary Art.
[‡] María José: Carmen Waugh's daughter.
[§] Queen of Sheba: Legendary queen of immense wealth of Ethiopian or Arabian origin.
[¶] Santa Lucía Hill: Hill in the midst of the city of Santiago de Chile, with a popular market of herbs and handmade products at its base.
[**] Cecilia Leblanc: Chilean who worked in the Nicaraguan Ministry of Culture during the Sandinista decade.
[††] Morazán, Sergio: Meneses's husband, known to be a great chef.

Interrogantes

¿Quién comprendió a la mujer rescatada de haber sido
la cabellera flotante entre los nenúfares?
¿Quién osó penetrar su real intimidad
para encontrar la uña en el pecho?
¿Quién escuchó su grito solitario en la madrugada?
¿Quién vió su cuerpo recogido, fetal, entre las sábanas?
¿Quién escuchó el sollozo en el trasfondo de sus palabras?
¿Quién descubrió la sombra gris debajo de sus párpados maquillados?
¿Quién, su mano crispada entre la cruz y el puño?
¿Quién vió en la sensualidad de sus hombros
la corva sombra del agobio?
¿Quién supo acariciar sus pechos
con la ternura que se da a un recién nacido?
¿Quién le penetró las entrañas y se le acomodó
como manso pájaro en el tibio cuenco?
¿Quién le da a esa mujer su verdadero sitial en el paraíso?

Questions

Who understood the woman rescued from becoming
long hair floating among water lilies?
Who dared penetrate her true intimacy
to discover the claw in her breast?
Who heard her lonely scream at daybreak?
Who saw her huddled, fetal body among the sheets?
Who heard the sob in the background of her words?
Who discovered the gray shadow beneath her tinted eyelids?
Who sensed her hand clenched, half-cross, half-fist?
Who saw in her shoulders' sensuality
the curved shadow of exhaustion?
Who knew how to caress her breasts
with tenderness given to newborns?
Who thrust into her body and was welcomed
like a gentle bird in the warm hollow?
Who gives that woman her rightful place in paradise?

[Translation by Andrés G. Tucker]

Vivas estamos

A Michèle, a Daisy, a mis hermanas poetas

Vivas estamos sobre su memoria.

      I

La osadía intelectual
de la adoradora de la diosa blanca,
Virginia Woolf, preparando el rito,
la palabra mágica, invocadora
del andrógino ordenador del caos.

Sólo en sus manuscritos la armonía
bajo el bombardeo a su casa
en Tavistock Square.

Ella escribiendo:
     "Gotas de sudor en la frente
     de la señorita La Trobe",
presagio de su propio fin.

Todo está consumado,
     "La vejez es el camino
     natural hacia la muerte".
Y se sumergió con serenidad
en las apacibles aguas del Ouse.

Alive Are We

For Michèle,* for Daisy,† for my sister poets

Alive we are upon their memory.

    I

The intellectual audacity
of the white goddess worshipper,
Virginia Woolf,‡ preparing the ritual,
the magic word, prophetess
of the androgynous orderer of chaos.

Harmony only in her manuscripts
with bombing over her house
in Tavistock Square.

And she writes:
    "Drops of sweat on the brow
    of Miss La Trobe,"
premonition of her own end.

All is consummated.
    "Old age is the natural path
    toward death."
And she serenely submerged
in the gentle waters of the Ouse.

---

* Michèle Najlis (Granada 1946): Contemporary poet and friend of Meneses, author of several collections of mystical poetry (see Chapter II).

† Daisy Zamora (Managua 1950): Contemporary poet and friend of Meneses; vice-minister of Culture under the Sandinistas; author of poetry collections that show disconformity with the situation of women (see Chapter II).

‡ Virginia Woolf (1882-1941): English novelist, essayist and critic; analyst of the situation of women and the possibility of an androgynous consciousness; defender of a woman's access to "a room of her own" in order to meditate and write; committed suicide in the Ouse River. Also mentioned in "Heart in the Open," a prose-poem not published in a collection.

II

Poco le duró el sueño a Sylvia Plath.
Apresada en lo doméstico.
Aturdida entre la libertad y el desamparo.
Expuesta como bebé desangrado
para ser arrastrado por el mar.
El alma columpiada:
Eros o Tánatos hasta sucumbir,
el día preparado con la rigurosidad
de un orfebre,
cuando de rodillas
metió su cabeza rubia
en el horno de la estufa de gas.

III

Alfonsina, apasionada,
consciente que ningún canto
sería más alto que su propia vida de mujer,
se defendió con torrentes de carcajadas
que la llevaron hasta el llanto
y amó hasta la consumación de sus días.

¡Tanto fuego, sólo las olas
de Mar del Plata
pudieron aplacar!

Vivas estamos sobre su memoria.
Inolvidables hermanas que nos precedieron.
Poetas, criaturas agónicas, sobrevivientes,
¡Triunfalmente vivas estamos sobre su memoria!

II

Short lived was the dream of Sylvia Plath*
Trapped in domesticity.
Dazed between freedom and helplessness.
Exposed like a bloodless baby
to be carried out to sea.
The soul swung back and forth:
Eros† or Thanatos‡ until she succumbed,
the day prepared with the precision
of a goldsmith,
when on her knees
she put her blond head
into the gas-filled oven.

III

Alfonsina,§ impassioned,
aware that no song
would be as lofty as her own life as a woman,
defended herself with torrents of laughter
that left her in tears
and loved until the consummation of her days.

Such fire only the waves
at Mar del Plata
could placate!

Alive are we upon their memory.
Unforgettable sisters who came before us.
Poets, agonizing creatures, survivors.
Triumphantly alive are we upon their memory!

---

* Sylvia Plath (1932-1963): U.S. poet and novelist who explored themes related to identity, women's consciousness, and mental illness among women writers; committed suicide at age 30.

† Eros: God of love in Greek mythology.

‡ Thanatos: Personification of death in Greek mythology.

§ Alfonsina Storni (1892-1938): Argentine poet and playwright who reclaimed a woman's point of view toward love and challenged men's social privilege; considered an early modern feminist voice; suffering from cancer, she threw herself into the ocean.

Convocatoria a la belleza

No soy la primera mujer que recorre su rostro
y descubre la intensidad de lo vivido
en el peso de sus párpados abultados
sobre el hundimiento de los ojos.

El pliegue vertical en la confluencia de las cejas
hondura del paso de las preocupaciones.
Los paréntesis de la risa abiertos
de la nariz a las comisuras
(hondamente pronunciadas) de los labios
y el cuello de anfibio que ya perdió su elasticidad

Tal visión descarnada en el espejo,
me lleva, mujer del mestizaje,
a recurrir al consejo de mis mayores:
cuidar la armonía del rostro con el corazón.
       Y eso me hace inmortal.

Mayo 1998

Poema del desamor

He visto a la mujer rondar el cetro,
el centro de su vida misma.
Ensayar la sonrisa más seductora de Eva
descalzarse ante el amado
y poner la ofrenda sagrada de su cuerpo
en las manos del hombre desconcertado
ante la abundancia.
¿En qué momento les crecieron los días,
esa distancia insalvable entre los dos?
¿Qué trampa les ha jugado la vida
 a éstos mil veces sorprendidos por la aurora?
¿Qué secretos arpegios habrá de pulsar ahora
para conducirlo de nuevo al paraíso?
¿Qué cantos de sirena? ¿Qué música encantada?
¿Qué incienso? ¿Qué aliento para convocar de nuevo el fuego?

Enero 2000

Beauty Contest

I am not the first woman who examines her face
and discovers the intensity of her life
in the weight of puffy eyelids
over sinking eyes.

The vertical crease at eyebrow juncture,
depth from traces of worries.
The parentheses of laughter opened
from the nose to the corners
(deeply pronounced) of the mouth
and the amphibian neck that has lost its elasticity.

Such a stark vision in the mirror,
leads me, a mestizo woman,
to heed the advice of my elders:
secure the harmony of the face with the heart.
        And that makes me immortal.

May 1998

Poem on Disaffection

I have seen the woman circle the scepter,
the center of her own life.
Try Eve's most seductive smile,
bare her feet before the beloved
and place the sacred offering of her body
into the hands of the man disconcerted
by such abundance.
When did their days grow long,
and the distance between them unbrigeable?
What trick did life play on these two
a thousand times surprised by the dawn?
What secret arpeggios must be strummed now
to draw him again to paradise?
What siren songs? What enchanted music?
What incense? What breath to reignite the fire?

January 2000

Esa mujer está loca

Esa mujer está loca
la he dejado hablando con su sombra.
Hace poco sabía que la oficina de correos
era la casa azul y blanco, un puente
para comunicarse con el mundo
por teléfono, por telégrafo, por carta.
Hoy no encontró buzón para las cartas,
ha llegado sin brújula a cualquier calle
donde le señalan la gasolinera
con su tienda abierta e iluminada
las 24 horas como un velorio.
Allí le recibirán la carta, —le dijeron—
pero ha hurgado en el insondable vacío
del viejo bolso desguindado en su hombro
y no hay rastros de la exigua ganancia de la semana
esfumada entre el pasaje de bus,
el pago proporcional de agua del puesto comunal
y las tres horas diarias de luz de la única bujía.
Esa mujer está loca,
sigue dialogando con su sombra.
Ha visto máquinas en unas casas
por las que se envían y se reciben mensajes,
y ella está más incomunicada que nunca.
Esa mujer está loca,
pero aún teme perder la cabeza,
por eso se aferra a su sombra.

2000

That Woman Is Crazy

That woman is crazy
I left her talking with her shadow.
A moment ago, she knew that the post office
was the blue and white building, a bridge
to communicate with the world
by telephone, by telegraph, by letter.
Today, she did not find the box for letters,
she arrived without compass at some street
where they pointed to the gas station
with its mini-mart open and lit up
24 hours a day like a wake.
"They'll take your letter over there," they told her,
but she's dug into the bottomless vacuum
of the old bag falling off her shoulder,
and there's no trace of her week's meager earnings,
vanished between bus fare,
her share of the communal water,
and her daily three hours of light from a single bulb.
That woman is crazy,
she still dialogues with her shadow.
She has seen machines in houses
for sending and receiving messages,
yet she is more disconnected than ever.
That woman is crazy
but still fears losing her mind,
that's why she clings to her shadow.

2000

Virgo

No conoció varón ni vibró ante voz masculina.
Sus labios se cerraron herméticos al primer beso.
Sus ovarios se endurecieron
como dátiles secos del desierto.
Su útero fue la entrada inviolada
a la caverna de la soledad.

Sus manos no recorrieron
rostro ni espalda de hombre;
a cambio sujetaron agujas
y tejieron ajuares para niños ajenos.

Su máxima aspiración se cumplió
cuando en su féretro colocaron
el lirio blanco de las vírgenes prudentes.
Falo florecido para nadie.

Virgo

She knew no man nor trembled at a male voice.
Her lips sealed hermetically at the first kiss.
Her ovaries grew hard
like dry desert dates.
Her uterus was the unviolated entryway
to the cavern of her solitude.

Her hands traced neither
face nor back of man;
instead, they wielded needles and
knitted layettes for others' babies

Her highest aspiration was reached
when in her coffin they placed
the white lily of prudent virgins.
Phallus flowered for no one.

La María Shangai

Voluptuosa se desparramaba
como ninguna en la cama.
A su puerta la fila de imberbes adolescentes
se frotaban las manos heladas
en la calurosa tarde de iniciación.

María Shangai fue puerto
donde amainaron las primeras tempestades.

Las matronas y el obispo la condenaron en vida
y se golpearon el pecho ante sus cenizas.

Los hombres le agradecieron sus buenos oficios
en rubricar la condición de machos de su descendencia.
Ahora ella duerme plácida
el sueño de las justas.

Nadie se atrevió a lanzar la primera piedra.

María Shanghai*

Voluptuously she writhed
like no other woman in bed.
At her door, the line of smooth-faced adolescents
rubbed their cold hands
on the hot afternoon of initiation.

María Shanghai was the port
where first storms were calmed.

Proper ladies and the bishop condemned her alive
and struck their chests before her ashes.

Men thanked her for her good offices
in certifying their descendants as macho men.
She now placidly enjoys the
sleep of the just.

No one dared cast the first stone. †

---

* María Shanghai: Meneses explains that María Shanghai, maternal and educative in her work, was the sexual initiator of generations of young men from "decent" families. According to the double moral standard of the time, women should remain virgins until marriage; but for men, the more women they had, the more manly or macho they were considered, and they began to frequent brothels from age 13 or 14. For a while, Meneses wondered whether this custom was not an advantage for men, since they could resolve their sexual impulses, whereas women's sexuality was repressed. Later discussions with men, however, revealed such encounters as occasionally traumatic, given the contrast between the conception of love as a beautiful thing and those first sexual relations with prostitutes who could be brusque and less than ideal as women. But also, this was a means for the boys to define themselves as heterosexual machos, as required by patriarchy.

† "No one dared cast the first stone": Reference to the Bible story of the compassion of Jesus for the adulteress (John 8:7): "If any one of you is without sin, let him be the first to throw a stone at her."

Cuando sólo un árbol te sostiene

Sonreír cuando los ojos están serios.
(Dicen que el aburrimiento
          es una forma de agresividad).
Podredumbre de nuevo.
Pero no en los suburbios
de los excluidos como se espera.
El cieno está en el centro del salón,
del país maquillado como viejo travesti
enmascarando las huellas de su senectud,
la mueca que no llega a ser sonrisa.
Pura fachada. Detrás el marasmo.
En los rescoldos del tiempo
hundo mi desesperanza
y a pesar de ello,
la pasión por un día mejor para todos, persiste.
El anhelo de recuperar la belleza total
como el follaje en los brazos generosos del limonero
que veo a través de la ventana cada amanecer.

When Only a Tree Sustains You[*]

Smiling when the eyes are serious.
(They say that boredom
        is a form of aggressiveness).
Putrefaction once again.
But not in the slums
of the excluded, as you might think.
The slime is in the center of the salon,
of the nation made-up like an old transvestite
masking traces of his senectitude,
the grimace not quite a smile.
Pure façade. Behind it, paralysis.
In the embers of time
I bury my desperation
and, despite this
persists the passion for a better day for all.
Yearning to recover full beauty
like the foliage in the generous arms of the lemon tree
I see outside my window each dawn.

---

[*] Inspired, according the poet, by testimony from a Jewish Holocaust concentration camp survivor. Chilean author María Luisa Bombal (1910-1980) explored a similar theme in her short story, "The Tree."

Viaje hacia el interior

He iniciado el viaje al centro de mí misma,
el necesario retorno a las cosas elementales:
un río y su lecho de piedras blancas y pulidas,
flores silvestres —copa de miel para las mariposas—
y atardeceres aturdidos por las chicharras.

Busco la fuente primigenia,
la materia acuosa en la que me formé,
la silenciosa y plácida cavidad
donde mis células se reprodujeron
con la magnificencia galáctica del Big Bang.

Indago por ese origen de vida,
de donde ya han emergido hijos de mis hijas
el misterio desplazándose sobre las aguas,
las partículas vivas y dispersas
apareciendo y desapareciendo.

—Tanto afán por ordenar el caos!
—y si decido quedarme quieta
como una tabla de surf, suelta,
sobre el vaivén de las olas?

Mayo 1998

Journey toward the Interior[*]

I have begun the journey to the center of myself,
the necessary return to elemental things:
a river and its bed of smooth, white stones,
wildflowers —cup of honey for butterflies—
and afternoons buzzing with cicadas.

I seek the primary fountain,
the aqueous material in which I was formed,
the silent, placid cavity
where my cells were reproduced
with the galactic magnificence of the Big Bang.[†]

I search for that origin of life,
from which children of my daughters already have emerged,
the mystery spreading out over the waters,
the live, disperse particles
appearing and disappearing.

—Such desire to order the chaos!
And what if I decide to stay quiet
like a surfboard loose
on the ebb and flow of the waves?

May 1998

---

[*] (See the poet's comments on this poem in Chapter II.)
[†] Big Bang: The theory that the Earth, and, therefore, life, began as the result of an explosion of enormous magnitude.

In extremis

> *¿Qué se hace a la hora de morir?*
> *—Rosario Castellanos*

Quizás sumida en la inconsciencia
o en el ámbito del dolor insoportable
nos lleguen a los oídos los ruidos cotidianos del hogar.
El clic del vaivén del lampazo.
El estrujante voltear de las páginas del diario
que lee tu pareja o el pariente cercano.
El timbre del teléfono anunciando una llamada
que ya perdió su sentido.
El chorro de agua del lavatrastos
un perro ladrando al paso del desconocido.
La cortina levantada por el viento
que toca con dedos invisibles
el cedazo de las ventanas.
Ruidos que preceden al gran silencio
umbral de la reconciliación consigo misma
cielo o infierno
—recuperación o pérdida
acaso definitiva, de la esencia del ser?

Julio 2000

In extremis

What does one do at the hour of death?
—Rosario Castellanos[*]

Perhaps submerged in unconsciousness
or in the realm of intolerable pain
the daily noises of home come to our ears.
The back and forth click of the mop.
The chrinkling turn of newspaper pages
that your partner or a close relative reads.
The telephone ring announcing a call
that has lost its meaning.
The rush of water in the dishwasher,
a dog barking at a passing stranger.
The curtain raised by the wind
that touches with invisible fingers
the window screens.
Noises that precede the great silence
threshold to the reconciliation with herself
heaven or hell
—recovery or loss,
perhaps definitive, of the essence of being?

July 2000

---

[*] Rosario Castellanos (1925-1974): Mexican writer (see References).

POEMS AND OTHER POETIC
PUBLICATIONS NOT IN COLLECTIONS

Invocación en días calurosos

Digo fuego y tu abrazo me abrasa.

1998

Analiza tu vida

Analiza tu vida
que ya está programada.

A lo mejor ya vieja, las canas te pesen
y te hagan bajar la cabeza

porque tu herencia será lastre
y tus descendientes,
indefensos insectos adheridos.

Invocation on Hot Days

I say fire and your embrace scorches me.

1998

Analyze Your Life

Analyze your life
that is already programmed.

When you're an old woman, grey hairs might weigh on you
and make you bow your head

because your legacy will be useless
and your descendants,
defenseless, smashed insects.

A Guillermo, Guardafronteras y hermanos

Hoy escuché el poema que nos dedicaste,
y me di cuenta del eco de nostalgia
que te dejamos en el pecho.
¿Cómo decirte que pactamos para siempre
y hacerte sentir que aún aquí nos batimos por la vida?

¡Cómo hacerte llegar este puño trenzado,
a lo mejor de un conjunto de debilidades
que unidos alcanzan su fuerza vigorosa?

¿Con qué palabras deslizarnos en tu pozo tirador
para musitar en tu oído nuestra presencia
y ofrecerte nuestros cantos para llenar tu vigilia?

1983

Guardafrontera

Quisiera escribirte con las trazadoras
El mejor poema de amor en la noche,
Llenar tu cantimplora con el agua más fresca
De nuestros ríos
Y balancear tu hamaca
Con las suaves ondas del lago
Convertirme en ceiba umbrosa
Sobre tu calurosa trinchera
Y poblarte la mente de recuerdos gratos
A la hora de la tregua en la línea de fuego.

Guardafrontera, Guardabarranco de la libertad
Guardador de nuestra soberanía.

1983

To Borderguard Guillermo and His Brothers and Sisters

Today I heard the poem you dedicated to us,
and sensed the echo of nostalgia
we left in your heart.
How can I tell you that we bonded forever
and make you feel that, even here, we're fighting for life?

How to send you this fist woven,
perhaps, from a bunch of weaknesses
which, united, achieve their vigorous power?

With what words to slip into your foxhole
and murmur our presence in your ear
and offer you our songs to fill your vigil?

1983

Borderguard *

I'd like to write you with tracer bullets
The best love poem at night,
Fill your canteen with the freshest water
From our rivers
And rock your hammock
With the soft waves of the lake,
Turn into a shady ceiba tree
Over your hot trench
And populate your mind with fond memories
At the hour of the lull on the front line.

Borderguard, Guardabarranco† of liberty,
Guardian of our sovereignty.

1983

---

* Published in the poet's campaign journal, where she explains that she improvised this poem after returning from the war zone and that it was immediately set to music by Grupo Pueblo.
† Guardabarranco: National bird of Nicaragua. The name literally means "ravine-guard."

Maestro, tu voz

> *Veo sus cosas ya insostenibles,*
> *deshabitándose.*
> —Pablo Antonio Cuadra, Oración por Joaquín Pasos

Que nos seas vos ahora
el que regresa a reconocer su ausencia
cuando el ala sutil del Ángel
ya te hizo traspasar el Paraíso.

Una rauda piel de jaguar
prendida a los ojos relampagueantes
iluminan ahora el bosque.
El Maestro de Tarca al fin encontró su puerto.
Dejó aullantes sirenas con sus cabellos
extendidos en la noche
cuando un cielo oscuro pronosticó tempestades
al solitario Capitán en la proa.

Mástiles y velas rendidas al vendaval
regresan tus versos en las encrespadas olas
como las conchas y caracoles tornasolados.
Brillan y nos dicen de nuevo tu palabra de eternidad.
Tu voz ha anclado en el tiempo.

Noviembre 4 del 2005

Leído el 4 de noviembre de 2005 en homenaje al aniversario de su cumpleaños. Publicado en *ANIDE* 4.10 (Dic. 2005): 8-9.

Master, Your Voice

> *I see his things already unsustainable,*
> *emptying themselves.*
> —Pablo Antonio Cuadra,* Oration for Joaquín Pasos

You are the one now
who returns to recognize his absence,
when the Angel's subtle wing
has crossed you into Paradise.

The swift jaguar skin
hung on flashing eyes
light up the woods now.
The Teacher of Tarca found his port at last.
He left wailing sirens with their hair
stretched into the night
when a dark sky foretold storms
to the solitary Captain at the prow.†

Masts and sails surrendered to the windstorm,
your verses return on rippling waves
like iridescent shells and sea snails.
They sparkle and repeat to us your word of eternity.
Your voice has anchored in time.

November 4, 2005

Read on November 4, 2005, at a homage to Cuadra's birthday. Published in *ANIDE* 4.10 (Dec. 2005): 8-9.

---

* Pablo Antonio Cuadra (Managua 1912-Nov. 4, 2002): Renowned poet of the Nicaraguan Vanguard, fiction writer, playwright, and essayist. This poem contains intertextual references to works by Cuadra: the poetry collection, *The Jaguar and the Moon* (1959) and the 11 poems under the title, "The Teacher of Tacna" in *Songs of Cifar*.
† "when a dark sky foretold storms / to the solitary Capitain in the prow": Allusion to Cuadra's metaphor in a 1978 essay, "The Ship is Still at Anchor," just before *La Prensa* newspaper was shut down, which refers to the dictator Somoza as a ship's capitain who denies the rights of his crew.

Corazón en pampa

Fuí concebida en acto de apasionada joven de diecisiete años. Según me cuentan, me deslicé imperceptiblemente a la vida una fría madrugada en Matagalpa, rodeada de tías abuelas, vírgenes virtuosas que afanadas bañaron mi cuerpo de aceites y agua tibia y perfumada.

Me bautizaron con un nombre poético y vital, combinación del de mi madre: Vida, sinónimo de Eva, la mujer expulsada del paraíso, y del que aparecía el 28 de mayo de 1944, en el Almanaque de Bristol: Luz, de Nuestra Señora de la Luz, mujer elegida entre todas las mujeres para Madre de Dios.

Según la ubicación de los astros a la hora de mi nacimiento, pertenezco al signo Géminis, por lo tanto soy pagana y mística, terrestre y celeste, versátil, con talento para ser muchas cosas, pero fundamentalmente poeta.

Acorde a la cultura a la que pertenezco, mi padre me dio el apellido con el que me incorporé a la vida civil y más tarde a la literaria.

Fui una niña quieta y ensimismada, con algunos pocos focos de atención, por ejemplo, el momento en que la vieja tía Elvira abría su cofre de madera y exponía la miscelánea de: vestidos doblados, novenas, rosarios, estampas de Primera Comunión, Recordatorios de difuntos y dentro de un sobre, discretamente reposando, una foto amarillenta por el paso de los años de un galán en pose de Rodolfo Valentino, dedicada amorosamente a ella en hermosa letra Spencer.

Me dormía con los cuentos de la tía Adelina y me despertaba bajo la cariñosa mirada de ojos verdes de la tía Pastora. Rezaba por todas las causas justas del mundo y por las ánimas del purgatorio a quienes las tías sacaban de pena cada año en la Cuaresma, entrando y saliendo del Templo en un rito simbólico. Quise ser querubín, me gustaba sentirme elegida.

En mi infancia, las tías me contaron las maravillas del paraíso terrenal despertándome la vocación de santa, de tal manera que a los siete años me quedaba hipnótica y de rodillas, bajo los fulgurantes rayos de oro que circundaban la hostia expuesta en el altar los días Jueves, o atorozonada contemplaba el cuerpo de un Cristo con expresión agónica:

"El hombre quebrantado sufre y calla / La corona de espinas lo lastima / No lo alcanza la befa de la plebe que ha visto su agonía tantas veces".

Heart in the Open

I was conceived in the act of a passionate 17-year-old girl. As they tell me, I slipped imperceptibly into life on a cold morning in Matagalpa,* surrounded by great-aunts, virtuous virgins who eagerly bathed my body with oils and warm, perfumed water.

They christened me with a poetic, vital name, a combination of my mother's, Vida, synonym of Eve, the woman expelled from paradise, and the name in the Bristol Almanac for May 28, 1944, Luz, from Our Lady of the Light, the woman chosen among all women to be the Mother of God.

According to the location of the stars at the time of my birth, I belong to the sign of Gemini, which means that I am pagan and mystic, terrestrial and celestial, versatile, with the talent to be many things, but fundamentally, a poet.

As is customary in the culture to which I belong, my father gave me the surname I used to join civil and, later, literary life.

I was a quiet, pensive child, with just a few points of rapt attention, for example, the moment Great-Aunt Elvira would open her wooden chest and display the miscellaneous collection of folded dresses, prayer books, rosaries, first communion cards, remembrance cards for the dead, and inside an envelope, discretely resting, a photo yellowed by the passing years of a handsome young man in a Rudolph Valentino pose, lovingly dedicated to her in beautiful Spencer script.

I went to sleep to Aunt Adelina's stories and woke under the warm gaze of Aunt Pastora's green eyes. I prayed for all the just causes in the world and for the souls in purgatory whom my aunts released from suffering each year during Lent, entering and leaving the church in a symbolic ritual. I wanted to become a cherub; I liked to feel chosen.

During my childhood, my aunts told me of the wonders of earthly paradise, wakening in me the desire to be a saint. So at age seven, I would kneel hypnotized under the brilliant golden beams encircling the host displayed on the altar on Thursdays, or uneasily contemplate the body of Christ with its dying expression:

"The broken man suffers in silence / The crown of thorns wounds him / He hears not the distain of the crowd that has often witnessed his agony."

---

* Matagalpa: City in the northern Darien Mountain Range, birthplace of Meneses.

Los primeros catorce años los viví en ocho ciudades, donde nuestra familia compuesta de seis hermanos con los que jugué de pequeña madre, se trasladaba de acuerdo a los transferimientos que ordenaban a nuestro padre militar, de esa manera absorbí la geografía de mi patria, arraigándome en ella con la fuerza de una planta simbiótica.

Parte de los estudios primarios los realicé en el Colegio Ramona Rizo de Matagalpa, donde su Directora, mujer soltera, de recia personalidad, era a la vez fogosa líder del partido conservador y se caracterizaba por el dominio de la oratoria; a ella debo mis primeras composiciones literarias y la fuerte emoción que todavía me provocan las marchas entonadas por las Bandas de Guerra los días patrios.

Los estudios secundarios los realicé en el Colegio de la Asunción, donde las religiosas me fomentaron la idealización de la realidad, la radicalidad del Evangelio, la honestidad personal. A los catorce años en vez de escribir el diario como lo hacían mis contemporáneas, empecé a escribir poemas con versos rimados. De Rubén Darío recuerdo a mi padre con la voz engolada leyéndome "La cabeza del Rawí" a la altura de mis diez años; Amado Nervo y Gustavo Adolfo Bécquer fueron mi inseparable compañía. Me estremecía escuchar a una compañera de estudios declamando "Entierro de pobres", de Azarías H. Pallais.

En el romanticismo de los dieciséis años recibí de regalo los *Veinte poemas de amor y una canción desesperada* de Pablo Neruda. Los poetas de la vanguardia nicaragüense, la traducción de poesía norteamericana realizada por José Coronel Urtecho y Ernesto Cardenal completaron los libros amigos.

A los diecinueve años me conquistó el que iba a ser mi esposo durante trece años. Fuimos felices diez de ellos, tuvimos cuatro hijos que adoro. A los trece años nos divorciamos por motivos ideológicos, la revolución estalló con fuegos pirotécnicos en mi pueblo y en mi corazón; me entregué a ella apasionadamente. Leí entonces a los poetas cubanos y

The first fourteen years I lived in eight different cities, where our family of six children, for whom I played the little mother, moved according to the transfers ordered for our military father. This is how I absorbed my country's geography, rooting myself in it with the power of a symbiotic plant.

Part of my primary studies was at the Ramona Rizo School in Matagalpa, whose director, a single woman with a forceful personality, was also the fiery leader of the conservative party and excelled at oratory. To her I owe my first literary compositions and the strong emotion still evoked in me by marches played by military bands on national holidays.

I did my secondary studies at the Asunción School, where the nuns instilled in me the idealization of reality, the radicalism of the gospels, and personal honesty. By age fourteen, instead of keeping a diary like my peers, I started to write poems in rhyming verses. I remember my father's booming voice reading me "The Rawi's Head" by Rubén Darío[*] when I was around 10. Amado Nervo[†] and Gustavo Adolfo Bécquer[‡] were my inseparable companions. I would tremble hearing a classmate declaim "Burial of the Poor" by Azarías H. Pallais.[§]

In the romanticism of age sixteen I was given Pablo Neruda's[¶] *Twenty Love Poems and A Song of Despair*. The Nicaraguan Vanguard poets, and the translation of U.S. poetry by José Coronel Urtecho[**] and Ernesto Cardenal[††] rounded out the group of book friends.

At nineteen, the man who would be my husband for thirteen years won me over. We were happy for ten of those years, and we had four children, whom I adore. We divorced for ideological reasons; the revolution exploded with fireworks in my country and in my heart; I passionately surrendered myself to it. I read Cuban poets and Mayakovsky,[‡‡]

---

[*] Rubén Darío (1867-1916): The greatest poet of Spanish American Modernism (see References).

[†] Amado Nervo (1870-1919): Mexican modernist poet, author of mystical, sentimental, and intimate poems.

[‡] Gustavo Adolfo Bécquer (Sevilla, Spain 1836-Madrid 1870): Great Spanish romantic poet; along with Pablo Neruda, one of the most read by young people in the Americas.

[§] Azarías H. Pallais (1885-1954): Priest and postmodern poet, a rebel against hierarchies and inherited literary forms; "a contestatory priest who made a true profession of faith in favor of the poor" (Ramírez).

[¶] Pablo Neruda (1904-1973): Chilean poet; Nobel Prize for Literature, 1971; his poetry spans Vanguardism, leftist political commitment, love, and the elemental things of daily life.

[**] José Coronel Urtecho (1906-1994): One of the greatest poets of the Nicaraguan literary Vanguard movement (see References).

[††] Ernesto Cardenal (1925): Priest and poet; minister of Culture under the Sandinistas (see References).

[‡‡] Mayakovsky, Vladimir (1893-1930): Soviet futurist poet and dramatist who praised

a Mayakovsky. Descubrí a Ana Ajmátova, a Rosario Castellanos, y las biografías de Frida Kahlo, Tina Modotti; "El cuarto propio" de Virginia Woolf; Elena Poniatowska.

Viví a fondo el compromiso social como expresión de la fe que se me había enraizado desde la infancia y encontré a Cristo encarnado en la historia. Me afirmé mujer como ser histórico con derechos y oportunidades iguales.

Fuí capaz de encontrar el amor de nuevo a los cuarenticinco años y de contar con la audacia de mi compañero de igual edad, para asumir la convivencia cotidiana. Este compromiso espontáneo lo renovamos día a día, sorteando las mil y una trampas de la vida, resolviendo la mutua entrega y posesión a la vez que la libertad de los espacios de cada uno. Amo su alegría y vitalidad, su abrazo poderoso.

Continúo encontrando causas por las cuales luchar y vivir, me enorgullecen mis amigas mujeres crecidas, extraordinarias y me enternecen los amigos varones que tratan de crecer aún contra sus propios intereses y de transformar la realidad para construir un mundo para todos(as).

Una vez dije que no podía separar la revolución, la fe y la poesía, sigo pensando igual, porque el centro de todo es el AMOR.

and discovered Anna Akhmátova,* Rosario Castellanos,† and the biographies of Frida Kahlo‡ and Tina Modotti,§ Virginia Woolf's¶ "Room of One's Own," and Elena Poniatowska.**

I profoundly lived social commitment as an expression of the faith rooted in me since childhood, and I discovered Christ incarnate in history. I affirmed myself as a woman, a historical being with equal rights and opportunities.

I was able to find love again at age forty-five and count on the audacity of my partner of the same age to begin daily life together. We renew this spontaneous commitment each and every day, avoiding life's thousand and one traps, balancing mutual surrender and possession as well as the freedom of each one's space. I love his cheerfulness and vitality, his powerful embrace.

I continue to find causes for which to struggle and live; my extraordinary, grown women friends make me proud, and I am moved by male friends who are trying to grow, even against their own interests, and transform reality in order to build a world for everyone, male and female.

I once said that I could not separate revolution, faith, and poetry, and I still think the same, because the center of everything is LOVE.

[Translation by Andrés G. Tucker & María Roof]

---

the Russian Revolution of 1917 but satirized the new regime. Also mentioned by Meneses in the poem "Pedro: Just Now, I Have Been Remembering…," *Air that Calls Me*, and "Inquiries," *All is the Same and Different*.

* Anna Akhmátova (1889-1966): Pseudonym of Anna Andréievna Gorenko, Soviet poet associated with St. Petersburg/Leningrad, who abandoned her early poetry on love and feminine intimacy to link her personal tragedy to that of Russia. Also mentioned in "Travel Notes," *Air that Calls Me*, and "Inquiries," *All is the Same and Different*.

† Rosario Castellanos (1925-1974): Mexican writer (see References). Meneses dedicates the poem "That Woman" to her and cites her in the epigraph to "Reckoning," *Flame in the Wind*; she includes her in the group of important Mexican poets in "Death Notices Crowned by Fame," *All is the Same and Different*.

‡ Frida Kahlo (1910-1954): Mexican painter who established her own place in art history, despite her marriage to the great muralist Diego Rivera; known for autobiographical paintings with elements of popular culture.

§ Tina Modotti (1896-1942): Italian photographer residing in Mexico; political activist in international struggles, including support for Sandino in Nicaragua and for Soviet Communism; subject of a poem by Pablo Neruda and the novel *Tinísima* by Elena Poniatowska.

¶ Virginia Woolf (1882-1941): English novelist, essayist and critic; analyst of the situation of women and the possibility of an androgynous consciousness; defender of a woman's access to "a room of her own" in order to meditate and write. Also mentioned in "Alive Are We," *All is the Same and Different*.

** Elena Poniatowska (Paris-1933): Mexican fiction writer, essayist, and journalist of French, Polish, and Mexican heritage; known for her interweaving of journalism and fiction in examinations of reality through the testimony of witnesses telling their own stories.

Reflexión en blue sobre New Orleáns

Junto a los ríos de Babilonia
estamos sentados y lloramos
acordándonos de Sión.
Mirando los rascacielos de Babilonia
y las luces reflejadas en el río
las luces de los night clubs y los bares de Babilonia
y oyendo sus músicas lloramos.
    "Salmo 136", Ernesto Cardenal.

De Centroamérica, la colonia hondureña es la más grande que reside en New Orleáns, esto en gran parte se explica por el puente de intercambio cultural que de hecho se estableció debido a la presencia de la United Fruit Company (UFCO) en Honduras cuya contraparte está en este puerto del sur de los EE UU.

New Orleáns tiene una identidad multicultural muy rica, marcada fuertemente por las culturas francesa (emigrantes del Canadá), española y africana.

Matriz del jazz aunque aficionados hacen que se dispute este mérito con New York. A pesar de mis frecuentes visitas a esa singular ciudad del sur de los EE UU, fue hasta en el penúltimo viaje que caí en la cuenta que el aeropuerto, hoy convertido dolorosamente en improvisado y gigantesco hospital, lleva el nombre del maravilloso trompetista Louis Armstrong, aunque no fue tanto mi despiste, pues luego supe que recientemente al finalizar la última década, fue cuando el Congreso votó por unanimidad para asignarle tal nombre a la puerta de entrada de la capital del jazz.

Reflection in Blue on New Orleans[*]

Next to the rivers of Babylon
we sit down and weep
remembering Zion.
Seeing Babylon's skyscrapers
and lights reflected in the river
lights from nightclubs and bars in Babylon
and hearing their music, we weep.
    —*Ernesto Cardenal, "Psalm 136"*[†]

The largest Central American colony residing in New Orleans is Honduran, largely explained by the bridge of cultural exchange established by the presence of the United Fruit Company in Honduras, with its counterpart in this southern port city of the U.S.

New Orleans has a very rich multicultural identity, strongly marked by French culture, including immigrants from Canada, as well as Spanish and African cultures.

Birthplace of jazz, although some devotees think this honor belongs to New York. Despite my frequent visits to this remarkable city in the U.S. South, it was only on my next-to-last trip that I realized the airport, today sorrowfully converted into a gigantic, improvised hospital, bears the name of the marvelous trumpeter Louis Armstrong. I didn't know this, not just due to my distraction, but because it was only recently, at the end of the last decade, that the Congress voted unanimously to assign that name to the port of entry to the capital of jazz.

My son Carlos Rodolfo was the first to sound the alarm for family

---

[*] Context: The massively destructive hurricane Katrina that hit the Louisiana coast on August 29, 2005.

[†] Compare the beginning of the Biblical version of the Psalm, in which Babylon is the city of non-peace, of oppression, and Zion, the familiar name of Jerusalem, is symbol of peace and communion among humankind:

>By the rivers of Babylon we sat and wept
>when we remembered Zion.
>There on the poplars we hung our harps,
>for there our captors asked us for songs,
>>our tormentors demanded songs of joy;
>>they said, "Sing us one of the songs of Zion."
>How can we sing the songs of the Lord
>>while in a foreign land?
>
>(Psalm 137, New International Version)

Mi hijo Carlos Rodolfo, fue el primero en darnos la campanada de alerta a sus familiares de Nicaragua, avisando que salía con su familia hacia Baton Rouge. Paralelamente se desplazaban a Houston y Tennessee, hermanos, tíos y primos. Al hablar con mi madre y hermana Annabella, me contestaron que ellas esperarían el último llamado y en efecto, al avisar el Alcalde que la población debía evacuar la ciudad, lo hicieron. De esa manera una familia completa nicaragüense, la mía, entrenada en guerras, exilios y emergencias provocadas por fenómenos naturales, lograba ponerse a salvo. Sólo mi cuñado, Humberto Alvarado, veterano de la guerra de Viet Nam, decidió quedarse en su casa en Metairie. Inmediatamente después del huracán mi hermana logró comunicarse con él, pero la llamada se cortó y no se ha vuelto a saber de él.

En mi amplia familia está la muestra de nuestra problemática nacional, unos salieron al exilio político, amenazadas sus vidas y confiscadas sus casas y sus bienes; otros debido al creciente desempleo, buscando mejores opciones de vida.

Ahora Katrina ha dejado a varios de ellos, de nuevo sin hogar. Uno de mis primos escribe y nos da el primer recuento: "mis padres y primas perdieron sus casas, yo confío que encontraré la mía ya que supuestamente en mi barrio, el agua subió 'solamente' cuatro pies. Ahora mis hijos tienen 12, 10 y 8 años, las edades que teníamos nosotros, los hermanos, cuando tuvimos que salir al exilio dejando nuestro país, a nuestros amigos y compañeros de colegio, ahora probablemente entenderán mejor lo que les contamos su mamá, cuando dejó Cuba y yo cuando dejé Nicaragua. Mi hija está lamentándose por haber dejado su diario, depositario de mil confidencias, añora a sus amiguitas y apenas tenemos unos cuantos días de haber salido y estar con toda la incertidumbre sobre el retorno".

Pueblos en diáspora permanente los nuestros. Por segunda vez y quién sabe por cuántas veces más, distintos grupos de centroamericanos llenos de añoranza, exclamarán con el salmista: "¡Cómo cantar en tierra extraña las canciones de Sión!"

Continúo viendo consternada las imágenes de la inundación colosal tragándose el barrio francés, "French quarter" y su encanto colonial, las bellísimas casas de la Calle San Charles, la Clínica Oschner prestigiada meca de la clase pudiente centroamericana en busca de salud y los bellísimos cementerios de Lafayette, donde numerosos centroamericanos reposan. Con el corazón oprimido observo el llanto, el desconcierto de quienes apenas sobreviven. La guitarra gigantesca que todavía pendula en la zona de night clubs, donde el trombón y la trompeta están guardando un pesado silencio.

members in Nicaragua, telling us he was taking his family to Baton Rouge. At the same time, brothers and sisters, uncles, and cousins were heading for Houston and Tennessee. My mother and sister Annabelle told me they would wait until the last call and, when the mayor told the residents to evacuate, they did. This is how an entire Nicaraguan family, mine, trained through wars, exiles, and emergencies caused by natural phenomena, managed to get to safety. Only my brother-in-law, Humberto Alvarado, a Vietnam war veteran, decided to stay in the house in Metairie. Immediately after the hurricane my sister was able to talk with him, but she was cut off and has not heard from him again.

In my large family you have the sample of our national problematic—some went into political exile, their lives threatened and their houses and belongings confiscated; others, due to growing unemployment, left seeking better options for their lives.

Now Katrina has left several of them homeless again. One of my cousins writes and gives us the first report: "My parents and cousins lost their homes; I trust I will find mine intact, since in my neighborhood, the water supposedly rose "only" four feet. My children are twelve, ten, and eight years old now, the same age we were when we had to go into exile, leaving behind our homeland, our friends, our schoolmates; maybe now they will better understand what their mother told them about abandoning Cuba and I told them about leaving Nicaragua. My daughter, complaining about leaving behind her diary, repository of a thousand secrets, already misses her friends, and it's been just a few days since we left, with total uncertainty about a return."

Peoples in permanent diaspora are ours. For the second time, and who knows how many more, different groups of Central Americans, full of longing, will exclaim with the Psalmist: "How can we sing the songs of Zion in a foreign land?"

In dismay I continue watching the images of the colossal flood swallowing the French Quarter and its colonial charm, the beautiful homes along St. Charles Street, the Oschner Clinic—prestigious mecca for upper class Central Americans seeking health, and the beautiful cemeteries of Lafayette, where many Central Americans are laid to rest. With a heavy heart I observe the grief, the confusion of those who barely survive. The huge guitar that still hangs in the night club area, where the trombone and the trumpet are keeping a heavy silence.

The inexplicable slowness and inability of the government of the

La inexplicable lentitud e incapacidad del gobierno de la nación más poderosa de la tierra. Una ciudad construida dos metros bajo el nivel del mar sin medidas de prevención adecuadas. El malestar general haciéndose eco interminable porque no llegan los recursos humanos, logísticos y financieros con la misma eficiencia que se envían a los frentes de guerra invasora.

¿Por qué razón el último llamado de evacuar la ciudad, no fue planificado, conducido, garantizado por las autoridades locales en lugar de dejar a la voluntad individual y a las posibilidades de cada quien el obligado éxodo? "Sálvese quien pueda" parece ser la traducción de esa orden final.

El Presidente llega de sus vacaciones, fresco, renovado, se hace acompañar de su antecesor y de su padre, también antecesor. Acuerpamiento para enfrentar tamaña responsabilidad de cuya magnitud parecía aún no darse cuenta y sobre la que aparentemente va tomando conciencia, día a día. Pero la tragedia le sobrepasa y gobiernos de naciones amenazadas, bloqueadas, tienden el puente: Venezuela, petróleo barato para auxiliar a los damnificados más pobres. Cuba, un valioso contingente de 1500 médicos y 26 toneladas de medicinas. Atención profesional altamente calificada y disposición ética sin límites, (muchos podemos dar fe de esas cualidades), tenemos la certeza que médicos cubanos se desplazarían eficientemente por la ciudad inundada de aguas pantanosas y fétidas para atender al centro de todo desarrollo: el ser humano.

"I have a dream", dijo Martín Luther King, y yo le rezo a ese gran pacifista para que el gobierno de su país se reconcilie con quienes amenaza, que acepte la ayuda por la meta superior de la pronta recuperación de sus pueblos del sur. Para que se haga la paz desde lo interno de los EE UU y que desde las aguas del Mississippi comience a surgir esa nueva humanidad reconciliada con el universo, armónica, bella y profunda como una serenata de soul a la luz de la luna.

Septiembre 2005

most powerful nation on earth. A city built two meters below sea level without adequate means of prevention. General unrest echoing endlessly, because the human, logistical, and financial resources do not arrive with the same efficiency as they are sent to the frontlines of invasive wars.

Why was the last call to evacuate the city not planned, conducted, and guaranteed by the local authorities, instead of leaving the obligatory exodus to individual will and the possibilities of each person? "Save yourself if you can" seems to be the translation of that final order.

The president arrives from his vacation, refreshed, renewed, and gets his predecessor to accompany him, and his father, also a predecessor—support to face such a large responsibility, whose magnitude he still seems not to grasp and apparently grows to comprehend only day by day. But the tragedy surpasses him, and the governments of threatened and blockaded nations extend their offers: Venezuela, cheap oil to help the poorest victims; Cuba, a estimable contingent of 1,500 doctors and 26 tons of medicine—highly qualified professional care and unlimited ethical attitude (many of us can attest to those qualities). We are certain that Cuban doctors would circulate efficiently throughout the city flooded by fetid swamp waters to attend to the central element in all development: human beings.

"I have a dream," said Martin Luther King, and I pray to that great pacifist that his country's government will reconcile with those whom it threatens, accept their help in the name of the greater goal of a quick recovery of the southern cities; that peace be made within the U.S., and that beginning to rise out of the waters of the Mississippi is that new humanity reconciled with the universe, harmonious, beautiful, and deep like a soul serenade by the light of the moon.

September 2005

Palabras para el último encuentro

Desde el balcón de tu habitación
vi por primera vez el parque
tapizado de blanco
y quise dar fe de lo visto
bajando los tres pisos
para tomar de la capota de un auto
la escarcha que moldeé entre las manos
como un goce tardío de la infancia
disfrutado en mi otoño.
Nunca había visto la nieve
y fue el frío que la antecede
el que me trajo a esta ingrata
misión familiar de acompañarte.

Te encuentro atado a un lecho
del que ya no volverás a levantarte
y siento que no podré hacer gran cosa,
como cuando niños, y montados
en el martillo volador que subía, bajaba
y rotaba vertiginoso
en el parque de diversiones
apresé contra mi pecho a Meriulda y a vos
para que no se me fueran por el agujero negro
de la ventana donde aparecían
y desaparecían las luminarias,
el asfalto, la gente y las estrellas rutilantes
del cielo decembrino de Managua.

Son meses de batallar contra esa cosa mala
que se te enquistó en el pecho y la cabeza
y que vos y quienes te amamos,
conjuramos todos los días
para que desaparezca,
para que se disuelva, para que no exista.

Pero supe que ya empezabas a contar tus días

Abril 2010

Words for the Last Encounter

From the balcony in your room
for the first time I saw the park
upholstered in white
and I wanted to confirm what I saw
running down three flights
to scoop from a car's hood
the frost that I molded in my hands
like a late childhood delight
enjoyed in my autumn.
I had never seen the snow,
and the cold that precedes it
brought me on this unwelcomed
family mission of accompanying you.

I find you bound to a bed
from which you will never again arise
and I feel that I cannot do much,
like when we were kids, riding
on the flying hammer that rose, fell
and spun dizzily around
at the amusement park
I pulled Meriulda close to my chest and you too
so you wouldn't fall through the black hole
of the window where appeared
and disappeared lights
asphalt, people, and twinkling stars
in Managua's December sky.

It's been months of battle against that thing
that took hold in your chest and brain
and you and all who love you
implore every day
to disappear,
to dissolve, to no longer exist.

y quisistes amenizarlos con las canciones
de Enrique Guzmán y "la novia de México"
de nuestros amores de adolescencia;
viendo a James Dean y su desasosiego
en Rebelde sin causa
o a Cantinflas que siempre nos hacía
reír con sus retahílas,
y así todo estaba bien;
hasta que llegaba el dolor y su punzada
nos sacaba del sueño de la vida
y dejábamos la risa, para aplicar el paliativo
que finalmente te dejaba dormido.

Un día de esos fue miércoles de ceniza
y vos, agnóstico por elección,
de puro amor por tu hermana,
me aceptaste la cruz que te dibujé
en la frente, diciéndote:
      "por tu reconversión y sanación",
mientras sonreías, pienso yo, con beatitud,
porque todo acto de amor nos aproxima
a ese mar infinito del que salimos
y al cual ineludiblemente vamos a retornar.

¿Qué día te irás? me preguntaste dos veces
y yo te respondí, falta bastante,
y si me voy, regreso pronto,
sabiendo ambos que todo era incierto
porque tu vida se nos escurría como el tiempo,
aunque esto lo guardáramos como el mejor secreto
de nuestra historia común.

Y así llegó el día
en que te observé lejano y distante
de lo que te rodeaba,
la habitación cargada de recuerdos,
Elisa y los chicos captados magistralmente

But I knew that you were already counting your days
and you wanted to brighten them with songs
by Enrique Guzmán and "Mexico's Sweetheart"
from our loves of adolescence;
watching James Dean and his restlessness
in Rebel Without a Cause
or Cantinflas, who always made us
laugh with his funny sayings,
and everything was all right;
until the pain and its stabbing
pulled us from the dream of life
and we abandoned laughter to apply the palliative
that finally let you sleep.

One of those days was Ash Wednesday
and you, agnostic by choice,
out of pure love for your sister,
accepted the cross I drew
on your forehead, saying to you:
      "for your reconversion and recovery,"
as you smiled, I think, with beatitude,
because every act of love draws us
toward that infinite sea from which we emerged
and to which, inevitably, we shall return.

Which day are you leaving? you asked me, twice,
and I answered, not for a long while,
and if I go, I'll be back soon,
both knowing that all was uncertain
because your life was slipping away from us like time,
though this we hid as the best kept secret
in our common history.

And so the day came
when I noticed you far away and distant
from what surrounded you,
the room loaded with memories
Elisa and the children masterfully captured

por tu cámara mientras jugaban en la grama;
los retratos de la tía Teresa al carbón y al óleo
y la foto de Carolina, con su escrutadora
mirada a los seis años.

Algo me dijo que habías iniciado el viaje.

Llegó entonces la madrugada
con el asma premonitoria y tu prisa
al pedirme: ¡la fecha, la fecha!
que me esforcé en contestar con serenidad.

Después ya nada.
Vertí unas cuantas gotas de agua
que parecieron refrescar un poco tu garganta.

Hermanito....hermanitooo!
¿Por qué tenés el rostro tan frío
y las manos, y los pies?...te gritó mi corazón.
Y te froté, te dí masajes, te puse calcetines,
revisé el aparato de calefacción,
te arropé mejor con la frazada.
Pero ya nada te volvió el calor.

Oré desde el fondo de mi alma
entregándote al Ser de todos los sueños,
y te despedí, asegurándote,
que yo siempre regresaría adonde estés
para volver a nuestros juegos infantiles
la casita en el patio bajo el árbol de mango en Ocotal;
el pequeño fogón de barro
y la mesa con los trastecitos
servida por tu hermana mayor
que de nuevo te llamaría
a vos, y a todos nuestros hermanos
a ese convivio definitivo
del que ya no nos volveremos a separar.

by your camera as they played on the grass;
the portraits of Aunt Teresa in charcoal and oil
and the photo of Carolina, with her penetrating
gaze at age six.

Something told me you had begun your journey.

Then, came morning
with its telltale asthma and your haste
to ask me, The date! The date!
that I forced myself to answer serenely.

Then, nothing.
I poured a few drops of water
that seemed to slightly refresh your throat.

Little brother…. little brotherrrr!
Why is your face so cold
and your hands, and your feet?... my heart cried to you.
I rubbed you, gave you massages, put your socks on,
checked the heater,
tucked the blanket around you.
But nothing brought warmth back to you.

I prayed from the depth of my soul
surrendering you to the Being of all dreams,
and said goodbye, assuring you
that I would always return to wherever you are
to play our childhood games again
the little house on the patio under the mango tree in Ocotal;
the small clay oven
and the table set with dishes
served by your older sister
who again would call
you and all our brothers and sisters
to that definitive gathering
from which we will never again part.

April 2010

References in the Poems

Bonanza: Mining town in the North Atlantic area of Nicaragua, where Meneses spent vacations with her maternal Great-Aunt Virginia Valle, wife of Leslie N. Hoey, a U.S. mining engineer. Virgina was one of the Valle Girls, whom Meneses also visited in the northern city of Matagalpa.

Ernesto Cardenal (Granada 1925): World-famous Catholic priest known as a poet and the first minister of Culture under the Sandinistas after their revolutionary victory in 1979. With José Coronel Urtecho he translated modern U.S. poetry in a widely read anthology of U.S. poetry (1949). His poem, *Zero Hour* (1960) established exteriorism—objective, narrative poetry made up of elements from real life and written in a conversational manner, in contrast to interiorism, which relayed the internal world using elaborate metaphors and symbols. Cardenal's works encompass a broad variety of themes, from *Psalms* (1964) against capitalism and totalitarianism, *Oration for Marilyn Monroe* (1967), *Homage to American Indians* (1969), *National Song* (1972) and *Cosmic Canticle* (1989), which "represents a new, much more ambitious stage in his poetry, where he uses the parameters of quantum physics to explore the existence of human beings, love, and death as a function of the universe, a theme that will be continued in *Telescope on a Dark Night* (1993)" (Ramírez). In 2003 Cardenal published the third volume of his memoires as an "explosive" book, *La revolución perdida* [The lost revolution].

Rosario Castellanos (Mexico, D.F. 1925-Tel-Aviv, Israel 1974): Prolific Mexican poet, fiction writer, essayist, dramatist, professor, diplomat, and pioneer feminist writer. She denounced historical discrimination against women and indigenous Mexicans and proposed the necessity to find "another way to be human and free." Her M.A. thesis, *Sobre la cultura femenina* (On feminine culture, 1950), essay *Mujer que sabe latín* (Woman who knows Latin, 1973), and play *El eterno femenino* (The eternal feminine, 1975) express her concerns regarding lives of women. Her stories in *Álbum de familia* (Family album, 1971) show the frustration of women disillusioned by marriage and motherhood.

José Coronel Urtecho (Granada 1906-Managua 1994): Poet, fiction writer, essayist, and historian, the greatest figure in the literary Vanguard movement in Nicaragua. At age twenty-one, he returned from studies in the U.S. with deep knowledge of modern poetry there, "an influence and mark that would permeate from then on, not only the Vanguard generation, but all Nicaraguan poets in succeeding generations" (Ramírez). With Ernesto Cardenal he translated U.S. poetry in the widely read anthology, *Antología de la poesía norteamericana* (Anthology of U.S. poetry, 1949). He criticized bourgeois social values, experimented with different poetic forms, and along with Cardenal established exteriorist poetry, meant to be objective and include unadorned elements from real life related in a conversational style.

Rubén Darío (Félix Rubén García Sarmiento, Metapa, Matagalpa 1867-León 1916): The greatest poet of Spanish American Modernism. He revolutionized poetry written in Spanish by creating new rhythms and musicality. Known as a "child poet," given his early facility in writing rhyming verses, he traveled as a young man to Chile, where he worked as a journalist and published poems and stories in his first collection, *Azul* (Blue, 1888). Living in Buenos Aires, he began to be recognized for his poetry and published *Prosas profanas* (Profane Prose, 1896), reflecting an exotic, precious Modernism that he later rejected. With the defeat of Spain in 1898 and ensuing U.S. aggression in Latin America, Darío reaffirmed his Spanish heritage and rejection of northern hegemonic pretensions. In 1905 in Spain, he published his most meaningful collection of poems, *Cantos de vida y esperanza* (Songs of Life and Hope), and other books. In failing health, he returned to Nicaragua in 1915 and died there. "His funeral services lasted a week and were a glorification. He was buried with the honors due a Prince of the Church at the Metropolitan Cathedral, where he had been baptized. The history of literature in Spanish should be divided into before Darío and after Darío.... In Nicaragua, Rubén Darío has more than just literary meaning, because he incarnates the cultural identity of the nation. The fact that a poor country during the dark 19th century was able to produce a universal genius of his caliber represents a synthesis and, at the same time, a permanent impulse that was to mark Nicaragua as a national entity" (Ramírez).

Roberto Fernández Retamar (Havana 1930): Cuban poet and essayist committed to the Cuban and Sandinista Revolutions, known for his recasting of the Latin American problematic in terms of a struggle against foreign exploitation (*Calibán*, 1971). In the 1980s, Meneses established a supportive relationship with him which was of importance for her emotional clarity at the time, since literally all her family had gone into exile and only her Great-Aunt Adelina and one daughter, Vidaluz, remained with her. Meneses recognizes the richness she derived from the cultural exchange and friendship of a Marxist poet and a Christian poet in the unique context of the Sandinista Revolution, a friendship that is reflected in the poems from that period.

Carlos Fonseca Amador (Matagalpa 1936-Zinica 1976): One of the three founders of the Sandinista National Liberation Front (FSLN) in 1961. He was a theoretician of revolutionary struggle and a combatant who was exiled several times. He was killed in the mountains of Zinica and became a martyr of the Revolution.

FSLN (Frente Sandinista de Liberation Nacional): Sandinista National Liberation Front founded in 1961 by Carlos Fonseca, Tomás Borge, and Silvio Mayorga. It was first called the National Liberation Front, but Fonseca insisted on adding "Sandinista" to the title in 1962. It organized uprisings throughout the country over the next decade and a half and assumed leadership of the rebellions against the Somoza regime in the mid 1970s. On July 19, 1979, it made its triumphal entry into Managua, after forcing Anastasio Somoza Debayle to flee the country.

Intertextuality: The allusion in one literary text to another, without citing it directly.

Carlos Ernesto Martínez Rivas (Guatemala 1924-Managua 1998): A child poet, like Darío and Pasos. He was known for his verbal precision, dense verses, and restructuration of language based on Spanish Golden Age poets of the 16th and 17th centuries. Intolerant of sloppiness in printed texts, he published only one collection, *La insurrección solitaria* (Solitary insurrection, 1953). "Epitome of the image of the poète maudit, ... the rebelliousness of his poetry against the bourgeois spirit ... led him also in life to rebel against society and even against himself" (Ramírez). Ernesto Cardenal considered him the best poet of the "Three Ernestos" who influenced Nicaraguan poetry during the 1970s—himself, Martínez Rivas, and Ernesto Mejía Sánchez.

Ernesto Mejía Sánchez (Masaya 1923-Mérida, Yucatán, Mexico 1985): One of the leading members of the generation of Postvanguard Nicaraguan writers. He resided in Mexico from early on. A professor, poet, fiction writer, and critic, he was a determined adversary of the Somoza family dictatorship. He created a new genre, the prosema, a brief lyrical text written in prose. He was one of the "Three Ernestos" who influenced poets of Meneses's generation, along with Cardenal and Martínez Rivas.

José M. ("Chepe") Mendoza: Member of the Sandinista military, son of a Nicaraguan father and Argentine mother. Meneses notes: He grew up and was schooled in Estelí and Managua, joined the popular insurrection, and as a military man fought in the war against the counterrevolutionaries. He was well-connected outside the country, and it is said that he participated in the 1980 execution of former Nicaraguan dictator Anastasio Somoza Debayle in Paraguay. He joined a guerrilla action in another Latin American country, where he died. The cover of his posthumous anthology of poetry indicates: "*Cuerpo a tierra* [Body to the ground; in military usage, "Drop to the ground"], read in the light of the poet's death, acquires the relevance of a written act of commitment to the liberation of the American continent that became a poetic act when it was honored in blood." Ernesto Cardenal's prologue states that this young poet emerged from the Ministry of Culture's Poetry Workshops and ends the words of praise for the combatant's life and work with a terribly prophetic judgment: "May that body so long frozen, before it is united with the land for which it died, be like a damning shout against those senior leaders who will never, ever again be revolutionaries."

Joaquín Pasos (Granada 1914-Managua 1947): Nicaraguan writer of poetry and fiction and member of the literary Vanguard movement. Like Darío and Martínez Rivas, he wrote poetry easily as a child. His poetry and prose works "are fused into one single poetic identity to cast a revolutionary challenge to Nicaraguan literature and leap forward to creation.... He uses the same techniques in his prose as in his poetry: metaphor, rhyme, chaotic enumeration, imagination, humor, and shows the same purpose for prose as for poetry.... Joaquín Pasos was a Creationist, because the poet who taught him and influenced him the most was [Chilean] Vicente Huidobro [who proclaimed his theory of Creationism in 1917], his teacher and, even more, his father" (Valle-Castillo, Prólogo). Uruguayan novelist and critic Mario Benedetti considers his apocalyptical *Canto de guerras de las cosas* (Song on the wars of things), on global destruction wraught by World War II, "one of the deepest and most authentic poems ever written in Latin America." With José Coronel Urtecho Pasos wrote a satire on cultural ignorance, *Chinfonía burguesa* (Bourgeois chimphony, 1931). He was incarcerated several times for his denunciations of the Somoza family in humor magazines.

Penelope: A weaver in Greek mythology and symbol of wifely faithfulness to her husband. In the epic poem *Odyssey*, attributed to Homer (8th century B.C.), during the 10-year absence and presumed death of her husband, Odysseus, after the siege of Troy, she resisted all offers of marriage, refusing to give an answer until she finished the cloth she was weaving. At night, she unraveled what she had woven during the day, thus fending off suitors until Odysseus returned.

Germán Pomares (Chinandega 1937-Jinotega 1979): An early member of the Sandinista National Liberation Front (FSLN). A guerrilla leader of humble rural origins, he died in combat. His autobiography was published posthumously in 1989, using his nom de guerre, "El Danto": *El Danto: algunas correrías y andanzas* ("El Danto"/The Tapir: some travels and wanderings).

Prosema: A genre created by Mejía Sánchez that consists of a brief lyrical text written in prose.

Rainer Maria Rilke (Prague, then-Austria 1875-Montreux, Switzerland 1926): Writer who began as an abstract symbolist but later searched for the meaning of art and death in his poems and novels. He wrote in his *Duino Elegies* (1923) that every angel is terrifying, because a weeping person embraced by an angel would be "consumed in its overwhelming existence," since "beauty is nothing but the beginning of terror."

Luis Rocha (Granada, 1942): Nicaraguan poet, colleague of Meneses in the Department of Culture, Central American University (UCA). He collaborated on several cultural publications (*La Prensa Literaria, El Pez y la Serpiente*) and was director of *El Nuevo Amanecer Cultural,* the literary supplement to *El Nuevo Diario.* Author of *Domus Aurea* (1969); *Poemas* (Poems, 1970); *Ejercicios de composición* (Composition exercises, 1974); *Phocas, versiones e interpretaciones* (Phocas, versions and interpretations, 1983), which won the Rubén Darío Latin American Poetry Prize; and *La vida consciente* (Conscious life, 1996), an anthology of poetry and prose.

Leonel Rugama (Estelí 1949-Managua 1970): "Rugama died in a one-sided battle against National Guard troops in an eastern neighborhood of Managua in 1970. He is respected in literature not for his heroic action, but because he created in his poems a new language, very intense, with no more adornments than those of reality itself. His poems, which were not many, were collected for the first time in a special issue of the journal *Taller* (1970) and later in a book, *La tierra es un satélite de la luna* ([Earth is a satellite of the moon] 1983)" (Ramírez).

Augusto César Sandino (Niquinohomo 1893-Managua 1934): The U.S. first sent Marines to intervene in Nicaragua in 1833, occupied the country off and on after 1894, and continually from 1912 to 1925. Sandino led a number of protests that resulted in their return in 1926 and the commencement of the first Central American counterinsurgency war against a people's army.

Sandino's guerrilla forces were never defeated. The Marines left in 1933 after training a National Guard force to replace them, and Liberal candidate Juan Bautista Sacasa assumed the presidency in 1933. Sandino made peace with the new government but, after agreeing to disarm his troops in 1934, he was killed on orders from the head of the National Guard, Anastasio "Tacho" Somoza García.

Somoza Dynasty: Anastasio "Tacho" Somoza García was named head of the U.S.-created National Guard in 1933. He tricked rebel leader Augusto César Sandino into surrendering his arms and had him murdered in 1934. He overthrew President Juan Bautista Sacasa in 1936 and held the power, if not always the titular presidency, until 1956, when he was murdered by poet Rigoberto López Pérez. "Tacho's" elder son, Luis Somoza Debayle, was president 1956-1963. Somoza associate René Schick Gutiérrez presided until 1967. He was succeeded by Luis Somoza Debayle's brother, Anastasio "Tachito" Somoza Debayle, also head of the National Guard, who had graduated from the U.S. Military Academy at West Point in 1946. "He was the only West Point graduate in history to receive an army as a graduation present" (Pezzullo 17). He married Hope Portocarrero, his cousin and a U.S. citizen, and had five children, the oldest of whom was his assumed successor, Anastasio "El Chigüín" Somoza Portocarrero—born in Tampa, Florida, like his mother—who studied at Harvard Business School, the Royal Military Academy at Sandhurst, England, and Ft. Benning, Georgia, in U.S. Army courses. After 1977 he was commander of the infamous EEBI—the Basic Infantry Training School (Escuela de Entrenamiento Básico de la Infantería), which was accused of brutal acts of repression. "Tachito" was routed by a popular uprising in July 1979 led by the Sandinista National Liberation Front (FSLN), fled to Miami with his top ministers, and was assassinated in Paraguay in 1980.

Álvaro Urtecho (Rivas 1951): Poet, professor, and literary critic who wrote the prologue to Meneses's third collection, *Flame in the Wind*. His own poetry finds its inspiration in philosophical and meditative poetry of the Spanish Renaissance and Baroque periods, and also in Rainer Maria Rilke and Carlos Martínez Rivas. His collections include: *Cantata estupefacta* (Amazed cantata 1986), *Cuadernos de la provincia y Esplendor de Caín* (Provincial notebooks and Cain's splendor, 1994), and *Tumba y Residencia* (Tomb and residence), 2000.

Valle Girls: Meneses's unmarried maternal great-aunts with whom she spent vacations in the northern town of Matagalpa: Elvira, Adelina, and Victoria ("Toya"). A fourth sister, Virginia, married Leslie N. Hoey, from the U.S., head of gold smelting at the Neptune Gold Mine Company in Bonanza. Other Valle sisters were: Elida de Genie and Dalila, mother of Vida Robleto and grandmother of Vidaluz Meneses, who died at age 33.

Vanguard: Literary movement in Nicaragua in the 1930s and '40s, which called itself antiacademic, antibourgeois, and antimodernist. Vanguard poets attacked rhetoric literature and the falsification of the poetic legacy of Rubén Darío and proposed conversational poetic discourse and the use of dialogue, collage, free verse, humor, and experimentation with poetic form. Catholic anti-yankees, they favored a nationalism based on a caudillo, a strong-man in the style of the first in the Somoza dynasty, Anastasio Somoza García. Although they later abandoned this political position, they were still accused as extreme right-wingers. The main Vanguard poets were: José Coronel Urtecho (1906-1994), Joaquín Pasos (1914-1947), Pablo Antonio Cuadra (1912-2002); Luis Alberto Cabrales (1901-1974), Manolo Cuadra (1907-1957), Alberto Ordóñez Argüello (1913-1991), Luis Downing Urtecho (1913-1983), and Octavio Rocha (1910-1986).

Annotated Bibliography on Vidaluz Meneses and Works Cited in References

Vidaluz Meneses: Poetry Collections

Llama guardada (Guarded Flame). Managua: Tipografía Asel, 1975.
El aire que me llama (Air that Calls Me). Managua: Unión de Escritores de Nicaragua e IMELSA, 1982.
Llama en el aire (Flame in the Wind). Col. Letras de Nicaragua 36. Managua: Editorial Nueva Nicaragua, 1990.
Todo es igual y distinto (Poemas 1992-2001) (All is the Same and Different (Poems 1992-2001). Managua: Centro Nicaragüense de Escritores, 2002.
Sonreír cuando los ojos están serios (Smiling when the eyes are serious). San José: C.R.: Editorial Lunes, 2006. Includes some 30 poems selected by Meneses on the occasion of the 5th International Poetry Festival celebrated in San José, Costa Rica, in 2006. The only poem not previously published in the author's collections is "Analiza tu vida"/ "Analyze Your Life," included here in the last section, "Poems and Other Poetic Publications…".

Vidaluz Meneses: Other Writings Related to Life and Works

La lucha es el más alto de los cantos. Diario de campaña, Brigada Cultural Leonel Rugama (Struggle is the highest of songs. Campaign Diary, Leonel Rugama Cultural Brigade). Managua: Anamá, 2006.

"Catolicidad y mestizaje, fuentes ecuménicas en los Escritos a máquina de PAC" [Catholicism and Mestizoism: Ecumenical Sources in Pablo Antonio Cuadra's Typewritten Messages]. <http: www.escritorasnicaragua.org/vm-catolicopac.html. 28feb06>.

Critical Articles on Poetry by Vidaluz Meneses

Anta San Pedro, Teresa. "El callado feminismo en la poesía de Vidaluz Meneses" [Quiet feminism in poetry by Vidaluz Meneses]. *El pez y la serpiente* 42 (July-Aug. 2001): 73-90. Also on ANIDE web site: <http://www.escritorasnicaragua.org/vm-crit-callado.fem.html>.

▻ This innovative and well-reasoned analysis incorporates unpublished comments by Meneses.

▻ In a 2000 personal interview with the critic, Meneses stated that Central American men, even those who like to consider themselves modern, liberal, and fair-minded, are not ready to accept feminist discourse and have not assimilated the concept of equality between men and women. Women who write with the energy, passion, and aggressivity typical of male discourse are judged immoral and brazen. "Gentlemen" dismiss and disparage their work as "a passing lunacy" from the pen of "so-called feminist writers," such as Ana María Rodas (Guatemala) and Gioconda Belli (Nicaragua).

▻ Meneses believes that women writers should seek non-conflictive forms of expression in order to wage a productive battle. Anta San Pedro sees this belief as the basis for the poet's elegant, sharp but discreet irony, her demure silence and measured language that eschews melodrama, sarcasm, and grandiloquent statements ("Ebb Tide," "Inventory of A Modern Man," "Today"). Women's rebellion, the denunciation of social ills, and attacks on tyrannical social institutions and oppressive bourgeois morality are presented discreetly ("Woman, 1950s").

▻ The poet's expression of sensuality is natural, pure, quiet, and intimate rather than exhibitionist ("Today").

▻ Poetry serves as a gnoseological instrument to probe the world rather than a means to express the known. The poet embarks on an internal exploration of her own being.

▻ Love is nourished by daily occurrences and allows us to forget metaphysical concerns ("Surprised, Happy," "Autumn Stroll").

➤ Experiences are not unique; life is cyclical; and everything is repeated. But poetry can become eternal.

➤ Meneses's prescient expression in "All in All" that the ashes of love lost will be nourishment for future relationships belongs to a postfeminist period and is almost inconceivable in Spanish America in 1980, when the poem was written. The female subject in the poem does not consider herself a victim or inferior to men; she knows what she wants and is determined to get it.

➤ Silence is the greatest theme and the most effective discursive method in Meneses's poetry; silence creates a space for communication to be achieved ("'He Who Has Ears to Hear'"). In her psychological introspection and philosophical profundity, omissions and silences become expressive, even sharp and caustic, in a world where their message is obscured by noise ("That's Life," "I Awake Chasing A Song").

➤ In "Cakchiquel Woman," Meneses's commitment as a subject in History is extended beyond the present. She gives voice to the historically voiceless and creates a female Amerindian hero—a woman hero-subject, not a heroine-object— who represents the forgotten indigenous Penelopes condemned to aborting the life engendered in their being with the same brutal force used by the Spanish conquistadors to create it.

Aragón, Alba Fabiola. "Revolution in Space and Time: The Work of Four Nicaraguan Women Poets, 1969-1989." Undergraduate Thesis, New College of the University of South Florida. Director José Alberto Portugal. 1999.

➤ Detailed, insightful analysis of contrasting conceptions of time and space and implications, such as "Body, Territory, Text: Grounding the Revolution," in poems by Michèle Najlis, Meneses, Ana Ilce Gómez, and Gioconda Belli, with an appendix of selected poems and translations.

➤ Meneses translations with Aragón's titles as translated:
From *Guarded Flame*:
1. "Yo amanezco persiguiendo un canto" / "I Awaken, Following a Song" (p. 121).
1. "Es la vida" / "Life" (122).
2. "Todos los días" / "Everyday" / (123).
3. "Alguna noche insomne" / "Some Sleepless Nights" (123).
4. "Cuando yo me casé" / "When I Got Married" (124).

From *Air that Calls Me*:
1. "Diciembre 7" / "December 7" (143).
2. "Última postal a mi padre, General Meneses" / "Last Postcard to My Father, General Meneses" (143).
3. "Compañera" / "Compañera" (144).

From *Flame in the Wind*:
1. "Sorprendido, feliz" / "Synthesis" (144).

Guzzo, Cristina. "El conflicto entre la familia y la patria en Vidaluz Meneses" [Conflict between family and nation in VM]. *Volver... a la fuente del canto: Actas del I Simposio Internacional de Poesía Nicaragüense del Siglo XX (Homenaje a Pablo Antonio Cuadra)*. Ed. Jorge Chen Sham. Managua: Asociación Pablo Antonio Cuadra, 2004. 331-40.

▷ Links Meneses's poetry to a Central American collective struggle, beyond its concrete historical circumstances.

▷ A social consciousness based on religious charity and social class privileges generates Meneses's mystical and militant poetry.

▷ Political differences between Meneses and her father reflect a broader generational gap throughout Latin America in the 1960s-70s, especially among middle and upper-middle class, university-educated youth raised in the Christian messianic tradition. Particular to Meneses is her non-confrontational, testimonial documentation of the struggle as a dialogue across generations.

▷ Meneses's feminism takes a domestic form, the legacy of one generation of women to the next, common in women's writing and, especially, in societies with indigenous matriarchal structures, as in Central America ("My Aunt Adelina," "Mother," "Daughter," "Looking at Her Photograph").

▷ Christian ethics undergird the revolutionary conviction, the humble, non-emphatic tone in Meneses's lyrical voice ("Small Homage," "Night Duty"), and an earthbound mysticism ("Voluntary Labor"), that is condensed in her poetic testament in "Wailing Wall."

Jaeger, Frances. "Otros héroes, nuevas utopías: la mujer revolucionaria y la poesía nicaragüense" [Other heroes, new utopias: revolutionary woman and Nicaraguan poetry]. *Otros testimonios: voces de mujeres centroamericanas*. Comp. Amanda Castro. Guatemala: Letra Negra, 2001. 115-26.

▷ Poets Daisy Zamora, Michèle Najlis, Gioconda Belli, and Meneses deconstruct monolithic, marginalizing, patriarchal revolutionary discourses and create new discourses that incorporate plurality and multiplicity, including women's contributions to the Revolution.

▷ Within messianic discourse, female poets can opt to position themselves as the (virgin) mother/creator of the revolutionary leader, who is male and occupies the center (Belli).

▷ The poets use messianic and utopian revolutionary discourses in order to create non-traditional messiahs/heroes who are: female (Belli, Meneses, Zamora), popular in origin (Najlis), or collective (Najlis, Zamora).

▷ Revolutionary discourses are used to: (1) expand traditional utopias to include a prelinguistic paradise, where the only language is love (Zamora) or one's own internal song (Najlis); or (2) to portray a revolutionary utopia that admits disorder and chaos as a necessary condition for its own creation (Belli, Meneses).

Jaeger, Frances Betty. "Constructing the Self through Otherness in the Works of Gioconda Belli, Daisy Zamora, Michèle Najlis, Vidaluz Meneses and Rosario Murillo." Ph.D. dissertation, University of Illinois Urbana. 1997.

Jiménez, Luis A. "En torno al palimpsesto: tres etapas en la poesía de Vidaluz Meneses" [Regarding the palimpsest: three stages in VM's poetry]. *Volver... a la fuente del canto: Actas del I Simposio Internacional de Poesía Nicaragüense del Siglo XX (Homenaje a Pablo Antonio Cuadra)*. Ed. Jorge Chen Sham. Managua: Asociación Pablo Antonio Cuadra, 2004. 341-53.
▶   Poet Daisy Zamora includes Vidaluz in the group of women poets who appeared in Nicaragua during the explosive decade of the 1960s and showed three thematic affinities that continued for the next 30 years: emphasis on family experiences before and after marriage, consciousness of being women, and social projection toward a poetry of action or action in poetry.
▶   The concept of palimpsest is useful for understanding poems such as "In the New Country," where the national present is written like a poem: created, erased, and rewritten. Meneses writes, erases, while leaving remnants of previous discourses, and rewrites three stages in her life and works, reflecting the history of Nicaragua.
▶   1st stage: Women introduced as subjects into literary discourse, with a (self-) reflection on the mystical and pagan worlds, heaven and earth, life and death, and inclusion of details of daily life, monotony, and tedium.
o "When I Married" is an ironic text that condemns and subverts sexist values in macho culture, such as the idealization of women in myths and false stereotypes.
o "Snapshot of a Marriage" questions the gender binary, as analyzed by Rosario Castellanos, in the social construction of women within patriarchal societies. Silence in the poem serves as a sort of palimpsest.
o "I Have Seen" returns to the previous theme of death and includes the body of the subject-woman, excluded since the 18th century from gender-based discussions about "the new man" (never "the new woman," though she was present in Latin American literature as early as the 19th century, and before, if we consider the 17th-century Mexican poet, Sor Juana Inés de la Cruz). The explicit ideological dialogue in the poem's composition is repeated throughout Meneses's work—a mixture of commitment and resistance of literary personae, due to their concern for the [individual] human subject, translated

into a political belligerence expressed in indefatigable struggles in defense of marginalized and exploited "subalterns" on the periphery of hegemonic discourses.

▶ 2nd stage: Inspired by the social and economic transformation resulting from the Sandinista Revolution, women assume a militant role as creators, with a (self-) reflection on their new identity as active, goal-oriented historical agents, no longer interested in daily life and its myriad details. Flames previously ignited are extinguished, in order to permit a new fire or renewed life rising from the ashes (palimpsest).

o "All in All" reinforces the idea of not looking back on the past.

o "Land Recovered" employs the antithesis life/death and repeats the palimpsest of putting aside the past to erase it and create anew. The repeated Meneses tactic of stating forward-looking newness continues in other texts.

o "Flight" also employs the antithesis of fall-ascension to describe the female subject and the Revolution. In many other texts of this period, the poetic voz is linked to the people, women, and the new political process in Nicaragua: "Compañera," "Forever Eve."

o "Reckoning" shows the poetic voice returning to her father's house, then erasing that space to substitute another, which implies the liberation of women.

o "That Woman" proclaims the birth of the "new woman."

▶ 3rd stage: Sameness and otherness. Sameness despite ludic palimpsest references.

o "Jurassic Evocation" reveals an internal landscape of ludic masks of sameness.

o "Love at Any Time" reflects women's pride in generational continuance.

o "Life with Life" presents the continuum of life and death.

López Miranda, Margarita. "Algunos textos claves en la evolución poética de Vidaluz Meneses" [Some key texts in the evolution of poetry by VM]. Lecture delivered May 31, 2001, at Managua's Instituto Nicaragüense de Cultura Hispánica. <http://www.escritorasnicaragua.org/mlm-vmeneses.html>.

▶ This interesting study reviews critical praise for Meneses's poetry and ties the thematic axes of her creativity to life experiences as a humanist, revolutionary, woman, and poet.

▶ Characteristic of Meneses is her early maturity and capacity for reflection, found also in works by Ana Ilce Gómez, Michèle Najlis, Gioconda Belli, and Daisy Zamora. Early poems contain themes that will become constant, such as the consciousness of being female and a critical perspective on religion in "When I Married." From the beginning, her visions and themes were broad, deep, and universal.

- Completely in control of her craft, in recent works Meneses tries more experimentation with musicality, plasticity, and intertextuality with literature, art, religion, family, nature, politics, popular culture, feminism, and the Greek-Roman legacy.
- Four periods are identified in Meneses's aesthetic and ideological evolution, roughly corresponding to each published book, though many poems correspond to more than one stage. Selected poems are analyzed for transcendental themes in Meneses's cosmovision: identity as a woman, family, rebellion and social criticism, humanism in the form of belligerent Christianity, desire for individual and community transformation and spiritualization, and correspondence between personal and poetic intents.
- Texts in *Guarded Flame* show perfect balance between their semantic-ideological level—themes, motifs, symbols, literary figures—and formal stylistic level—forms and composition of stanzas, syntaxis, rhetorical and poetic devices. "When I Married" combines colloquial language with quotes from church matrimonial liturgy to redefine the traditional paradigm of a new wife as a modern protest against antiquated social models. Women's self-definition is contrasted to the oppressive social mores.
- "Reckoning" reevaluates the contradictory nuptial experience and the sublimation of traditions expressed in "When I Married." Women are no longer seen as sacrifical lambs led to the sacrifice because they are now self-defining in their search for partners. No concessions to social traditions are made, and women's hearts remain intact even among the debris of the past. Meneses establishes a dialectic between love/lack of love, illusion/disillusion, tradition/rupture that evolves into a new, hopeful experience in the present.
- "Last Message to My Father, General Meneses" expresses the debate between compassionate love and the moving, though inevitable, rupture between personal affection and political history. As Daisy Zamora observed, sentiments as well as historical judgements like those in this poem were possible only after the 1979 Sandinista revolutionary triumph. The equal status Meneses affords to herself and to her father in their final combat corresponds to a postfeminist era in which women express their sense of equality with men. "Postal" in the title [in Spanish] refers to a love-inspired message. This poem expresses Meneses's soul divided between Christian children's love for parents and commitment to social revolution.
- *All is the Same and Different* shows thematic variation, experimentation, reaffirmation of the female "I," and maturity in reflection.

Mc Callister, Rick. "La sobrevivencia en un mundo pos-histórico: Todo es igual y distinto de Vidaluz Meneses" [Survival in a posthistorical world: All is the Same and Different by VM]. *ANIDE* 10 (Dec. 2005): 45-55.

➤ With humor and irony, *All is the Same and Different* emphasizes universal truths against market-based and postmodern values: the real, not the virtual ("Office Girls"); love in opposition to dehumanization ("Love at Any Time"); personal experiences, not ideologies ("Confiding A Secret," "Itinerary/97"); local diversity, not cultural homogenization, and creativity in the face of neoliberal obsession with profits ("May Lullaby").

➤ "Paco" evidences "the clandestine histories of little countries" in its tale of resistance to foreign powers and collaborative national governments; recovery of the past to construct the future.

➤ "That Woman Is Crazy" decries the privatization of public functions that leaves the poor in "cybernetic exile," with no access to communication and comprehension. The woman's "critical schizophrenia" appears in "Virgo" to demonstrate the useless sterility of dual-standard sexual requirements for females.

➤ Self-definition in the face of the mystery of death and exploration of the sounds and scenes of daily life allow us to create new cultural weapons against a future imposed by others ("In extremis").

Moyano, Pilar. "'Raíces que rompen el tiesto': Transgresión y espacio poético en la obra de Vidaluz Meneses" ["Roots that break the pot": transgression and poetic space in works by VM]. <http://www.escritorasnicaragua.org/vm-crit-raices.html; euram.com.ni/pverdes/Verdes_Culturales/.../verdes_culturales_ 158.htm>.

➤ This penetrating study incorporates the critic's interviews with Daisy Zamora and Meneses to shed light on works by poets who began publishing in the 1960s and 1970s.

➤ Much of Meneses's poetry posits the question: What does it mean to be a woman? Her work is a poetic inquiry into the tension women experience when they face socially imposed imperatives, as well as a battle against a literary tradition that disparaged and marginalized women writers.

➤ Meneses would agree with critics who affirm that social structures are tied to linguistic structures. Poetry subverts the codes and clichés of ordinary language and is an essential instrument for social transformation.

➤ Self-definition by women as literary and social subjects constitutes a transgression of sociocultural conventions and imbues patriarchal traditions with new meanings. Writing can be a tool to destroy myths and roles limiting women, but the cost of such transgression is high, as Meneses suggests when recalling those who succumbed to suicide ("Alive Are We"). They were pioneers who dared to challenge the suppositions of patriarchy, and they survive in writings by women who triumph in letters.

▶ According to Zamora, she, Meneses, and others were women writers of transition, and their generation was crippled by the historical moment from which there was no escape. Their sacrifice might lighten the load for their daughters.

Palacios Vivas, Nydia. *Voces femeninas en la narrativa de Rosario Aguilar.* Managua: Ediciones del Siglo/JEA, 1998.

▶ A long and detailed "General Panorama of Central American Women's Literature," in this study of fiction by Nicaraguan Rosario Aguilar (1938), identifies a group of women who, in the 1960s, began to publish poetry of high quality outside women's usual themes: love, death, religion, and poetry for children. These writers prepared the way for the creation of poetry committed to social and political change.

▶ Poets reflecting this new position of Nicaraguan women are: Michèle Najlis, Ana Ilce Gómez, Ligia Guillén, Christian Santos, Gioconda Belli, Daisy Zamora, Meneses, and Yolanda Blanco.

▶ In the 1960s universities welcomed women into traditionally male majors (law, engineering, economics), bringing a sense of professional and political responsibility to middle-class women, who broke with assigned social roles and joined the political struggle against the Somoza dictatorship.

▶ Meneses "subverts and reconstructs Biblical and Greek myths, in order to show the situation of women who bear the brunt of the ideological weight of tradition" (63). She constructs for women a self-image that redefines them outside patriarchal strictures ("When I Married," "Reckoning," "Small Death," "Cakchiquel Woman.").

▶ Meneses deconstructs misogynist codes in her portrayals of women in literature and popular culture and proposes a new self-affirming woman capable of participating in the construction of a new Nicaragua ("Forever Eve," "The New Skirt," "All in All," "Compañera," "Flight").

Peters, Kathryn M. "Practice in the Translation of Poetic Discourse: A Translation of Selected Poems from *Llama en el aire* by Vidaluz Meneses. M.A. Thesis, University of New Mexico. 1993.

▶ Translations of 46 of the 80 poems in *Flame in the Wind*, several of which we have reworked here and designate Peters as cotranslator.

▶ The preface provides a brief biographical sketch of Meneses, thematic and structural analysis of several poems, and comments cogently on translation "puzzles, choices and dilemmas."

▶ Important thematic threads are Meneses's ideological conflicts with her father and other family members and experiences as a member of the educated upper-class intelligentsia of the Sandinista Revolution.

➤ The poet's conversational style at times resembles an internal monologue or flow of consciousness.

➤ "Last Message to My Father, General Meneses" uses a conversational style combining nostalgia and irony. The use of pronouns, especially the familiar form of address in the verbs [marked as either "tú" or "vos"], places the poem's female subject in a position of equality with the father, thereby leveling gender and generational superiority/inferiority paradigms. This personal account expresses a transpersonal reality: the vast ideological schisms in families in Nicaragua and throughout Central America.

Raquidel, Danielle. "Mirada hacia los elementos en la poesía de Vidaluz Meneses"[A look at natural elements in VM's poetry]. <http://www-ni. el-nuevodiario.com.ni/archivo/2001/julio/4-julio-2001/cultural/cultural2.html>; and <http://www.dariana.com/diccionario/Vidaluz_Meneses2.htm>.

➤ This interesting study of the elements of nature in Meneses's poetry explores the layering of natural images charged with metaphorical meaning.

➤ Air and fire, the elements most often used in the titles of Meneses's poetry collections, are intangible and ungraspable, yet complementary. They suggest immateriality and define a subjectivity that seeks the freedom they enjoy. Air and fire contrast to temporality and measurement. They represent love, passion, inspiration, and desire for change ("December 7th").

➤ The contradictory nature of fire, which can produce destruction but also regeneration, can symbolize rapid change. In Meneses, fire represents the internal/external duality that attracts the poet like moths to a dangerous flame.

➤ Air represents flight in many poems, as well as life and the Revolution ("Flight," "Daughter").

➤ Water and earth often appear in their pulverized or segregated forms, as rain, mist, and dust. Water has multiple symbolism: the passing of time, blood, love, life, death, renovations ("Land Recovered"). Characteristic of Meneses's poetry is the vaporous nature of water as rain and steamy rivers, suggesting fertility and also irreality, doubt, insecurity, and solitude ("'He Who Has Ears to Hear'").

➤ Water is often used is the sense of deep security, as in the maternal womb ("On A Sleepless Night").

➤ Water is also the river of death but with regenerative power ("I Have Seen").

➤ Earth is linked to the path that leads to knowledge and self-possession ("Compañera," "Forever Eve," "Wailing Wall").

➤ A constant in Meneses's poetry is the association of imagination with earthly and cosmic space. This space is a refuge, but humankind tries to destroy it ("I Have Seen"). Meneses is a daughter of the cosmos; hers is a world that values intuitions, primitive impressions—a natural world with a human logic that opposes everything artificial, such a mechanical routines.

Urtecho, Álvaro. Prólogo. Vidaluz Meneses. *Llama en el aire*. Letras de Nicaragua 36. Managua: Editorial Nueva Nicaragua, 1990. 11-16.

▸ In this prologue to *Flame in the Wind*, the critic highlights the collection's lyrical, warm, and intimate tone, which demonstrates that feminine sensuality is not at war with intelligence, and that confessional emotional extremes, resentful femininity, and "screaming ovaries" do not make for good poetry.

▸ Lauds the poet's intelligent precision in word choice and rejection of the narcissistic exhibitionism that characterizes much of poetry by Nicaraguan and other women.

▸ Finds from the poet's first writings a preference for brief, highly concentrated forms that suggest a sharp, elegant sense of discreet irony, especially to unmask the negative forces of lies and alienation, the castrating and paternalistic bourgeoisie's false morality, and oppression by institutions against freedom, beauty, and imagination.

▸ Believes that the poet consciously attempts to exorcise not only the threatening fantasies of traditional society, but also the artificial paradises of the "American Way of Life," and the specter of mechanized life in bureaucratic offices, full of monotony and lack of authenticity.

▸ A constant in the poet's works is the attempt to clarify the meaning of human relations, through analysis and psychological introspection, like Daisy Zamora and Ana Ilce Gómez.

▸ A convincing and, at times, dramatic dialectic exploration of a difficult duality begins with *Air that Calls Me*: the individual subjectivity in History and a liberating humanist project. The poet identifies openly with the people.

▸ Like Rosario Murillo, Gioconda Belli, and Daisy Zamora, Meneses's works register the impact of the Sandinista Revolution, which redefines individual subjectivity relative to the collective experience. Meneses presents the Revolution as causing an organic transformation of nature and all of life.

▸ The more reflective poems in this work, *Flame in the Wind*, show greater interiorization of the external world and an emphasis on the impermanence of love because it is both historical and human.

Interviews with Vidaluz Meneses

Cabestrero, Teófilo. "Vidaluz Meneses: 'Hay tres cosas en mi vida que no puedo separar: la poesía, mi fe cristiana y la revolución'" [VM: "There are three things in my life that I cannot separate: poetry, my Christian faith, and the Revolution]. *Revolucionarios por el Evangelio: Testimonio de 15 Cristianos en el Gobierno Revolucionario de Nicaragua*. Pról. Pedro Casaldáliga. Bilbao: Desdée de Brouwer, 1983. 209-45.

➤ Cabestrero incorporates many of his own observations, not originally part of the interview, to provide a broad historical context. At the time of this interview, Meneses had published two books of poetry and was general director of Libraries and Archives at the Ministry of Culture.

➤ Meneses mentions her preferred Nicaraguan poets: Joaquín Pasos, Carlos Martínez Rivas, Ernesto Cardenal, and martyred poets Leonel Rugama, Ricardo Morales Avilés, Fernando Gordillo.

➤ Nicaragua's poets are its prophets: they denounce injustice and announce the coming of a new society based on love, justice, and peace.

➤ Democratizing culture is the challenge for a popular, democratic revolution.

➤ Meneses calls her style lyrical and intimist, expressing the personal. Almost all her poetry is an X-ray of the internal process she has lived as a person, so her poetry is her life.

➤ As a child, living with her devout great-aunts, the Valle girls, she imbibed all types of solemn religious ceremonies and has had a certain mystical tendency throughout her life.

➤ In the Revolution, Meneses believes her poetry is fuller and freer, and her Christianity is more effective and authentic.

Heyck, Denis Lynn Daly, ed. "Vidaluz Meneses." *Life Stories of the Nicaraguan Revolution*. New York: Routledge, 1990. 227-241.

➤ Interviews conducted in 1986, 1987, 1988, edited to remove questions.

➤ Three sections:
o Political Lives (Violeta Chamorro, Commander Doris María Tijerino, Reynaldo Antonio Téfel, public officials, a professor, a graduate student).
o Religious Lives (an anti-Sandinista monsignor, a nun, members of Christian base communities, public officials, mother of President Daniel Ortega, Meneses).
o Survivors' Lives (uprooted rural workers, small business owner, physician, school principal, potential emigré to U.S., high school student).

➤ Succinct 12-page overview of Nicaraguan history to late 1980s.

Randall, Margaret. *Risking a Somersault in the Air: Conversations with Nica-*

raguan Writers. Trans. Christina Mills. Ed. Floyce Alexander. San Francisco: Solidarity Publications, 1984.

▷ Informative, sensitive interviews from 1983, some published in Managua cultural supplements to newspapers.

▷ The interesting introduction explores the place of poets and poetry in Nicaraguan society and writer participation in the Sandinista government.

▷ Photographs of writers and others.

▷ Five women included —Meneses, Michèle Najlis, Gioconda Belli, Daisy Zamora, and Milagros Palma— and nine men —Sergio Ramírez, Lizandro Chávez Alfaro, Carlos Guadamuz, Beltrán Morales, Ernesto Cardenal, Omar Cabezas, Francisco de Asís Fernández, Julio Valle-Castillo and Tomás Borge.

▷ Vidaluz Meneses interview, "We Cannot Talk about the Revolution in the Third Person" (41-54), focuses on her poetry collections, relationship with father, schooling, the Ministry of Culture, and the Writers Union (ASTC).

▷ Translation of Meneses's "Mi tía Adelina" as "To My Aunt Adelina" (53-54).

---. *Sandino's Daughters Revisited: Feminism in Nicaragua*. New Brunswick, NJ: Rutgers UP, 1994.

▷ Interviews conducted in 1992 with 12 women previously interviewed for her *Sandino's Daughters: Testimonies of Nicaraguan Women in Struggle* (1981) and others. Daisy Zamora was the only writer in the original book.

▷Included are: Meneses, Michèle Najlis, Daisy Zamora, and Gioconda Belli. Others are indigenous woman physician Mirna Cunningham; worker Diana Espinoza; lawyer Milú Vargas; intelligence officer and former nun Aminta Granera; military and political leaders Doris Tijerino and Dora María Téllez; organizer of the gay and lesbian movement and AIDS outreach leader Rita Arauz; journalist Sofía Montenegro.

▷ The very informative introduction, with detailed historical annotations, highlights tensions between women's issues and national struggles, family structures, U.S. impositions, repression under the Somozas, Catholicism and Liberation Theology, women's organizations, women warriors, and the new feminist movement.

▷ Brief biographical data, circumstances of the interview, and Randall's initial impressions of the person precede interviews. She likens Meneses's "serene and amiable exterior" to that of Sor Juana Inés de la Cruz or Joan of Arc.

▷ Meneses interview, "As a Woman, I Think It Was Worth Living the Revolutionary Process" (144-67), emphasizes early schooling and literary experiences, Christian praxis, distancing from father and husband, separation

from children, cultural work, and women's advancements under the Sandinistas.
➤ Meneses translations by Margaret Randall:
1. "About the Revolutionary and Some of Her [sic] Weaknesses" (146) of "Del revolucionario y algunas de sus debilidades."
2. "Wailing Wall," (147), partial translation of "Muro de lamentaciones."
3. "Last Post Card to My Father, General Meneses," (157-58) of "Última postal a mi padre, General Meneses."

"Un secreto para mí sola (Testimonio)" [A secret for me alone (testimony)]. Dir. Rossana Lacayo. Managua: INCINE, 1988. Documentary film on the life of Meneses.

Translations of Poetry by Vidaluz Meneses

"Instant Marriage." A translation of "Instantánea conyugal." Trans. Kate Peters. Harvard Review 9 (1995): 97.

Ixok Amar·Go: Central American Women's Poetry for Peace. Ed. Zoë Anglesey. Penobscot, Maine: Granite, 1987.
➤ Monumental bilingual collection: 600+ pages, 180+ works by 55 well-known and lesser known writers, including more Costa Rican and Panamanian poets than other anthologies, with several poems in indigenous languages and Jamaican creole, translated into Spanish as well as English, and stated preference for "literary" rather than "literal" translations. Introductory bilingual general essay on women writers in each country, photograph, and six to eight lines about each poet, with titles of published collections.
➤ Nicaraguans: Luz Marina Acosta, June Beer, Gioconda Belli, Yolanda Blanco, Marianela Corriols Molina, Ana Ilce Gómez, Meneses, Rosario Murillo, Michèle Najlis, Christian Santos, Mariana Yonüsg (born in Venezuela), Daisy Zamora.
➤ Meneses translations:
1. "I Read Your Letters" (344-45) of "Vigilia." Translation by Nancy Esposito.
2. "I Write to You Now" (346-47) of "Te escribo ahora." Translation by Nancy Esposito.
3. "The Earth Recovered" (348-49) of "La tierra recobrada." Translation by Zoë Anglesey.

Lovers and Comrades: Women's Resistance Poetry from Central America. Ed. Amanda Hopkinson. Trans. Amanda Hopkinson and members of the El Salvador Solidarity Campaign Cultural Committee. London: Women's Press, 1989.

▷   An excellent and influential collection of important poetry, presented not chronologically or by the poets' national origins, but—more coherently for the poetry itself—under general rubrics that signal the directions of many Latin American women in the 1970s and 1980s: Roots of My Song, Bright Country, Woman in My Time, Lovers and Comrades, In the Struggle, and Time of Awakening.

▷   An unfortunate omission, due to "lack of available contemporary material" (xix), excludes writers from Panama and Honduras, where important resistance poetry had been written by Diana Morán, Bertalicia Peralta, Bessy Reyna, Moravia Ochoa, and Consuelo Tomás (Panama), Argentina Daley, Waldina Medina (Honduras). Poets included:

Costa Rica: Eulalia Bernard, Janina Fernández, Ana Istarú.
Cuba (considered Central American in a geopolitical and cultural sense): Soledad Cruz, Nancy Morejón, Reina María Rodríguez, Excilia Saldaña, Mirta Yáñez.
Guatemala: Alaíde Foppa, Luz Méndez de la Vega, Carmen Matute, Ana María Rodas.
El Salvador: Claribel Alegría, Maura Echevarría, Jacinta Escudos/Rocío América, Claudia Lars.
Nicaragua: June Beer, Gioconda Belli, Marianela Corriols Molina, Esmeralda Dávila, Gloria Gabuardi, Ana Ilce Gómez, Meneses, Rosario Murillo, Michèle Najlis, Cony Pacheco, Christian Santos, Daisy Zamora.

▷   Meneses translations:
1.   "Poet or Avenging Angel" (4), "Poeta o ángel terrible."
2.   "Mother," (56), "Madre."
3.   "Last Postcard to My Father, General Meneses," (56), "Última postal a mi padre General Meneses." The note on the circumstances of General Meneses's death is erroneous.
4.   "Minimum Homage" (110), "Mínimo homenaje."
5.   "In the New Country" (134), "En el nuevo país."

Nicaragua in Reconstruction & at War: The People Speak. Ed., trans. Marc Zimmerman. Studies in Marxism 17. Minneapolis: MEP, 1985.

▷   Illustrative subtitle: "A Collage of Chronology/Analysis/Poetry/etc. Portraying Insurrection, Reconstruction, Cultural Revolution & U.S. Intervention. Poetry by Gioconda Belli, Ernesto Cardenal, Rosario Murillo & Other Nicaraguan Poets."

▷   Follow-up to *Nicaragua in Revolution: The Poets Speak* (1980), by Zimmerman et al.; similar dramatic interweaving of historical analysis, chro-

nologies, and poetic material; chocked full of information and poetry.
- Emphasis on political and testimonial poetry almost exclusively by Nicaraguans, including many non-professional poets; English text only; many photographs of street scenes; detailed treatment of final insurrection against Somoza (1977-79) and first phase of Reconstruction to early 1985.
- Lack of index reinforces collective purpose but hampers the search for contributions by individual authors. Incomplete bibliographical data for poems and brief biobibliographies reduce usefulness for scholarly research.
- Meneses poems:
1. "In the New Country" (118), "En el nuevo país."
2. "Minimal Homage" (168), "Mínimo homenaje."
3. "To Guillermo Frontierguard & His Brothers and Sisters" (267), unpublished in poetry collections but included in Meneses's cultural brigade campaign diary, *La lucha es el más alto de los cantos* (2006).
4. "Note for Angela" (276), "Nota para Ángela."
5. "Compañera" (278), "Compañera."

Open to the Sun: A Bilingual Anthology of Latin-American Women Poets. Ed. Nora Jacquez Wieser. Van Nuys: Perivale, 1979.
- An early anthology that recognized the many good women poets.
- Works selected to disprove the charge of sentimentality and confessionalism in poetry by women.
- Emphasizes poetry written after 1950.
- Includes from Uruguay: María Eugenia Vaz Ferreira, Delmira Agustini, Juana de Ibarbourou, Amanda Berenguer, Nancy Bacelo, Cristina Meneghetti; Argentina: Alfonsina Storni, Olga Orozco, Alejandra Pizarnik; Chile: Gabriela Mistral, Francisca Ossandón; El Salvador: Claudia Lars; Brazil: Cecilia Meireles; Mexico: Rosario Castellanos; Costa Rica: Eunice Odio; Peru: Blanca Varela; Puerto Rico/Colombia: Olga Elena Mattei; Cuba: Belkis Cuza Malé; and "The Nicaraguan Group": Mariana Sansón, Lygia Guillén, Meneses, Ana Ilce Gómez, Gioconda Belli, Yolanda Blanco.
- Meneses translations by Nora Weiser:
1. "When I Married" (116-17), "Cuando yo me casé."
2. "Warnings" (118-19), "Advertencias."

Poets of the Nicaraguan Revolution: An Anthology. Comp. and trans. Dinah Livingstone. London: Katabasis, 1993.
- Bilingual anthology. Excellent selection of revolutionary poetry from 1954-1990. Helpful introduction to literary and cultural issues under the Sandinistas, detailed chronology of political actions 1954-1990, brief biographies of poets, and translator's explanations in notes.

➤ Thirty-six of the best known poets, including Ernesto Cardenal, Daniel Ortega, Tomás Borge, Julio Valle-Castillo, poet-martyr-combatant Leonel Rugama, Afro-Nicaraguan David Macfield.
➤ Eight important women political/cultural figures and poets: Luz Marina Acosta, Gioconda Belli, Ana Ilce Gómez, Meneses, Rosario Murillo, Michèle Najlis, Dora María Téllez, Daisy Zamora, as well as three literary teachers and workshop participants: Martha Blandino, Cony Pacheco, and Lesbia Rodríguez.
➤ Meneses translations:
1. "Voluntary Work" (226-29), "Trabajo voluntario."
2. "Wailing Wall" (230-31), "Muro de lamentaciones."

Volcán: Poems from El Salvador, Guatemala, Honduras, Nicaragua, A Bi-lingual Anthology. Ed. Alejandro Murguía and Barbara Paschke. San Francisco: City Lights, 1983.
➤ A small but rich sampling of "a volcano ready to erupt" (xii)—"poems of war, exile, love, and death" by "descendants of poet-warriors who fought the early struggles dating back to the European invasion of Central America" (xi).
➤ Nicaraguan poets: Ernesto Cardenal, Gaspar García Laviana, Carlos José Guadamuz, José Coronel Urtecho, Carlos Martínez Rivas, David Macfield, Ernesto Mejía Sánchez, Carlos Rigby, Leonel Rugama, Fanor Téllez, Iván Uriarte, Roberto Vargas, Gioconda Belli, Meneses, Rosario Murillo, and Daisy Zamora.
➤ Meneses translation by David Volpendesta: "Cachikel Woman" (114-15), "Mujer cachikel."

Women and Revolution in Nicaragua. Ed. Helen Collinson. London: Zed, 1990. Cites a Meneses poem, "In the New Country" (7), "En el nuevo país," from *Lovers and Comrades: Women's Resistance Poetry from Central America* (134).

Selected Works in English on Nicaraguan Poetry

Beverley, John and Marc Zimmerman. *Literature and Politics in the Central American Revolutions.* Austin: U of Texas P, 1990.
➤ Two chapters, "Nicaraguan Poetry from Darío to Cardenal" and "Nicaraguan Poetry of the Insurrection and Reconstruction," derive important general characteristics and link poetry to details of the political process.
➤ Works by "The Six," women poets who supported or worked for the Revolution (Gioconda Belli, Yolanda Blanco, Meneses, Rosario Murillo,

Michèle Najlis, Daisy Zamora) are described as expressing the emergence of a "new woman," who offer "an emancipatory conception of female identity without completely negating its origins in the concrete experiences of women as mothers, daughters, lovers in a given time and place" (106).

Dawes, Greg. *Aesthetics and Revolution: Nicaraguan Poetry, 1979-1990.* Minneapolis: U of Minneapolis P, 1993.
➤ Challenges Beverley and Zimmerman's interpretations of interactions between political and symbol realms. Dawes sees aesthetics as inextricably bound to social relations of production, and he presents not "a primer in aesthetics and revolution nor in Nicaragua poetry, but rather a theoretical and sociohistorical intervention on aesthetics, revolution, and Marxism" (xix).
➤ Devotes chapters to Pablo Antonio Cuadra and Ernesto Cardenal.
➤ His "Feminist and Female Self-representation in Revolution" omits Meneses but looks at Gioconda Belli, Ana Ilce Gómez, Michèle Najlis, and Daisy Zamora and the negotiation of class and gender. He concludes that gender roles and sexuality, as social constructs, "territories—the family, motherhood, reproduction—that have in patriarchal societies traditionally been considered female," were both challenged and reinforced under the Somozas as well as the Sandinistas (111). The women poets present the problematic relation between feminism and socialism.

Nicaragua in Revolution: The Poets Speak. Ed. and trans. Bridget Aldaraca, Edward Baker, Ileana Rodríguez, Marc Zimmerman. Studies in Marxism 5. Minneapolis: Marxist Educational Press, 1980.
➤ An innovative, alternative approach to illustrate the process leading to the 1979 Sandinista victory and to promote international solidarity for reconstruction.
➤ A bilingual poetic collage "in which one narrative voice breaks off and cedes to another and in the process a collective poem of Nicaragua's century-long struggle for national liberation is written" (1).
➤ Poem fragments illustrate the two-page descriptions of sections:
o 1. Nicaragua under Imperialism and Sandino's Uprising (1898-1933).
o 2. The Tyranny (1936-1956).
o 3. The Struggle Continues (1956-1979).
o 4. The March to Victory (1970-1979).
➤ Over 40 Nicaraguan poets, although Ernesto Cardenal is featured most prominently; mainly includes the (now) best-known male poets; poet-combatant-martyrs Leonel Rugama and Carlos Fonseca Amador; Afro-Nicaraguan David Macfield.

▶ Gioconda Belli cited frequently; brief incursions by Michèle Najlis and Christian Santos. No other women poets mentioned (except Mexican Judith Reyes).

▶ Interweaving of poetry by international supporters: Pablo Neruda (Chile), Nicolás Guillén (Cuba), Otto-René Castillo (Guatemala), Pedro Mir (Dominican Republic), Rafael Alberti (Spain), Rogelio Sinán (Panama).

▶ Useful eight-page history of Nicaragua to 1979 and brief list of important dates from 1821 independence to 1979 Sandinista victory. Bio-bibliographies of principal poets.

▶ Lack of an index hampers the search for contributions by individual authors. Incomplete bibliographical data reduces usefulness for scholarly research.

Poets of Nicaragua: A Bilingual Anthology, 1918-1979. Ed. and trans. Steven F. White. Greensboro: Unicorn, 1982.

▶ "Reverses the glow of the cultural imperialism that has inundated Nicaragua" and shows poetry as a rich export production, since "Nicaragua has produced literary riches that equal and even surpass those of larger and more developed countries" (editor, viii).

▶ Poets selected are largely major writers of the Postmodernist, Vanguard and Postvanguard periods, 1910s-60s, including Alfonso Cortés, Salomón de la Selva, José Coronel Urtecho, Pablo Antonio Cuadra, Joaquín Pasos, Juan Francisco Gutiérrez, and Ernesto Mejía Sánchez. More contemporary poets are Carlos Martínez Rivas, Ernesto Cardenal, Ernesto Gutiérrez, Francisco Valle, Álvaro Urtecho, and Ana Ilce Gómez, the only woman included among the 13 poets.

▶ Grace Schulman's introduction places each poet within a broader literary and political context.

▶ Succinct introduction to each poet. Very helpful Selective Bibliography of poets' publications and translations into English (books), and selection of Useful Anthologies and Useful Studies, including several in English.

White, Steven F. *Modern Nicaraguan Poetry: Dialogues with France and the United States.* Lewisburg: Bucknell UP/London: Associated University Presses, 1993.

▶ An innovative exploration of twentieth-century Nicaraguan poetry in terms of two family resemblances or poetic affinities: one focused on the poetic word and metareality deriving from French authors (Baudelaire, Rimbaud, Mallarmé, Supervielle), the other interested in poetic versions of history and verisimilitude linked to U.S. forebears (Whitman, Pound, Eliot, Masters).

➢ Scholarly study, by a well-regarded poet himself, of seven major (male) authors presented in White's *Poets of Nicaragua: A Bilingual Anthology, 1918-1979* (1982): Alfonso Cortés, Pablo Antonio Cuadra, Carlos Martínez Rivas, Joaquín Pasos, Salomón de la Selva, José Coronel Urtecho, and Ernesto Cardenal.

➢ Subverts premises of Eurocentric cultural dependence to propose international dialogue with U.S. and French works as a means to create a Nicaraguan literary identity, a "mimetic independence."

➢ Extensive notes and bibliography.

Other Works Cited

Arellano, Jorge Eduardo. *Literatura nicaragüense*. Managua: Distribuidora Cultural. 1997.

Benedetti, Mario. "Joaquín Pasos o el poema como crimen perfecto." *Letras del continente mestizo*. Montevideo: Arca, 1967. <http://www.dariana.com/diccionario/joaquin-pasos2.htm>.

Cardenal, Ernesto. *Flights of Victory/Vuelos de victoria*. Ed. and trans. Marc Zimmerman. Willimantic, Conn.: Curbstone, 1988.

Garvin, Glenn. "Hostility to the U.S. A Costly Mistake." *Miami Herald*. July 18, 1999. http://www.fiu.edu/~yaf/sand71899.html.

Mantero, José María. "Poesía post-sandinista: el regreso de la metáfora." http://www.dariana.com/diccionario/novedades-2.htm.

Peralta, Humberto. "Palo de Mayo, tradición de nuestra Costa Caribe." *El Nuevo Diario*. May 9, 2005. <http://archivo.elnuevodiario.com.ni/2005/09-mayo-2005/opinión/ opinión-20050509-07.html>.

Pezzullo, Lawrence and Ralph Pezzullo. *At the Fall of Somoza*. Pittsburgh: U of Pittsburgh P, 1993.

Ramírez, Sergio. "Literatura Nicaragüense." *Enciclopedia de Nicaragua*. Barcelona: Océano, 2002. <http://www.sergioramirez.org.ni/conferencias/La%20literatura %20Nicaraguense.htm>.

Rey, Alberto. "Social Correlates of the Voseo of Managua, Family and Neighborhood Domains." *Hispanic Journal* 16.1 (1995): 39-53.

Rodríguez Rosales, Isolda. Personal communication. Oct. 23, 2006.

Urbina, Nicasio. "Pablo Antonio Cuadra: la construcción de un imaginario nacional." <http://www.dariana.com/Panorama/p_cuadra3.html; and ... p_cuadra 4, 5, 6 and 6ª.html> .

Valle-Castillo, Julio. Prólogo. Pasos, Joaquín. *Prosas de un joven*. Ed. Julio Valle-Castillo. Managua: Editorial Nueva Nicaragua, 1994.

Valle-Castillo, Julio, ed. *El siglo de la poesía en Nicaragua*. Vol. I: *Modernismo y vanguardia* (1880-1940). Vol. II: *Posvanguardia* (1940-1960). Col. Cultural de Centro América, Serie Literaria 14. Vol. III: *Neovanguardia* (1960-1980). Col. Cultural de Centro América, Serie Literaria 15. Managua: Fundación Uno, 2005.

Whisnant, David E. *Rascally Signs in Sacred Places: The Politics of Cuture in Nicaragua*. Chapel Hill: U of North Carolina P, 1995.

Zamora, Daisy. *La mujer nicaragüense en la poesía: antología*. Col. Letras de Nicaragua 39. Managua: Nueva Nicaragua, 1992.

INDEX

1960s 41-45, 49, 500, 504
1970s 44-45, 49-50, 510
1980s 132, 166, 510
1990s 156, 158
"About the Revolutionary and Some of His Weaknesses" 373, 509
abuse, physical, emotional 72, 134, 156-157, 259
Acosta, Luz Marina 80, 168, 509, 512
Adelina (great-aunt) 73, 74, 102, 107, 112, 141, 153, 176, 255, 325, 473, 491, 496
adolescence 39, 41-45, 173, 403, 405, 407, 411, 487
Afro-Caribbean 21, 38, 161-165, 337, 339, 513
Aguilar, Rosario 149, 504
Air that Calls Me 38, 67, 147-153, 321, 323, 433n, 475n, 477n, 496, 498, 506; poems 251-319
Akhmatova, Anna 277, 433, 477
Alegría, Claribel 84, 171-172, 510
Alemán, Arnoldo 28, 118, 120, 122, 135-137
Alemán Ocampo, Carlos 75
"Alfonso" 146-147, 193
"Alive Are We" 158, 160, 447n, 503
"All In All" 152, 313, 323, 357n, 498, 500, 504
All is the Same and Different 156-161, 277n, 305n, 371n, 373n, 375n, 397n, 475n, 477n, 496, 502, 503; poems 395-463
Alvarado, Humberto (brother-in-law) 481
Alvarado Meneses, Moisés (nephew) 415
Álvarez, María José 43
Álvarez, Rolando 120
Álvarez Montalván, Emilio 137
Amador Kühl, César 66
Ambroggio, Luis Alberto 139
AMLAE (see Luisa Amanda Espinosa Association of Nicaraguan Women)
AMPRONAC (see Association of Women Facing the National Problematic)
"Analiza tu vida" 467, 496
Anglesey, Zoë 24, 295, 353n, 355n, 509
Anta San Pedro, Teresa 148, 152-153, 167, 497-498
anti-Somoza 51-53, 62, 73
Aragón, Alba Fabiola 25, 178, 298, 301, 498-499
Arbenz, Jacobo 131, 419n, 421
Arce, Bayardo 68
Arellano, Jorge Eduardo 24, 78, 333n, 515

Argeñal, Hilda 69
Argüello, José 172
Argüello, Telma 43
Argueta, Manlio 24
Ashby, Claudia 293
Asociación Nicaragüense de Escritoras (ANIDE) (see Nicaraguan Association of Women Writers)
Association of Women Facing the National Problematic 132
Astorga, Lidia 60
Astorga, Nora 60
Asunción School 38, 41-44, 69, 99, 142, 475
Atlantic Coast (see Caribbean Coast)
Autonomous Women's Movement in Nicaragua 132, 135
"Autumn Stroll" 371, 498
Avilés, Álvaro 70, 391
Avilés Cevasco, Álvaro 70, 391
Azucena Torres, Alba 375
Bailón Dixon, José 38, 62
Baltodano, Mónica 88
Bank, Amy 115
Barahona, Amelia 77, 80, 82
Barreto, Pepe 69
Barricada 59, 77, 83, 85, 345
Barrios de Chamorro, Violeta 28, 68, 76, 107-108, 125, 134-136, 507
Base Committees 69-71, 88
Beatles 45
Bécquer, Gustavo Adolfo 173, 475
Beer, June 161, 337, 509, 510
Belli, Gioconda 41, 43, 92, 94, 131, 146, 177, 497, 498, 499, 500, 501, 504, 506, 508, 509, 510, 511, 512, 513, 514
Belli, Regina 123
Benedetti, Mario 172, 309, 493, 515
Bermúdez, Juanita 65, 93
Bernheim Espinosa, Edmundo (husband Carlos's cousin) 56, 66-68
Betancourt, Virginia 78
Beverley, John 25, 512-513
Bible 24, 147, 156, 160, 179, 191n, 199n, 215, 219n, 227, 303n, 313n, 359n, 381, 389, 433n, 457n, 479-481
Blanco, Yolanda 24, 504, 509, 511, 513
Blandón, Erick 59, 86
Boaco 35, 116
Boff, Leonardo 105

Bolaños, Enrique 29, 136
Bonanza 33-36, 39-40, 48, 102, 157, 159-160, 175, 205, 245, 263, 490, 496
"Bonanza" 147, 205
Borge, Tomás 27, 64, 68, 94, 492, 508, 512
Bosch, Juan 62
boyfriend 38; boyfriend-poet (Carlos) 45-48, 110, 150, 173
Brautigam Beer, Donovan 162-164
Bravo, Alejandro 86, 115-116
Brecht, Bertolt 371, 373, 437
Britton, Rosa María 58
Brooks Saldaña, Ronald 339
Brown, Colin 65
Brown, Nelson 77
brothers, brothers & sisters 37-39, 60, 72, 489
Cabezas, Omar 387, 508
Cabrales, Julio 43
Cabrales, Luis Alberto 168, 333, 496
Cabrera, Martha 36, 118-123, 126-127, 160
"Cakchiquel Woman" 148-149, 279, 498, 504, 512 (as "Cachikel Woman")
Calasanz School 82
Calero, Alonso 106
Calero Portocarrero, Adolfo 92
Camoapa 35, 36, 37
Cantarero de Meneses, Dolores (grandmother) 417
Carballo brothers 65
Cardenal, Ernesto 20, 28, 54, 74-80, 82-88, 92, 96, 101-104, 106, 137, 150-151, 160, 168-169, 171, 176, 285, 335n, 345n, 475, 479, 490, 492, 493, 507. 508, 510, 512, 513, 514-515
Cardenal, Fernando 70, 102-105
Cardenal, Lorenzo 70
Cardenal, Salvador 149
Cardenal de Delgadillo, Tere 54
Caribbean 365
Caribbean Coast, región 33, 35-36, 38, 61, 106, 120, 209, 337, 339, 367, 490, 515
Carrión, Gloria 43
Casaldáliga, Pedro 105, 507
Castellanos, Rosario 100, 178, 347, 357, 425, 463, 477, 490, 500, 511
Castellón, Blanca 177
Castillo, Chema 64
Castillo, Ernesto "Tito" 52
Castro, Patricia 124

Catholic Church, Catholics, 36-37, 89, 105-106, 120, 136, 168, 496, 497, 508
Catholic Women of Austria 122
Celerín, Sonia 23
Centeno Gómez, Carmen 173
Central American University (UCA) 49, 52, 60, 65, 122-123, 125; Meneses as dean 112-118, 126, 129-130, 132, 155, 164, 166, 183, 494
Centro Ecuménico Fray Antonio de Valdivieso (see Valdivieso Center)
Centro Nicaragüense de Escritores (CNE) (see Nicaraguan Writers Center)
Centroamérica School 50, 82, 183
Cerna, Lenin 68
Cevasco, Graciela 70, 391n
Chamorro, Carlos Fernando 77, 85
Chamorro, Claudia 68
Chamorro, Cristiana 126
Chamorro, Jaime 69
Chamorro, Pedro Joaquín 28, 52, 53, 62, 68, 125
Chamorro, Rafael 54, 70
Chavarría, Ricardo 70
Chávez, Hugo 137
Chávez Alfaro, Lizandro 86, 508
children (see also daughters) 35, 49-51, 55, 69-74, 91-102, 107, 111, 141-142, 148, 153, 160, 178-179, 183, 207, 231, 235, 239, 287, 325, 373, 383, 475, 509
"Children" 269
Chile 40, 50, 81, 115, 149, 443, 459, 491, 493, 511, 514
Christian identity 38, 100, 491, 507
Christian prayer group 54, 66, 69, 145, 391n
Christianity, Christians 51-52, 68, 105, 142, 156, 169, 174, 179, 499, 502, 509
CIA 95
CILCA (International Congress on Central American Literature) 24, 25, 107
Civil Coordinator 122-127, 138, 175
clandestine, anti-Somoza acts 64-66, 69
class. socioeconomic 19, 38, 41, 44, 49-51, 53, 58, 74, 76, 82, 124, 132, 134, 136, 140, 155, 213, 481, 499, 504, 505, 513
Clinton, Hillary 135
coffee harvest, 72, 95, 101, 373, 379, 383, 385-387
Coloma, Fidel 80, 84
Colombia 64-66, 76, 511
commitment 19-20, 33, 38, 44, 51-52, 68-71, 100, 104, 120, 131-133, 148, 477, 500, 502
communism, communists 43, 51-52, 56, 81
compaction of ministries 87, 102-103

"Compañera" 149, 301, 499, 500, 504, 505, 511
"Confiding A Secret" 34, 35, 407, 503
Conrado, Guillermo 62
Coordinadora Civil (see Civil Coordinator)
Córdova, Carmen Dolores 70
Córdova Rivas, Rafael 28, 90
Coronel Urtecho, José 150, 168-169, 333, 343n, 423n, 475, 490, 493, 496, 512, 514-515
Corriols Molina, Marianela 509, 510
corruption 51, 66, 120, 135-137
Cortázar, Julio 81, 84, 106, 172, 443n
Cortés, Alfonso 146-147, 193, 514-515
Cortés Domínguez, Guillermo 138
Costa Rica 28, 75, 149, 169, 335n, 441n, 496, 509, 510, 511
counterrevolution, "Contras" 28, 69, 92, 94-95, 98, 117-118, 387, 493
Criquillon, Ana 115
Cruz, Arturo 28
Cuá 151, 285
Cuadra, Pablo Antonio 51-52, 125-126, 145, 168, 175, 471, 496, 497, 499, 501, 513, 514-515
Cuba 19, 44, 59, 81, 86, 92, 107, 114, 137, 277, 291, 301, 331, 363, 367, 391n, 475, 481, 483, 491, 510, 511, 514
cultural brigade 72, 89-92, 373
Dambach Colony (Managua) 77
Dawes, Greg 25, 513
Darío, Rubén 77, 80-81, 165, 167-169, 173, 177, 411n, 475, 491, 492, 493, 496, 512
"Daughter" 153, 305, 499, 504
daughters 39, 99, 108-109, 111-112, 160, 411, 461, 504
De Nueda, Auxiliadora "Chilo" 385
death 34, 37, 57, 60, 64, 70, 150-151, 155, 158-159, 173-174, 179, 227, 233, 247, 239, 271, 283, 285, 287, 295, 331, 371, 391, 393, 425, 427, 463, 493, 494, 500, 501, 504, 512
"December 7th" 299, 498, 505
Delgadillo, César 54
Delgado, Violeta 126
democratization 80, 82-86, 108, 117-118, 134-139, 507
depression 107-111, 125, 128
d'Escoto, Miguel 93
Díaz, Claudia 81
divorce 70-73, 92, 475
Dominican Republic 19, 53, 62, 514

Doña Hope (see Portocarrero, Hope)
Doña Violeta (see Barrios de Chamorro, Violeta)
Donne, John 391
double moral standard for boys & girls 41, 457, 503
drugs 45, 99, 114, 141
earthquake (1972) 27, 36, 50, 75
"Ebb Tide" 261, 497
El Jícaro 38, 62, 253, 263
El Salvador 24, 92, 510, 511, 512; massacre of Jesuits 70, 389
elections of 1990 20, 28, 60, 107-108
Elisa (sister-in-law) 100, 487
Espinosa, Auxiliadora 91
Espinosa Ramírez, Virginia 81
evangelical churches 105-106
Esposito, Nancy 353n, 355n, 509
"Every Day" 245, 498
exteriorist poetry 84, 146, 150, 171, 490, 491
faithfulness in relationships 46-48, 134, 279, 357n, 365n, 493; unfaithfulness 46-47, 110-111, 128, 237n, 419
"Familiar April" 149-150, 285
family relations 20, 39, 70-71, 72-74, 92-102, 137-138, 140-141, 178-179, 291, 499, 502, 505
father (Edmundo Meneses Cantarero) 34-35, 38, 40-43, 46-47, 51-54, 57, 61-62, 64-65, 72, 94, 128, 141, 148, 173, 237, 253, 357, 473, 475, 499, 501, 505, 508, 509; father, death of 55-61, 99, 100-101 121, 174, 307, 391; father as a victim 61-62 (see also "Last Message to My Father, General Meneses")
father-in-law 50, 57
Federation of NGOS (FONG) 122, 124
female body (see women's bodies)
feminism 20, 45, 51, 131-133, 135, 140, 147, 149, 151-153, 321, 490, 497, 499, 502, 506, 508
Fernández, Francisco de Asís 84, 508
Fernández Retamar, Fernando 107, 137-138, 154, 165, 283, 319, 353, 359, 491
Ferreti, Walter "Chombo" 60
Fierro, Pepe 129
finances (personal) 49-50, 73-74, 101-104, 108-112
"First Lady" 67, 77, 297
Flakoll, Darwin "Bud" 171-172
Flame in the Wind 89, 153-156, 187, 191n, 197n, 211n, 219n, 227n, 229n, 231n, 235n, 243n, 245n, 257n, 261n, 265n, 279n, 287n, 291n, 293n,

299n, 301n, 303n, 305n, 307n, 309n, 313n, 319n, 437n, 477n, 495, 496, 497, 498, 504-505; poems 321-393
Fletes de Chamorro, María Elena 54, 70
"Flight" 293, 501, 504
Fonseca, Carlos 27, 62, 92, 291, 377, 492
"Forever Eve" 323, 501, 504, 505
Franco, Rita de 77
Freire, Paul 45
Fromm, Erich 45
FSLN (see Sandinista National Liberation Front)
Fuentes, Napoleón 146
Galeano, Eduardo 172
Gandhi 279
García Canclini, Néstor 103
gender studies 114-115, 132
Gil Yépes, Graciela 85
Girardi, Giulio 105
Gold, Janet 107
Gómez, Ana Ilce 131, 146, 171, 177, 498, 501, 504, 506, 509, 510, 511, 512, 513, 514
Gordillo, Fernando 89, 176. 507
Gorky, Maxim 199
Gorostiaga, Xabier 112, 115, 126, 166
gospels, radicalism of 69-70, 120-121, 142, 179, 475
Graham, Mercedes 169
Granada 35, 88, 109, 169, 183, 335n, 345n, 447n, 490, 493, 494
grandchildren 34, 39, 70, 84, 100, 145, 162, 341, 461
Guarded Flame 145-148, 175, 321, 496, 498, 502; poems 182-249
Guardia, Gloria 149
Guatemala 24, 45, 53-56, 59, 100-101, 131, 145, 148, 279, 281, 419n, 492, 497, 510, 512, 514
Guerrilla Army of the Poor (EGP) 59, 101
Guevara, Alejandro 106, 108
Guevara, Ernesto "Che" 373, 391n
Guido, Lea 88
Guillén, Adriana ("Carla Rodríguez") 51, 75, 92, 146
Guillén, Arnoldo 89
Guillén, Ligia 51, 92, 146, 504, 511
Gutiérrez, Carlos Alberto "You" 65
Gutiérrez, Ernesto 345, 514
Gutiérrez, Gustavo 105, 140
Gutiérrez, Hans 331

Gutiérrez, María Antonieta 45
Gutiérrez, María del Socorro 69
Gutiérrez, Octavio (uncle) 55, 99, 140
Gutiérrez Sacasa, Juan Ignacio 66, 69
Guzzo, Cristina 25, 153, 156, 179, 499
Hassan, Moisés 28
"He Who Has Ears to Hear" 191, 498, 505
"Heart in the Open" 152, 277n, 305n, 447n, 473-477
Hernández, Leopoldina (housekeeper) 64
Herrera, Rafaela 441
hippies 44
Hoey, Anna Bessie (godmother) 34, 36, 37
Hoey, Leslie N. (great-uncle) 33-34, 36-37, 147, 153, 171, 174-175, 205, 351, 490, 495
holistic view 117, 124, 126-127
Holland 123, 138
Honduras 28, 29, 62, 95, 97-99, 101, 131, 419n, 479, 510, 512
Hopkinson, Amanda 24, 265n, 291n, 307n, 510
house in Managua 50, 108-111, 130, 139; parents' house outside Managua 101, 111-111-112, 139; Morazán's handcrafted house 130-131
Howard University 21, 25, 161
Hurricane Katrina 121, 137, 479-483
Hurricane Mitch 29, 121-124
Hurtado, Isolda 138
"I Awake Chasing A Song" 229, 498, 498
"I Have Seen" 201, 500, 505-506
"I Sense the Soft Murmur" 22, 241
"I Write to You Now" 355, 509
Icaza, Carlos Rodolfo (first husband) 48-51, 54-56, 64-66, 70, 72-74, 92-102, 110-112, 128, 145, 148, 152, 183, 475
Icaza, Marina 65
Icaza Meneses, Carlos Rodolfo (son) 35, 55, 89, 93-95, 99-100, 137, 141, 162, 223, 269, 341, 381, 481
Icaza Meneses, Karla Dolores (daughter) 22, 84, 89, 94-95, 97, 99-100, 108-109, 124, 130, 163, 221, 223, 267, 269, 381, 411, 413
Icaza Meneses, Mariano Edmundo (son) 25, 37, 70, 95-100, 110, 153-154, 269
Icaza Meneses, Vidaluz (daughter) 95, 97-100, 107, 109, 110, 124, 130, 141, 154, 269, 381, 411, 491
illiteracy 28, 49, 106, 146, 177
"In extremis" 463, 503
"In the New Country" 291, 500, 510, 511, 512

INDESA 80
indigenous 36, 60, 120, 147-148, 205, 279, 281, 337, 490, 498, 499, 508, 509
"Inquiries" 277n, 305n, 371n, 373n, 375n, 431, 475n, 477n
Institute of Culture 81
International Monetary Fund 134
"Inventory of a Modern Man" 189, 497
"Itinerary/97" 439, 503
Jaeger, Frances 25, 499-500
Jäger, Willigis 174
Jalapa 89, 90, 353n
Jiménez, Luis A. 175, 500-501
Jinotega 57-58, 60-61, 253n, 417, 494
"Journey toward the Interior" 158-160, 461
"Juan Meza" 76-79
Juana Inés de la Cruz 321, 500, 508
Juárez Polanco, Ulises 138
Julio Cortázar Museum 81
Junta of National Reconstruction 22, 28, 68, 69, 75, 90
"Jurassic Evocation" 15, 401, 501
Justo Rufino Garay Theater Group 89
Kalthoff, Adela 98-99
"Karla Dolores" 22, 267
"Katati" 75
Klimenko, Boris 277, 431
La Colonia Supermarkets 73
La Limonera camp 89-92, 377
La Prensa 28, 51-52, 69, 125, 145, 170, 289n, 471n, 494
Lacayo, Ramiro 75
Lacayo, Rossana 43, 509
Lacayo Parajón, Francisco 86-87, 115, 130, 170
"Land Recovered" 295, 501, 504, 509 (as "The Earth Recovered")
Lanzas, Milagros 70
Lara Manning, Alejandro 64
La Salle Pedagogical Institute 82
"Last Message to My Father, General Meneses" 52, 59, 153, 174, 307, 498, 502, 505, 509, 510
Lenin, Vladimir 375, 433
Leningrad 277n, 319, 431, 477n
León 35, 38-40, 45, 47, 63, 88, 327, 345, 387n, 491
Leonel Rugama Cultural Brigade 89-92, 116, 176, 178, 469, 497, 511
Lewites, Herty 111-112
Liberation Theology 44, 52, 105, 166, 508

libraries 50, 74, 77, 80-81, 87, 132, 146, 161, 164, 507
"Life with Life" 423, 501
Lila (mother's sister) 38-39
literacy campaign 28, 74, 80
Livingstone, Dinah 24, 379n, 393n, 511-512
Lobo, Tatiana 149
"Looking at Her Photograph" 153, 162, 341, 499
López, Amando 56, 70, 389
López Miranda, Margarita 80, 138, 157, 501-502
Lot's wife 303, 313
"Love at Any Time" 403, 405, 501, 503
Luisa Amanda Espinosa Association of Nicaraguan Women 132
Macfield, David 161, 337, 512, 514
Mairena, Miguel 121-122
Mantero, José María 24, 515
Mántica family 73, 79, 81
Marenco, Nicho 73
Martínez, Ángel 145-146, 183
Martínez, Chuchú 96
Martínez Peláez, Severo 45
Martínez Rivas, Carlos 169-171, 299, 335n, 343n, 345n, 427, 429n, 492, 493, 495, 507, 512, 514-515
Matamoros, Ximena 383
Marxism, Marxist 45, 68-69, 71, 105, 140, 359, 375n, 433n, 435n, 491, 513
Matagalpa 33-37, 39, 61, 63, 73, 127, 253, 255, 263, 265, 325, 351, 473, 475, 490, 491, 492, 495
Matillo Vila, Joaquín 81-82
"May Lullaby" 161-164, 413, 503
May Pole 161-163, 337n, 369n, 413, 515
Mayakovsky, Vladimir 305, 433, 475
"Mayaya June Beer" 161-162, 337
Mayorga, Lourdes 43
Mayorga, Silvio 27, 62, 492
Mc Callister, Rick 25, 503
McCurdy, Nan 121-122
Medrano Matus, Piedad 177
Mejía Godoy family 39
Mejía Godoy, Armando 81
Mejía Godoy, Carlos 75, 151, 285
Mejía Sánchez, Ernesto 162, 169, 171, 325n, 341, 345n, 425, 492, 494, 512, 514
Mendoza, José "Chepe" 391, 492
Meneses, Annabella (sister) 37, 481

Meneses, Dalila (sister) 38, 56, 100
Meneses, Edmundo (brother) 35, 100, 141, 253, 485-489
Meneses, Jairo (brother) 35, 60, 141
Meneses, Meriulda (sister) 37, 141, 253, 485
Meneses, Ulda (sister) 34
Meneses Cantarero, Edmundo (see father)
menstruation 39-41
Methodist Church 122-123
Mexico 19, 44, 47, 64, 116, 133, 156, 169, 425, 477n, 490, 492, 511, 514
Military Academy (Managua) 34, 58, 61, 63
Ministry of Culture 19-20, 28, 67-68, 71, 74-88, 92, 114; dismantling 102-105
Miranda, Mayra 82
Miranda, Nelly 115-116, 119
Mistral, Gabriela 173, 511
"Mistress of Her Song" 165, 411
Mojica, Iván 54, 57
Mojica, Otto 54, 57
Mokorón War 62
Molieri, Carlota 146
Molina, Uriel 42, 104-106, 118-119
Moncada, Adilia 75, 155, 385
Monimbó 60
Montealegre, Margarita 43
Morales, Beltrán 43, 508
Morales, Luis 81
Morales, Óscar "Moralitos" 63
Morales Avilés, Ricardo 68, 507
Morales Carazo, Jaime 79
Moravian Church 36, 120
Morazán, Sergio (second husband) 110-111, 122, 125, 128-131, 157, 399, 443
Morazán Elvir, Francisco 131, 419
Moscow 277, 305, 319, 375, 419, 431, 433
mother (Vida Robleto) 20, 33-38, 42, 46-47, 52, 55-61, 72-73, 94, 101, 124, 130, 134, 139, 141, 239, 265, 291, 293n, 391, 407, 473, 481, 495
"Mother" 153, 265, 499, 510
mother-in-law (Clementina Sotomayor de Espinosa) 49, 53-55, 73, 97, 101, 148, 207
Movimiento de Renovación Sandinista (see Sandinista Renovation Movement Party)
Moyano, Pilar 151, 157-158, 178, 503-504
Murguía, Alejandro 23, 512
Murillo, Rosario 82-88, 89, 102, 131, 177, 500, 506, 509, 510, 512, 513

"My Aunt Adelina" 153, 325, 499, 508
Najlis, Michèle 41, 43, 112, 118-123, 127, 131, 145, 146, 177, 447, 498, 499, 500, 501, 504, 508, 509, 510, 512, 513, 514
National Archive 77-78, 87, 385n, 387n
National Guard 19, 27, 38, 41, 53-55, 58, 61, 63-64, 89, 124, 285, 307, 494, 495
National Library 77-78, 80, 82, 87, 104, 385n, 387n, 475
National Theater 66-67
neoliberalism 50, 120, 134, 140, 397, 503
Neptune Gold Mine Company 36, 496
Neruda, Pablo 173, 443n, 475, 477n, 514
Nervo, Amado 173, 475
newspaper column, "Voice of the Nicaraguan Woman," 51, 75
Nicaragua, Carlos 65
Nicaraguan Association of Women Writers (ANIDE), 20, 138
Nicaraguan Writers Center (CNE) 20, 138
"Night Duty" 353, 499, 509 (as "I Read Your Letters)
Non-governmental Organizations (NGOs) 20, 121-124
Norway 115, 138
"Note for Angela" 303, 511
Núñez, René 88
nuns 38, 40-44, 57, 71, 142, 281, 475, 507
Ochoa, Moravia 97, 510
Ocotal 37-39, 96, 263, 489
"Office Girls" 399, 503
"On A Sleepless Night" 235, 498, 505
"On the Side Most Fragile" 37, 153, 174, 351
Quirós, Ana 124
Oquist, Paul 80
Organization of American States (OAS) 53, 62, 136
Ortega, Daniel 28-29, 50, 79, 83, 85-88, 90, 102, 104, 111-113, 136-137, 507, 512
Ortega, Humberto 50, 62, 68
Ortega Hegg, Manuel 80, 138
Ortega-Murillo administration 80, 136-137
Osses, Esther María 96-97
Pacheco, Cony 510, 512
Pacific Coast 36
"Paco" 419, 503
Palacios Vivas, Nydia 14, 147, 149, 177, 504
Pallais, León 52
Panama 23, 58, 61, 95-97, 149, 509, 510, 514
Pancasán 63
Pancasán musical group 79, 89, 91

Parrales, Edgar 70
parties (social) 38, 41-47
Paschke, Barbara 23, 512
Pasos, Joaquín 147, 251, 471, 492, 493, 496, 507, 514-515, 516
Pasos Marciacq, Ricardo 129-130
Pastor, Edén "Cain" 373n
Pastora "Pastorcita" (mother's sister) 55, 99, 101, 140
Pastora (great-aunt) 473
patriarchy 72, 132, 147, 157, 457, 493, 500, 503-504, 513
Patriotic Military Service 70, 179, 391n
peace accords 99, 106, 112, 123
"Pedro, Just Now I Have Been Remembering" 21, 305, 433n, 475n
Penelope 148, 279, 357, 365, 493, 498
Peralta, Humberto 162-164, 515
Pérez, Cony 385
Pérez, Eunice (sister-in-law) 60, 141
Pérez, Teresa (housekeeper) 64, 93, 102, 107, 114
Pérez Díaz, Mayra Luz 112
Pérez Vega, Reynaldo (brother's father-in-law) 60, 141
Perezalonso, Carlos 319
Peters, Kathryn 150, 189n, 191n, 197n, 209n, 217n, 227n, 243n, 249n, 261n, 265n, 277n, 295n, 291n, 363n, 369n, 504-505, 509
Pezzullo, David 175, 495, 515
Pineda, Gustavo 114
Plath, Sylvia 158, 449
"Poet or Terrible Angel" 329, 510 (as "Poet or Avenging Angel")
poetry workshops 82-84, 493
polio 34-35
Pomares, Germán 89, 92, 377, 494
poor people, poverty 19, 41-42, 44, 51, 69-70, 74, 79-80, 101, 106, 116-117, 121, 134-137, 140, 158, 166, 225, 289, 475, 483, 503
popes 105, 135, 154
Portocarrero, Hope 66-68, 297, 495
post-traumatic stress syndrome 36, 123
Powell, Carlos 123
Prego, Irma 155, 335
Presley, Elvis 44-45
Pushkin, Alexander 375, 433
"Questions" 156, 445
Ramírez, Dorel 384
Ramírez, Ileana 70
Ramírez, Sergio 20, 24, 28, 74, 90, 93-94, 104, 108-109, 138, 383n, 490, 491, 492, 494, 508, 515

Ramírez de Espinosa, Gladys 76
Ramos, Helena 138, 150, 177
Randall, Margaret 23, 142, 145, 299, 307, 325, 508-509
Raquidel, Danielle 147, 505-506
"Reckoning" 357, 501, 502, 504
Red Cross 64
Reed 122
"Reflection in Blue on New Orleans" 137, 479-483
revolution (not Sandinista) 117, 140, 142, 165
Revolutionary government 43, 60, 74, 88, 104, 112, 134, 507, 508, 511
Rey, Alberto 21, 515
Reyes, Carlos 62
Reyes, Rodolfo 75
Rigby, Carlos 161, 163, 337, 512
Rilke, Rainer Maria 21, 195, 329, 494, 495
Río San Juan 106-107, 138, 333, 423n, 441
Rivas, Gabry 173
Rivas, María Amanda 124
Robelo, Alfonso 28, 68-69
Robelo, Ernesto 70
Rocha, Luis 52, 145, 147, 271, 494
Rocha, Vilma de la 138
Rodríguez, Ileana 102-103, 106-107, 113-114, 116-117, 513-514
Rodríguez, Lesbia 103, 512
Rodríguez Rosales, Isolda 22, 515
Rothschuh Tablada, Guillermo 83
Rueda, Francisco 89
Rugama, Leonel 89, 345, 377, 494, 507, 512, 514
Ruíz, Henry 59
Ruth Palacios Folkloric Dance Group 89
Saballos, Ángela "Angelita" 42, 43, 47, 110, 117, 132, 138, 156, 172, 303, 383n
Sacasa, Juan Bautista 27, 495
Sáenz, Carlos 122-123
Saint Petersburg 277n, 319, 431, 433, 477n
Sallick, Morris & Jeannette 69
Sampson, Dinorah 66
San Carlos 107, 122
San Francisco Libre 121-123
Sánchez, Hilario 60
Sánchez, Karla 146
Sanchez, María Teresa 131, 138, 177
Sánchez, Roberto 66, 90

- 531 -

Sandinista Association of Cultural Workers (ASTC) 83, 89, 508
Sandinista National Liberation Front (FSLN) 20, 22, 27-28, 53, 59-60, 62-63, 65, 69, 75, 103, 108, 118-119, 136-137, 285, 291, 297, 373n, 383n, 387n, 492, 495
Sandinista Renovation Movement Party 20, 138
Sandinista Revolution 19-20, 33, 43, 50, 58-59, 64, 491, 501, 502, 505, 506, 507, 513
Sandinista Youth 95, 383n
Sandino, Augusto César 27, 37, 168, 253, 353, 377, 419n, 477n, 494-495, 513
Sandoval, Julio César 71
Sandoval, Martha 71
Sansón Argüello, Mariana 131, 138, 177, 511
Santa Claus 37, 39
Santos, Christian 138, 504, 509, 510, 514
"Scenes from Jalapa (La Limonera Military Unit)" 91-92, 377
Schick Gutiérrez, René 27
Selva, Mario 145
Selva, Salomón de la 514-515
Sevilla, Nadina 70
sexuality 41-43, 427, 455, 459, 513
Silva, Fernando 145
Silva, Fernando Antonio 145
Sinán, Rogelio 97, 514
"Sketch" 38, 253
"Small Death" 227, 504
"Small Homage" 291, 499, 510-511 (as "Minimal Homage")
"Snapshot of a Marriage" 217, 500, 509 (as "Instant Marriage")
Sobrino, Jon 105
Socialist Realism 83-84, 199
Solentiname 79, 106-109
Somoto 39, 64, 90, 175
Somoza family, Somozas 82, 291, 492-493, 495, 508, 513
Somoza Debayle, Anastasio "Tachito" 27-28, 49, 51, 53, 58, 65-68, 73-74, 76, 100, 168, 297, 339n, 471n, 492, 493, 495, 504, 515
Somoza Debayle, Luis 27, 62, 495
Somoza García, Anastasio "Tacho" 27, 63, 168, 495, 496
Somoza Portocarrero, "El Chigüín" 53, 495
Stadthagen, Mercedes 92-94, 101
Storni, Alfonsina 158, 449, 511
Struggle is the Highest of Songs 89, 176, 497, 511
Suazo, César (cousin) 38-39, 407
Subtiava 88

suicide 156, 160, 175, 447-449, 503
"Surprised, Happy" 359, 498, 499 (as "Synthesis")
"Sweating Virgin" 89
Sweden 87, 88, 130
Tarot 285n
"Tarot" 22, 367
Téfel, Reynaldo Antonio 51, 136, 507
Tejada, David 63
Téllez, Dora María 508, 512
Téllez, Fanor 146, 512
Terán, Marta 129-130
"That Woman" 100, 178, 347, 477n, 501
"That Woman Is Crazy" 158, 453, 503
"That's Life" 243, 498
"The New Skirt" 287, 504
Tijerino, Doris 59, 68. 507, 508
"To Borderguard Guillermo and His Brothers and Sisters" 469, 511 (as "To Guillermo Frontierguard & His Brothers and Sisters")
"To Pavel" 22, 199
"Today" 207, 497
Torres, Dolores "Lola" 116
Torres, Hugo 89
Torres Rivas, Edelberto 45
"Triptych on Death" 174, 247-249
"Triptych to Remember" 58, 70, 391
Trujillo, Rafael Leónidas 62
Tucker, Andrés G. 25, 445n, 477n
Turcios, Froylán 99
Ubilla Baca, Napoleón 62
UCA (see Central American University)
UNAN University 47
United Nations 53-54, 80, 146
United States 19, 23, 33, 27-28, 36-37, 44, 61, 63, 80, 92-95, 97, 99, 101, 107, 113, 117, 136, 137-139, 141, 150, 163, 166, 168, 171, 201n, 205n, 215n, 253, 291, 293n, 297, 303, 333n, 341n, 343n, 351, 381n, 387n, 419n, 475, 479-483, 490, 491, 494-495, 496, 507, 508, 510, 514-515
University reform 113-118
Urbina, Nicasio 24, 515
Urtecho, Álvaro 153-155, 159, 171, 495, 506, 514-515
Utopian Club 129-130
Valdivieso, Antonio de 120

Valdivieso Center, Friar Antonio de Valdivieso Ecumenical Center 104, 118, 120-124, 131, 158; Meneses as executive director 119-124
Valle, Francisco 77-78, 514
Valle Girls (great-aunts) 33, 37, 39, 189, 255, 257, 265n, 281, 325, 407, 409, 473, 490, 496, 507
Valle, Indiana 45-47
Valle, Virginia (great-aunt) 33. 36, 37, 147, 171, 205, 245, 351, 490, 496
Valle-Castillo, Julio 24, 82, 102-103, 154, 168-170, 425, 493, 508, 512, 516
Vanegas, Leonel 44, 89, 116
Vanguard literary movement 167-169, 333, 251n, 425, 471n, 475, 490, 493, 496, 514, 516
Vannini, Margarita 125-126
Vargas, Óscar-René 49, 113
Vásquez, Jaime 77
Vásquez, Raúl "Pablo" 65
Vega Sánchez, Boris 65
Venezuela 40, 61, 85, 94, 137, 483, 509
Vice-Minister of Culture, Meneses as acting 74, 76, 87-88, 96, 168, 174
Violeta Barrios de Chamorro Foundation 125-126
Vijil Teyssere sisters 43
Villalta, Orlando 51-52, 59
virginity 40-41, 455
"Virgo" 455, 503
Vivas, Antonina 75, 82, 155
Vogl, María Elsa 79
Volpendesta, David 279, 512
"Voluntary Labor" 379, 499, 512 (as "Voluntary Work")
"Wailing Wall" 155-156, 345n, 393, 499, 505, 509, 512
"Warnings" 215, 511
Waugh, Carmen 81, 443
Wieser, Nora Jacquez 24, 219, 511
Wheat, Valerie 139
Wheelock, Jaime 68
"When I Married" 48, 50, 147, 153, 219, 357n, 498, 500, 502, 504, 511
Whisnant, David E. 25, 515
White, Steven F. 24, 333, 514-515
"Woman, 1950s" 155, 335, 497
women, change agents, heroes, warriors 140, 148-149, 279. 383, 493, 498, 499, 501, 502, 508, 509, 513
women, rural 53, 149, 151, 285
women, university studies 19, 49, 177, 504
women in relationships 72, 128, 133-134

women officials 88, 137
women working outside home 49, 325, 379
women writers & artists 131-132, 146, 149, 169, 176-177, 179, 447-449, 477n, 497, 503-504, 506, 509, 510, 511, 513
women's bodies 20, 39-41, 289, 323, 411, 498, 500
women's identity, ways of being 178, 503, 512
women's issues 117, 122, 124, 131-134, 151-158, 335, 445, 447-449, 467, 477, 500-501, 508
women's organizations 132, 508
women's resistance 19, 53, 285, 499, 510
Wong, Carlos 97
Woolf, Virginia 158, 447, 477
World Bank 137
"You Said" 22, 195
Zambrana Godoy, Ricardo 124-126
Zamora, Daisy 24, 71, 73, 75, 77, 85-87, 112-13, 131, 146, 171, 176-178, 447, 499, 500, 501, 502, 503, 504, 506, 508, 509, 510, 512, 513, 516
Zimmerman, Marc 25, 291, 301, 303, 510-513, 515
Zúñiga, Édgard 120

1. Meneses with godmother Anna Bessie Hoey, Bonanza, 1948.

2. Miss American Nicaraguan School, 1961.

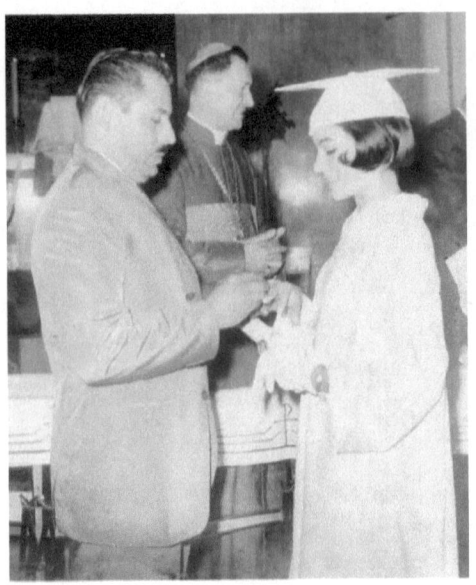

3. Graduation from La Asunción, 1965. Father places school ring on her finger. Behind, Nuncio Msgr. Portlupi.

4. "When I Married…," with father and mother, 1966.

5. *La Nación* (Guatemala) reports shooting of Nicaraguan Ambassador, General (ret.) Edmundo Meneses Cantarero, Sept. 1978, quoting his daughter, "May my father's blood serve to bring peace to my country."

6. Press conference, Ministers of Culture Armando Hart (Cuba) and Ernesto Cardenal (Nicaragua). Nicaraguan delegation included Meneses, Mercedes Stadthagen, Adriana Guillén. Cuban delegates: Haydée Santamaría, Roberto Fernández Retamar. Havana, Nov. 1979.

7. Official visit to Petrogodost as Director of Libraries and Archives, July 1981.

8. Meeting of writers Luis Rocha, Claribel Alegría, Augusto Monterroso, Carlos Martínez Rivas, Fernando Silva, José Coronel Urtecho, Roberto Fernández Retamar, Sergio Ramírez, Tomás Borge, Ernesto Cardenal, Ernesto Mejía Sánchez, Omar Cabezas, Vidaluz Meneses. Managua, 1982.

9. Open air poetry reading, 1984.

10. Poetry reading with Daisy Zamora, 1984.

11. "Revolución es el triunfo de la poesía" (Revolution is the triumph of poetry), reading on a "Poetry Tuesday" at the Ruben Darío National Theater, with critic Julio Valle-Castillo. 1985.

12. Family remaining in Nicaragua, 1985: daughter Vidaluz, Meneses, son Mariano, housekeeper Teresa Pérez and her son Eddie, Great-Aunt Adelina.

13. Coffee harvest, 1985.

14. Executive Director of the Valdivieso Ecumenical Center, Meneses carries aid to the town of San Francisco Libre ravaged by Hurricane Mitch, Oct. 1998.

15. Lifetime friends, journalist Ángela Saballos and poet Michèle Najlis, reception for founding of the Federation of Central American Women Writers, Managua, March 2002.

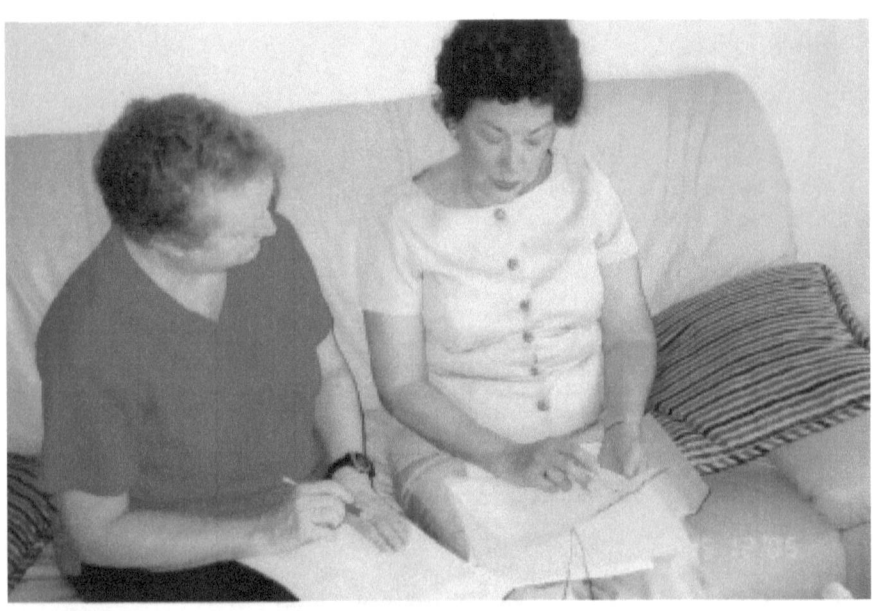

16. Reviewing poetry with editor-translator Maria Roof, Washington, DC, 2009. Photo by Françoise Pfaff.

17. Cover of diary (published 2006) of Cultural Brigade at front lines in Contra war (1983). Courtesy Anamá Ediciones.

Impreso en Estados Unidos
para Casasola LLC
Segunda Edición
MMXV ©

www.ingramcontent.com/pod-product-compliance
Lightning Source LLC
Chambersburg PA
CBHW021823220426
43663CB00005B/117